THE POLYGAMISTS

A History of Colorado City, Arizona

by Benjamin G. Bistline

The Polygamists: A History of Colorado City, Arizona
by Benjamin G. Bistline

Publisher's Cataloging-in-Publication Data

Bistline, Benjamin G.
    The Polygamists : a History of Colorado City, Arizona / Benjamin Bistline. – 1st ed.
      p.cm.
    Includes bibliographic references and index.
    LCCN: 2004100938   (pkb : alk.paper)
    ISBN: 1-888106-74-3
1. Mormon Fundamentalism–Arizona–Colorado City–History. 2. Mormon Fundamentalism–Utah–Hildale–History. 3. Polygamy–Utah–Hildale–History. 4 Polygamy–Arizona–Colorado City–History. 5. Persecution–Arizona–Hildale–History–20th Century. 7. Colorado City (Ariz)–Church history. Hildale (Utah)–Church history. Title.

BX8680.M534C64 2004   289.3'79159–dc20

Printed in the United States of America

Featured on www.agreka.com

Agreka, LLC
800 360-5284
www.agreka.com

Dedication

To my wife Annie and our sixteen children, of whom two are living in polygamy. For all their love, patience, consideration, and support they have given me during the ten years I have spent writing and compiling this history.

Glenn, John, Quentin, Patrick, Deslie, Terri, Diane, Nephi, Suzie, Marcus, Jasper, Fred, Kirby, Ida, and Billy. I love and respect each and every one of you. And our precious two-year-old Luann, who was killed in1961 by a drunk driver.

You have been the greatest family that any man could ever hope for.

Pappy (Benjamin Bistline)

Contents

Preface

"History is simply a record of man's intelligence; or lack of it."

Bart Anderson

What our people did not realize is described in the polygamist's Law Book, the Doctrine & Covenants.

"We have learned by sad experience that it is the nature and disposition of almost all men, as soon as they get a little authority, as they suppose, they will immediately begin to exercise unrighteous dominion." D&C 121:39

The faithful people of Colorado City gave their time, talents, money, devotion, and ongoing hard work to build their community, trusting all the while that their leaders would behave honorably and do right by them. Much of the money accumulated by the leadership-controlled UEP Trust had actually come from the people themselves: through work that produced income to the UEP, through periodic requested donations, and through regular tithing of 10 percent of their income. This same money was used to purchase land for the Trust and the people were "allowed" to build their homes on it.

The leaders acted as if the money was rightfully theirs and did not belong to the people who had produced it. The leaders did not see themselves as stewards over this money and accountable to the people. They seemed only accountable to themselves.

> Lorin Woolley, who claimed he had been commissioned in 1887 by a prophet of God to keep plural marriage alive, perpetuated the movement by calling a Priesthood Council of men to "govern and make decisions together" to oversee it and keep it going. He emphatically taught them what he had been taught: Not to organize, not to proselyte, not to hold public meetings, not to set up a United Order, and not to collect tithing money from the people. Just quietly teach about plural marriage and live it in secret.

But John Yates Barlow, one of the men on the Council apparently came to believe he alone had been given the Keys of the Priesthood, which polygamists believed was a bestowal by God upon a man so righteous that he should have supreme power over others on earth. This attitude of dictator type power by John Y. Barlow was used to organize the polygamists, proselyte to gain new members, set up a United Order, and collect tithing money from the people. He taught this One Man Rule to those around him, to the leaders who would succeed him, and to his sons whom he expected would one day take their rightful place and rule. As years passed the "one man" was called a prophet and his direction to the people was taught as coming from God and was not to be questioned. Otherwise, one's eternal salvation was in jeopardy.

As more time passed older men needing more wives were taught to take child brides before the girls were attracted to boys their own age, plural wives were told to apply for government assistance, boys competing with older men for wives were driven out of the community, and men out of favor were "evicted" from their homes and their wives and children reassigned to a more compliant man.

This "unrighteous dominion" described in the Law Book would grow into an unprecedented dictatorship secretly hidden away in a remote corner of America. It would grow and mushroom and eventually come full circle, creating a stranglehold on the people they never imagined. And one most do not even recognize today.

In 1989 I was asked by a person I met if a history had ever been written about Short Creek (Colorado City, Arizona). I realized that such a history would be important to future generations, because those persons who had seized political and religious control of the community years ago were lying about its history in order to justify their power takeover and the One Man Rule.

Since I have been associated with the polygamists all my life and have lived in Short Creek since 1945, I supposed I could compile as accurate a history as any other person living here. So I began gathering information and documents. In 1995 I became discouraged about finishing the project, because it was so hard to obtain documents from the Fundamentalists that would tell the true history.

I was, however, able to obtain some important letters written in the 1940s and 1950s that became public record due to a lawsuit filed in 1987. I also obtained some journals of the early Fundamentalist leaders. These, along with the printed sermons of Leroy Johnson, polygamist Prophet, and several sermons of other leaders, have been sources for this history. Very important, however, is the fact that I have been an eyewitness to almost all that has occurred and I have kept a detailed journal all these years.

One major event greatly influenced me to complete this work. Martha Sontag-Bradley compiled a history of the government raids in Short Creek and the history surrounding it. Published in 1993 by University of Utah Press, *Kidnapped From That Land* has interesting facts and observations. She spent two or three weeks living in Colorado City, gathering information for her book. This information was all obtained from and through the Barlow Family and the residents they carefully selected. Thus it reflected only what the leadership wanted the world to hear.

While reading the book, I became so incensed in regards to the manipulation of truth by the Barlows that my determination was renewed to finish this work. That way, there will be an opposing historical view of Short Creek history so future generations will have an opportunity to determine for themselves what the truth might be.

My hope in writing this history is to try and portray that the things taught to the followers of the Fundamentalist Cult are NOT fact and that once a person begins to question such, only then will they be able to see the truth in the matter and be able to take steps to break out from under its grasp.

The hold that these religious leaders have on the people and the community is powerful because of misconceptions and outright lies. Even though many of the people *suspect* that things are not right, they don't have the facts.

My goal for this book is to dispel the lies, reveal the truth as it was from the beginning, and help the polygamist members regain control over their own lives and property. Most of these people are honorable, honest, hardworking citizens simply trying to faithfully live their religious beliefs. Any people who are faithful in their hearts to a religion (any religion) can be manipulated by unrighteous leaders. Knowing the truth will help them over time develop a more open society, and one where they feel free to pose questions to their leaders and receive truthful answers. These people deserve to be depicted as they really are and not lumped into the same pile with those who abuse. For in any society, abuses occur, and those abuses are abhorrent wherever they occur.

Let's begin with the following clarifications.

The fundamentalist group leadership in Colorado City has never been organized like The Church of Jesus Christ of Latter-day Saints (LDS) with a president, two councilors, and twelve apostles. They began with a Priesthood Council. The fundamentalists consider themselves a sub-culture of the LDS Church.

In 1929, Lorin Woolley formally began the fundamentalist movement and called three men, Leslie Broadbent, John Y. Barlow, and Joseph Musser, setting them apart as "High Priest Apostles," an office that the Mormon Church never had. Joseph Musser later claimed in 1935 that this office of High Priest Apostle was a higher office than that of the president and prophet of the LDS Church.

In 1933 Woolley called three more men, Charles Zitting, LeGrand

Woolley, and Louis Kelsch to the same office of High Priest Apostles. He instructed them that their only authority was to keep plural marriage alive. They were not to organize a church, not collect tithing money, not to proselyte, not to hold public meetings, but they were allowed to hold cottage meetings in the homes of friends to discuss the gospel and teach that polygamy should be lived.

At the Senior Member of this council's death, the next one in seniority, according to the order in which they were called, would become the senior member, and was to lead the Council. All decisions were to be made as a Council, *not by one man.*

Woolley died in 1934, leaving Leslie Broadbent the leader. Broadbent died in 1935, leaving John Barlow as the leader. In the 1940s John Barlow called seven more men: Leroy Johnson, Marion Hammon, Guy Musser, Rulon Jeffs, Richard Jessop, Carl Holm, and Alma Timpson.

Barlow died in 1949, leaving Joseph Musser as the leader.

Musser died in 1954 leaving Charles Zitting as leader. Zitting died later the same year.

The next two council members, LeGrand Woolley and Louis Kelsch, declined to lead any group or organization, reverting back to Woolley's instructions *not to organize.* Leroy Johnson, John Barlow's protege, then assumed the leadership position, and was the leader until 1986 when he died. Rulon Jeffs next assumed the leadership position and when he died in 2002, his son Warren Jeffs took over.

A lawsuit was filed in 1987 against the United Effort Plan, a business trust originally set up to protect the property of the polygamists, but used by the leadership to acquire deeds to the homes some of the members had built on UEP property. For lawsuit purposes, these men who had assumed power and control of the organization came up with the name "Fundamentalist Church of Jesus Christ of Latter Day Saints" (FLDS) *claiming* they were an organized church and had been since 1830 when Joseph Smith organized the Mormon Church. They did this in order to legally hide behind a church entity.

In the lawsuit was the first time the name FLDS was ever used. It does not identify the polygamist group before 1987. In the 1940s they did identify themselves as Fundamentalist Mormons, but never claimed to be a church, only a Priesthood group called together to keep plural marriage alive.

Here are the lies the Barlows began circulating among the polygamists.

Lie 1
The succession of Priesthood leadership and authority from God was as follows: Lorin Woolley, John Barlow, and then Leroy Johnson.

(To legitimize their claim of a One Man Rule, they eliminated the names of those leaders in the Priesthood Council who had believed in and followed Wilford Woodruff's counsel to govern the principle of plural marriage *as a group*. With the change to a one man rule, they began calling the man a "prophet." They could not eliminate Lorin Woolley since he was the one who started the movement, but they discredited his teaching to make all decisions as a group with Lie 2.)

Lie 2
The revelation given to Wilford Woodruff in 1880 that proclaimed all apostles (council members) *having the same authority – was from Satan –* and not from God.
(Convincing the people this lie was true paved the way for One Man Rule.)

Lie 3
The United Effort Plan (UEP) was a *religious and charitable trust*, not a business trust as is declared in the original trust document. The property that had been donated by people to the UEP belonged to the *prophet*, not the listed beneficiaries (individual members) of the trust.
(This allowed the leadership to claim they owned and controlled the property people lived on and therefore they could evict anyone who disagreed with them at any time, forcing them from their home, their family, their job. In effect, casting them out.)

Now read the history of our people, which began in Short Creek, Arizona, (which became Colorado City), then a neighboring community was created on the Utah side of the valley and named Hildale, Utah. And finally, because of a split in the group, another nearby community was developed and named Centennial Park, Arizona.

Acknowledgements

I would like to thank my editor Linda Taylor for all her work and the support she has given me, and my daughter Diane, and my granddaughters Chelesa and Ashley for all their help with the computer and typing. I am grateful to John Llewellyn for introducing me to his publisher because without this help my book would not have been published. I appreciate and thank Bob Curran for his support.

I would like to thank the following people who provided research material: Max and Nancy Anderson, John Dougherty, Jay Beswick, Lorin Webb, Keith Pipkin, Elaine Johnson, Richard Van Wagner, Brian Hales, Don Bradley, Dorothy Zitting, and Don and his wives Earlene and Katy.

And most especially I would like to thank my wife Annie. She labored long and hard to transfer my manuscript from an old word processor into a computer program. I am most grateful for her patience, understanding, and for helping me in so many ways throughout my life and this project.

Introduction

Polygamy (plural marriage), a basic principle of The Church of Jesus of Christ of Latter-day Saints (the Mormons), was introduced by Joseph Smith, Church founder in 1843 at Nauvoo, Illinois. It was not accepted as a tenet of the Church until 1852, after the Mormons under the leadership of Brigham Young settled in Utah Territory. Brigham Young became the leader of the Mormons after Joseph Smith was assassinated in June of 1844.

Joseph Smith established a city in the State of Illinois, which he called Nauvoo. Due to Joseph Smith's controversial doctrine much antagonism was generated among people living in the surrounding area. Joseph Smith ordered a printing press destroyed that had published a paper exposing his polygamist relationship with several women. This led to his arrest and incarceration in jail in Carthage, Illinois, a neighboring community about 13 miles from Nauvoo. Three other men, his brother Hyrum, John Taylor, and Willard Richards were also in jail with him. A mob stormed the jail killing Joseph Smith and his brother Hyrum. John Taylor was severely wounded and Willard Richards escaped with barely a scratch. John Taylor recovered from his wounds and eventually became the third president of the Mormon Church in 1880.

After the assassination of Joseph Smith, the Mormons were in a leaderless state of confusion. Brigham Young, president of the twelve apostles of the Church, assumed the leadership position and led the people out of their confusion, establishing order among the church. The assassination of Joseph Smith did not stop the persecution of the Mormons. In the winter of 1845-46 the Mormons were driven from Nauvoo. Crossing the Mississippi River, they began their trek westward. Following the Missouri river upstream, they stopped in the area of Council Bluffs, Iowa, and established a camp along the Missouri river bottomlands, remaining there the summer of 1846. Many of the saints contracted malaria and cholera, resulting in many deaths among the refugees, who were scattered in the deplorable camps among the mosquito-infested willows and marshes. Brigham Young himself, suffering severely, became a victim of malaria, coming very close to death.

In the spring of 1847 Brigham Young led a vanguard of a little over one hundred people across the great plains, toward the great Basin of the Rocky Mountains, settling around the great Salt Lake. Thousands more would follow.

Brigham Young was sustained as the president of the Church in 1848 and by 1852 he introduced polygamy to the people as a requirement to reach the highest place in heaven. In 1862 Congress passed the Morrill law prohibiting polygamy, which the Mormons resisted on the grounds that it was unlawful interference with religious belief and practices, thus unconstitutional. This law remained practically a dead letter until 1882, when Brigham Young decided to test the validity of the Morrill law. His secretary George Reynolds offered himself as a test case to go before the Supreme Court to test the constitutionality.

Brigham Young died on August 29,1877. Three years later John Taylor was sustained as the president of the Mormon Church. The Reynolds case ascended the territorial tribunals and by 1879 was argued before the United States Supreme Court, which ruled the Morrill Act to be constitutional. Church leaders and members were greatly disappointed and George Reynolds went to prison. However, in light of the failure of the Morrill Act to stem the perceived polygamy menace, the U.S. Congress passed the Edmunds Act in 1882 that provided imprisonment and fines for the practice of plural marriage. It also prevented polygamists from voting and serving on juries.

In 1887 Congress considered The Edmunds-Tucker Bill. This bill threatened to confiscate all church property (except chapels) in excess of $50,000, and to dissolve the church as a corporate entity. This law was approved in 1890 by the Supreme Court. Following that, the Manifesto of 1890 was issued by Wilford Woodruff, fourth president of the Mormon Church, prohibiting any further polygamist marriages.

Many of the Mormon people did not accept this manifesto and in defiance to these laws of the land and this rule of the Church continued in the living of polygamy. A few of these people gravitated to a spot on the Utah/Arizona border called Short Creek (the name was changed to Colorado City in 1961) and established a society based on their beliefs in polygamy, and a United Order, where all possessions and acquisitions were owned not by the person, but by the group and were for the use of everyone participating. Each person was responsible for and to all others in the group.

THE POLYGAMISTS

"They have been shielded…by the geographic circumstances of Arizona's northern most territory – the region beyond the Grand Canyon that is best known as The Strip. Massive cliffs rearing north of Short Creek's little central street provide a natural rock barrier to the north. To the east and west are the sweeping expanses of dry and almost barren plateaus before the forests begin. To the south is the Grand Canyon. It is the most isolated of all Arizona communities. Short Creek is 400 miles by the shortest road from the Mohave County seat of Kingman. Short Creek is unique among Arizona communities in that some of its dwellings actually are in another state."

A description by Arizona Governor Howard Pyle in 1953.

Stephen V. Jones, assistant topographer to the second Colorado River expedition of John Wesley Powell, in describing his impression of the area, entered in his diary on Saturday, April 6, 1872: "(We) made Short Creek at 1 p.m. A dirty little stream not fit to drink."

In 1872, Short Creek, so named because of the short distance from the canyon to the lake bed it emptied into (a distance of about three miles), indeed seemed an unlikely place for a city to be established. There was very little water, the one most important necessity for the establishment and growth of a pioneer city. The only asset was the good grasslands in the area, making it suitable for the grazing of livestock.

During the period from 1867-1900, Short Creek Valley was "herd ground" for cattle owned by the Mormon Church. The springs in the Upper Canyon and also those at nearby Cane Beds to the southeast and Canaan to the northwest were headquarters for prosperous ranches that utilized the luxuriant forage on the Arizona Strip. The Mormon Church owned the ranch at Canaan. The Maxwell brothers owned the ranch in the mouth of Short Creek Canyon. Most of the other cattle on the Arizona strip were owned by the United Order (Mormon Church) based at Orderville, Utah.

The first permanent settlers did not move to Short Creek until about 1914 when Jacob Lauritzen came to the valley. Eventually, with the help of his brother and sons, he installed an irrigation ditch from Water Canyon that was adequate for watering about 200 acres. James Black and his family moved to Short Creek from Ferron, Utah, in April 1918, and helped the Lauritzens complete the ditch.

Water Canyon, a left hand fork from Creek Canyon, about one mile from the canyon mouth, produced the most water for Short Creek. The ditch, bringing the water from the canyon, was about three miles long. It was constructed by hand with the aid of horses and scrapers and was completed in one summer. The first half-mile of the ditch was run in 8 inch concrete pipe, the pipe sections being three feet in length. These pipe sections were hand carried for this half-mile distance before being set in place. The ditch was then hand dug for the remaining two and a half miles to the potential farmland. The water emptied into a reservoir where it was stored overnight and was used to water the fields in the daytime.

One "water right" was one eight hour natural stream flow. These water rights were granted to people (besides the Lauritzens) who worked on the ditch. Some of these included James Black and his family, Isaac Carling, and Elmer Johnson. The Blacks traded their water rights in the ditch to the Lauritzens for land and water rights to springs in the mouth of the main Short Creek Canyon, just above the junction of Water Canyon. They established a small farm there and called the spot The Garden of Eden.

In the 1930s an attempt was made to construct an irrigation ditch out of the canyon for the south side of the valley, but due to the small amount of water from the main canyon, it was not successful in these early times.

The first permanent settlers on the south side of Short Creek were Frank Colvin and his wife Elizabeth, who moved from Pipe Spring in the summer of 1914, where they had been living in the old Mormon fort, about 15 miles east of Short Creek. Pipe Spring Fort had been built in the 1870s under the direction of Brigham Young and the ranch supervisor Anson Perry Windsor.

The building consisted of two sandstone structures facing each other across a courtyard enclosed by wooden gates, which became known as Windsor Castle. Windsor and his family used the fort as headquarters for the cattle herds that he managed for the LDS Church. Even before the fort was completed a relay station for the Deseret Telegraph system was installed, connecting this remote outpost on the Arizona Strip to other Mormon settlements and Salt Lake City, Utah. This was the first telegraph line to enter the Arizona Territory. However, the location of the territorial boundary was not known to the builders, making them unaware of this fact.

In the 1880s and 1890s the remote fort at Pipe Spring became a refuge for wives hiding from federal marshals enforcing anti-polygamy laws. A number of women and children hid at Pipe Spring to save their husbands and fathers from prosecution. Faced with the confiscation of Church property, the Mormon Church sold Pipe Spring Ranch. Between 1895 and 1923 it remained in private hands. It was an oasis in the desert where travelers would stop to refresh themselves and several families lived there from time to time. On May 31,1923, President Warren G. Harding signed the proclamation setting aside Pipe Spring National Monument, which it remains to the present time.

The Blacks later moved out of the canyon and settled on the south side of the Creek. Two of Elizabeth Colvin's brothers also settled at Short Creek – Leroy Johnson in 1926, and Elmer Johnson in 1932. Another brother, Price Johnson and a brother-in-law, Carling Spencer, moved there about the same time. These two were probably the first polygamists to move into the area since the Mormon Church outlawed polygamy.

Price Johnson and Carling Spencer embraced polygamy under the sanction of John Woolley (father of Lorin Woolley), a man who claimed he had been given a commission to continue to marry people in polygamy after the Church outlawed it in 1890.

When John Taylor became (the third) President of the Mormon Church in 1880, there was a spirit of revolt among its members against polygamy. The Church had accepted polygamy in 1852 as a law pertaining to salvation in heaven, but the price of salvation became very high for the majority of the members. The desire for statehood was uppermost in the hearts of many members of the church, polygamist and non-polygamist as well. All were chafing under the yoke of territorial "carpet-bag" government, local self-government being denied them. Congress had enacted measures against polygamy and the Supreme Court of the nation had declared these laws constitutional.

Many men were being imprisoned for disobedience to the Civil law and rumors were reaching the people in Utah Territory that the United States would grant political emancipation if they would conform to these Civil laws. Also, there were threats of a confiscation of all Church property and the disfranchisement of all Church members who refused to compromise. It only became natural that concerned members would seek some kind of an agreement with the Civil Government. The pressures had become so severe that President John Taylor was forced into hiding lest the civil authorities put him in prison.

John Taylor went into hiding in 1884 and remained so until his death in 1887. While in hiding he remained in Salt Lake and Davis Counties, moving between the homes of people he could trust, often staying just one step ahead of the authorities. He was wanted because he was a polygamist but vigorously because he was the President of the Church. He had trusted bodyguards with him at all times. During this period there were mass arrests among the Latter-day Saints practicing polygamy, resulting in many men going to prison.

The following is a partial account of events that a man by the name of Lorin

Woolley later claimed to have taken place at his father's home during these tremulous times. It alleges that a self-appointed committee drafted a manifesto to discontinue polygamy for President Taylor's consideration and these are the events he described. One of the men Lorin claims was present for these events, who he says witnessed all that occurred, denied that he had been witness to any of the events described by Woolley. (Chapter 1 Notes provide more details of these events.)

"On September 26, 1886, George Q. Cannon, Hyrum B. Clawson, Franklin S. Richards, and others met with President John Taylor at my father's residence at Centerville, Davis County, Utah, and presented a document for President Taylor's consideration.

"I had just got back from a three days' trip, during most of which time I had been in the saddle, and being greatly fatigued, I had retired to rest.

"Between one and two o'clock P.M., Brother Bateman came and woke me up and asked me to be at my father's home where a manifesto was to be discussed. I went there and found there were congregated Samuel Bateman, Charles H. Wilkins, L. John Nuttall, Charles Birrell, George Q. Cannon, Franklin S. Richards, and Hyrum B. Clawson.

"We discussed the proposed Manifesto at length, but we were unable to become united in the discussion. Finally George Q. Cannon suggested that President Taylor take the matter up with the Lord and decide the same the next day. Brothers Clawson and Richards were taken back to Salt Lake. That evening I was called to act as guard during the first part of the night, notwithstanding the fact that I was greatly fatigued on account of the three days' trip I had just completed.

"The brethren retired to bed soon after nine o'clock. The sleeping rooms were inspected by the guard as was the custom.

That night two guards at the D. O. (code name for President Taylor's hiding place), Lorin C. Woolley and Henry Charles (Little Charles) Birrell, bore witness to a remarkable event. Although Lorin had checked the locked door and windows of the President's bedroom, "a light of intense brilliance appeared under the door." Lorin was "at once startled to hear voices of men talking there." He distinguished "three distinct voices, one was that of 'the Boss' (President Taylor), the other two were strangers. The three voices continued until about midnight, when one of them left and the other two continued." Lorin's father and other members of the household witnessed the brilliant light and heard the voices beyond the door, which continued until dawn. When President Taylor emerged from his room that morning "We could scarcely look at him because of the brightness of his countenance."

"He stated, 'Brethren, I have had a very pleasant conversation all night with Brother Joseph (Smith).'

"I said, 'Boss, who is the other man that was there until midnight?'

"He said, 'Brother Lorin, that was your Lord.'"

John Taylor had received a revelation, which he wrote in his own hand:

The Revelation September 27, 1886:

My son John, you have asked me concerning the new and everlasting covenant, how far it is binding upon my people.

Thus saith the Lord: All commandments that I give must be obeyed by those calling themselves by my name unless they are revoked by me or by my authority. And how can I revoke an everlasting covenant?

For I, the Lord, am everlasting and my everlasting covenants cannot be abrogated nor done away with; they stand forever. Have I not given my word in great plainness on this subject? Yet have not great numbers of my people been negligent in the observance of my law and the keeping of my commandments? And yet I have borne with them these many years, and this because of their weakness because of the perilous times. Furthermore, it is more pleasing to me that men should use their free agency in regard to these matters.

Nevertheless, I the Lord, do not change and my word and my covenants and my law do not; and as I have heretofore said by my servant, Joseph, all those who would enter into my glory must and shall obey the law. And have I not commanded men that if they were Abraham's seed and would enter into my glory, they must do the works of Abraham? I have not revoked this law, nor will I, for it is everlasting and those who will enter into my glory must obey the conditions thereof; even so, Amen.

"We had no breakfast, but assembled ourselves in a meeting. I forget who opened the meeting, I was called to offer the benediction. I think my father, John W. Woolley, offered the opening prayer. There were present at this meeting, in addition to President Taylor: George Q. Cannon, L. John Nuttall, John W. Woolley, Samuel Bateman, Charles H. Wilkins, Charles Birrell, Daniel R. Bateman, Bishop Samuel Sedden, George Earl, my mother, Julia E. Woolley, my sister, Amy Woolley, and myself. The meeting was held from about nine o'clock in the morning until five in the afternoon without intermission, being about eight hours in all. (Polygamists refer to this as "The Eight Hour Meeting.")

"After the meeting referred to, President Taylor had L. John Nuttall write five copies of the revelation. He called five of us together: Samuel Bateman, Charles H. Wilkins, George Q. Cannon, John Woolley, and myself.

"He then set us apart and placed us under covenant that while we lived we would see to it that no year passed by without children being born in the principle of plural marriage. We were given authority to carry this work on, they in turn to be given authority to ordain others when necessary, under the direction of the worthy senior (by ordination), so that there should be no cessation in the work. He then gave each of us a copy of the Revelation."

It must be pointed out here that there is no *written* testimony of anyone other than Lorin Woolley of these ordinations taking place, and the written account was not accomplished until forty-three years later in 1929.

Joseph Smith proclaims that "Out of the mouths of two or three witnesses shall all things be established." Even Joseph Musser (the man most responsible for the Fundamentalist movement) does not provide the evidence of these "two or three witnesses."

Quoting from *Truth*, a monthly magazine he published, he states: "There are a number of the brethren now living who heard not only Lorin Woolley and Daniel R. Bateman, but also John W. Woolley, relate the incidents of the meeting referred to, and their story agrees in all essential details" (*Truth*, vol. 2, p 126).

Daniel Bateman, in a written statement: "The proceedings of the meeting, as related by Brother Woolley (Lorin), are correct in every detail. I was not present when the five spoken of by Brother Woolley were set apart for special work, but have on different occasions heard the details of the same related by both Lorin C. Woolley and John W. Woolley, and from all the circumstances with which I am familiar, I firmly believe the testimony of these two Brethren to be true" (*Truth*, vol. 2 p. 120).

Daniel Bateman's testimony presents a question. If he was not present when these ordinations took place, can he be considered as a legitimate witness? There is no other written testimony of anyone witnessing these ordinations (Note 1).

George Earl apparently was approached many times during his life by Fundamentalists seeking corroboration of the Lorin Woolley story. Each time he was approached, he denied that he had been witness to any of the events described by Woolley, although he affirmed his respect for the Woolley family (Note 1).

In all fairness it must be acknowledged that John W. Woolley was aware of what his son Lorin was telling people. There is no written record that he ever contradicted Lorin's claims. Before John Woolley's death in 1928, J. Leslie Broadbent and John Y. Barlow published a pamphlet. These two men were associated with the Woolleys and were eager to not only live polygamy but also wanted to get the message to the general LDS Church membership that there was a Priesthood established outside of the Church commissioned to keep the Principle alive. The General Authorities had declared polygamy no longer a necessary tenet of the LDS doctrine and were excommunicating those who still advocated it be lived.

It was in September of 1927 that this pamphlet first appeared, entitled

Celestial Marriage, with a big question mark on the front cover. The little pamphlet was read by many people and created some controversy among the general LDS Church membership and some began asking questions of their Bishops (pastor of a congregation) concerning the doctrine advocated in the booklet.

In June of 1928 it became necessary to print additional copies of the pamphlet. The compilers of the pamphlet did not put their names on the first printing, leaving questions as to who they were. This was due, no doubt, because of the fear of persecution that they felt might result from its being published.

However, on the preface page of the second printing this statement appeared: "The compiler's name isn't necessary to a consideration of the subject treated. As a matter of fact it is just a setting forth of what the leaders and scriptures say in an effort to determine amid conflicting statements, what the law really is, without any effort, on the part of the compilers to say what in his opinion, the law might be. On the other hand the party responsible for the work has in no way tried to evade the issue, having at the time of its first publication, in September 1927, informed men in high positions and low, who did it."

When a third printing was put out in May 1929, the compilers did put their names on the preface page. In part it says: "Grateful acknowledgment is here made of the assistance of John Y. Barlow in searching the record for the enclosed quotations." It is signed by J. L. Broadbent, Compiler. This was the first propaganda material put out by the Group that was to become known as the Polygamist Fundamentalists.

It is not disputed that John Woolley was performing plural marriages up until the time that he died. Just what the connection between his actions in these matters has to do with the claims of his son Lorin is unclear. One such marriage was for Price Johnson, who at the time was living at Short Creek. (This marriage was actually performed by Joseph Musser under John Woolley's direction, before Musser was ordained by his son, Lorin Woolley.)

In about 1928, Price Johnson took his two brothers, Leroy and Elmer, to Salt Lake City to meet John Woolley. The two brothers were convinced of the truthfulness of John Woolley's calling and desired to enter into polygamy themselves. Elmer was successful in finding a girl who would marry him as a second wife, but Leroy was unable at this time to enter the "principal" (plural marriage).

John Woolley died December 13, 1928. This, according to Lorin Woolley, left him as the only survivor of the five men to whom John Taylor had given the special commission to keep polygamy alive. Lorin Woolley felt the necessity of setting other men apart to carry on with the special commission given him by President Taylor. Six more men were set apart to carry on after his death. The names of these men in the order they were ordained: Joseph Leslie Broadbent,

John Yates Barlow, Joseph White Musser, Charles Fredrick Zitting (Note 2), LeGrand Woolley, and Louis Kelsch.

Lorin Woolley designated J. Leslie Broadbent the second Elder (Note 3). He specifically told these men that the only commission they had was to keep plural marriage alive.

They were told not to organize, not to proselyte, and not to collect tithing. Lorin Woolley's hope was that people could remain in the Church and live plural marriage in secret.

The Mormon Church, however, began excommunicating all the polygamists that had been sealed by this group of men, calling them apostates. Lorin Woolley died September 18, 1934, leaving Leslie Broadbent as the senior member of the Group (Note 4).

Leslie Broadbent died in 1935, leaving John Barlow the senior member of this group of men who were beginning to be referred to as the Priesthood Council (also called the Council of Friends.)

John Barlow had tried on different occasions to get John and Lorin Woolley to organize the people and set up a United Order, but was rebuked every time. After their deaths, he approached Leslie Broadbent with these same ideas but was met with the same disapproval.

With the passing of Broadbent, John Barlow became the new leader, putting him in a position to move ahead with his dream of setting up the Order. He was soon promoting the other Council members to let him start a United Order.

About this time some of the people living at Short Creek went to Salt Lake and offered their property to the Priesthood Council as a gathering place for the polygamists. The Priesthood Council, due to Lorin Woolley's instruction, *felt it would be improper to set up any kind of an organization* so declined the offer. John Barlow, however, wanted to accept this opportunity to set up a United Order, and since he was now the senior member of this Council, he began working on the other members to allow him to do such and was successful in getting Joseph Musser's consent. Charles Zitting agreed to help somewhat, but the other two members, LeGrand Woolley and Louis Kelsch, were much slower to have anything to do with it. Joseph Musser's support, however, was all that John Barlow felt he needed, because Musser was well loved and respected among the followers of these men who were now referring to themselves as the Group.

It is a popular misconception that Short Creek was chosen as a gathering place for the polygamists because it straddled the state line. This is not true. Short Creek was chosen because the people there offered their property to the Priesthood Council, and John Barlow, senior member of the Council, was looking for a place to start a United Order.

Leroy Johnson was one of the property owners at Short Creek who had made the offer to their brethren in Salt Lake, to help set up a haven for the polygamists to gather. He became very intimate with John Barlow and a mutual bond of trust was established between these two men that never ended

In 1935, John Barlow, along with Joseph Musser and a few others, which included Richard and Fred Jessop, made a trip to Short Creek to apprize the situation. It was a hard trip because there were few paved roads and the automobiles of the 1930s were not too dependable. After a grueling trip, the group did arrive at Short Creek. Meetings were called and plans were talked about to turn the isolated spot into a beautiful place.

Joseph Musser made prophecies of things that would come to pass. Among these prophecies were that a temple would be built on a small hill south of the community called Berry Knoll, so named in memory of two brothers, Robert and Joseph Berry and Isabella, wife of Robert, who were killed by Indians nearby during the Black Hawk uprising of the 1860s. He also prophesied that Short Creek would become a garden spot of the west, one acre of land producing more food stuff than 10 acres of the best farm land in Davis County, Utah.(As of 2004, neither of these prophecies has come to pass.)

The group then went back to Salt Lake City, where Barlow and Musser began soliciting men who would participate in a United Order Movement. Some were asked to take their families and move to Short Creek while others were solicited to consecrate money to finance the project. They were successful in getting about six men to move their families to Short Creek, joining with the original settlers there.

This small Group became the nucleus Barlow needed to establish a society where people could live Plural Marriage *and* the United Order according to their religious beliefs.

When news of the polygamists settling at Short Creek was received by the County Officials in Kingman, Arizona, they felt it was necessary to stop this influx of lawbreakers moving into Mohave County. The County Sheriff was sent to Short Creek in the late summer of 1935 and he arrested a few of these polygamists on the charge of open and notorious cohabitation. A trial date was set for September 6, 1935. The trial took place at the Short Creek School house with the local Justice of the Peace, Jacob Lauritzen, presiding. After being convened for about a half hour, the cases were all dismissed because of improper pleadings prepared by the County Attorney and the prisoners were set free. New complaints were then prepared and served on two of the men, Price Johnson (brother of Leroy) and Carling Spencer. Their cases were to be moved to Kingman for final disposition.

After turning themselves in to the sheriff, Price Johnson and Carling Spencer were taken to Kingman in the fall of 1935. In a preliminary hearing they were bound over to the District Court and the trial was set to come up in December of 1935, at which time they were released on bail and returned to Short Creek to prepare for the trial.

The trial began on December 9, 1935, and lasted for four days with Judge J. W. Faulkner presiding, E. Elmo Bollinger as the prosecuting attorney, and Victor J. Hayek acting for the defense. Evidence was shown that the defendants were living polygamously and raising children in that relationship. In each case the defendants were adjudged guilty and were sentenced to serve 18 months to two years in the Arizona State Penitentiary at Florence, Arizona. On January 7, 1936, they were taken to Florence to begin their prison sentence. The defense appealed their cases but to no avail. These men had never been accused of any crime and were only living polygamy as a tenet of their religion.

Both of these men had big families at Short Creek and the care of their families had been trustingly left to the responsibility of the United Order. Because they had contributed their property, making them members of the Order, they felt confident their families would be taken care of. But they weren't.

John Barlow, the United Order Leader, failed to provide even the basic essentials for them; in fact, when some of their relatives in Glendale sent a few meager relief supplies to Price and Carling's families, Barlow confiscated them, using them himself, much to the disgust of the contributors. Some of the small children of these men were afflicted with lifetime maladies resulting from the malnutrition they suffered at this time.

These developments did not slow Barlow from developing his United Order. It is impossible to estimate how much donated money was spent to set it up. This was a time when the Nation was coming out of the Great Depression and any money given to the project was with great sacrifice to the donors.

A United Order was set up by Barlow, calling it "The United Trust," and was filed in the Mohave County courthouse in Kingman, Arizona. *The document declared what each participant contributed and that all members would be equal owners in the trust.* Also, there would be no rich nor poor, but all will be equal.

This document was copied by Barlow from a document drawn up by Joseph Musser a few months earlier in Salt Lake City, Utah. The United Trust was the name chosen by Musser for an association that was established in Salt Lake City by the "Group," in their efforts to live the United Order. A man by the name of Charles Owens was buying a farm in the Union area of Salt Lake Valley. He was unable to make the payments and was faced with foreclosure on the property. He went to the Brethren and offered the place to them for a United Order Movement, but they would have to redeem it.

A committee of five men: John Barlow, Joseph Musser, Louis Kelsch, Arnold Boss, and Charles Owens had met to discuss the organizing of a United Order. In this meeting Owens stated:

"It has been demonstrated to me that I cannot succeed temporally except through the spirit of the United Order and I am ready to turn in all I have, permitting the Priesthood to handle the same as they see fit. I recognize those of the Great High Priests as being the mouthpiece of God on the earth."

Charles Owens later joined a united order group in the Bountiful, Utah, area led by Eldon Kingston. This group claims that when J. Leslie Broadbent was the President, he declared Eldon Kingston his Second Elder, thus leaving him as the Worthy Senior when Broadbent died in 1935. But that didn't happen and Kingston eventually started his own group.

In Joseph Musser's journal, under the date of June, 1935, he writes:

"On 11th. spent day at home of Bro. Owens in Union Dist. 40 acres which he asks the privilege of putting in a co-operative movement looking toward the establishment of the United Order. He wants no guarantees or promises, but recognizing the Priesthood as he does, is prepared to give over everything to them. Presidents Barlow, Kelsch, and myself went over the farm carefully... unintelligible....Bro. Owens also presented some plans looking to the establishment of a Service Exchange Corporation (an even exchange of goods), for the consideration of the brethren."

Joseph Musser was appointed to draw up a document for the organizing of a United Order. He further writes in his journal, Saturday (June 22, 1935): "Working on Trust papers and met with the same six brethren (including myself) at 6 P.M. and read papers, which were unanimously approved. Name of Company – United Trust."

The operations at Short Creek were assumed under this same Trust organization. The affairs there were placed under the direction of John Barlow, while Joseph Musser was to take charge of the Salt Lake department.

Again from Musser's journal (July 20, 1935):

"John Y. Barlow to have full charge of operations at Short Creek, using his judgment and taking action as occasion requires: J.W. Musser, with the help of the brethren here (Salt Lake) to have like jurisdiction in Utah in the absence of Prest. Barlow."

The United Trust was established in Salt Lake and had some measure of success. The situation at Short Creek, however, was a different story. The members there began complaining about John Barlow's management of affairs in the organization. Joseph Musser wrote Barlow a letter offering some advice. The advice was received with contempt and Barlow made certain threats. "W. Barlow (John's brother) came up on 4th. and informed me in detail of conditions at Short Creek, and certain threats Bro. Barlow made against me for imaginary wrongs. Am nonplussed. It has annoyed me beyond expression. Will have the matter settled before my council if necessary."

This disagreement between John Barlow and Joseph Musser led to a confrontation over the situation. John Barlow was "invited to come up with a view to adjust matters at Short Creek." (Musser's Journal, August 24, 1935).

Musser did indeed have the matter settled before his council. The Priesthood Council decided that Barlow should be removed from the managing position at Short Creek. From Musser's Journal:

"Friday 18th.(1936). On 13th. we held Council meeting, and decided John should discontinue his active management of affairs at S.C. except in spiritual matters, and that the brethren locally there should organize and manage their own affairs, free from domination of the Priesthood."

This was a hard blow to John Barlow. The United Order Movement at Short Creek was his dream venture. He was not about to give up his control there. Determined to succeed, he returned to the community and related an altered story to the men there. He told them that the Council had decided to let the members choose who they wanted for their leader, that Joseph Musser wanted him out of the leadership position, but that the rest of the Council thought he should remain in control because of him being the President, that if the people did what the Council wanted, they would vote for him to continue to run things, thus overriding Musser's desires.

He was successful in convincing them to do just that, vote him to remain in the leadership position. When Joseph Musser learned of these developments, he, along with Louis Kelsch and Daniel Bateman, made a trip to Short Creek to confront Barlow on his actions.

Musser's journal, November 8, 1936:

"Thursday Louis and I had a personal talk with Bro. John Y. Barlow. We pointed out our fears that under the present set-up the group could not prosper; that there seemed a disposition toward a one man rule; that many of the Saints were complaining; that the present arrangement was not in accordance with the spirit of the action of the Priesthood recently taken, whereby it was advised that Bro. Barlow resign from the management of the affairs of the group and confine his labors more particularly to the spiritual field; That our work was especially along the line of keeping faith in patriarchal marriage alive, and not in the directing of colonizing.

"Bro. Barlow was asked if he claimed to hold the Keys of Priesthood, which he answered in the negative, saying, however, that he had dreamed of a personage coming to him and handing him a bunch of keys, and leaving without explanation. He did not know that that had any significance.

In later years, after his death, the sons of John Barlow changed the original account of his dream to say that the man who appeared to him was Joseph Smith, and that the keys he gave him (in this dream), were indeed the Keys of The Priesthood. (Which gave him supreme authority over the people.)

Musser's journal continues.

"On Friday 13: Priesthood met at 9 a.m. at home of Sister Colvin. Twelve of the local brethren were present, also Elders Kelsch, Bateman and Musser (13 instead of twelve present).

"Elder Kelsch stated the purpose of our visit, asking several questions of the brethren, and eliciting the following information: The action taken by the Priesthood in Salt Lake had been voted (by the members at Short Creek) adversely, mainly on account of supposing it to have been the submission of Bro. Musser and not the action of the Priesthood.

"That, ignoring the action and recommendations of the Priesthood, they (Short Creek members) had organized, using the form of United Trust, placing Bro. Barlow at the head, and were now operating under that agreement....

"The majority expressed the belief that Bro. John Y. Barlow held the keys to priesthood and was the mouth-piece of God on earth, and with some this was the only reason for accepting Bro. Barlow's Management of affairs. Elders Covington and I.W. Barlow expressed emphatic dissent, stating they did not believe Bro. B. held the keys to Priesthood, but that he did have authority to seal and was the senior member in the Priesthood group, and as such presided at the meetings of the group, etc." (Sealed used herein describes marriage for eternity.)

"J.W. Musser explained his views on Priesthood matters:
"That the special mission and labors of the Priesthood group was to keep plural marriage alive; that we were not called upon to colonize only as the Lord might dictate such a move; that it was the feeling of the Priesthood that the affairs of the Saints should be conducted by them in their local communities and not by the Priesthood,...that the time had not come for the establishing of the United Order...the Lord had not revealed to him who held the Keys to Priesthood, but that Bro. Barlow, by reason of his seniority in ordination presided over the group;.... He expressed his unshaken faith in the fertility of the soil and that the section involved would yet become a very choice spot, yielding in abundance, and would be a place where protection would be assured the Saints against their evil enemies; But that this condition would be brought about through the faithfulness of the Saints and not otherwise. There must be no autocratic rule. The agency of every individual must be respected. That no man should refuse his neighbor help when it was needed, even though the neighbor may not be a member of a TRUST GROUP."

Ignoring these feelings of the other Brethren, Barlow went ahead and copied the document that Musser had drawn up in Salt Lake City, even using the same name United Trust, changing the names of the members and the assets on the trust document to be different from those on the Salt Lake venture, then filing the trust document in the Mohave County Court House at Kingman, Arizona.

Barlow immediately began experiencing problems in his new Order. To have all things in common proved to be an impossibility, for those who controlled the money and supplies were living better than the lay members, many of whom were living on the verge of starvation. This situation caused many bitter feelings and led to the distrust of the followers in their leaders, because the leaders were those who controlled the money and supplies.

On November 8, 1936, Price Johnson and Carling Spencer were released from the prison at Florence, Arizona. They had served 11 months of their sentence, which was shortened through good behavior. When these two men returned home they found to their dismay that some changes had taken place. The Order, *as they had known it*, was in the throes of breakup with John Barlow promoting his new United Trust.

The Order had not properly taken care of the families of the two imprisoned men. The men felt they had spent their prison time pretty much ignored, their families were unjustly treated by their friends, and especially by the leaders. Carling Spencer withdrew from any of the doings of the Group. He eventually sold his property in about 1945 and moved to Mexico. Price Johnson, in the spirit of brotherhood, went to John Barlow and, in humility, confessed his betrayed feelings and some of his shortcomings, hoping to bond their relationship. He was a little critical of the action of the brethren, especially that of John Barlow, but supposed he had spoken with Brother Barlow in confidence. Much to his disappointment, he heard the things come back to him from other people of the community. John Barlow had told other members that since Price was complaining, he was weak in the faith; this undermined the confidence of the people towards Price Johnson. When Price learned what had happened, he withdrew from the society and moved over to Glendale, Utah (Note 5). He did keep in contact with the group, moving back to Short Creek in about 1946. After living there a few years, he then moved on to other places.

Probably the main criticism by these two men was the unjust treatment of their wives and children not being cared for while they were in prison. This touched them deeply, for they had supposed that by donating their property and consecrating all of their worldly possessions to the United Order, the Order would take care of their families while they were suffering as martyrs for the cause.

Soon after these happenings an offer was made for Leroy Johnson to go to a place on the Colorado River called Big Bend, where Riveria, Arizona, now stands and share crop on a farm there. He moved his family there and began farming, hopeful of helping to supply the pioneers of Short Creek with food stuff. John Barlow made a trip to Big Bend to visit with Leroy and offer encouragement. Before he left Short Creek he put Leonard Black, one of the natives of Short Creek, in charge of the Sunday School class. It was only a short time after Barlow's leaving, until other members felt that he did not have the authority to leave Leonard Black in charge of anything.

A special meeting was called, wherein the trustees of the United Trust were removed by membership vote and replaced by other members. Warren Black, older brother of Leonard, was called to Kingman for jury duty at this time. He went by way of Big Bend and informed John Barlow and Leroy Johnson of these developments. John Barlow's comment: "We organized the Trust and we can dissolve it." They claimed they went to Kingman and officially dissolved the United Trust, but there is no written record they did so (Note 6). John Barlow returned to Short Creek and returned the deeds of the property back to the owners. This put a stop to the movement and most of those who were not original settlers moved back to Salt Lake City.

Because of a water rights dispute concerning the use of the Colorado River water at Big Bend, Leroy Johnson was forced off the farm there. He moved back to Short Creek where a few of the Group were still struggling to survive under John Barlow's leadership. The Woolsey ranch near Cedar City, Utah, was leased. Leroy Johnson, John Barlow, and their families moved there. Richard Jessop leased a farm nearby in New Harmony and, along with their families, these few men stayed loyal to "Uncle John (Barlow)." They continued to work under the old United Trust and lived a form of the United Order. (Within the polygamist community, it is customary to call people "Uncle" or "Aunt" as a matter of respect, rather than just using their first name.)

After the breakup of the united order effort (John Barlow and Leroy Johnson were in Cedar City, and Richard Jessop was in New Harmony), things in Short Creek returned to somewhat the same as it was before the United Order experiment. While John Barlow had given the deeds of property back to the former owners, some, Leroy Johnson being one, had told him to keep the property, saying, "I have consecrated this to the Lord and I want you to keep it." It seems that the United Trust may have still been a legal entity.

John Barlow and some of these men remained loyal to the concept of the United Order and still lived under the guidelines of the United Trust. They were able to farm in New Harmony and the Woolsey Ranch, thus surviving the conditions of the times. Because of the property that was owned by the Trust at Short Creek, they continued their ties there, trying to farm some of the land, but not with much success because of the lack of water. An effort was made at this time to bring an irrigation ditch from the canyon to bring water to the fields on the south side of the creek, but there was very little water coming from this source and the hope was to mostly catch the flood waters when it rained. This project never did succeed at this time and the old ditch line remained unused for several years, a monument to the hard labor of these early pioneers and their diligent efforts. Warren Black bought out the little store that had been started by John Spencer and with the help of his mother, Sara Black, ran the little store and the U.S. Post Office for several years.

The next few years were a time of struggling to survive for these families. The hardships and trials they endured together created a strong bond of kinship between the families of John Barlow, Leroy Johnson, and brothers Richard and Fred Jessop. These ties of kinship were strengthened also by the intermarriage between families. John Barlow married another wife. Leroy Johnson and Richard Jessop also married another new wife each, while Fred Jessop also became a polygamist in these years. Along with the financial struggle to survive, another event occurred to hinder the progress of these hard working people.

In 1939, Richard and Fred Jessop were arrested at New Harmony for unlawful cohabitation. Their trial began on September 19, 1939, at Saint George, Utah. Richard Jessop chose to be tried before a jury and in just six minutes of deliberation he was declared guilty. He was sentenced to serve from one to five years in the State Penitentiary at Salt Lake City. Execution of the sentence was stayed pending an appeal to the State Supreme Court.

Fred Jessop waived his right to jury trial and was acquitted by the Court (Judge Will T. Hoyt) on lack of evidence. On March 27, 1940, the Utah Supreme Court reversed the lower Court's decision in the case of Richard Jessop. Among the points of error cited was insufficiency of evidence. This victory caused hope among the struggling group. Their faith was renewed and with optimism and hard work they set about the job of establishing a city at Short Creek.

World War II came to the United States in 1941 and with it a time of prosperity for the whole country. Members of the group in the Salt Lake City area became involved in war time production, earning high wages. Joseph Musser's monthly magazine *Truth*, kept him in close touch with many of these people. John Barlow still believed the United Order would work and convinced some of the Council to try it once again. In 1942 a new Trust was organized, called the United Effort Plan, and the migration of people to Short Creek began again, hoping to establish the "Order of Enoch" (a united order group described in the Book of Mormon). This new United Effort Plan was designated a Common Law Trust.

The Priesthood Council decided it would be safer to organize the association as a business, rather than a religious trust "to Safeguard our interests at Short Creek." The purposes of establishing a trust was for protection from losing the property, due to either mortgage foreclosure or from confiscation by the government because of the living of polygamy, which was against the law. The most important reason for establishing the United Effort Plan was for the security and protection of the members, both from outside influence as well as unjust management within the Group itself. For these reasons the organization must be founded under the laws of the land and be subject to these laws at all time. Such was the stated intentions of the Leaders at the time of its organization.

Note 1: Joseph Musser writes in his journal under the date of September 22, 1929:

Sunday, 22: "At noon met Loren C. Woolley, Dan R. Bateman, Jno. Y. Barlow and J. Leslie Broadbent in my office, to get from Pres. Woolley and Bateman their statement for future generations, of Prest. Taylor's experience in referring to the circumstances surrounding his receiving the revelation of 1886. It was a glorious occasion and gave me great comfort of mind and spirit. Adjourned to Friday 6 P.M."

These statements of Woolley and then Bateman were written down by Joseph Musser and then signed by them. The statements are found in *Truth*, (a monthly magazine Musser began publishing in 1935) vol. 2 p. 118. The complete statements are as follows, beginning with Lorin Woolley:

"On September 26, 1886, George Q. Cannon, Hyrum B. Clawson, Franklin S. Richards, and others, met with President John Taylor at my father's residence at Centerville, Davis County, Utah, and presented a document for President Taylor's consideration.

"I had just got back from a three days' trip, during most of which time I had been in the saddle, and being greatly fatigued, I had retired to rest.

"Between one and two o'clock P.M., Brother Bateman came and woke me up and asked me to be at my father's home where a manifesto was to be discussed. I went there and found there were congregated Samuel Bateman, Charles H. Wilkins, L. John Nuttall, Charles Birrell, George Q. Cannon, Franklin S. Richards and Hyrum B. Clawson.

"We discussed the proposed Manifesto at length, but we were unable to become united in the discussion. Finally George Q. Cannon suggested that President Taylor take the matter up with the Lord and decide the same the next day. Brothers Clawson and Richards were taken back to Salt Lake. That evening I was called to act as guard during the first part of the night, notwithstanding the fact that I was greatly fatigued on account of the three days' trip I had just completed.

"The brethren retired to bed soon after nine o'clock. The sleeping rooms were inspected by the guard as was the custom.

"President Taylor's room had no outside door. The windows were heavily screened.

"Some time after the brethren retired and while I was reading the Doctrine and Covenants, I was suddenly attracted to a light appearing under the door leading to President Taylor's room, and was at once startled to hear the voices of men talking there. I was bewildered because it was my duty to keep people out of that room and evidently someone had entered without my knowing it. I made a hasty examination and found the door leading to the room bolted as usual. I then examined the outside of the house and found all the window screens intact. While examining the last window, and feeling greatly agitated, a voice spoke to me, saying, 'Can't you feel the Spirit? Why should you worry?'

"At this I returned to my post and continued to hear the voices in the room. They were so audible that although I did not see the parties I could place their positions in the room from the sound of their voices. The three voices continued until about midnight, when one of them left, and the other two continued. One of them I recognized as President John Taylor's voice.

"I called Charles Birrell and we both sat up until eight o'clock the next morning.

"When President Taylor came out of his room about eight o'clock of the morning of September 27, 1886, we could scarcely look at him on account of the brightness of his personage.

"He stated, 'Brethren, I have had a very pleasant conversation all night with Brother Joseph' (Joseph Smith). I said, 'Boss, who is the man that was there until midnight?' He asked, 'What do you know about it, Lorin?' I told him all about my experience. He said, 'Brother Lorin, that was your Lord.'

"We had no breakfast, but assembled ourselves in a meeting. I forget who opened the meeting, I was called to offer the benediction. I think my father, John W. Woolley, offered the opening prayer. There were present, at this meeting, in addition to President Taylor; George Q. Cannon, L. John Nuttall, John W. Woolley, Samuel Bateman, Charles H. Wilkins, Charles Birrell, Daniel R. Bateman, Bishop Samuel Sedden, George Earl, my mother, Julia E. Woolley, my sister, Amy Woolley, and myself. The meeting was held from about nine o'clock in the morning until five in the afternoon without intermission, being about eight hours in all.

"President Taylor called the meeting to order. He had the Manifesto, that had been prepared under the direction of George Q. Cannon, read over again. Then he put each person under covenant that he or she would defend the principle of Celestial or Plural Marriage, and that they would consecrate their lives, liberty and property to this end, and they personally would sustain and uphold that principle.

"By that time we were all filled with the Holy Ghost. President Taylor and those present occupied about three hours up to this time. After placing us under covenant, he placed his finger on the document (the proposed manifesto to discontinue polygamy), his person rising from the floor about a foot or eighteen inches, and with countenance animated by the Spirit of the Lord, and raising his right hand to the square, he said, 'Sign that document – never! I would suffer my right hand to be severed from my body first. Sanction it, never! I would suffer my tongue to be torn from its roots in my mouth before I would sanction it!'

"After that he talked for about an hour and then sat down and wrote the revelation which was given him by the Lord upon the question of Plural Marriage. Then he talked to us for some time, and said; 'Some of you will be handled and ostracized and be cast out from the Church by your brethren because of your faithfulness and integrity to this principle, and some of you may have to surrender your lives because of the same, but woe, woe, unto those who shall bring these troubles upon you (Three of us were handled and ostracized for supporting and sustaining this principle. There are only three left who were at the meeting mentioned: Daniel R. Bateman, George Earl and myself. So far as I know those of them who have passed away all stood firm to the covenants entered into from that day to the day of their deaths).

"After the meeting referred to, President Taylor had L. John Nuttall write five copies of the revelation. He called five of us together: Samuel Bateman, Charles H. Wilkins, George Q. Cannon, John Woolley, and myself.

"He then set us apart and placed us under covenant that while we lived we would see to it that no year passed by without children being born in the principle of plural marriage. We were given authority to carry this work on, they in turn to be given authority to ordain others when necessary, under the direction of the worthy senior (by ordination), so that there should be no cessation in the work. He then gave each of us a copy of the Revelation.

"I am the only one of the five now living, and so far as I know all five of the brethren remained true and faithful to the covenants they entered into and to the responsibilities placed upon them at that time.

"During the eight hours we were together, and while President Taylor was talking to us, he frequently arose and stood above the floor, and his countenance and being were so enveloped by light and glory that it was difficult for us to look upon him.

"He stated that the document, referring to the Manifesto, was from the lower regions. He stated that many of the things he had told us we would forget and they would return to us in due time as needed, and from this fact we would know that the same was from the Lord. This has been literally fulfilled. Many of the things I forgot, but they are coming to me gradually, and those things that come to me are as clear as on the day on which they were given.

"President Taylor said that the time would come when many of the Saints would apostatize because of this principle. He said 'one half of this people will apostatize over the principle for which we are now in hiding, yea, and possibly one half of the other half' (rising off the floor while making this statement). He also said the day will come when a document similar to that (Manifesto) then under consideration would be adopted by the Church, following which 'apostasy and whoredom would be rampant in the Church.'

"He said that in the time of the seventh president of this Church, the Church would go into bondage both temporally and spiritually and in that day (the day of bondage) the One Mighty and Strong spoken of in the 85th Section of the Doctrine and Covenants would come.(Heber J. Grant was seventh President, from 1918 to 1945.)

"Among many other things stated by President Taylor on this occasion was this: 'I would be surprised if ten percent of those who claim to hold the Melchizedek Priesthood will remain true and faithful to the Gospel of the Lord Jesus Christ, at the time of the seventh president, and that there would be thousands that think they hold the Priesthood at that time, but would not have it properly conferred upon them.'

"John Taylor set the five mentioned apart and gave them authority to perform marriage ceremonies, and also to set others apart to do the same thing as long as they remained on the earth; and while doing so, the Prophet Joseph Smith stood by directing the proceedings. Two of us had not met the Prophet Joseph Smith in his mortal lifetime, and we – Charles H. Wilkins and myself were introduced to him and shook hands with him."

(Signed) Lorin C. Woolley.

Daniel R. Bateman, being present while the above experience was related by Brother Woolley, testified as follows:

"I was privileged to be at the meeting of September 27, 1886, spoken of by Brother Woolley, I myself acting as one of the guards for the brethren during those exciting times.

"The proceedings of the meeting, as related by Brother Woolley, are correct in every detail. I was not present when the five spoken of by Brother Woolley were set apart for special work, but have on different occasions heard the details of the same related by both Lorin C. Woolley and John W. Woolley, and from all the circumstances with which I am familiar, I firmly believe the testimony of these two brethren to be true."

(Signed) Daniel R. Bateman.

The Polygamist leaders rely on this statement of Lorin Woolley for their claim of Priesthood authority from God to perform plural marriages. In August of 1949, one of the men who Lorin Woolley claims was at this meeting in 1886, made a statement refuting Woolley's story.

Statement of George Earl:
"I have been approached during the past many years by scores of men endeavoring to secure my signature to a statement that I was at the meeting where President (Taylor) was purported to have stood in the air and delivered a powerful sermon upon a certain doctrine and that heavenly messengers visited him, etc. Never did I see or hear any such things and I doubt if anyone else did, but I hereby solemnly affirm that I saw nothing supernatural like that, nor heard such a sermon and I firmly believe it could not have escaped my observation had it occurred.

"I am absolutely now the sole survivor who was present during those eight months, and I feel it my duty to present these facts before the world, inasmuch as some aspersion had been cast upon my name by those seeking to subvert the truth. I always have had the feelings of the highest regard for all the Woolley family and still do."

George Earl apparently was approached many times during his life by Fundamentalists seeking corroboration of the Lorin Woolley story. Each time he was approached, he denied that he had been witness to any of the events described by Woolley, although he affirmed his respect for the Woolley family.

Although Lorin Woolley originally claimed that George Earl was one of the thirteen present at the eight-hour meeting, Earl's denials have caused Fundamentalists to later repudiate this claim and to pretend that he only occasionally entered the house between chores and therefore in truth would not remember the details. Joseph Musser later gave the following apology:

"Another man is yet living who is said to have been at the meeting referred to. He was at the time a young chore-boy, passing in and out of the house from time to time, and while he recollects such a gathering as having taken place, his memory as to details is not such as to constitute him a reliable witness. This man is George Earl, now residing at Centerville, Utah. George Earl, in a recent interview, while disclaiming a recollection of the details of the meeting referred to, with emphasis stated that after a life-long acquaintance with John W. Woolley, Lorin C. Woolley and Daniel R. Batemen, he considers them to be men of probity and strict honesty and that their testimony on any question can be relied upon."

The following statement is typed and then signed by George Earl:

Centerville, Utah

August 2nd, 1949

To whom it may concern:

I am making this statement of my own free will and choice, with no duress nor pressure from any person. And it is truthful and I hope will have a good effect.

As a young English convert I came to Utah nearly sixty-five years ago and in my middle teens I secured employment on the John W. Woolley farm in Centerville. I was as one of the family, taken into their confidence and ate at the same table as they.

In the late eighties I saw come to the Woolley home and remain there for perhaps eight months the following, although all of them did not remain constantly there, the following: President John Taylor, George Q. Cannon, Joseph F. Smith, Angus Cannon and Joseph E. Taylor. I repeat, I ate with them, helped guard them and knew all the routine that went on from day to day.

I attended the meetings on Sundays, including Fast meetings. President Taylor presented me with a five dollar gold piece, with which I purchased a small trunk, and I still have it in my possession. I at times carried their mail to the Church office in Salt Lake City on horseback. I remember Charley Wilkins and Samuel Batemen well. I heard President Taylor sing "A Poor Wayfaring Man of Grief" at a night party.

Now for the crux of the letter. I have been approached during the past many years by scores of men endeavoring to secure my signature to a statement that I was at the meeting where President Taylor was purported to have stood in the air and delivered a powerful sermon upon a certain doctrine, and that heavenly messengers visited him, etc. Never did I see or hear any such things, and I doubt if anyone else did, but I hereby solemnly affirm that I saw nothing supernatural (sic) like that, nor heard such a sermon, and I firmly believe it could not have escaped my observation had it occurred.

I am absolutely now the sole survivor who was present during those eight months, and I feel it my duty to present these facts before the world, inasmuch as some aspersion has been cast upon my name by those seeking to subvert the truth. I always have had the feelings of the highest regard for all the Woolley family, and still do (*The Polygamy Story: Fiction and Fact*: by J. Max Anderson, Publishers Press, Salt Lake City, 1979. Anderson's book is out of print but can be found at libraries and rare book sellers.).

Note 2: The Autobiography of Charles Zitting, p. 60.

"One day in the early spring of 1932, I was called into a meeting of this (the) Priesthood Council and notified that I had been called by revelation from God through their senior member, to be ordained a Patriarch and an Apostle to our Lord Jesus Christ.... About two months later, another brother (LeGrand Woolley) and I met again with this Priesthood Council.... We were ordained as Patriarchs and Apostles of the Lord Jesus Christ. I was ordained first and the other brother (LeGrand Woolley) followed right after me. The members of this Council..., in order of seniority were Lorin Woolley, Joseph Leslie Broadbent, John Yates Barlow and Joseph White Musser. Brother Woolley presided and directed Brother Broadbent to be mouth in setting me apart.

"Sometime later another brother (Louis Kelsch) was called by revelation into this Council....In ordaining me to this office in the High Priesthood Council, Brother

J. Leslie Broadbent used the following words .... 'Brother Charles Fredrick Zitting, we, thy brethren unitedly place our hands on your head and by the authority of the Holy Melchizedek Priesthood in us vested and by virtue of our office and calling, we ordain you to be a Patriarch and Apostle of our Lord Jesus Christ and we confer on you all the Keys, Power, and authority that we ourselves hold, together with the privileges and responsibilities belonging to this holy office. We forgive you of all your transgressions and say unto you dear brother, be faithful and clean before God to the end and your joy will be great. We bless you with wisdom and understanding that you will be able to discharge your duties with God's approbation and in due time receive the confirmation of your calling under the hands of your Saviour Jesus Christ, when you will meet him and converse with him as one man converses with another.

"'Now dear brother be of good cheer and abide in God's Covenants to the end. By the authority of The Holy Priesthood vested in us, we seal these blessings on your head and we do it in the name of our Lord and Saviour Jesus Christ, Amen.'"

"In giving us instructions at this meeting, Lorin Woolley informed me that he used the same words in effect, when he ordained Brother J. Leslie Broadbent and others to this High Priesthood Council.... Every man must be called of God by revelation given to the senior Apostle or President of this Priesthood Council. This one man is known as the Senior President or President of Priesthood. When he dies, the next worthy or qualified Apostle in seniority in this council becomes President of Priesthood automatically as they all hold the same keys, power and authority.... He said, he had no right to even suggest a name to heaven for this high position.... A person is first chosen by the Council in heaven and then a messenger comes here to reveal the man chosen to the President of Priesthood. Then the Priesthood Council here votes on him and the results are taken back to the Priesthood Council in heaven, who calls the man by revelation through the President of Priesthood."

Note 3: From Charles Zitting Autobiography, p. 65.

"Before President Lorin C. Woolley passed away he instructed us of the Priesthood Council in gospel doctrine, endowments, ordinances and all essentials pertaining to this holy calling.... We met once a week, Thursday evenings. About two months before we completed our work, a messenger from heaven visited Brother Woolley and told him the time was short and we would have to meet twice a week in order to complete our work. This messenger was Brother John W. Woolley, who held the keys of Priesthood before his son, Lorin C. Woolley. Therefore, we met twice a week and I remember well the night we finished our work, it was a very solemn occasion.

"After finishing, Brother Lorin C. Woolley arose and said to Brother J. Leslie Broadbent, who was next in seniority in this Priesthood Council: 'Brother Leslie, you are to me as Oliver Cowdery was to the Prophet Joseph Smith, before Oliver Cowdery apostatized. You are second elder to me and you are now to take charge until I come.'

"As he said this the tears streamed from his eyes and we were all in tears. Little did we realize that this was the last time that Brother Lorin C. Woolley would be with us, but he must have known it. Soon after this meeting he had a stroke and was confined to his home in Centerville until his death a few months later.

"His death left J. Leslie Broadbent in charge as President of Priesthood. This body of Priesthood has continued the School of the Prophets from the days of the Prophet Joseph Smith until the present time (1946) .... Not long after the passing of Apostle Lorin C. Woolley, President J. Leslie Broadbent, at a School of the Prophets, took lead in a prayer circle wherein we all offered our lives to God for the establishment of the principle of salvation. This was Brother Broadbent's last meeting with us. A day or two later, he contracted pneumonia and died.... This left Brother John Y. Barlow in charge as Senior President of the Priesthood Council (End from Zitting's Journal)."

September 18, 1934, entry in Joseph Musser's journal states: "Lorin Woolley died. J. Leslie Broadbent and John Barlow had been ordained to the Priesthood Council sometime in March, 1929. Lorin Woolley had designated J. Leslie Broadbent the second Elder some ten months before he died."

Note 4: On September 7 the Stake Presidency and High Council of Zion Park Stake met with the members of the Short Creek Branch of The Church of Jesus Christ of Latter Day Saints in the same school house where the trial of the polygamists had been held the previous day. The members of the Branch were asked to sign a loyalty oath to the Church and its leaders and to promise to refrain from living polygamy. Those who would not comply to their request were threatened with ex-communication.

The following is the loyalty oath that the Zion Park Stake Presidency asked the church members at Short Creek to sign (*Truth*, vol. 1, p. 121)
Short Creek, Arizona, September 7, 1935

To the Stake Presidency and High Council of Zion Park Stake and to whom it may concern:

I, the undersigned member of Short Creek Branch of the Rockville Ward of The Church of Jesus Christ of Latter Day Saints, declare and affirm that I without any mental reservation whatsoever, support the Presidency of the Church, and that I repudiate any intimation that any of the Presidency or Apostles of the Church are living a double life, and that I repudiate those who are falsely accusing them, and that I denounce the practice and advocacy of Plural marriage as being out of harmony with the declared principles of the Church at the present time.

Note 5: A letter from Price Johnson to John Barlow.
Glendale, Utah Aug. 5th, 1937
John Y. Barlow
Short Creek, Arizona

Dear Brother:

I believe the time has come when I must give you plainly and frankly my attitude with regard to "United Order" at Short Creek. As you know, I am, and have been for sometime, out of harmony with the way the Order has been managed, and am sending you my resignation from the United Order there, and my reasons for taking this step. In doing it I am fully aware that I will be misunderstood, but I will at least be at peace with myself.

My reasons are as follows: 1st, When I came from the Prison I was determined to live, if possible, this Order, Which I know to be an essential law of the Gospel, and must be complied with at least in spirit, if we expect to be exalted in the presence of God. I had full confidence in you and believed that you would straighten things out and make the movement a success. But I soon found out that it was not a United Order, but a dictatorship and Edmond Barlow was the sole dictator. His treatment of me and my family amounted to actual and serious persecution. Not for personal reasons but because I was concerned for the safety of the movement, I made a complaint to you. You pretended to be in sympathy with me but whispered to some of my friends that I had lost the Spirit of the Lord, and that I was unreliable, unstable and non dependable.

I believe you made this statement without understanding the facts in the case. And to refute the charge, I refer you to my past life and the fruits thereof. When the Lord made known to me that it was my duty and privilege to obey the law of Abraham I was alone in this part of the country in upholding by word and actions in this holy principle, and I was alone in it for several years thereafter. I was ostracized and shunned by my former friends. But the Lord depended upon me to uphold the law, and I did it, and when I found where the authority lie I entered the principle. Since then I have never flinched nor faltered in my determination to organize and set in order my family and lead them in righteousness toward God and His eternal glory. I honestly cannot (see) where I can be accused of being non-dependable or unreliable when it comes to upholding and sustaining principles of righteousness.

2nd: I believe you have erred in making the statement that the Mighty and Strong one had come (in 1886) to set God's house in order. If such was the case why did not John Taylor or the Woolley's proceed to act on the instructions there given? I agree with you, Brother John, that we need no more revelations on doctrine until we live up to what we already have, but I disagree with you when you say that you or anyone else have the right to organize any order or branch of the Kingdom of God without definite instructions from the Lord. I believe that men who are living the Patriarchal law, or who would live it if given the opportunity, have the right to unite together for the purpose of living the United Order according to their knowledge, but no one has the right without appointment and instruction from the Lord to organize or appoint its officers, and I had this in mind when I joined with the brethren here in asking you and your associates to assist us in living the United Order. My mind has not changed on this question. I believe this group should be allowed the privilege to organize themselves and appointing those whom they wish to preside over them, unless the Lord speaks.

I am writing this in genuine sorrow and disappointment. My family at Moccasin has been entirely ignored by the "Order." In a case like this, my first duty is to them, and I am taking this step in order that I might take care of this obligation. I have chosen this time when you, according to your statement, are about to come into some means, that I may not be accused of selfishness. According to my understanding of the Law of Consecration, a man is a steward over the property the Lord may place in his hands. After his family had been provided for, the surplus goes for the building up of the Kingdom of God. When I find a people who are determined to keep all the commandments of God, including the law of Consecration, when this people are determined to obey the law of honesty, the law of chastity and the law of obedience, when they demonstrate beyond any shadow of doubt that they are led by the revelations of God and that they have that Spirit burning in their bosom, then you will find me in the first ranks, with a determination to dedicate myself, my family and all I possess to the building up of the Kingdom of God on earth.

I am not writing this in the spirit of bitterness or hatred. I love the people of Short Creek, and want you to count me as a friend. I love the Gospel which includes the law of love and charity. I will not knowingly do anything that would deprive me or anyone else of the blessings that follow obedience to the Gospel of the Son of God.

Your brother in the Gospel,
Price W. Johnson.

Note 6: John Barlow told the members of the United Trust that he and Leroy Johnson had gone to Kingman and officially dissolved the Trust, but there is nothing in the County records showing that this was ever done. The operations at Short Creek, by the people who remained working with Barlow, were carried on under the name of the United Trust into the early 1940s, when the new Order was implemented under a different name. This evidence shows that Barlow probably told the dissenters that the Trust had been dissolved only to have them leave the community so he could keep control of the affairs there. This act of deceit on the parts of Barlow and Johnson betrays their true motives in regards to the future of the Priesthood work at Short Creek. Their plan was to always keep control of affairs there.

This was the beginning of an underlying Cabal that would plague the Short Creek Polygamists throughout their history and any decisions ever to be made concerning this group would be controlled by this Barlow Cabal.

The United "Effort" Plan

In June of 1935, Joseph Musser sent out the first issue of the *Truth* Magazine. A front page paragraph reads:

"A complete breakdown threatens the monogamistic order of marriage, the boast of modern civilization, has failed. Gnawing at its very vitals, to which the glorious principle of marriage is slowly but surely succumbing, are the death dealing agencies of infidelity, birth control and divorce. The remedy is comprehended in God's order of marriage known today as Celestial or Patriarchal Marriage (polygamy). It was revealed to Abraham by the Lord and in the present Dispensation was restored through the Mormon Prophet, Joseph Smith."

The *Truth* Magazine, a monthly publication, was circulated widely among the Ward members of the LDS Church throughout the Inter-mountain region. Joseph Musser used the magazine as a forum to promote the ideas of the Priesthood Council. The Lorin Woolley story was told of how the former Church president John Taylor had set a group of men apart to keep polygamy alive in the event the Church abandoned it. Statements from the early presidents of the Mormon Church on the necessity of living polygamy were quoted extensively.

It was not long until Musser acquired a number of followers who began seeking him out for counsel and advice. Little groups of people sprang up throughout the Western region of the United States, from Idaho to Southern California. As early as 1933, the Priesthood Council began holding cottage meetings in the Salt Lake Valley to tell their followers of the special commission that had been given them to keep polygamy alive.

After the advent of *Truth*, Joseph Musser spent much of his time traveling throughout the region teaching the groups that began asking more about the special calling these men had been given. One such group of followers was located in Eastern Idaho around the St. Anthony area. These people would gather money to buy Joseph Musser a bus ticket from Salt Lake City and request him to come and hold cottage meetings, to teach them the story of the Priesthood Council. It was in December of 1938 that Musser made his first trip to St. Anthony, Idaho, to meet with the little group. This was after the breakup of the United Trust at Short Creek, but the principle of the United Order was still an important part of the teachings of the Priesthood Council. A man by the name of Jonathan Marion Hammon, who was living at St. Anthony, became a member of this group and was to become a very prominent figure in this history.

Marion Hammon had always been an active member of the LDS Church. When he first heard the story of polygamy being lived in his day and time, he became interested and began to investigate the claims of the "Priesthood Group." When Joseph Musser met Marion Hammon, a bond of confidence and friendship was formed similar to the bond between Leroy Johnson and John Barlow. Musser and Hammon believed much the same way as to how the Gospel should be lived, including United Order.

After several trips to Idaho, Joseph Musser advised the people there to move into northern Utah to be closer to the main Group. In June of 1940 Marion Hammon moved to Millville, Cache County, Utah, where a group of the polygamists were living. He lived there less than a year before moving on to Salt Lake City. Only a few months after moving to Salt Lake, he received a surprise. One day after Sunday meeting, Brother Musser asked him to come over to his house, he wanted to talk to him. Marion was very disturbed over this invitation. It seems he had been having family problems. He had recently entered the principle of Plural Marriage and due to the problems this had caused in his household, he was afraid that Brother Musser was going to chastise him for not doing better with managing his family affairs. Imagine his surprise when Joseph Musser informed him he had been selected to be a member of the Priesthood Council.

Thus in 1941, John Barlow had "felt inspired" to call two men, Leroy Johnson and Marion Hammon, into the Priesthood Council. Because of the instructions Lorin Woolley had given them, the other Council Members gave him a certain amount of opposition. Lorin Woolley had taught them the order of how new members should be selected: "A man must be suggested by the Council on the *other side* (heaven) first and then presented to the senior or key man of the council on the earth and he takes it up with *his council* and when they pass on the man then word is sent back, by a messenger if you please, to the council on the other side, who in turn would send word back to set that man apart" (Note 1). When Barlow was asked by the other Council members, "Have you had a revelation?" He answered, "No, I just feel inspired that we should call them."

Since he was the President of the Priesthood Council, he believed he had the authority to act on his own volition, not necessarily needing *revelation from heaven* to justify his actions. Since the late 1930s he had been teaching his close friends and associates that only one man held the power and authority to manage the affairs of the Polygamists and *since he was that one man*, it was within his right to choose these men to be in HIS council.

Thus the other men of the Priesthood Council could not act until the one man in charge gave them permission. It was under these circumstances that he was able to convince Joseph Musser and Charles Zitting to allow him to ordain Leroy Johnson (his close friend) and Marion Hammon to the Priesthood Council. Louis Kelsch and LeGrand Woolley never did endorse the proposition, they only agreed to "not stand" in John Barlow's way.

John Barlow had decided to ordain Leroy Johnson to the Priesthood Council before he had received fully the permission he needed from the other Council members, and proceeded on his own to do so. Leroy Johnson was ordained by John Barlow at Woolsey Ranch on May 21, 1941. (Some of the witnesses to this event: Fred Jessop, Dan Jessop, Louis and Joe Barlow).

On June 6, two weeks later at Salt Lake City, Leroy Johnson and Marion Hammon were officially ordained by John Barlow and Joseph Musser. In later years, Leroy Johnson would claim that John Barlow ordained him at the Woolsey Ranch two weeks before Marion Hammon was ordained. Marion Hammon related that they were both ordained the same time at Salt Lake City, Leroy being ordained only 15 minutes before he was. It seems that Barlow was determined that Leroy be ordained before Marion. Since he needed Musser's help to bring in the money to finance the new United Order Movement they were about to launch, he could not afford to alienate him at this crucial time. By ordaining Leroy in secret, it was assured that he would be senior over Marion, no matter what happened later. It turned out there was no problem with Musser regarding Leroy's being ordained before Marion, so things worked out for John Barlow.

By 1941, Barlow was pretty much in control of affairs at Short Creek. He had defied the decision of the other Council members in regards to his resigning from the management position there and he began advocating that another effort be made toward establishing the United Order. After the failure of his first venture, it took a few years to convince the other Brethren to go along with the idea, but by 1941, the Priesthood Council members were ready to try again "to establish a place of refuge" that would precede a United Order. They decided to begin by establishing THE UNITED EFFORT PLAN (UEP), which would provide their "place of refuge."

On March 15, 1941, Joseph Musser and others left Salt Lake City for Short Creek. They made it to the Woolsey Ranch (near Cedar City) that day and spent the night with John Barlow. The organization of the new United Effort Plan was discussed among the Brethren. Leroy Johnson, Richard Jessop and Fred Jessop were very much a part of these planning sessions. The group of Brethren went on to Short Creek the next day where meetings were held. On March 26, 1941, a special meeting was called where the community members were presented with a letter dated March 20, 1941 (Note 2), listing the assets for the previous United Trust. The letter was a plea to the people to help raise money to pay the indebtedness of the old Trust. Also the letter made it clear that "pending a more complete organization, or of entering into a united order under instructions of the Lord, the contributors proceed under a United Effort Plan." A "board of control" would manage the plan. The members of this board were: John Y. Barlow, Joseph W. Musser, Charles F. Zitting, Louis A. Kelsch, Otto Holm, Carl Fischer, Leroy Johnson, Richard Jessop, Joseph Jessop, and Moroni Jessop. The Group struggled on under this setup until late 1942.

In October of 1942, a committee left Salt Lake City and went to Short Creek to set up the new trust to facilitate "living toward the United Order." Some of the men in this committee were: John Barlow, Joseph Musser, Marion Hammon, George Dockstader, Guy Musser (son of Joseph), and Rulon Jeffs. After returning to Salt Lake City, a trust document was drawn up. An association was formed called The United Effort Plan. The trustees were: John Y. Barlow, president; Leroy Johnson, vice-president; Joseph W. Musser, secretary and treasurer; Marion Hammon and Rulon Jeffs as trustees. The document was signed by these trustees and officers on November 9, 1942. It was filed and recorded in Mohave County Courthouse, Kingman, Arizona, on August 8, 1944.

The trust document of the United Effort Plan was somewhat different from the document of the previous United Trust. The United Trust had given the members power to vote who the trustees and officers would be. The United Effort Plan *did not allow this protection to the members.* "Trustees" were appointed by the organizers of the trust. Any new trustees would be appointed by these trustees. *The members would have no say or control in matters governing the association in any way.* The organizers were determined to have the United Effort Plan succeed even at the cost of the free agency of its members.

The complete Trust Document of the United Effort Plan is as follows:
DECLARATION OF TRUST OF THE UNITED EFFORT PLAN
DECLARATION OF TRUST, STATE OF UTAH, COUNTY OF SALT LAKE

KNOW ALL MEN BY THESE PRESENTS: That we, the subscribers and trustees hereto have this 9th day of November, 1942, entered into an agreement and contract to create a trust under which the appointed and constituted trustees hereunder shall be empowered to operate as hereinafter set forth.

To this end the subscribers associate themselves together in the formation of a trust for the purposes hereinafter stated, and without personal liability to the members hereof or to the public. It is intended and proposed that all others than the subscribers hereto who may become members in this association ipso facto agree to accept the terms of this instrument and declaration of trust to all intents and purposes as if they were the original subscribers hereto. Further, it is understood and agreed that we and such other members as may hereafter come into said association are associated together merely and solely for the purpose of being cesti que trustents of the trust hereby created, thus being entitled to the equitable and beneficial interests of all profits and property, both personal, real and mixed, of the trust estate hereby created in accordance with their respective just wants and needs as determined from time to time by the board of trustees and as the trust estate may be able to respond thereto.

The association shall be known as the UNITED EFFORT PLAN.

We do now covenant and declare that the following are and shall be the fundamental articles of said trust by which we and all persons who at any time hereafter may transact any business with said trustees pertaining to the trust shall be bound and concluded. The contracting parties and trustees herein signify and confirm by their signatures to this instrument their acceptance of all its terms and their obligation to perform and discharge the duties imposed by this instrument.

John Y. Barlow, Leroy S. Johnson, Joseph W. Musser, J. Marion Hammon and Rulon T. Jeffs are hereby designated trustees of said trust, with powers and duties, and the limitations of the same, as hereinafter set forth.

Article #2

Joseph W. Musser, Trustee, is to fill the office of Secretary, and Joseph W. Musser, Trustee is to fill the office of Treasurer, and shall perform each other duties as are necessary and usually performed by such officers in a similar business; but it is specifically understood that they shall have no power to bind the trust by contract except as such powers are delegated to them in writing by a majority of the trustees, or by a resolution passed at a regularly called meeting of the trustees.

Article #3

John Y. Barlow, trustee, shall be President of said association with powers, duties, authority and rights to do all things necessary in assisting to carry out the purposes of said trust as hereinafter set out, and said trustee, acting with the other trustees, is hereby empowered to execute all contracts, deeds, transfers, and assignments and other instruments to pass title to property, bind the trust estate as may be deemed essential to the interests of the trust; provided, however, that in the absence of the President or in the event of his inability to act through sickness or otherwise, the Vice-President may act in such duties; such instruments also being signed by the Secretary or Assistant Secretary in attestation, with the seal of the association impressed thereon.

Article #4

Leroy S. Johnson, trustee, shall act as Vice-President of said Association.

Article #5

The trustees aforesaid and their successors in trust shall hold the legal title to all property that may be acquired by or for the benefit of the trust estate, and shall have and exercise exclusive management, disposition and control of the same, subject to the terms and provisions of this Declaration of Trust.

Article #6

The trustees may appoint a General Manger, Assistant Secretary, Assistant Treasurer, or other officers who may or may not be trustees, and the respective duties of whom shall be designated by the Board of Trustees from time to time.

Article #7

The Board of Trustees shall not be less than three, nor more than nine in number; provided, that upon their own initiative and their own action the Board of Trustees may increase the board membership to any number deemed advisable for the best interests of the trust, and may choose additional trustees in accordance with such action.

Article #8

The purpose and object of the trust shall first be charitable and philanthropic, its operations to be governed in a true spirit of brotherhood; and to accomplish such purpose, it may engage in any and all kinds of legitimate business ventures; provided, however, that such endeavors of adventures of whatsoever name or nature shall in no wise conflict with the Constitution of the United States, or the constitutional laws of the land where such operations may be carried on.

Article #9

The trustees shall not be liable to the members of the trust estate for error in judgment in prosecuting and managing the trust property, interest or business, nor for any act done by them in the course of such management, nor for omission to act in the execution of this trust, except such acts as involve bad faith on their part; nor shall they be liable for the acts of omissions of each other, nor for the acts or omissions of any officer, agent, or servant appointed or acting for them; and should they or either of them be held personally liable on any tort or breach of contract in the prosecution of the trust estate, they or either of them will be entitled to indemnity out of the trust estate to the extent of such liability.

Article #10

The trustees shall have authority to fix all salaries or other compensation, both for themselves and for other employees or agents of the trust and may pay the same out of the trust funds; and such salaries of compensations shall be reasonable and consistent with the purposes and condition of the trust estate.

Article #11

A trustee or other officer may be removed at any time for cause, misconduct, or breach of trust, by a majority vote of said trustees at a special meeting called for the purpose; and upon the death, removal, or resignation of any trustee or other officer such vacancy or vacancies may be filled by the remaining members of the Board of Trustees.

Article #12

Membership in the trust estate is established for the signers of this instrument and who form the first Board of Trustees, by the conveyance to the trust estate of the following described property, situated in Mohave County, State of Arizona, to-wit: Commencing 80 rods north of the south-west corner of Section 32, Township 42 north, Range 6 west, Gila and Salt River Meridian; and running thence east 240 rods; thence north 66 rods more or less to the county road, thence west along south boundary of county road 240 rods to a point 72 and one half rods to the place of beginning, thence south 72 and one half rods to the place of beginning, containing 104 acres, more or less. Also Lot 6 and the southeast quarter of the southwest quarter of said section 31. Also Lots 3, 4 and 5 and the southeast quarter of the northwest quarter Section 6, Township 41 north, all being in Range 6 west. Also lots 1, 2, 3, and 4 and the south one half of the north-west quarter, the south-east quarter of the north-east quarter Section 1, Township 41 north of range 7 west, of above Meridian in Arizona. Containing in all 619 acres more or less. Also, beginning at a point 40 rods south of the northeast corner of Section 6, Township 41 north, Range 6 west, above Base and Meridian, and running thence north 40 rods to place of beginning, and containing 5 acres more or less.

Evidence of membership shall be shown in the books of the association. A membership certificate may, in the discretion of the trustees, be issued to each member; but such certificate shall not be transferable, nor carry title to any of the property or assets of the trust.

The proceeds arising from the operations of the trust estate shall be used by the trustees for the performance of this trust as herein provided, and any profits arising from the conduct of the business shall become part of the corpus of the trust fund. The trustees are hereby authorized to set aside from time to time such portions of the net income as they may think proper as a surplus out of which to declare dividends; provided, however, that from time to time the said trustees may make a division of the trust fund or property as may by them be deemed advisable to individual members of the trust, or all of them, strictly in accordance with their just wants and needs; and provided, further, that the trustees may render needed assistance to non-members of the trust when deemed wise by them. Further and additional membership shall be established and added to by the consecration of such property, real, personal or mixed, to the trust in such amounts as shall be deemed sufficient by the Board of Trustees; provided, however, that any member may be expelled or excluded from the trust for actions prejudicial to the interests of the trust, by a majority vote of the Board of Trustees, at a special meeting of the Board called for that purpose; and provided, further, that any member being thus expelled or excluded from the association shall have no further claim upon the trust estate.

Article #13

This trust shall continue for such time as the business proves to be advantageous but may be terminated sooner by the trustees if they deem it advisable to do so for the best interests of the trust estate and the members thereof.

Article #14

Membership in said association shall not entitle the member to any part of the trust property, either personal, real or mixed; nor to the right to call for a partition or division of the same, or for an accounting; nor shall any member have any right to amend, alter, or terminate this trust; provided, however, that amendments may be made to this Declaration of Trust by a majority vote of the Board of Trustees.

The trustees shall have no power to bind the members personally, and the members and all parties whosoever extending credit to, contracting with, or having any claim against the trust, shall look only and solely to the funds and property of the trust for payment under such contract or claim, or for any debt, damage, judgements or for any money or property that may otherwise be due or become due or payable to them from the trustees, so that neither the trustees or members at any time shall be personally liable by themselves, or by any contract which any officer or agent of the trust shall give or enter into. It shall be the duty of the trustees to refer to this Declaration of Trust and to stipulate that any contract or obligation entered into by them shall be subject to all the terms and conditions of this Declaration of Trust.

Further, it is declared that any person who shall accept a membership in said trust ipso facto becomes a party to this Declaration of Trust and shall be bound and concluded by all the terms and conditions thereof.

Article #15

The death of a member or trustee during the continuance of this trust shall in no wise operate to terminate the trust, nor shall it entitle the legal representative of the deceased member or trustee to an accounting or to take any action in court or elsewhere against the trustees.

Article #16

The original of this Declaration of Trust shall remain a part of the files of the Board of Trustees. It may, however, be recorded in the offices of the county recorders in the states wherein the property of the trust may be located. The general office of the trust shall be at Salt Lake City, Utah, unless and until it be moved elsewhere by act of the Board of Trustees. The trust may also establish branch offices by action of the trustees.

Article #17

In the event of the termination of this trust the then members of record shall participate in the distribution of all the properties belonging to said trust estate, and the assets shall be distributed upon the basis of share and share alike.

Article #18

To eliminate any question which might be raised as to the intention of the parties to this instrument, as well as cestui que trustents, it is hereby stipulated and declared that the purpose is to create a trust and not a partnership.

Article #19

The trust shall have a seal which shall be of such form and device as the trustees may determine; and it may be changed from time to time.

IN WITNESS WHEREOF, WE, the trustees and original contracting parties under this Declaration of Trust, sign our names in duplicate, original in authorization, the day and year first above written.

John Y. Barlow
Leroy S. Johnson
J. Marion Hammon
J.W. Musser
Rulon T. Jeffs
STATE OF UTAH
COUNTY OF SALT LAKE
SS

Before me, the undersigned authority personally appeared _____ known to me to be the persons whose names are subscribed to the foregoing instrument and severally acknowledged to me that they executed the same for the purposes and consideration therein expressed and in the capacity therein stated. Given under my hand and seal this 9th day of November, 1942.

Charles F. Zitting
(Notarial Seal)
Notary Public, residing at Salt Lake City, Utah. Commission expires October 29, 1943.

Filed and recorded at the request of J.W. Musser, Sec. Aug. 8, A.D. 1944 at 9 o'clock A.M. in Book 31 of Misc. p. 597-600, Records of Mohave County, Arizona.

Mary E. Carrow, # 25423
County Recorder.

The following addendum was added to the UEP Trust document in 1946.

CERTIFICATE OF AMENDMENTS TO DECLARATION OF TRUST OF THE UNITED EFFORT PLAN BE IT HEREBY RESOLVED:

"That ARTICLE III of the Declaration of Trust of THE UNITED EFFORT PLAN shall be amended to read as follows:

"John Y. Barlow, Trustee, shall be President of said association until incapacitated by removal, resignation or death, with powers, duties, authority and rights to do all things necessary in assisting to carry out the purposes of said trust as hereinafter set out, or as in the future amended: and said Trustee, as President upon being duly authorized by resolution of the Board of Trustees, is hereby empowered to execute all contracts, deeds, transfers, assignments, and other instruments to pass title to property and otherwise bind the trust estate, as may be deemed essential to the interests of the Trust; provided however, that in the absence of the President, or in the event of his inability to act through sickness or otherwise, the Vice President may act in such capacity; such instruments also being signed by the Secretary or Assistant Secretary in attestation, with the seal of the association impressed thereon.

"That the third paragraph of ARTICLE XII which paragraph now begins: The proceeds arising from the operations, etc., of said Declaration of Trust shall be amended to read as follows:

"The Trust is designated a non-profit organization. The proceeds arising from the operation of the trust estate shall be used by the Trustees for the performance of this Trust as herein provided, and any profits arising from the conduct of the business shall become part of the corpus of the trust fund. From time to time the said Trustees may make a division of the fund or property as may by them be deemed advisable, to individual members of the Trust, or all of them, strictly in accordance with their just wants and needs as determined by the said Trustees; and provided further, that the Trustees may render needed assistance to non-members of the Trust when deemed wise by them.

"That ARTICLE XIII of said Declaration of Trust shall be amended to read as follows:

"This Trust shall continue for one hundred years from date hereof, but may be terminated sooner by the Trustees, if they deem it advisable so to do, in the best interest of the trust estate and the members thereof.

"AND BE IT FURTHER RESOLVED that the Secretary or Assistant Secretary be hereby authorized and instructed to file a certified copy of this resolution adopting these amendments in the offices of the Recorders in the respective counties in which the original Declaration of Trust are or may hereafter be recorded."

STATE OF UTAH: COUNTY OF SALT LAKE:

I, Rulon T. Jeffs, Trustee and Assistant Secretary of THE UNITED EFFORT PLAN, a common law trust, having its principal office in Salt Lake City, Utah, being sworn, depose and say that the above is a true and correct copy of a resolution adopted by unanimous vote of the Board of Trustees at a meeting duly held on April 6, 1946; and that the same appears of record in the minutes of said meeting.

(SEAL)

ss RULON T. JEFFS
Assistant Secretary

Subscribed and sworn to before me this 10 day of April, 1946. (Notarial Seal) ss LEONE ERICKSON Commission Expires June 6, 1949.

Notary Public.
Filed and Recorded at Request of
The United Effort Plan, May 2 AD, 1946
at 9 o'clock A.M. in Book "33" of
Miscellaneous, p. "150-151",
Records of Mohave County, Arizona.
Mary E. Carrow County Recorder. #28834.
1153 Third Ave. Salt Lake City, 3, Utah.

After this document was drawn up and filed, one of the committee members, George L. Dockstader, who had assisted in its creation, made this statement:

"It (the trust document) is straight from Hell. A man would be absolutely crazy to ever subscribe to such a document." (It is interesting to note that George L. Dockstader did indeed join the United Effort Plan and move to Short Creek, where he taught in the public school for five or six years).

The organizers believed that such strict control was necessary to insure the survival of the association, and for the benefit and good of the members.

Marion Hammon was appointed by the UEP Board of Trustees, to be the General Manager of affairs at Short Creek. He moved his family there in late 1942 and became active in this managing role. Under his direction the UEP flourished, and the next few years at Short Creek were a time of limited growth. This was not so much because of management or production there, but rather because of new members who were turning in (donating) property and money. New converts throughout the Inter-mountain region would sell their homes, move to Short Creek, and consecrate the money to the Priesthood. Some who had small farms would "turn them in," thinking the Group would use them for production of commodities to help in feeding the people.

It is sad to look back and realize just how naive these sincere and trusting people were. Not one of these farms was ever used to support the members of the UEP. To the sad disappointment of the contributors, any real estate outside of Short Creek that had been consecrated to the Priesthood, was almost immediately sold and converted to cash. It is almost unbelievable to look back at the records of the UEP and see the thousands of dollars obtained this way. The money was not used to build the trust, but rather was given to the trustees as salaries for their support.

Some of these new members were already polygamists. Those who were not hoped that by this show of confidence (giving all they possessed) would earn them the blessings of obtaining additional wives so they could become polygamists. As it turned out, getting these plural wives would not be easy. Even after a man would make consecrations, he still had to prove himself in the eyes of the Priesthood. All marriages within the Group had to be sanctioned by one of the Priesthood Council members, but getting their approval often proved complicated.

In the 1930s and 1940s, the Priesthood Council members acted on their own in these matters. If a member of the Group would ask one of them to perform a marriage, the individual council member would act on his own feelings as to whether or not he would allow such to happen. This caused little cliques to spring up among the Group. Each council member would have his own little following and much competition would develop between these factions. If a man wanted another wife, the first step to take was to give money, property or service to one of these council members, thus winning favor enough to receive the "blessings of the Priesthood."

The people of Short Creek during the 1940s were divided into three cliques. One clique followed John Barlow (Leroy Johnson), one followed Joseph Musser (Marion Hammon) and a third group believed that to worship a "man" was a false principle. This group supposed they could be honest men, living the commandments as outlined in the Doctrine & Covenants (rule book of the Priesthood Group) and still gain the blessings of living the Principle (polygamy). It was this third group that suffered the most out of the people at Short Creek. By not aligning with one of the council members and accepting all they said as scripture, "without any mental reservations," they cut themselves off from further blessings. The men who received the blessings (wives) were those who sided with either John Barlow's or Joseph Musser's clique.

As the General Manager of the UEP, Marion Hammon felt the responsibility of improving the standards and living conditions of the people in the community. He was young in age and experience, being only 32 years old when called into the Priesthood Council, but he had high hopes and ideals. One project he felt important was the necessity of building a meeting house, where the people could be called together and be taught how to obtain the high goals he envisioned.

He began construction on the meeting house in February of 1943. As the General Manager, he supposed that he would receive full support from the people and the other council members. He was supported by Joseph Musser, but John Barlow opposed the project and he began to undermine Hammon's efforts. Barlow did not go to him directly and state his disagreement, but rather talked among the members of his clique, saying, "We are not a church house building people." (No doubt referring back to the teachings of Lorin Woolley). "The county school house is sufficient for a meeting place for us." He felt that building efforts should be spent on homes and industry.

John Barlow had more influence among the people at Short Creek than did

Marion Hammon. Construction was started on a home for Fred Jessop (Barlow clique), with a chicken coop next to it, with the idea of raising chickens as a commercial venture. The work on the church house was abandoned, while Fred Jessop's house and chicken coop was soon completed. These were the first buildings of any importance to be completed by the United Effort Plan at Short Creek.

In the 1930s the Civilian Conservation Corps (CCC) established a camp at Short Creek.

     The CCC had brought a 2" water line from Jans Canyon to the camp. The water rights of the spring belonged to the Lauritzen family (not members of the Group) and when the CCC left the area, the pipe line became the property of the Lauritzen's. This new house of Fred Jessop's was built close to this pipe line, and he obtained permission from the Lauritzens to use the water. His house had the one luxury that few other Group members had – running water.

     Along with the chicken business, the UEP obtained a sheep herd. For summer range, the sheep were kept at a ranch in Johns Valley, near Bryce Canyon. This ranch had belonged to Newel Steed, who had donated it to the Priesthood. For winter range, the sheep were moved to Short Creek, where they could forage on the desert. A sawmill was also on the Steed Ranch at Johns Valley and the Polygamists operated this mill to supply lumber to build houses. This sawmill was moved to the Kaibab Forest, near Jacob's Lake, Arizona, in about 1946 and lumber was sold to help bring in money for the Group. Also some agriculture ventures were acquired, not so much at Short Creek because of the lack of irrigation water, but other places such as a farm at Bloomington, and another at Widstoe. The Widstoe Ranch was also in Johns Valley, near the Steed Ranch. Mostly it was used for raising cattle, but some crops such as potatoes and alfalfa were raised.

Fred Jessop was appointed to act as bishop for the United Effort Plan. A store house was established at his home (the brooder building was converted for this purpose), and the Group began living United Order. Fred would purchase the groceries and bring them into town. On three days a week, Monday, Wednesday and Friday, he would pick up the grocery lists of the members in the morning and in the afternoon he would deliver the groceries back to the people of the items the store house had. This was the system for the people "having all things in common," a United Order.

     All income made by families was turned in to the Order and each family would receive back through Fred's store house what they needed to survive. Times were hard, but the people were willing and they believed progress was being made. Just as it seemed they might be experiencing a degree of success, the powers of evil were turned loose against them.

On the morning of March 7, 1944, F.B.I. agents and U.S. Marshals raided the polygamists, both at Short Creek and in Salt Lake City. Forty-six people were arrested on charges of conspiracy and the Mann and Lindberg Acts. The defendants were placed in county jails to await their trial dates, or for bonds to be raised. March 20th was set for the day to hear their pleas, only 13 days after the arrests. While the defendants were in jail, they were re-arrested on charges brought under state statutes, fifteen of them being charged with unlawful co-habitation and thirty-four with conspiracy to promote the practice of unlawful co-habitation.

The federal charge of conspiracy was based upon an alleged violation of Federal code: "which denounces as a crime the mailing of obscene matter." It was alleged that the mailing of the *Truth* Magazine came under this statute, that the magazine was "obscene, lewd and lascivious." The Mann Act cases were based upon a husband traveling from one state to another with his alleged plural wife. The kidnaping cases against three of the defendants resulted from a man taking his intended wife to another state for marriage. The man driving the car and his wife, who was with him, were included in the indictment.

On March 18, 1944, the conspiracy indictment against the *Truth* Magazine was quashed. U.S. District Judge L. Foster Symes ruled there was nothing in the *Truth* Magazine that could be construed as "obscene, lewd or lascivious." The *Truth* Magazine only teaches what the early Mormon leaders taught, that polygamy was and is a necessary part of the Mormon religion. "In conclusion it might be said that the natural reaction to reading a publication setting forth that polygamy is essential to salvation is one of repugnance and does not tend to increase sexual desire or impure thoughts." The decision of Judge Symes was appealed by the Government to the U.S. Supreme Court, but the High Court refused to hear the appeal. On June 7, 1944, Judge T. Blake Kennedy, U.S. Federal Court, passed sentence on the six Mann Act and the three kidnaping cases, having been previously declared guilty. Prison terms of from one year and a day to four years and a day were ordered. Names of the men at Short Creek convicted on the Mann Act charge: Lawrence Stubbs, Theral Dockstader, and Vergel Jessop. These men were sent to Federal prison at Tucson, Arizona.

During these turbulent times, while these persecutions were being carried out against the polygamists, the Brethren attempted to comfort the Saints at Short Creek. A letter of encouragement, dated August 30, 1944, was sent, signed by some of the Priesthood Council: John Barlow, Joseph Musser, Leroy Johnson, and Rulon Jeffs. Guy Musser (son of Joseph) and Rulon Jeffs had been called into the Priesthood Council sometime in 1943. (Note 3)

The letter has a tone of apology for the lack of financial support from the Brethren at Salt Lake City. The burden of hiring lawyers to defend the men in court cases was using all the resources the leaders could raise. This left the Saints at Short Creek pretty much to themselves, to try and earn their own support. It was during these times that the people there had the hardest times of survival. At one time they were reduced to eating rutabagas that a sympathetic farmer from the little town of Antimony, Utah, had given them. All the members of the Group were suffering because of the persecution against them. This only forced them to stick together, to try and help each other and, in so doing, brought them closer spiritually. Under these circumstances, the letter most surely gave them encouragement. However, the persecutions continued.

On October 10, 1944, thirty-one defendants were adjudged guilty of conspiracy to encourage the breaking of the laws of the State (Utah) with reference to unlawful co-habitation. Each was sentenced to serve a year in the county jail in Salt Lake City. Notice of appeal was given to go before the State Supreme Court. The defendants were allowed to remain free on bail until this decision. On February 7, 1945, the cases of Fred Jessop and Edson Jessop of Short Creek, charged with unlawful co-habitation, were dismissed at St. George by Judge Will L. Hoyt, for lack of evidence.

On May 12, 1945, fifteen defendants appeared before Judge Van Cott. They had been found guilty of unlawful co-habitation about one year before and had been sentenced to an indeterminate term of from one to five years in the State Penitentiary, Salt Lake City, Utah. The defendants had exhausted all appeals and on this date were committed to the custody of the sheriff to carry out the sentence. The men of the group connected with the Priesthood Work at Short Creek: John Y. Barlow, Joseph W. Musser, Charles F. Zitting, Louis A. Kelsch, and Alma A. Timpson. It was a sad day for the polygamists at Short Creek when their leaders were sent to prison.

The leadership at Short Creek was temporarily left to newly appointed members of the priesthood council: Leroy Johnson, Marion Hammon, and Richard Jessop (Richard Jessop was called to the Priesthood Council in early 1945). The publishing of The *Truth* Magazine was left in the hands of Guy Musser (son of Joseph) at Salt Lake City. Affairs at Short Creek were conducted adequately the next few months under the leadership of these men.

After only seven months, some of the leaders who had been sent to prison were released on parole. On December 15, 1945, the Utah Board of Pardons granted parole privileges to eleven of the prisoners after they signed a statement agreeing "To refrain hereafter from advocating, teaching or countenancing the practice of plural marriage or polygamy" (Note 4). Four of the prisoners would not sign the Manifesto and remained in prison to serve their full time. Charles Zitting and Louis Kelsch were two of the four. John Barlow, Joseph Musser, and Alma Timpson were among the eleven who signed to get out (Note 5).

The signing of this Manifesto by the Group leaders caused bitter feelings among some members at Short Creek. They felt the leaders had betrayed them. After all, the reason they had left the LDS Church was because of the Manifesto signed in 1890. They wanted to know how these men could justify themselves in what they had done. The best explanation given was this: "We (Barlow and Musser) had to get out to carry on Our Work (that of keeping polygamy alive)."

The conditions in the prison were such that the health of the older Brethren was fast deteriorating. If they were required to serve out their full sentences, it was questionable whether or not they could live them out. These reasons did little to satisfy the feelings of those criticizing their actions. That was not all. After the Brethren were out of prison and returned to their homes, they didn't live up to the agreements of the manifesto they had signed. They violated every covenant in it. They went back to cohabiting with their plural wives; they went right on performing plural marriages for others, and they went right on preaching and teaching it to their followers.

This made it even harder for the ones questioning their behavior. These were mostly those of the third clique, who had not aligned themselves behind Barlow or Hammon. They began questioning the worthiness of leaders that would make agreements with no intention of ever living up to them. This led them to believe that maybe they did not hold the High Priesthood they claimed they held. Within a few months, this dissension spread thoughout the community. Many became unhappy with the way the leaders had squandered the money. Some began asking for some kind of security for the equity they had put into the Trust. They wanted something in writing to guarantee that they would not lose their Stewardship, or means they had of earning a living if the UEP would break up. By asking for something in writing to protect themselves, these dissenters only caused more discord and loss of confidence of the leaders towards them, especially when they confronted the leaders with the Written Word (Doctrine & Covenants) to support their requests.

The leaders were not willing to grant their requests: "Give unto him a writing that shall secure unto him his portion" (Note 6). Their defense was: "We are not living the United Order, but only a step toward it, thus we are not bound by the commandments in the written word." Some of the men that this stand was directed against, came to realize, "If this is a United Effort only, the United Order will be easy."

In early 1946, John Barlow called Carl Holm to be a member of the Priesthood Council. This brought the number to six men that he had called. Carl was only about 30 years old at the time. He had lived near Idaho Falls, Idaho, and had inherited a pretty large farm from his father, about the time he was married. He sold the farm and turned the money in to the UEP. He was placed in a leadership position at a very young age. He was very inexperienced for such a calling, as was proven a few years later when the leadership of the UEP placed him as the General Manager at Short Creek.

Now that Carl Holm was a member of the Priesthood Council, he was automatically recognized as a Trustee of the United Effort Plan. A letter signed by Rulon Jeffs, assistant secretary of the UEP, was sent to Carl Holm congratulating and welcoming him as such. This letter was dated June 29, 1946 (Note 7). The calling of Carl Holm to the Priesthood Council only made matters worse in the eyes of the Dissidents. They were very critical of Barlow calling such a young and inexperienced man to be a leader over them and demanded that some changes be made in the operation of the UEP, where they were concerned. The leaders concluded that something must be done to satisfy these unhappy dissidents.

By the first of 1948, it was pretty much recognized that the UEP had failed in so far as the hopes of its organizers. The strife between the cliques had brought things pretty much to a general break up. In order to keep the United Effort Plan together, the leaders decided to make a compromise with their unhappy followers. *They did not concede that a compromise was being made*, but rather called it "A higher step." In March of 1948, a letter was distributed among the people of Short Creek. The letter (Note 8) was signed by John Y. Barlow, Joseph W. Musser, J. Marion Hammon, Guy Musser, Rulon T. Jeffs, and Richard S. Jessop (Leroy Johnson was in Old Mexico, having been sent there by John Barlow to start another Community).

The letter made it clear that "we are not living the United Order, nor have we been living it. We are living 'toward' it. The United Effort Plan was organized to protect our operations legally. That by working on a community basis, be prepared to live the full law as the Lord requires it, and as he intends vindicating it by issuing inheritances" (See D&C 85). The leaders felt it was time to issue these inheritances by granting *perpetual leases on property to the members* to come under: "The exclusive management of the members receiving the same."

The letter further outlines: "this, then, places every man on his own, to reap the benefit of his labors and the more energetic he is the more he is entitled to for the support of his own family."

The idea of granting leases came about because of the complaints of the Dissidents (those of the third clique), who went to Joseph Musser with their grievances. He wrote up a rough draft of a lease that said:

"Leases: John Bistline: Terms: In consideration of past consecrations; a lifetime lease, not subject to termination by reason of conscientious beliefs."

This draft resulted in the following lease presented to the Dissidents.

"LEASE: THIS INDENTURE, made this day of _____ , 19___ , between The United Effort Plan, a common law trust, with principal office at Salt Lake City, Utah, lessor, and _____ of _____, lessee; WITNESSETH: That for and in consideration of all consecrations, gifts and contributions heretofore made by lessee to lessor, and for the further consideration of $1.00 per year to be paid by lessee to the lessor yearly in advance, the lessor has let and by these presents does grant, demise, and let unto the lessee and his heirs, for the life time of lessee and his heirs, the following described tract of land in _____ County, State of _____ , to-wit; Subject to the following terms and conditions: It is agreed that if default shall be made in any of the covenants herein contained, then it shall be lawful, upon thirty days notice, for the lessor to re-enter said premises and to remove all persons therefrom.

The lessee hereby covenants to pay to the lessor the rent as herein specified, and to pay the annual rent or charge assessed or imposed on said premises and for the use of water, if any water assessment (where irrigation is included), and to pay all taxes assessed against said land.

The lessee covenants that he will not assign this lease, nor any interest therein, or let or underlet the whole or any part of said premises, without the written consent of the lessor, under penalty of forfeiture and damages.

The lessee covenants that he will live on said premises in peace with his neighbors and members of the United Effort Plan; and so long as lessee continues to live in peace and conduct himself as a Christian, lessor covenants that the lessee, in paying the said yearly rent and performing this and other covenants aforesaid, shall and may peaceably and quietly have, hold, and enjoy the said demised premises for the term aforesaid.

And it is further understood that the covenants and agreements herein contained are binding on the parties hereto and their legal representatives.

IN WITNESS WHEREOF the parties hereto have set their hands and seals the day and year above written. The United Effort Plan, by (the President) ss/ _____ , (by the Secretary) ss/_____.

A committee was appointed to oversee these operations: Richard Jessop, J. Marion Hammon, and Joseph S. Jessop, "to preside over the Saints of Short Creek." Also, "we recommend, however, that your problems be taken to the Presiding Elders (above named) and not to Brother Barlow direct in his poor state of health." The letter further explains, "our plan is to satisfy those only who feel it desirable to have exclusive jurisdiction leases – these latter people are now placed on their own." There was mention in the letter to "clear off all indebtedness as quickly as possible." Further the members were told to support their own families, pay their tithing (10 percent of all income), and each head of household was to give Fred Jessop thirty dollars a month to take care of the widows (Fred was still acting as the Bishop).

This breakup of the UEP was a hard trial for John Y. Barlow. He had hoped the people would support him, and the UEP could have succeeded. He said he endorsed the actions of the other council members in allowing members to have leases, but in his heart he did not accept it. Back in 1938, he had spent many hours walking the streets of Short Creek, telling anyone who would listen to him that "in order for the United Effort Plan to work, we will have to raise a generation of people, teach them as we raise them how to make the plan work." He had told them "If I can get just one man to go along with me I will keep the UEP alive." He had been successful in getting a few people to follow him: Leroy Johnson, Richard Jessop, Fred Jessop, and a dozen or so young men in their early twenties.

Marion Hammon left Short Creek and, after a few weeks in Old Mexico, he moved back to Salt Lake City, making his own way outside of the UEP. Joseph Musser more or less spent his time with the people in Salt Lake City and had very little to do with Short Creek after 1948, pretty much leaving John Y. Barlow to do as he pleased.

The members who thought they were going to get leases of their property were very disappointed because John Y. Barlow would not allow these leases to be honored.

Anyone who insisted on getting a lease was simply told they were no longer a member of the United Effort Plan. Because there was *nothing in writing* (no certificates of membership had been issued), they felt it impossible to get the security on their homes that the leases might offer. These discouraged members began to move out as best as they could. The UEP leaders refused to assist them in any way. These disillusioned men would leave the community, most of them going to Salt Lake City, working there for up to two years in some instances, before they could earn enough money to move their families out.

At the beginning of 1949, most of the dissatisfied members had left Short Creek. Leroy Johnson was in Old Mexico with a small group of people whom John Y. Barlow had sent down there to try another experiment (Note 9). Barlow had been stricken with a malady that left him pretty much bedridden, spending most of his time now in Salt Lake City. The managing of affairs at Short Creek was left in the hands of Richard Jessop, Carl Holm (newly appointed council member), and Fred Jessop (not a member of the Priesthood Council).

With the dissidents gone, Marion Hammon out of the picture, and Joseph Musser no longer bothering him, John Barlow made one last effort to establish the United Effort Plan before he died. In the latter part of 1949 he made one last trip to Short Creek to accomplish just that. Every man over the age of 16 was called to a special Priesthood meeting one Sunday morning at the home of John Barlow, a small house where one of his young wives (age 15) lived.

The men attending this meeting were instructed as to the purpose of the meeting. They were each given the opportunity of joining with the UEP in this last struggle for its survival. All chose to support him in this endeavor. They were then each placed under covenant that they would support the UEP and its leaders with everything they had. They agreed to devote their full time, their money, property, and talents to its up-building and survival. The men involved in this collusion were mostly young and zealous. They had grown up in the association of John Barlow,

Leroy Johnson, and Richard and Fred Jessop. They were willing to accept the things told them by any of these men, especially John Barlow.

After this meeting Barlow asked Fred Jessop to make him a promise that when he died, Fred would take care of his sons, seeing to it that they would never suffer for lack of material things. Also to see to it that they would be included in the managing of affairs of the UEP. Fred made him this promise with a sacred covenant that he honored for the rest of his life, putting these sons of John and Mattie (his sister) Barlow above the support of his own brothers when his own father died, also leaving a number of young children. John Barlow had extracted this same promise from Leroy Johnson a few years before. John Barlow then returned to Salt Lake City. He never returned to Short Creek again.

Towards the end of 1949, the experiment in Old Mexico was called off. John Barlow sent for Leroy Johnson to come to Salt Lake City. It took over a week for the mail to reach him in Mexico. He finished up affairs there and then started for Salt Lake City as soon as he could, leaving the moving of his family to his son Orval, along with others who had been sent there to help him. He did not reach Salt Lake City before Barlow died, arriving there a few hours late. He was sorrowful that he had not been able to talk with Barlow before he passed on. He had expected to receive special instruction as to the running of the UEP and the Priesthood Work.

John Barlow died on December 29, 1949. A few days before he died, he sent word to Alma A. Timpson (on Christmas day) that he wanted to see him. Because of it being Christmas day, Timpson waited until the next day to call on Brother Barlow. When he went into the bedroom where John lay (on his death bed), he received chastisement for not coming the day before. Brother Barlow told him to get the other Brethren of the Council to ordain him a member of the Priesthood Council. Timpson and the other Council members (except Leroy Johnson, who was on his way from Mexico) went into the next room and the ordination was carried out (Note 10).

This brought to seven the number of men John Y. Barlow had called: Leroy S. Johnson, J. Marion Hammon, Guy H. Musser, Rulon T. Jeffs, Richard S. Jessop, Carl O. Holm, and Alma A. Timpson. Of the council that Lorin Woolley had called in the 1930s, four men were still alive: Joseph W. Musser, Charles F. Zitting, LeGrand Woolley, and Louis A. Kelsch.

As next in line Joseph Musser became the recognized President of the Priesthood Council. He had been sick when he came out of Utah State Prison in 1945 and before John Barlow's death, he suffered the first of a series of strokes that would leave him in an incapacitated state (and eventually caused his death in 1954). Soon after Barlow's death Joseph Musser attempted to call a new member to the Priesthood Council, filling the vacancy left when Barlow died. He presented the name of Rulon Allred to the Council, but was met with rejection, the other members not sustaining him in this decision. He decided to go ahead and call Allred anyway, ignoring their objections. In calling Rulon Allred, Musser was following John Barlow's example of "One Man Rule," even against the advice of his council.

In April of 1950, in Salt Lake City, Utah, Joseph Musser stood before a general meeting of the polygamists and announced he had received a revelation to call Rulon Allred into the Priesthood Council. He told the other Council members who were present that he wanted them to help him with the ordination after the meeting. When the meeting was over, Richard Jessop was the only Council member to come forward to assist President Musser in confirming Allred. With the other Council members milling among the congregation, Joseph Musser and Richard Jessop placed their hands on the head of Rulon Allred and ordained him to the office of Patriarch and Apostle (High Priest Apostle).

Later that evening, Richard Jessop was "called on the carpet" by the Council members for his actions. According to Jessop's beliefs and teaching he had done no wrong. Joseph Musser was the recognized priesthood head and had the authority to receive revelation for the people in such matters. The other council members did not approve of Allred's calling and they spent all night and until noon the next day convincing Jessop of his error in following Musser's leadership. Richard Jessop finally gave in and went with the other council members on the issue. In later years he would say that when he assisted Joseph Musser in Allred's ordination, all they gave him was a blessing. This was probably the only concession of conscience that Richard Jessop ever made on Priesthood Matters.

After the calling and ordination of Rulon Allred, the other Council members turned against Joseph Musser, telling the people that due to his sickness he was now incompetent to be the leader. This caused a split among the group, with some following the Council, while others placed their allegiance with Musser. Joseph labored with the Council members to accept his leadership but was unable to convince them he had done right in regards to Allred's ordination. His own son Guy was his most bitter opponent. In January of 1952, in a special priesthood class held once a month where only selected members were invited (School of the Prophets), a member of the class made these observations (Note 11).

"I wanted a clean start before the Lord in the New Year and so I called upon Brother Guy on New Year's evening and stated the reasons for my visit. He immediately began to denounce Brother Allred. I protested to the best of my ability. In the face of my protests, Brother Guy said, (1) 'R.C. Allred is a devil! He has tried for the last 15 years to split up the Priesthood. (2) My father is incompetent and is not able to give any man the apostleship. Rulon has not got it! (3) Rulon C. Allred has used my father as a pissing post. If I wanted to use the same policy that Rulon is using, we could get father to do whatever we wanted him to do. (4) Certain of the Brethren have come to me and offered to take Brother Allred's life if he continues to maintain his stand'."

In Joseph Musser's mind, there was nothing he could contribute to help the Priesthood Council. They had openly rejected him and his position as President. In light of this, he decided to call new members to the Council, leaving the others, who would not accept his leadership, to go their own way.

In 1952, Joseph Musser, as President of the Priesthood, called six men to the Apostleship, thus establishing a *new* Priesthood Council. These six, along with Rulon Allred, filled the Council to the required number of seven. The names of the six: John Butchereit, Eslie Jensen, Owen Allred, Marvin Allred, Joseph Thompson, and Lyman Jessop (Owen and Marvin Allred were brothers to Rulon, Lyman Jessop was a brother to Richard Jessop).

The Priesthood Group in Salt Lake City was split about fifty-fifty, with about half of them following Joseph Musser and his new council, while the remainder followed the old Priesthood Council of John Barlow. The Group at Short Creek, however, followed the old council almost one hundred percent. This Priesthood controversy took place at Salt Lake City and the people at Short Creek were pretty much following Leroy Johnson (under Charles Zitting) by this time. None of them were firsthand witnesses to what had transpired at Salt Lake City. Their only knowledge of the events was what the Council related to them. This, of course, was information designed to support their stand on the controversy. Joseph Musser was portrayed as old, senile and incapacitated, no longer capable to lead the Lord's Work. Joseph did attempt to explain his actions to the Saints at Short Creek, but the leaders there would not allow him to address the people in any public meeting.

In July of 1952, Joseph Musser, along with Lyman Jessop and Wayne Handy, made a trip to Short Creek, the purpose being to justify his actions to the people there. He met with Leroy Johnson, Richard Jessop, and Carl Holm, asking them to call a meeting so he could talk to the people. This they were reluctant to do. Lyman Jessop, in his journal, writes about this meeting (Note 12):

"Brother Joseph asked Roy (Leroy Johnson) to state how he felt toward him, so Roy said that he knows that Joseph holds the keys to the Priesthood and he (Roy) will sustain him in that position in love and loyalty (Leroy said) 'I stood by John (Barlow) until the end. I will support you as I did him'. Joseph responded, 'That's fine'."

These men did not allow Brother Musser to talk to the People, even in light of their professed loyalty. Leroy, in spite of his expressed allegiance, then made this statement to Musser: "We are under covenant to do what we are doing and we cannot change from that course and we have no arguments to make. If the Lord wants to use an incapacitated leader (referring to Joseph Musser standing before him) to lead some people astray, that is the Lord's business." These bitter feelings from Leroy surprised Musser very much.

After a few moments of thought, Musser told Leroy that the time would come when he (Leroy) would be in the same incapacitated condition and that the Group at Short Creek would be split to smithereens (This prediction of Joseph Musser pretty much came true).

Joseph Musser and his companions returned to Salt Lake City. This was the last attempt he made to regain the loyalty of the people at Short Creek. The two polygamist groups became split and a wide gap came between them. The people following Joseph Musser's (Rulon Allred) group have grown more in numbers than the Barlow (Leroy Johnson) group. The Musser group have maintained warm and friendly feelings towards the Barlow group, but these feelings have not been reciprocal. Over the years, the people of Short Creek have been bitter towards the "Allred Group" and resent any attempts of friendship from them.

The polygamists at Short Creek were loyal to Leroy Johnson's leadership (under Charles Zitting). With all dissidents gone, the next year was one of peace and good feelings. The group in the main were young people, loyal to John Barlow's teachings and eager to follow their Priesthood Leaders. There was some civic progress in the community. The people were still living United Order, getting commodities from the UEP storehouse. The little store and post office building was purchased from Warren Black by David Broadbent (son of J. Leslie Broadbent). His mother Fawn Broadbent was appointed postmistress. The store was named Short Creek Supply. A new store building was constructed (on the corner of Central St. and Township Ave.) and the Post Office was moved to a room in the new store. Aunt Fawn Broadbent was store clerk as well as postmistress. Having a store in the community was a paradox because the members of the UEP were all living the United Order. They had no money (supposedly) to spend in the store. There was, however, a small need in the area for a store and gas station to serve the few outsiders who braved the rough dirt roads (it was 30 miles to Hurricane, the closest town), to get to the isolated area. This consisted mostly of the cattlemen who operated ranches in the area. It did seem that there was a certain class of local people who always had money to purchase what goods were not available in Fred's Store House. These people were the ones in Leroy's clique, those he felt to favor.

Besides the new store building, a few new homes were also built. Some of the Lauritzen property was purchased by Group members. Also a farm at Hatch, Utah, and another one near Alton, Utah, were purchased from E. J. Graff of Hurricane. Payments on these ranches at Hatch and Alton were made by the UEP, the money being earned from the projects sponsored by its leaders and managers. The payments on the Lauritzen property were made by Bill Cooke and his son Lynn, who were farming the property, raising chickens, and selling the eggs in the outside communities.

There is an inconsistency regarding the UEP leaders that should be related here.

Bill Cooke had been given the responsibility to make the payments on the Don Lauritzen property. The only income he could raise was from the resources of the farm. By using his ingenuity he established a way to earn money from the farm by selling eggs. Much to his surprise, he was approached by Leroy Johnson and scolded severely for running a business on the UEP property. He was informed that businesses on UEP property could only be run under the jurisdiction of those appointed by the trustees. He was told to get rid of the chickens and discontinue the enterprise. He obeyed the directive of Leroy. He did, however, feel unjustly done by and expressed his feelings to anyone who would listen. He was very surprised then, when a few months later he was called by the Priesthood to be set apart as a Patriarch. He felt he had been given the trial to prove his worthiness.

It should be noted here that the chicken business that was started some six or seven years earlier, under the jurisdiction of the UEP and turned over to Fred Jessop to run, lasted only about a year or so until it was abandoned because it was not successful.

This was a time of limited prosperity at Short Creek, and most everyone was encouraged. It appeared that nothing could stop the progress of the Priesthood in the building of the Kingdom of God. There were, however, some surprises in store for the peaceful community.

Note 1: The following is a copy of instructions from Charles Zitting.(Charles Zitting Autobiography)

Pres. Charles F. Zitting spoke upon the order pertaining to the calling of a man into the Priesthood Council, stating in substance as follows:

"I remember clearly the instructions of President Lorin C. Woolley. Brother Lorin recited the case of Dan Bateman who was a very dear friend of his and would have liked to have seen him in the Council for he was a faithful and good man. He suggested his name to the Lord and received the answer by a messenger from the other side, which was his own father, that it was none of his (Lorin's) business.

"Brother Lorin taught us the order in this way. A man must be suggested by the Council on the other side first and then presented to the senior or key man of the council on the earth and he takes it up with his council and when they pass on him then word is sent back, by a messenger if you please, to the council on the other side, who in turn would send word back to set that man apart and also give instructions when to set him apart. That is the order as taught to Brother Lorin C. Woolley by John Taylor as it was handed down by the Priesthood and received from the Savior.

"Now we do not deviate from this procedure, otherwise we would be out of order. Any man that receives authority other than that was, it is (then) just a delegated authority, and when a man that has delegated that authority to him dies, that is the end of his authority."

Note 2: UNITED TRUST HOLDINGS – UTAH AND ARIZONA (3-20-41) Short Creek:

Leroy S. Johnson land, 640 Acres (three homes)

Richard & Fred Jessop 130 acres

Total: 770 acres (Deeded land.)

LEASES New Harmony: 165 acres, three years to run. On 30 acres lessees get full crop for 1941 and 2/3 on balance. 70 acres from Mr. Smutz for 1941, on 2/3 crop basis. 70 acres from Mr. Taylor for 1941, on 2/3 crop. 25 A. Planted.

Cedar Ranch: 470 Acres of which 150 A. Are cultivated: 3/5 basis.

33 head of cows with bull-same basis.

Group Owns Outright:

9 head two year old heifers, some with calf

10 yearling calves

3 work horses; 3 saddle horses and pony.

Threshing machine	Hand plow
Tractor	Drill
Plows	Silo cutter

Disc	3 and a half sets harness
Harrow	Wagon rack
Potato planter	Trailer
Mowing machine	2 canning outfits

Indebtedness:
Taxes on Short Creek property $215.00
Due on threshing machine $65.00
On Government loan (drawing 5%) $1568.26
On Government loan (drawing 3%) $4226.15
Current bill for gas and oil $106.15

Now due on above:
Taxes $215.00
Store $106.15
Due December 1st:
On Government loan $824.00
On thresher 65.00 = 889.00

It is proposed to receive voluntary contributions to clear the indebtedness mentioned, and that the property, crops, etc. be under the control of the contributors. That, pending a more complete organization, or of entering into an United Order, under instructions of the Lord, the contributors proceed under a United Effort Plan, the property and contributions belonging to those fostering the plan. That contributions be used in meeting present indebtedness and future requirements. That the lands be worked as at present, the actual workers, with their families, being maintained out of the increments in accordance with their just wants and needs. Those contributing money or needed goods will be cared for in like manner. The policy of the brethren being to store grain and other food-stuffs, and to increase the herd, and accumulate other property, distribution of goods will only be made as actual needs arise. Each contributor, whether in money, goods, or labor, will receive proper credit on the books of the plan; and in the event of a disagreement or dissatisfaction in distribution, the matter may be arbitrated by the Priesthood Council, or such other Council as shall be agreed upon, whose decision shall be final and binding. Contributors wishing to withdraw from the plan may do so by forfeiting any contributions they may have made, but they shall not be permitted to make any claim on the remaining members or on the assets of the plan. A Board of Control shall be given the management of the plan, consisting, for the present, of John Y. Barlow, Jos. W. Musser, Charles F. Zitting, Lewis A. Kelsch, Otto Holm, Carl Fischer, Roy Johnson, Richard Jessop and Moroni Jessop.

Note 3: Letter to the people at Short Creek from the Brethren.
TRUTH PUBLISHING COMPANY
1153 Third Avenue
Salt Lake City, Utah
August 30, 1944

Dear Brethren of The United Effort Plan:

We feel impressed to write you setting forth some thoughts arising in our minds regarding your labors in this United Effort Plan. We desire to be frank and above-board in our expressions and suggestions; and above all things we want you to know that we are moved upon with only one major thought – that of the building up of the Kingdom of God on the earth.

It is because of this determination that the powers of darkness have made such a vicious attack upon us in the courts and elsewhere, and that Satan is using his utmost strength to defeat our efforts and plans. As his blows become harder our resistance must increase, and this can only be done as we improve our technique and more determinedly serve the Lord, whose servants we are.

The United Effort Plan is of the Lord. Its birth and growth thus far have been inspired of heaven. The plan can succeed only as it is advanced in humility, with determination and unselfishness, and with an "eye single to the glory of God." It is the one great step towards the Order of Enoch (Book of Mormon), which order enabled Enoch with his people to subdue the part of the earth they occupied, and to become translated (taken to heaven without dying a mortal death). We aim to reach the same goal. The part of the earth which you are engaged in subduing is as important to the Lord as that which Enoch's people became master of. Enoch's people achieved through the power of the Priesthood; it is through this same power that we are endeavoring to operate at Short Creek and other places.

Our interests are strictly in common, not one of us possessing that which is above the possessions of our neighbor who is identified with the Plan. And we want you and all our brethren engaged in this great movement to know, that you have our full support and confidence.

Our industry in the Short Creek unit comprises agriculture, livestock, sheep raising and lumbering. In Salt Lake County we have some small acreage being devoted mainly to truck gardening and dairying; and in Northern Idaho we are interested in a large cattle ranch, now being operated by Brother Hunter and family.

Each of these three units is under efficient management. J. Marion Hammon is the General Manager of the Effort, under the direction of the Board of Directors, his time being specifically devoted to the Short Creek unit. The unit here is under the management of a "Planning Committee", consisting of Davis L, Hunter, Rulon C. Allred and Joseph L. Jessop, under whose direction the Allred farm is being managed by Brother Allred, the Fischer farm and dairy by Karl Fischer, and the Fors farm by Axel Fors. The Idaho ranch is being managed by the Hunter Family. Our expansion has been rather abrupt and fast, and is handicapped by principally the shortage of man power.

When we stop to think of some fifty of our group being in legal jeopardy, many of them already under sentence of from one to five years in the penitentiary, and other cases in preparation for trial; all requiring a large outlay of money, legal fees, court costs, etc.; added to this is a large number of our boys in the armed forces of the country – when we consider these facts it is little wonder that our struggles are increased and that at times the burden seems heavier than we can bear.

Yet the Lord has been with us. His strength has been our succor and His promises have held us from falling. We have been singularly free from sickness and accidents; what few of the latter we have had, by the quick interposition of Providence, the damage had, in most cases, been remdied (sic). Our dear brethren, Isaac Carling and Joseph Lyman Jessop, Junior, were called home by Father, doubtless on important missions not fully understood by us.

There are some elementary business principles that must be adhered to enable the Effort to succeed, and these we feel are particularly important at the present time. The Short Creek Unit is divided into sub-units:

(a) Agriculture and livestock.

(b) Poultry.

(c) Lumbering.

(d) Sheep raising.

(e) Picking and canning fruit and vegetables.

(f) General trucking, peddling, etc.

This is under the direct management of Elder Hammon. He has his managerial lieutenants, each unit being operated under the direction of an assistant manager, etc.

The General Manager must be in close touch with the operations of each assistant manager at all times and his orders must be adhered to.

There should be one general bank account for the Short Creek Unit, in the name of the United Effort Plan. This being the parent company, our efforts should be to build up its credit and prestige.

Where thought wise, each assistant manager may have an expense account in an amount and for the purposes agreed to by the General Manager, each such account being at all times subject to the inspection of the General Manager. As revenues are received by each of these units, they should be deposited to the General Fund, or transferred to that fund as the General Manager shall direct. Through careful bookkeeping, each department or sub-unit will have credit for its income and be charged with its expenses. Since the General Manager renders a monthly report to the general office at Salt Lake City, this information is absolutely necessary, and the head of each unit or sub-unit should cooperate in getting this information into the hands of the manager at stated intervals. This plan is being strictly carried out here, and is most important. We realize how difficult it is for some to keep books and render reports, but this is the only method that will insure success to our effort, while a loose and haphazard course is bound to cripple our efforts.

One thing we should keep in mind, which you are doubtless well aware of, is that while building up a cash reserve, the Saints must first eat and have their pantries properly supplied; they must also have clothing, shoes, etc. The school children should be outfitted as well as may be. This should receive immediate attention. We wish we could send you some means to help in this matter, but our legal expenses, for the time being, are keeping our purse strings tight. Other essentials should receive as early attention as possible, such as providing proper homes, culinary water, heating facilities, bedding, dishes, etc. This latter need embraces a large field and will doubtless proceed as funds are available. We should endeavor to build up an emergency fund to be used only as emergencies arise. We should get our respective units free from debt and keep them free. Debts should be avoided wherever possible. Our enemies are ever on the alert to catch us in our weaknesses and destroy our efforts. We firmly believe that in the present wicked crusade against us in the courts it was expected we could not meet the financial demands of employing lawyers, providing bail, advancing appeal costs, etc., in consequence of which we would be whisked into prisons for long terms; and in that way – and that way only – their fiendish work would be successful. The Lord, however, in his benign kindness, foiled their designs and we are yet at liberty. We were out of debt and have consistently remained so for a decade. We hope to be able to continue this policy. It is good. By observing this admonition we shall, in time, be "lenders to many people and not borrowers", as the Lord promised ancient Israel.

Now, brethren, you, with us, are the leaders in this great work – the watchers at the gates. Israel looks to us for guidance. They will follow us as we lead and follow the Lord. Those of us who have weaknesses displeasing to the Lord must overcome them. If any have sinned they must repent before the Lord, for He will not tolerate sin. We, of all men, must cleanse ourselves from vain ambitions, jealousies, selfishness, hatreds (sic), prejudice and the like. We must be as a light upon the hill for all Israel to see and follow after. Your Joshua at Short Creek is Brother Marion. The Lord called him to that work. He is loyal and true. He is ably supported in that work by Brother Roy (Leroy Johnson). You should rally to their support with every ounce of strength you can muster and always assume a course that will breed loyalty and confidence. Remember the one thing the Lord especially hates (Proverbs 6:19) is he "that soweth discord among brethren." Better that we suffer wrong than do wrong. Let us use great care in sustaining one another. Ours is an eternal prize we are working for, to achieve which we must live the higher laws. We are building Celestially, which means we must live Celestial laws.

By taking a righteous course it will come to pass that "One man of us shall chase a thousand." "For thou art an holy people unto the Lord thy God, and the Lord hath chosen thee to be a peculiar people unto Himself, above all the nations that are upon the earth …. Thou shalt be blessed above all people: There shall not be male or female barren among you, or among your cattle," or flocks or fields. And the Lord will take away from thee all sickness…. There shall nothing cast their young, nor be barren in the land: the number of thy days I will fulfill."

These, brethren, are promises to you as leaders of this great work of establishing the economic law of heaven in your section. And as we give heed to these duties and promises we shall have faith to observe the economics of land: "And six years thou shalt sow thy land, and shall gather in the fruits thereof: But the seventh year thou shalt let it rest and lie still; that the poor of thy people (those who are not working with you) shall eat; And what they leave the beasts of the fields shall eat. In like manner thou shalt deal with thy vineyard and with thy olive yard. Six days thou shalt do thy work and on the seventh day thou shalt rest: That thine ox and thine ass may rest, and the son of thy handmaid, and the stranger, may be refreshed."

Aren't these great and glorious blessings worth striving for and sacrificing our feelings to obtain? They are meant for this group of people. You brethren are leading out, and are being watched by the Priesthood Council on each side of the veil. Much is expected of us. We are on trial.

Let it ever be kept in mind that to make money and accumulate earthly values is but secondary. Our first duty is to make Latter-day-Saints, first of ourselves and then of our sons and daughters and our other associates. Let our children grow up and mate and establish family relations, free from sin. They are the future strength of Zion. Many of them will be called to help build the temple and the New Jerusalem at Zion, and devote themselves to giving to the "Lost Tribes of Israel" their washings and anointings. The present UNITED EFFORT PLAN is blazing the way for us to become equal in all things; for, saith the Lord: "Zion must increase in beauty, and in holiness; her borders must be enlarged; her stakes must be strengthened; yea, verily I say unto you, Zion must arise and put on her beautiful garments.... And you are to be equal, or in other words, you are to have equal claims on the properties for the benefit of managing the concerns of your stewardship, EVERY MAN ACCORDING TO HIS WANTS AND HIS NEEDS, inasmuch as his wants are just...."Every man seeking the interest of his neighbor, and doing all things with an eye single to the glory of God." Remember that "I, the Lord am bound when ye do what I say, but when ye do not what I say, ye have no promise."

Brethren, give heed to those things. Clothe yourselves with the mantle of charity. Bury yourselves in the work of the Lord. Be the leaders of your families and respect the leadership over you and God will bless you far beyond your understandings or power to desire.

Your brethren in the Faith,
JOHN Y. BARLOW
JOSEPH W. MUSSER
LEROY S. JOHNSON
RULON T. JEFFS

Note 4: From *Truth*, vol.11, p. 218.
Manifesto of 1945:
To whom it may concern:
The undersigned officers and members of the so-called Fundamentalist religious group do hereby declare as follows:

That we individually and severally pledge ourselves to refrain hereafter from advocating, teaching, or countenancing the practice of plural marriage or polygamy, in violation of the laws of the State of Utah and of the United States.

The undersigned officers of the religious group above referred to further pledge ourselves to refrain from solemnizing plural marriages from and after this date contrary to the laws of the Land;

ss/ John Y. Barlow
ss/ J.W. Musser
ss/ A.A. Timpson
ss/ Edmund Barlow
ss/ Oswald Brainich
ss/ I.W. Barlow
ss/ Albert Barlow
ss/ R.C. Allred
ss/ Joseph Lyman Jessop
ss/ David B. Darger (and Heber K. Cleveland, who agreed orally).

Dated at Salt Lake City, Ut., this 24th day of September, 1945.

Subscribed and sworn by me the day and year above written.

ss/ George H. Carman, Notary.

(SEAL)

Note 5: From Charles Zitting Autobiography, p. 88:

The brethren had been suffering the jail sentence (fifteen polygamist men had begun a prison sentence on May 12, 1945 in Salt Lake City for living polygamy) for three months or more…. Little hints had been circulating around concerning a Manifesto in the making, which if signed would let the brethren out on parole …. When this paper was presented to one of the leading brethren (John Barlow), he and three others, (Joseph Musser, Charles Zitting, and Louis Kelsch) spent the afternoon discussing it out behind the prison barn…. Before they presented it to the others, the leading brethren (the four named above were all members of the Priesthood Council) explained that they wished to make it an individual matter and wanted everyone to use his own free agency in deciding whether he should sign it or not. They all agreed on that. I (Charles Zitting) read it over and felt that I couldn't sign it and told them why. When I went to my cell a little later than the rest I found that five of the brethren had already signed it. I went in tears and prayed more earnestly than I had ever prayed before in all my life. I felt that I could not sign it and I thought I was alone in my opposition. Several of the brethren worked late at the cannery that night. When they came to their cells they informed me they couldn't sign it either. It was the first time in my life that I had ever stood on the opposite side to John Y. Barlow and Joseph W. Musser.

I lay awake nearly all night long praying about it. I could not see that my stand against that paper could be changed. I pleaded to know the will of the Lord, promising Him if he would let me know His will I would stand unmoved and serve Him at all costs.

The following is a copy of the paper they asked us to consider (note that this is a little different than the paper that was eventually signed).

DECLARATION OF POLICY To whom it may concern:

The undersigned officers and members of the so-called Fundamentalist religious group, desiring to bring about peace and harmony within the church, and recognizing the futility of disobeying the laws of the land even in the practice of a religious belief, do hereby declare as follows:

That we individually and severally pledge ourselves to refrain hereafter from advocating, teaching or countenancing the practice of plural marriage or polygamy in violation of the laws of the State of Utah and of the United States.

The undersigned officers of the religious group above referred to further pledge ourselves to refrain from engaging in or from solemnizing plural marriages from and after this date….

When I saw the signatures already on it (John Y. Barlow and Joseph W. Musser had already signed it) I went to one of the brethren (John Y. Barlow) and asked if we shouldn't have prayed about it first before signing as the meeting behind the barn had not been opened nor closed with prayer.

He answered: "The Prophet Brigham Young said to pray about anything where you are in doubt and if the Lord doesn't answer you then use your best Judgement and he will uphold you in it. I have prayed about this for three months without him answering me and this is my best judgement."

I then spoke to another (Joseph W. Musser) and he argued he couldn't see any harm in signing it. He said he felt we would have to do something like this and he believed this was the best we could do. I left and went to my cell feeling very blue and alone. I was awake most of the night pleading with the Lord to keep me from making a mistake as I wished to do nothing but his will. I stayed in my cell all the next day reading chapters in Daniel and other parts of the Bible, also revelations of Joseph Smith Jr., John Taylor and Wilford Woodruff. In the late afternoon the Lord gave me a personal revelation for my family and me which is as follows:

"Thus saith the Lord to you my servant Charles:

"I the Lord know thy desires to serve me at all costs and have heard thy prayers and will answer thee by my voice out of heaven. Thou art much troubled in finding thyself in opposition to my servants John and Joseph, but you are only discharging the responsibility placed upon you and the privilege I gave you through them to use your own free agency in this matter and to speak as you are moved upon in defense of my work. Did I not inform my servant John Taylor that it was now pleasing to me that men should use their own free agency in regards to these matters?

"Nevertheless you must not waver but stand firm and be unmoved after taking a stand for God. The enemy have plainly informed you on many occasions that they intend to destroy my works. They seek the destruction of my faithful ones by pledging them to follow man instead of their God. Why should my people fear them more than me? Consider my servant Daniel and the three Hebrew Children, and my servant John Taylor in the brave stand they took for my work. Study the scriptures more diligently than you have heretofore and continue to call upon me for all of your brethren who are with you in prison and also those out of prison.

"You are much concerned about the health of my servants John and Joseph. Your stand can in no way injure their health nor shorten their days upon the earth.

"You must know for yourself if all the works of my servants over you are inspired by God and then you are a help to them in carrying the great load placed on my servants at this time. Did I not tell my servant Wilford Woodruff to not place yourselves in jeopardy to your enemies by promise as they seek your destruction and the destruction of my people? Did I not deliver you from the hands of the enemy when you placed your trust in me in the spring of 1931 and also delivered you and your wife Edna from them in the fall of 1944?

"Did I ever fail you when you placed your full trust in me or in my word?

"Will there be any faith left on the earth at my second coming?

"You are much concerned about your family. Have you not placed them in my hands? I am watching over them and it needs be that they also must be tested severely. Teach them to remain sober and prayerful and to not seek after the pleasures of this life while you are in jail as they must add to your strength.

"The enemy also seeks their destruction and their hearts must remain pure at all times toward their Lord and one another or they are not worthy to go where you go. They must strive to improve themselves each day as you are doing. If they neglect this council their children will dwindle in unbelief and if they abide in your council their joy will be full.

"You have asked for great blessings and your prayers have been recorded. Did you think you could receive those blessings without first being tested in your faith? Be a good soldier in the Kingdom of God and after the trial of your faith cometh the blessing.

"Now be diligent in the use of your time and talents and in the observance of my law, as your days on earth are numbered and be of good cheer until I come. Amen."

Charles stood firm to the testimony he had against signing that paper and was more convinced as days went by that it was from the lower regions and he put up a strong fight to convince all the brethren to decide against it.... Some of the brethren were anxious to be released so the paper was revised again and again with pressure from the outside in its favor getting stronger and stronger.... Charles writes in his journal; I didn't believe any of them would sign it but to my surprise, all of them did. This left only the five who had refused from the first who didn't sign it and one of these five later promised verbally to the specifications written in the document.

Charles states here that it was just 55 years ago on the very same day, September 24, 1890, that Wilford Woodruff signed his manifesto.

This revelation to Charles Zitting presents a question: Why was John Barlow unable to receive the word of the Lord in this matter? Is it possible that he did receive the Lord's word, but chose to ignore it because he could no longer stand the trial?

Note 6: From the Doctrine and Covenants, Sec. 51: 4-5
"And let my servant Edward Partridge, when he shall appoint a man his portion, give unto him a writing that shall secure unto him his portion, that he shall hold it, even his right and this inheritance in the Church, until he transgresses and is not accounted worthy by the voice of the Church, according to the laws and covenants of the Church, to belong to the Church.

"And if he shall transgress and is not accounted worthy to belong to the Church, he shall not have power to claim that portion which he has consecrated unto the bishop for the poor and the needy of my Church; therefore, he shall not retain the gift, but shall only have claim on that portion that is deeded unto him."

Note 7: The following is a letter to Carl Holm from Rulon Jeffs.
June 29, 1946
Elder Carl O.N. Holm
St. George, Utah
My Dear Brother Carl:
By instruction of the Board of Trustees, I have the honor of informing you of your recent appointment to the Board of Trustees of the United Effort Plan.
This bespeaks the love and confidence we have in you. We feel that the faith, integrity and talents with which the Lord has so richly endowed you will redound to the progress of this great and important work.
May the Lord bless and prosper you and yours and magnify you in your labors.
Sincerely your brethren,
ss/ By Rulon T. Jeffs,
Assistant Secretary
(Jeffs)

Note 8: A letter from the Brethren to the people at Short Creek.

Salt Lake City, Utah – March 27, 1948

TO THE MEMBERS OF THE UNITED EFFORT PLAN:

As there seems to be some lack of understanding regarding our present movement among our members, we will endeavor to make the matter clear, that there may be perfect harmony of purpose and desire.

Let us get this one fact in mind: We are not living the United Order, nor have we been living it. We are living toward it. The United Effort Plan, organized under the laws of the land, under which we are working, was organized to protect our operations legally, looking to eventually entering into the United Order; and our community plan is calculated to prepare us for this great order. It is true some of the Saints are living the Order in spirit, but the Saints in general are not yet prepared to live it in fact. Our operations in the southern units to date has had in mind the uniting of the Saints, that by working in a community basis and in a community spirit they may eventually be prepared to live the full law as the Lord requires it, and as He intends vindicating it by issuing inheritances (See Doctrine and Covenants, Section 85).

We have now lived for several years along communal lines and, we believe, have pretty well demonstrated our ability to take a higher step, and we now feel the time has come to receive perpetual leases on small tracts of land which shall be under the exclusive management of the members receiving the same. In line with this thought we are awarding each of the brethren a plot of land, with homes where possible, and as the Spirit of the Lord shall dictate; with the understanding that more may be allotted as present plots are cultivated and a greater area is needed.

Aside from these individual plots a large acreage is reserved to be planted into grain, hay, or, as time develops, in other communal crops, and in the increase of which the community at large may share in accordance with their labors in maturing such crops. This, then places every man on his own, to reap the benefit of his labors; and the more energetic he is the more he is entitled to for the support of his own family and for the Lord's Storehouse in the payment of tithes and surpluses.

We feel to appoint, with your approval, Elders Richard Jessop, J. Marion Hammon and Joseph S. Jessop as presiding elders, in the order named, to preside over both the spiritual and temporal welfare of the Saints in Short Creek, with what help they may require from time to time from other members of the Priesthood Council. These brethren will be available not only to counsel in spiritual matters but also in temporal, giving help as it may be required in the handling of leases. These brethren should be consulted freely and their counsel should be regarded as sacred and of the Lord. They will have the benefit of Brother Barlow's wise counsel and direction. We recommend, however, that your problems be taken to the presiding elders and not to Brother Barlow direct, as in his poor state of health he should be relieved of discussions of these matters as much as possible. Questions that the Presiding elders need ironing out can be presented to him.

It must be strictly understood that this change in our procedure in no way disrupts the present community plan. The brethren and sisters may from now on work separately upon their leases or they may form a community of interest understanding with others, either as a family or as a community of families. Our plan is to satisfy those only who feel it desirable to have exclusive jurisdiction over their lease, subject always, of course, to the action of the Lord through His Priesthood. These latter people are now placed on their own, with what labors they are willing to perform on the community farm, and from which they will receive their share.

Now brethren, is this present movement a letting down – a step in retrogression? Most positively no; it is a step in advancement. We are not attempting to live the fulness (sic) of the United Order, but live toward that Order until such time as the Lord may deem us worthy of being enlarged, and the present arrangement is in line with that enlargement.

Are we going back to tithing? We have never left this eternal principle. Our increase is tithed in accordance with God's revelation, D&C Sec. 119, and our surplus, when we have any, is also dedicated to the Lord.

In inaugurating this new plan it may be necessary for some of the brethren to seek work outside, to help complete their family budgets; and in such communal work as shall be instigated, all of the brethren should pay into the communal chest a tithe of their time as shall be conveniently arranged by the presiding elders.

Our growing need there is water. The digging of wells may well be a communal job as you may decide; and in this respect and in all other respects we remind the Saints of the importance of faith, and the absolute necessity of combining works with faith. We feel that there is water for that land, but we have got to go after it. It will not come of its own accord, at least until we have shown an iron determination to live the commandments of the Lord, and subdue the land. Faith without works is dead. The Lord blesses our efforts one step at a time. Let us make each step count. Those who take counsel and apply themselves industriously for the glory of God are entitled to His blessings.

It is our duty not only to get water, cultivate and plant the land, raise beautiful gardens, but also to bring our home affairs up to a higher level; have our homes a fit place for the Savior to come to. We should, as circumstances permit, plant orchards, shade trees, paint our homes, fences and outbuildings, and in all respects make our surroundings inviting and pleasant. Flowers play a large part towards beautifying home surroundings. Latter-day Saints should be examples to the world in all good things. Efforts along these lines will be pleasing to the Lord and will receive His blessings.

"The prayer of the righteous availeth much." Let each individual dedicate his labors to the Lord, pray over his crops, pray for water, and for the removal of the curse with which the land is infested. This land lease is a real endowment, and to receive its full benefits we must wrestle with the Lord.

Record keeping is important in connection with our labors. We should be prepared at any time to render an account to those entitled to know; and it should be the hope and effort of every head of family to produce in abundance, in both temporal and spiritual blessings, for the glorification of the Father, the beautifying of the earth, and for the feeding, clothing, educating and spiritual advancement of our children.

Now, let us observe the commandments of the Lord. "Behold, the Lord requireth the heart and a willing mind; and the willing and obedient shall eat the good of the land of Zion in these last days (D. & C. 64:34)."

We cannot stress too strongly the law of tithing and how careful the Saints should be in observing this law. The Lord said (D.& C. 64:23), "Behold, now it is called today until the coming of the son of Man, and verily it is a day of sacrifice, and a day for the tithing of my people; FOR HE THAT IS TITHED SHALL NOT BE BURNED AT HIS COMING." A hint to the wise is sufficient.

We understand there are some outstanding obligations that were contracted for the benefit of the community. These the community should take care of. We suggest that the Saints be called together by the presiding elders to discuss and arrange this matter on a fair and equitable basis, and clear off all indebtedness as quickly as possible; and let your creditors know what is being done regarding this matter, that your good credit may be kept intact.

Brethren, may the choicest blessings of the Lord be upon you, and may all our efforts be for the building up of the Kingdom of God. You are truly engaged in the work of the Lord.

Yours in the bonds of love,
John Y. Barlow
Joseph W. Musser
J. Marion Hammon
Guy H. Musser
Rulon T. Jeffs
Richard S. Jessop

Note 9: When this group of men arrived in Mexico conditions were much harder than they were in Short Creek. Marion Hammon and Newel Steed were able to stay and endure the hardships for only about one month. They then loaded their belongings and came back. Marion Hammon told John Barlow that he would only go back if he was shown a revelation from the Lord telling him to do so. John Barlow, to his credit, did not supply the revelation.

Before Newel Steed was sent to Mexico, he had turned in his ranch at John's Valley (Widstoe) to the UEP. John Barlow had mortgaged the farm and the money was soon spent. When Newel Steed returned from Mexico, the mortgage payment was past due. John Barlow had no way of making the payment, and intended to just let the bank foreclose, thus losing the farm. When Newel Steed learned of this, he became very irate over the matter. He went to the bank, making arrangements to pay back the money that John Barlow had spent. It took him twenty years to pay it off, but he was able to reclaim the farm. He withdrew from the association of the United Effort Plan and pretty much ran his own business, becoming quite successful. He was very bitter toward John Barlow for many years, not having a good word to say about him or his "worthless sons" for quite some time. He did, however, become associated with the people at Short Creek again in the early 1960s.

Note 10: From the journal of Ben Bistline:

Sometime in June, 1990, Don Cox and myself went to visit Alma Timpson. One of the things I asked him was to tell what happened when he was called into the Priesthood Council. The following is what Alma Timpson told us:

"John Barlow was on his death bed at Salt Lake. He sent word to me that he wanted to see me. It was Christmas day (Dec. 25, 1949), so I waited until the next day to go see him. He got after me for not coming sooner. He told me he wanted me to get the other brethren of the Council to ordain me a member of the Priesthood Council. I told him OK., I would take care of it. He reached up and taking a hold of my shirt, pulled me down toward him, and in a commanding voice said; DO IT. It was probably the last words he spoke before he died.

"I went into the next room where the Brethren proceeded to ordain me. Joseph Musser was mouth. I was not satisfied with his wording since his speech was halting due to a stroke he recently had. I asked Charles Zitting to redo it, which he did. Uncle Roy was not there, as he had been in Old Mexico and was on his way home. Brother Barlow died before Uncle Roy got to Salt Lake. He (Leroy) told me that he had received revelation on the way from Mexico that I was to be called, so all the Brethren were in harmony about my calling."

I then asked Alma Timpson about the wording of the prayer, what he was given when ordained.

He said "There are three things that must be said, namely, the person being mouth must say; 'I ordain you a High Priest, a Patriarch and an Apostle to the Lord Jesus Christ'."

I then asked, was the keys of Elijah given?

He looked somewhat surprised, but said; "No"!

Note 11: The following is a statement by John Butchereit. The statement was made before a class (School of the Prophets) which only selected members of the Polygamist Group were invited into. These men were put under oath to protect each other from lies about any class members. They had covenanted to not believe any rumors about any class members until they could face the member face to face and determine for themselves whether the accusation was true or false. Butchereit's statement follows:

1. Before I can approve of the minutes as read I must be satisfied that they are an actual verbatim account of what was said last Saturday night.

2. Those who were here all heard the statement of Brother Guy H. Musser: ie, that there would be no Court trial here. Some were not present and this issue was never voted upon. Could this be presented for a vote from the class?

3. Is this decision founded upon correct principles? A brother has been accused and a defender is refused a hearing.

4. President Jeffs stated that any conversation between a lay member and a minister could not be used as evidence in this circle. Where is the scriptural proof for this position (Is it not a decision for legal procedure in Courts of Law, but in conflict with the procedures of God)?

5. Would the class please indicate by the raising of hands if they uphold President Jeffs in this position?

6. Brother Russell Kunz said that the brethren all knew that when Brother Rulon C. Allred entered this class and took part the spirit of the Lord left the class. Does the class uphold Brother Kunz in this position by the upraised hand?

Compendium, pg. 286:

"That the Council should try no case without both parties being present or having had as opportunity to be present, neither should they hear one party's complaint before his case is brought up for trial, neither should they suffer the character of anyone to be exposed before the high Council without the person being present, and ready to defend him or herself; that the minds of the Counselors be not prejudiced for or against anyone whose case they may POSSIBLY have to act upon."

JOHN BUTCHEREIT'S PLEA BEFORE THE COUNCIL – JANUARY 26, 1952

Dear Brethren:

I feel the time of my termination has come. I ask the privilege to speak for a few minutes. In brother Timpson's address, Sunday night, he said to this effect: "Any priesthood position that has to be contended for is a usurped authority." Since in all my contacts with brother Allred, he has never so much as mentioned this subject to me, nor contended that he had any authority, and ever since Pres. Musser gave him this calling, the members of the Council have in every way contended against it, and have gone about behind his back, undermining his character and destroying his good name among the people, violating their sacred covenants in this class, not only speaking evil of him, but in listening to and upholding such evil reports, I must conclude from Bro. Timpson's remarks that the Council members are fearful of their position and authority and for this reason justify themselves in violating their covenants, etc. After much anxiety and prayer concerning these matters, I must say that I cannot and will not sustain you in the course you have taken. I am standing here in the defense of the Mouthpiece of God and a brother with whom I have covenanted before God "that I would not listen to, nor credit any derogatory reports against him, nor condemn him upon any testimony under heaven, except that which is infallible, until I could see him face to face, and that I would place unremitted confidence in his word, for I believe him to be a man of truth." Having heard things against Bro. Allred, as well as Bro. Bautista, I have had to warn some of my brethren to be careful, knowing them to be under this covenant. It was not until the President of the Priesthood, J.W.Musser, openly asked for a sustaining vote of Brother Allred and Brother Bautista in a Sunday night meeting, that I resolved to get a confirmation from my file leader, which he gave me unhesitatingly and with great force and clearness.

He said; "They are Apostles of the Lord Jesus Christ and hold the same authority as any man in the Council." I had a desire to follow the instructions by brother Guy H. Musser, which he made in a Monday night Priesthood meeting, when we were discussing the subject of apostasy. Referring to Lyman E. Johnson's case, he quoted: "Brethren, if I could believe Mormonism once more, as I used to do, I would give my life over and over again." Bro. Guy said, "I will give you a key which will help you; never let 24 hours pass without making reconciliation with the brethren, if necessary crawl in the dust on your bellies to do so." This was repeated again, after brother Charles interrupted him. I wanted a clean start before the Lord in the New Year and so I called upon Bro. Guy on New Year's evening and stated the reasons for my visit. He immediately began to denounce brother Allred. I protested to the best of my ability, stating that such a course constituted a violation of covenant and that if he felt that way about brother Allred, he never should have let him come into the class. He said he would not have done, except that he was approached by Bro. Allred, who asked to come into the class. (Since this conversation I have asked Pres. Musser and Bro. Allred about this and they both state that it is an untruth. That Bro. Allred was invited into the class as other members had been and no request to come into the class was made). In the face of my protests, Bro. Guy said:

1. R.C. Allred is a Devil! He has tried for the last 15 years to split up the Priesthood.

2. My father is incompetent and is not able to give any man the Apostleship. Rulon has not got it!

3. All who follow R.C. Allred work under a spurious Priesthood, and all his work is done unauthorized. I know he has not got the Apostleship.

4. My father, Jos. W. Musser, and John Y. Barlow put the members of the Council under Covenant, before he became sick, to never accept Rulon Allred as an Apostle; that he was an aspiring man (Of this Pres. Musser told me that it was a damn lie, and that if they would lie about what he said, they would lie about what John had said).

5. Bro. Guy said: "Our endowments will be given us, if we stand as a circle in the gap. There is no man that could try the people and the Council, as the Lord is permitting my father to do in his condition!"

6. Rulon C. Allred has used my father as a pissing post. If I wanted to use the same policy that Rulon is using, we could get father to do whatever we want him to do (This makes me wonder why men who would break their Covenants to destroy a brother, haven't been successful in getting Brother Musser to change his mind after so long a time).

7. (Brother Guy continued:) "Certain of the brethren have come to me and offered to take brother Allred's life, if he continues to maintain his stand."

8. "Some of the brethren have tried to put me next to father, but I am the 7th in the line down. My father cannot by-pass his whole council and put someone else ahead."

9. "The Council of the Priesthood is united in its stand against Brother Allred."

Brethren, before God, I testify to the truth of these things. They were so stated to me.

In Proverbs 6, the Lord says: "These six things doth the Lord hate, yea seven are an abomination in His sight. A proud look; A lying tongue; Hands that shed innocent blood; A heart that deviseth wicked imaginations; Feet that are swift in running to mischief; A false witness that speaketh lies and he that soweth discord among brethren.

I have made another attempt tonight to defend the head of the Priesthood, and the principles of truth and righteousness. God being my helper you may take my life, also, and step across my body before I will consent with you in the wicked accusations made against a servant of God behind his back. And I have ample evidence that this has been the policy of other members of the Council. You who have made such statements have broken your solemn covenants, and you who have sustained such things are as guilty as those who are accusers of the brethren. The Prophet Joseph said: "Anyone who goes about speaking evil against a brother, seeking to destroy his good name is prompted by the spirit of the Devil." Jos. Sm's Teachings, p. 358. The following accusations against Brother Allred were made openly in the Circle:

1. Brother Guy H. Musser said: "R.C Allred has used my father as a pissing post." To me this is an open assault upon Bro. Allred's character.

2. Bro. Russell Kunz also occupies this same position in stating in Bro. Allred's absence: "The spirit of God left this class when Bro. Allred came into this circle."

3. Bro. Hammon certainly became an instrument in prejudicing the minds of the circle when he got up and said: "We ought to vote upon this issue. I feel that I cannot

sustain Bro. Allred as a member of the Circle and I want to know if you will sustain me in this position." This shows prejudice.

4. Bro. Helmut Olschewski said in open circle: "Once my confidence has been destroyed in Rulon it cannot be restored again." This also shows that Bro. Helmut's confidence had been destroyed in Bro. Allred without his having given him an opportunity to defend himself, or before he had heard his side of the question.

5. Bro. Charles Zitting questioned the authority of his file leader when, in open meeting, he answered Bro. Bautista's question as to why he would not sustain him. Bro. Zitting said: "If it is done right, I might."

6. Pres. Rulon T. Jeffs and his father questioned the authority and wisdom of Pres. Musser when they both stated: "I cannot do it without the approval of the Council". This was relative to Pres. Musser's calling Bro. David (Jeffs) to the Council. I bring these items to your attention because it is written in Priesthood Items -2nd Edition-pg. 40;

"It is also well to note when the Twelve were finally chosen to THIS HIGHEST ORDER in the winter of 1843-4, it was by the direct command of God THROUGH HIS MEDIUM, which is the only way men are chosen for this apostolic order of the Priesthood." You are certainly guilty of high-handed procedure and are insubordinate to the mouthpiece of God, and my charges against you shall face you in the Judgment Day. Your motives are prompted by covetousness and jealousy and are well known to your file leader and to God, himself, whose mills may grind slow, but they grind exceedingly fine. I have nothing but pity for you, unless you repent, speedily. To me, Joseph W. Musser stands in the same position the Prophet faced when every man in his council, save two, stood against him, and this is the crowning experience of his mission in mortality.

I humbly request that these statements, which have been written to avoid having my words misstated and mis-represented, be attached to the minutes of the class as a permanent record of my confidence, respect, and unwavering faith in Joseph W. Musser as the mouthpiece of God. He has told me that, as the Lord lives, he has appointed no one to take his place, and that God has not, and that those who state otherwise are false prophets. I do not sustain Jos. W. Musser as a Prophet of God and someone else behind his back, as you brethren are doing. I have done my duty and I now, voluntarily, withdraw from this class and its hypocrisy. I know that the Gospel is true and that theseexperiences will only help me in my determination to give my all to His glorious work, upholding truth and justice, no matter what the consequences.

Amen.

Note 12: The following is taken from Joseph Lyman Jessop's (Uncle Lyman) diary; July 1, 1952: Wayne Handy and I picked up Bro. J.W. Musser at 4 a.m. and drove to Short Creek, Arizona. The purpose of this trip is to find out how the people feel toward Joseph Musser and the Priesthood callings made through him. Joseph conversed some with Carl Holm on this situation, and Carl seemed to feel like he would rather not have Joseph hold a meeting with the people. Joseph and I called upon my brother Richard Jessop, and Richard expressed a firm belief and testimony that Bro. Musser is the head of the Priesthood, and he would gladly call the people together in a meeting if Joseph desire it so – but Bro. Roy Johnson was away and is expected back this evening, so Joseph decided to wait until Roy was consulted.

July 2, 1952: After breakfast, at Joseph's desire we went to Berry Knoll, a mile or so out of town, a spot designated for a temple sometime.... We returned to Short Creek and found Bro. Roy Johnson in his car near Richard's house. We invited them into our car and Roy, Richard and Carl Holm, came and sat in our car for more than an hour: Bro. Joseph asked Roy to state how he felt toward him, so Roy said that he knows that Joseph holds the keys to the Priesthood and he (Roy) will sustain him in that position in love and loyalty. "I stood by John (Barlow) until the end. I will support you, as I did him." Joseph responded; "That is fine:" Bro. Carl Holm asked Joseph if he could make a statement. Joseph said; "Yes, go ahead." Then Bro. Carl made a lengthy statement to Joseph Lyman Jessop.

(He stated) "Bro. Musser should be in harmony with the Council, else, 'If you are not one, ye are not mine, saith the Lord'....

(I said) "he has stated the situation backwards, because the Council should agree with Joseph – not Joseph agree with the Council – if there is a difference in understanding;... I also referred to a story told me, that Bro. John Barlow had once made a statement concerning Bro. RCA (Rulon Allred) and that's the reason the Council would not sustain him. I have asked, 'What is that statement that they of the Council won't tell me.' Now I'd like to know, what that statement is. ... Is it a secret that is forbidden fruit to me?

"I asked again, 'Uncle Roy, is it a secret? Carl, is it a secret? Rich, is it a secret?' Roy said; 'We know some things, Lyman, that you don't know.'.... Joseph slowly shook his head at the expression of the brethren opposing him and said; 'I don't know what it is they have against me.' Roy said; 'We are under covenant to do what we are doing, and we cannot change from that course and we have no arguments to make. If the Lord wants to use an incapacitated leader (referring to Jos. Musser) to lead some people astray, that is the Lord's business.' ...Joseph (Musser) seemed to feel appalled at their persistent stand against him, and said to them; 'Well, you just as well go your way and we'll go our way.'" (Lyman's diary)

The following is from Owen Allred's (brother of Rulon) journal: January 24, 1953: Bro. Cook (Bill?) was at Butchereit's when we went there for a Council meeting. Bro. Cook feels that Joseph is mentally ill and has been for sometime. He tells me a story of Bro. John Y. Barlow having told him that Rulon Allred did not have the blessings he thought he did and that he, Rulon Allred, would claim that he, John, had given him a calling, which he had not given him. This claim of a story from John Y. Barlow to Bro. Cook is contrary to a statement from Sister Barlow (Aunt Suzie, John's wife), who said that John had told her of his giving Rulon that calling. (what calling this refers to is unknown to the author) Also, Guy (Musser) has admitted that he knew of Bro. John's giving Rulon that calling. And I (Owen) have talked with 3 others who were present when John gave Rulon that calling. I do not understand John telling Bro. Cook such a story: This is what Bro. Guy has to say about that situation: "My father, Joseph W. Musser, and John Y. Barlow put the members of the council under covenant before he became sick, to never accept Rulon C. Allred as an Apostle, that he was an aspiring man:" Brother Butchereit went right straight to Bro. Musser and Rulon and asked them about this. And this is what John Butchereit says: "Of this, Pres. Musser told me that it was a damnable lie, and that if they would lie about what he said, they would lie about what John had said."

The Infamous Short Creek Raid

In the early morning hours of July 26, 1953, Arizona Highway Patrolmen, Mohave County Sheriff's Deputies and Arizona National Guardsmen moved in on the people of Short Creek in military might. With red lights flashing, sirens sounding, and brandishing firearms, the military caravan in a cloud of swirling dust pulled up at the school yard fence where the citizens of the community had gathered to wait for them.

Speaking over a loud speaker to those in the school yard, Mohave County Sheriff Frank Porter announced, "This is the sheriff. You are all under arrest. Stay where you are." The invading officers then moved cautiously into the yard surrounding the group and began serving arrest warrants.

The officers had hoped they could surprise the polygamists, break into their homes, and catch them in bed with their unlawful wives to gather evidence to convict them. But the polygamists at Short Creek had been warned that the raid was coming.

In 1953, Charles Zitting was the recognized leader of the Short Creek (Barlow) Group. But it was the Allred (Musser) Group in Salt Lake City that someone in law enforcement or the press warned of the impending raid. Lyman Jessop, a member of Joseph Musser's Priesthood Council, quickly drove to Short Creek to warn the polygamists. Charles Zitting, living at Salt Lake City, had no home at Short Creek, but when he learned of the coming raid, he and his wife Elvera drove to Southern Utah to meet with the Priesthood Council members. He told them to take the women and children and leave Short Creek, to go into hiding with friends at Salt Lake City or other places. He had just spent three years in the Utah Penitentiary and knew firsthand the consequences of arrest. And, there were women and children involved. He believed they could then negotiate with the Governor and reach a compromise.

Leroy Johnson defied Charles Zitting, his recognized Priesthood Leader, and refused to take this message to the people. He said, "We are not going to run. We will stand up to them and ask the Lord to fight our battles. I will take the responsibility."

Charles made no effort to contend with Leroy over the issue. "If that's your decision, Roy, and you are willing to take responsibility, then I will stay here and be with the people when the law arrives."

Because of Leroy's decision, the Polygamists of Short Creek did not run. They had not been given any choice in the matter. They were told by Leroy they were going to stay and meet the invading force on the morning of July 26th, so putting on a brave face, they obeyed. This decision would cause much suffering for the women and children over the next two years. In fact, if not for an obscure Arizona Statute that council member Guy Musser searched out, the Arizona Welfare Department would have taken the children and adopted them to other families.

The Short Creek Raid was carried out after more than two years of investigation by the Arizona State Attorney General's office. The radio address on Sunday morning, July 26, 1953, by Arizona Governor Howard Pyle made the state's case to the public:

> "The evidence accumulated included alleged instances of statutory rape, adultery, bigamy, open and notorious cohabitation, contributing to the delinquency of minors, marrying the spouse of another and an all embracing conspiracy to commit all of these crimes along with various instances of income tax evasion, failure to comply with Arizona's corporation laws, misappropriation of the school funds, improper use of school facilities and falsification of public records."

But was the raid *really* just about the practice of polygamy, or was it motivated by something else.

The Polygamists were, in some degree, guilty of almost all of these charges. The one charge that started all this and was most responsible for causing the Raid was the *alleged misappropriation* of school funds. And that charge came about because of tax money ranchers were having to pay to help support the Short Creek School District.

In the 1950s, to support the schools in Arizona, funds came from the state, *and* from the local school district by way of a special tax levy (Note 1). About the only taxable asset in the small school District of Short Creek was the cattle industry on the Arizona Strip.

The ranchers who owned the permits to graze their cattle on the public lands in the Short Creek School District mostly lived in Utah, but they were expected to pay this tax levy and meet this tax burden. Due to the high birth rate in the polygamist community, the number of students grew each year and this became a real financial burden to the ranchers. They felt it was grossly unfair that they should be paying extra taxes to educate the increasing number of polygamist children.

In Arizona the school districts are unusually small, being controlled by

88

local Board Members elected by local residents. In the case of the Short Creek School District, the Polygamists controlled who these Board Members would be at every election. The Utah Cattlemen could not even vote in these elections, having no control at all. These local school boards were pretty much autonomous and could set the amount of the special fund from tax to be placed on the local district, or in this case, on the Utah Cattlemen.

In 1949 the Short Creek School levy required tax of a little less than one half of one percent on the assessed valuation. One cow was assessed at $25.00 (Real value was about $200.00). The total cost of the special tax fund for the Short Creek School in the 1952-1953 school year was about $7,000. By 1953 the percentage had almost doubled to just under one percent. Also, the assessed valuation had been raised to $35.00 per cow. This increase of the special fund was not caused due to increase of any appreciable number of students. The increase was due to other costs and expenses incurred by operation of the school.

In 1950, Louis Barlow, son of John Barlow, was hired by the Short Creek School Board as principal. The school property and buildings were run down when Louis took over. The only water supply was a shallow well with a windmill to pump the water. There was only a faucet in the school yard for drinking water, the water coming from a wooden storage tank on a tower by the windmill. The toilets were outhouses. There were no lawns or shrubbery of any kind.

Louis felt it necessary to improve these conditions a little. He went to the School Board and requested them to raise the Special School Fund. This in turn caused the tax levy to go up for the Cattlemen. Louis used this extra money to purchase a pressure pump for the well (with the help of the upper class boys, he was successful in digging another well, where the new pump was used). An army surplus generator was purchased, an old car motor was rigged to turn it, and the new pressure pump was used to successfully pump the water. Grass and shrubbery was then planted, greatly improving the school grounds. A 16mm movie projector was purchased and movies were brought into the community. Also, a school lunch program was established.

These were improvements that most other schools in Arizona had taken for granted, but they were a big advancement for the school children at Short Creek. The Cattlemen might not have complained about the cost increase of these improvements, except that in their opinion, Louis went too far and bought a school vehicle, an old 1946 Ford pick-up truck. Louis' younger brother Truman, an upper class student, spent time *and school money* for gasoline, driving all over town for any excuse, whether it was school business or not.

The ranchers complained to the Short Creek School Board, but it did no good. Only then did they take their complaints to the County level at Kingman.

The Short Creek School Board had in the past made an attempt to alleviate some of the cost increase to the Utah Cattlemen by recommending that nearby School Districts be combined into one, thus spreading the tax burden to a larger population. In 1951, there was only one school in the Short Creek School District, with about 65 students, but about 20 of them were from the Utah side of the community and Washington County, Utah, paid their tuition. Because the District was very small in area, it put the burden on just a few ranchers.

Three adjoining Districts had few or no students: Cane Beds, Pipe Valley, and the Tuweep Districts. The Cane Beds District had less than eight students, already attending school at Short Creek (Arizona law at the time required a minimum of eight students to hold school). The Pipe Valley and Tuweep Districts had no students at all. The Short Creek School Board asked that these Districts be combined with theirs.

The Mohave County Board of Supervisors and the County School Superintendent not only denied the request, but gave the dormant school districts to the Moccasin School District, which was barely meeting the minimum eight students needed to hold school. This decision was no doubt made by the County Officials due to the complaints of the Utah Cattlemen. The answer in their minds was *not* to increase the valuation of the Short Creek District, giving the local School Board more area to control, but rather to try and somehow stop the high increase of students in the District. To do this, they appealed for State intervention.

In his radio address to the public explaining his action, Governor Pyle stated in part: "…Arizona has mobilized and used its total police power to protect the lives and future of 263 children. They are the product and the victims of the foulest conspiracy you could imagine…." (Note 2).

July 24th, the anniversary of Brigham Young's 1847 entry into Salt Lake Valley, is celebrated by the Mormons as Pioneer Day. In the 1950s era, the 24th of July was probably the biggest holiday celebrated by the Polygamists at Short Creek. Group members would gather from far and wide to attend this event. The day would be spent with such activities as playing games, running foot races, and other general sports. A barrel of lemonade, cookies baked by the young ladies, and other refreshments were available throughout the day. In the afternoon a community dinner was served at the school house (the only place large enough). After everyone had eaten their fill, the school house would be cleared out, tables removed, and the hall prepared for an evening social. Old and young alike would enjoy dancing until midnight. Then they would gather on the dance floor and sing their theme song "Give Me A Home In The Heart Of The Mountains." All would then retire to their homes, feeling much lifted up because of the day's recreation and go to sleep with joy in their hearts. The Arizona State Officials knew of this day of celebration, and planned their raid knowing that all Short Creek Polygamists would be there.

Although Short Creek straddled the Utah/Arizona state line, Utah state officials did not participate with Arizona in this raid. However, one of the two roads leading into town came in from Utah. The Arizona task force divided into two contingents, sending one around to come in from the Utah side, thus blocking any escape route.

The detachment coming from the Arizona side stopped at Fredonia, about 40 miles east of Short Creek. After cutting the telephone lines (this telephone line only went about halfway to Short Creek, stopping at Pipe Spring National Monument and the small community of Moccasin), they moved out toward Short Creek on 40 miles of unimproved roads.

The group was made up of 100 law enforcement officers, including highway patrolmen, county sheriffs and deputies, superior and juvenile court judges, the state attorney general and his associates, policewomen, nurses, doctors, the Arizona National Guard, together with all the equipment to house, feed, and clothe the task force, as well as the citizens of Short Creek. There were also 25 carloads of news media and twelve Alcohol, Tobacco and Firearms (ATF) officers.

In the early morning hours of Sunday, July 26, 1953 (during the darkness of a lunar eclipse), the officers and their entourage stopped about two miles outside of Short Creek, both from the Utah and Arizona sides of town. They were waiting to coordinate their move on the community. Unbeknown to these officers, the citizens, having been forewarned, were gathered at the school yard waiting for them. The Polygamists, aware that the raiding force was coming, had dispatched sentries to the outskirts of town to wait for the invaders' arrival.

A warning signal had been arranged for these sentries to set off dynamite blasts when they had determined that the officers were ready to move into town. When these blasts were set off, it not only warned the citizens at the school yard, but also frightened the officers of the invading force. Not knowing what to expect, thinking perhaps they were being met with armed resistance, Mohave County Sheriff Frank Porter said, "Well, it looks like they want to fight, so let's go."

Turning on their sirens and flashing red lights, the caravan began moving in on the Polygamists at 4:00 a.m. Prepared for the worst, with weapons drawn, they were stunned to find the citizens gathered around the flag pole, singing patriotic songs. The officers, still with firearms drawn, began moving through the crowd making arrests. All adults were taken into custody. Any that were not named on warrants were arrested as John or Jane Doe.

At daylight a court was set up in the assembly hall of the schoolhouse. Each man was questioned and then booked under arrest. Judge J. Smith Gibbons from Apache County was there to read the charges against them. All the men were charged with the same crimes regardless of whether they were polygamists or not. They were then turned over to Sheriff Frank Porter of Mohave County and were locked in one of the school rooms to await transportation to the County Jail at Kingman.

The mothers and their children were presented to Judge Lorna Lockwood (Maricopa County) acting as Juvenile Judge. The children were declared wards of the state, then released into the custody of their mothers, who were told to take them home and wait for instructions. The mothers themselves were never arrested or taken into custody. There were nine older women who had no minor children that were arrested. One of these was Elvera Zitting, the wife of Charles Zitting who had accompanied him from Salt Lake City. She was not a resident of Short Creek, but had been arrested on a Jane Doe warrant.

The National Guard set up camp in a vacant field about one block from the school house. A mess tent was assembled to feed the officers, and the citizens of the community. The one small store in town was not allowed to open, depriving the people from their source of groceries. Everyone was forced to go to this compound for their meals. This proved so cumbersome and impractical that mothers were allowed to get food from the field kitchen and take it home to their children.

That evening the men were escorted to supper at the National Guard Camp. Buses had been ordered to take them to Kingman, but they never arrived. The men were loaded, three each, in the back seat of a patrol car, with two officers in the front. The long seven hour trip to Kingman began at 7:00 p.m. Traveling all night, they reached their destination at 4:00 a.m. the following morning, just 24 hours since the raid had begun. There were 31 men and 9 women (with no minor children) taken to Kingman in this caravan of police cars.

The State had planned to hold the children's hearings at Short Creek, bringing in the respective fathers from Kingman to confirm the identity as to which children belonged to whom. On Wednesday, July 29, the first of these men (two) were flown to the Kanab, Utah, airport, and then taken by automobile to Short Creek. They were returned to Kingman that same night. The next day three more men were flown up to their hearings. On Friday, five men came.

Leroy Johnson sent word with these men to have those who were still at Short Creek (the teenage boys who had not been arrested) to bring vehicles to Kingman because bail had been raised for their release. They expected to be out of jail the next day.

Three men at Short Creek had not been arrested (Dan Jessop, Joe Barlow, and Jack Cooke). Warrants had been issued for their arrest, but these were Arizona warrants and by staying in Utah, they were able to avoid being picked up. Because of rumors that the Washington County officials in St. George were planning to arrest those on the Utah side, Council Members at Salt Lake City directed these men to evacuate the women and children from the Utah side of the community. Word was sent to the Utah families, telling them to take only a small pack of clothing, a few blankets, and a little food and milk for their babies. They did not tell them where they were going, only that they would be walking quite a distance.

About 100 people gathered around midnight Thursday, July 30th, and began walking west, staying on the Utah side of the state line. After hiking along the foothills, through the sagebrush and trees, climbing through gullies, washes, and crossing through several fences, they crossed into Arizona about three miles west of Short Creek. Arrangements had been made for a truck to meet them, but it was not there. Rhea Kunz, a member of the Polygamist Group who lived in Hurricane, Utah, was there, however. She only had a small car, but used it to transport these tired souls a little further west, back into Utah and into the seclusion of the trees and rocks.

It had rained all night while they were hiking and the people were soaked through. When the sun came up in the morning, they spread their wet clothing and blankets on the rocks to dry. The babies were out of milk and what little food had been brought with them was gone. About 10:00 a.m. one of the three men, who had escaped arrest, brought water and milk, and also food for the older children and the adults.

Feeling safe on the Utah side, all waited for the truck scheduled to arrive sometime in the afternoon. But something went wrong and the men and older boys fled the area, leaving the women and children behind to wait for the truck. They soon learned that the driver of the rescue truck had been apprehended. Officials told these women and children they had to return to their homes in Short Creek. They promised that if they went back to their Utah homes, they would not be arrested. They convinced them that it was safe to return to their homes, so these women allowed the officers and matrons to transport them back, reaching home about sundown.

Due to the attempt made to evacuate the Utah women and children, the Arizona officials decided it would be best to take the children already in custody to Phoenix to continue the court hearings.

On Saturday morning, August 1st, the officers and matrons went to all the homes on the Arizona side of Short Creek. The mothers were told that the children were going to be taken to Phoenix and must be ready to leave in fifteen minutes. The bail had been paid for the men's release at Kingman, but the Sheriff would not release them, fearing trouble over the children being moved to Phoenix. The mothers told officials they would not allow the children to leave unless they could go with them. Due to the urgency of the situation, they were allowed to accompany the children to Phoenix.

The plan to fly the children to Phoenix had complications, so buses were scheduled. In the meantime, the women and children had been forced to wait at the school house all day, not being allowed to go home. It was a very tired and unruly group that climbed on the five buses at 5:00 p.m. to begin the long trip to Phoenix, over 500 miles away.

Non-stop – without adequate food, water or rest stops for the 43 mothers and the 177 children – was an unspeakable hardship. Kidnaped from their peaceful homes in the solitude of remote Short Creek, they were forced into a crime-ridden city. During 20 months of captivity, 17 more children would be born to these mothers.

The whole episode of the Short Creek Raid would gain national attention and become very unpopular in the state of Arizona. Public sentiment turned against Arizona Officials, and especially Governor Howard Pyle. It was not long until officials were regretting their actions.

The men in Kingman were released from the county jail in the afternoon of Saturday, August 1, the same day their families were being taken to Phoenix. The young men did not arrive in Kingman with the vehicles (a truck with a touring car loaded on it) to bring the men home until late in the evening. After these men coming from Short Creek related what had happened at home, Leroy Johnson, taking the touring car, left for Phoenix, hoping to contact the women and children and search out an attorney to begin the long legal battle of bringing them back home. The other men loaded on the truck and began the long journey home, arriving in the early morning hours.

On Monday morning the fathers, with the help of the older boys that had been left at home, began the task of going around the community and cleaning up the abandoned houses that had been vacated so abruptly. The hasty departure had left food on the tables to spoil in the hot summer heat, dirty dishes, uncooked bread in pans, dirty clothes to be washed, unmade beds, and all the housework that is necessary to running a home. All the men from the Arizona side of town, whose families were taken, were invited to Fred Jessop's home on the Utah side, where they met each night and morning to not only eat their meals, but also gather in a circle prayer, asking their Father in Heaven to watch over and protect their loved ones, taken so far away. In these prayers they would also plead for the release of their wives and children, asking that the hearts of the Arizona Officials would be softened so as to let them come home. These prayer meetings were faithfully attended by all members of the community, both from the Utah as well as the Arizona side for the entire time the people were gone (about 20 months).

In Phoenix, state officials began the process of relocating the families in homes throughout the state. The mothers were allowed to stay with their children who, being wards of the state, were placed on welfare for their subsistence. Since the mothers were under no restraint or arrest of any kind, the state would not pay for their keep. However, they were not at liberty to travel. If they were to leave their children, to even return home for a short visit, the state officials told them the children would be placed in foster homes, with intent to adopting them out to other parents. So by all reality, they were just as much captives as were the children.

The husbands and fathers were required to pay the state $30.00 a month for the support of the mothers, which was in turn, passed back to them when they received the monthly state welfare checks for support of the children. Due to the lack of money among the Polygamists, this $30.00 per month was hard to raise and the mothers would return this amount every month to Leroy Johnson so it could, in turn, be paid to the State the next month. This resulted in only making conditions harder for the families to survive while they were away from home. The small amount of money they received was far too little to adequately provide the necessities for their families. Had it not been for the help of kind friends these people made in their new surroundings, it would have been hard indeed to have survived.

On November 30, 1953, twenty-six of the Short Creek Polygamist men who had been arrested, appeared before Superior Court Judge Robert Tullar at Kingman, Arizona. In a plea bargain agreement they plead guilty to "Conspiracy to commit open and notorious cohabitation," a misdemeanor. On December 7, 1953, the 26 men were sentenced to one year suspended sentence and ordered to report to the Chief Probation Officer of Mohave County, Judge Charles Adorns, for probation. Judge Tullar ordered "That the bonds posted to assure the defendants appearance, be exonerated." The men were virtually free, while their wives and children were still held hostage. It would be more than another year from this time (December 1953) before the women and children would be free and allowed to return to their homes.

The school board trustees of the Short Creek School: Carl Holm, Melvin Johnson, and Joseph S. Jessop were among the men who plead guilty to the misdemeanor. Judge Tuller removed them as trustees of the Short Creek School District, #14. Their replacements were: Alfonzo Nyborg and Clifford Black of Short Creek, and David Roueche of Hurricane, Utah. The new trustees were sworn in by Mrs. Logsdon, Mohave County School Superintendent on December 27, 1953. School had started in Short Creek on August 31 with 8 Arizona students. On September 7th, 27 Utah students joined these at the Short Creek School.

The Mohave County School Superintendent, Mrs. Logsdon, refused the Polygamists the use of the school house for religious purposes, including funerals. Joseph S. Jessop (84 year-old grandfather to many of the people in Short Creek, including the school board member by the same name, and one of the men arrested and taken to Kingman), died on September 1, 1953. Because of the ban on using the school house, his funeral was held out of doors, in the front yard of Fred Jessop's house. Due to this discrimination, the Polygamist Leaders concluded they would have to provide their own meeting house. They decided to renovate the chicken coops at Fred Jessop's home and turn them into a meeting place. Also, by providing a building, it was hoped that the Washington County School Board at St. George, Utah, would consent to allowing a public school to be established on the Utah side of the community.

This work of remodeling began in September of 1953. Fred Jessop's home, which was used as a maternity clinic where all of the Polygamist's babies were born, had been known as "The Coop." This name was formally changed to "Hildale Home" at this time, to better identify with this clinic status. The chicken coops being rebuilt to use as a meeting place were joined on to the house, with only a breeze-way between them. The work of remodeling began by removing the old roof of the coops and raising the walls about four feet. A new roof was then reconstructed, the building closed in and put into use before the cold winter weather set in.

Washington County School Board did indeed establish a school there by 1954 and this building was leased to the County for that purpose. The new building was also sufficient for use as a meeting place for the religious meetings, and also dances and socials were held there. This was an advancement for the Polygamists, to own the building in which they held their religious meetings. Up until this time, all the meetings and socials had been held in the public school house. With this new Hildale School, it was necessary to provide more space for classrooms. With the income of the rent from the County, it would not be long until an addition would be built onto this building, allowing much needed room for the other uses of the community. This was not accomplished for another year, however. In the meantime other developments were transpiring.

Joseph Musser

On March 29, 1954, Joseph White Musser, senior Priesthood Council Member, died at Salt Lake City. The Polygamist Group at Short Creek did not recognize him as the President of Priesthood due to his ordaining Rulon Allred and of his calling a new Priesthood Council. Charles Zitting had been the recognized Priesthood Leader among the people in Short Creek for the last three or four years. Musser's death had very little impact at Short Creek. This is somewhat unjust, for history must give credit to whom and to where it is due. Had it not been for this man, "Saint Joseph White Musser," it is very likely there would never have been a Fundamentalist movement, or a Polygamist community at Colorado City today. Also, other Fundamentalist communities throughout the Mountain West would not exist. Joseph Musser was a dynamic person. He devoted the latter part of his life to establishing what he believed was the Gospel of Jesus Christ. It was because of such dedication that the Polygamists became so numerous and so well indoctrinated.

Joseph Musser was probably best known for his publishing of the *Truth* Magazine. He began publishing this monthly magazine in June of 1935. The *Truth* became the media used by the Priesthood Council to proclaim their doctrine among the people of the LDS Church. Along with the *Truth*, he also published numerous pamphlets and treatise', setting forth the doctrines of the Priesthood Group. It was Joseph Musser, along with Leslie Broadbent and John Barlow, who promoted Lorin Woolley (1929) into allowing them to write down his story, of how he received the special calling to keep Plural Marriage alive after the LDS Church abandoned it in 1890. It was also Joseph Musser, who in 1935, after the First Presidency of the Church publicly announced that "There is no authority on earth to perform Plural Marriages," either in the Church, or outside the Church, claimed there was a higher authority than what the President of the LDS Church held.

He published a pamphlet called "A Priesthood Issue," setting forth evidence that Joseph Smith had established a secret order of Priesthood called The Council of Friends. This Priesthood Order superseded any authority that the Church President held. The Priesthood Group that Joseph Musser and associates were members of, was of this higher order, thus placing them outside of the jurisdiction of the LDS Church Presidency. Of all the Priesthood Council Members, excepting for one small pamphlet put out with the help of Leslie Broadent in 1929, Joseph Musser is the only one who published any writings establishing the doctrines of the Polygamists. Without question, Joseph Musser is the most important person connected with the establishment of the modern day Polygamists. For this reason, it seems fitting to narrate a little of his history.

Joseph Musser was born at Salt Lake City on March 8, 1872, five years before Brigham Young died. At the age of 20 years old, he attended the placing of the Capstone on the Salt Lake Temple. From his journal, April 13, 1892: "I ascended the east middle tower of the Temple and touched the feet of the Golden Angel Moroni."

His formal school consisted of a "few years in the lower grades, never having attended high school or University." He did, however, work very hard at educating himself, learning shorthand and typing. He also studied extensively in law, gaining an understanding in this field.

He and Rose Barquist were married June 29, 1892. Less than three years later, on January 27, 1895, he received a call signed by President Wilford Woodruff to serve a mission in the Southern states. He was set apart by Apostles Brigham Young Jr., Heber J. Grant, and John W. Taylor and left for Alabama on April 13, 1895.

Joseph labored without purse or scrip. While on his mission his wife gave birth to their first son. Joseph Jr. was born July 24, 1895, just three months after Joseph's leaving home. Joseph Musser returned home and resumed his normal life of carrying out his increasing family responsibilities. In the early part of the year 1900, on the threshold of a new century, his peaceful life was interrupted. In his own words, here is what happened.

"When the Wilford Woodruff Manifesto was adopted (October 1890), I was not married. I had been promised in the Name of The Lord, by my Stake President some days after the Manifesto was published, that I would enter The Law. I believed it and later while courting my young lady, I told her I expected to enter that law of marriage. That when the time came I would take it up with her and we would make the selection of other wives together. Although I was taking her out of a plural family, she took the matter coolly, but she was true to her promise on that occasion.

"In December 1899, after receiving my 'Second Blessings' (Joseph had received a written invitation from President Lorenzo Snow, 5th LDS President, to receive Higher Anointings, which was attended to in November 1899, in the Salt Lake Temple), a messenger came to me from President Snow, stating I had been selected to enter Plural Marriage, and to help keep the Principle alive. Apprizing my wife of the situation, we both entered into prayer for guidance. At this time I hadn't the slightest idea whom to approach. The Manifesto had been issued and word had gone out from Bishops and Stake Presidencies that a definite stop had been put to the practice. Those assuming to enter the Principle would be handled. I was placed in a peculiar situation. God's Prophet told me to accept the Law and keep it alive. His subordinates said if I did so they would cut me off the Church."

It was not until the year of 1901 that Joseph married his second wife, Mary Hill. When he asked her father William Hill (a member of the Mill Creek Ward Bishopric) if he could marry Mary, her father told him it could not be done. In less than an hour after telling Joseph "no," Brother Hill returned and told him it was all right and he could go ahead and marry his daughter. Astonished at his change of heart, Joseph asked why he changed his mind. He answered that he had gone to apostles John Henry Smith and Mathias F. Cowley and put the question to them. They assured him it was all right and advised him to give his consent to the marriage. Mathias F. Cowley was the man who performed the marriage.

Joseph Musser married two more wives, bringing the number to four. His third wife was taken under the direction of President Joseph F. Smith (6th LDS President). His fourth was under the direction of Lorin Woolley in the 1930s. Apostles Mathias F. Cowley and John W. Taylor were disfellowshipped from the LDS Church and dropped from the Council of The Twelve because of performing plural marriages after the Manifesto. Mathias F. Cowley was allowed back in the Church but never reinstated to The Council of The Twelve. John W. Taylor was excommunicated and died as a non-member of the Church.

On February 16, 1914, Joseph had an interview with Francis M. Lyman, President of the Quorum of The Twelve. At this time Joseph Musser was a member of the High Council of the Granite Stake. Brother Lyman maintained it was a sin to enter into the relations of plural marriage since the Manifesto of President Woodruff. Joseph explained to him that he did nothing except through the council and ratification of the Members of his own Quorum. He was told he had no right to take counsel from members of the Quorum, but should have gone to the President of the Church. He was advised by President Lyman to resign his position in The High Council of Granite Stake. When Joseph related the circumstances of the interview to his File Leaders, the Stake Presidency, they advised him not to resign. He took their advice.

Joseph Musser became acquainted with Lorin Woolley in the 1920s. These events have been covered in a former chapter. It would not be amiss, however, to enter here an event that transpired prior to his meeting Lorin Woolley. From Joseph W. Musser Journal (Note 3): "In the year 1915 an Apostle (Joseph F. Smith) conferred upon me the sealing power of Elijah, with instructions to see that plural marriage shall not die out.... May 14, 1929, I was ordained a High Priest Apostle and a Patriarch to all the world by a High Priest Apostle (Lorin Woolley), and I was instructed to see that never a year passed that children were not born in the covenant of plural marriage."

Quoting further from this same journal: "I recall instructions given at the close of a prayer circle meeting held in the Salt Lake Temple in the early part of 1902. President Anthon H. Lund, a Counselor in the First Presidency was President of the Circle. We asked President Lund for a private audience after the close of the prayer. We made known to President Lund that children were being born to some of the Saints in the plural marriage relation and that they were not being recognized by the Church. We asked what should be done in such cases. His instructions came clear and emphatic.

"Brethren, you hold the Priesthood and stand at the head of your families. As your children are born you should give them a father's blessing and a name. When they reach the proper age for baptism, you should baptize them, confirm them members of the Church and confer the Holy Ghost in the usual manner. Be sure and keep the record and when the Church will receive it hand it in."

This short report on the early life of Joseph Musser is important in the history of the Polygamists. He was not a crackpot, but had been an active and faithful LDS Church member prior to his excommunication in March of 1921 and of his meeting Lorin Woolley. No doubt he would have excelled and gone far in the Church had he accepted the changes that were necessary to insure its survival against the political pressures that were opposing its principles at this critical time in Church history. Instead, he chose to stand up for the principles he believed in and in so doing, ended up fighting the very source of his blessings. When the opportunity presented itself to carry on, in what he considered the Higher Principles, he was in a prime position to "Take the ball and run," thus changing, not only his life, but the lives of a good many souls, both those living at the time and many more who were yet unborn. The effects of his efforts have, to this day, changed the history of the LDS Church and the Inter-mountain region, especially the states of Utah and Arizona.

With the passing of Joseph Musser, Charles Zitting became the next Council President for the Short Creek group. Rulon Allred became the leader of the Musser/Allred group at Salt Lake City. Since the Priesthood split, Charles Zitting had been acting as the leader for the Short Creek Group. When Musser died in March of 1954, Zitting moved into his leadership position without any opposition. His was to be a short rule.

Four months later, on July 14, 1954, Charles Zitting died, just twelve days short of being a year from the Short Creek Raid. Though his position of "President" had been accepted by the group, it had been a strained relationship because of the respect and influence that Leroy Johnson had over the people at Short Creek.

Charles Zitting was not a selfish man. He gave of his time and efforts freely. He was a considerate leader which enabled him to earn the respect of his followers. Had it not been that he was in the leadership position for such a short time, he no doubt would have been able to surpass the handicap of Leroy Johnson's efforts to undercut him.

Charles Fredrick Zitting

Charles Fredrick Zitting was born on March 30, 1894. He married Minnie Affleck on September 15, 1920. Because of Charles' belief in plural marriage, the union did not last. They were divorced about six years later. Charles wasted no time in getting married again. He convinced two other girls to marry him about one year later. John Woolley preformed the marriage for them, marrying one girl to him on August 13 and the other on August 30, 1927. Because of this decision to marry more than one wife, he was excommunicated from the LDS Church in November of 1928. He was arrested several times in his life because of his belief and practice of plural marriage.

The longest time he spent in prison was during the polygamist crusade in 1944. He and 14 others were sentenced to the Utah Penitentiary. All but four of these men signed a "manifesto" to gain parole after only spending a few months there. Charles was one of the men refusing to go against his conscience; by not signing, he remained in prison for the next 31 months before he was released. Because of this decision, he was later accused (long after his death) of going against John Y. Barlow, who was the Council President at the time and was arbitrarily "removed from the Presidency for turning against the Head," by the sons of

John Y. Barlow. It was while he was in prison that he wrote his memoirs. It was in these memoirs that he tells of being called into the Priesthood Counsel, this event taking place in the spring of 1932.

He was ordained a Patriarch and Apostle of the Lord Jesus Christ by Joseph Leslie Broadbent, who acted under the direction of Lorin C. Woolley. Charles remained faithful to his belief in the validity of this calling until his death. He would make no concession of conscience for any reason and suffered because of it. The worst of these being put upon him after his death by men claiming certain things had happened that, in fact, they have no proof of. These men believe that by discrediting Charles Zitting, they can then change the history of the Fundamentalist movement.

With the passing of Charles Zitting, there was a question among the Short Creek group as to who the next leader would be. The next legitimate leader in line was LeGrand Woolley. After him was Louis Kelsch. These two men were the last of the Council that had been called by Lorin Woolley. They both lived in Salt Lake City and by this time in history were not associated with the group at Short Creek. The people at Short Creek were following Leroy Johnson, a disciple of John Y. Barlow and a man whom both LeGrand Woolley and Louis Kelsch had refused to accept into the Priesthood Council at the urging of John Barlow in the 1940s.

Leroy went to LeGrand Woolley and asked if he was going to assume the position of leadership of the people at Short Creek. He was told by Woolley that the instructions of Lorin Woolley was *not to colonize* and he felt that he should not get involved in any such movement. He then went to Louis Kelsch with the same question. Kelsch gave a little different response. He first asked Leroy if he had any revelation on the matter. Leroy answered that he had not. Kelsch responded that he likewise had received no revelation on the matter. Leroy then asked Kelsch if he had any objection to him taking over the leadership of the group. Kelsch answered in this manner: "Roy, if you have what you think you have, you don't need my permission to go ahead."

This is somewhat different than what Leroy told the people at Short Creek. He said that Louis Kelsch had told him that he, Leroy, should go ahead and lead the people because Kelsch felt that the people at Short Creek did not have the confidence in him to allow him to be their leader. So under this pretext, Leroy Johnson became the undisputed leader of the "saints" and the Priesthood Work of the Short Creek Group (Note 4). Meanwhile, the persecutions from State Officials were still going on at Short Creek.

The State of Utah took a little different approach to solving the polygamy problem in the Utah portion of Short Creek. They decided to use one case, putting it through the courts, reasoning that it would be less costly to the taxpayers this way.

They chose for this test case the family of Vera (Johnson) Black, a plural wife of Leonard Black. Officers of the state picked up seven children (the youngest was left in the care of his mother) on June 4, 1954. These children were then placed in foster care. A writ of Habeas Corpus was filed in the Supreme Court of the State of Utah. The State Supreme Court ruled in the favor of Vera Black and ordered that the children be returned to their parents. In a matter of a few weeks the children were returned.

The State did eventually win the case. An offer was made to Vera and Leonard Black that if they would sign a paper promising not to live polygamy the children would be returned to them. They refused the offer.

On January 10, 1956, the children were picked up by officers from the State Welfare Department at Short Creek and placed in a foster home at Provo, Utah. This was very hard for Vera and Leonard Black to bear, not only losing their children but losing them at this time, for by January1956, the families of the people in Arizona had been released and allowed to return home.

In Arizona, the State Officials had picked four test cases to try in Court. The cases were each different in nature but covered the circumstances of the other cases there. The goal of the State was to take the children from their natural parents and adopt them out to other families.

An attorney in Salt Lake City had approached Guy Musser (a member of the Priesthood Council) and informed him that there was an Arizona Statute that prohibited the State from adopting children out without the consent of their natural parents. When Leroy Johnson told the attorneys that such a law existed, they responded they were unaware of such, but would find it if it did indeed exist. Leroy implied to the people that he had received inspiration about this statute, never acknowledging that Guy Musser had been the one to tell him of it.

On March 3, 1955, Judge Henry S. Stevens of the Superior Court of Maricopa County ordered the children returned to their parents, which was done on March 21, 1955. The wives and children were then free to come home. The State appealed the Court's decision but never regained the custody of the children. Thus ended the "Arizona State's crusade against the Polygamists of Short Creek." The Short Creek fiasco cost Governor Pyle his political career. He was never again elected to any public office in Arizona. He did, however, hold a position under President Eisenhower for a short time in the Federal Government at Washington D.C.

After the people returned home there was a time of peace at Short Creek. Life somewhat returned to normal. The United Order Movement continued for about a year or so and then the "Brethren" decided to put everyone on their own, asking that they simply contribute their time to community projects and pay their tithing.

Also about this time Vera and Leonard Black did indeed sign a statement agreeing to no longer live polygamy, making it possible for their children to be returned to them.

The families of Leroy Johnson did not return to Short Creek to live, but rather remained in Phoenix for a time. He began buying property in his own name, using tithing money paid to him by the people. He moved some of his family to the Manti, Utah, area, one of these places where he was buying property. Establishing himself there, he more or less began abandoning the people at Short Creek, where circumstances became very hard.

They were not accustomed to providing for themselves. They had not been schooled in managing money or of providing for their own families. Those with multiple families were the hardest hit. The management of affairs there fell on Richard Jessop, a Priesthood Council member, with Carl Holm, another Council member, assisting him; as also did Fred Jessop, who was not a member of the Priesthood Council.

These were very hard times for the people at Short Creek. They were unable to even pay the County taxes on the property, which only amounted to about three thousand dollars a year. The tax burden fell on the people at Salt Lake who were aligned with the group at Short Creek. This burden became unbearable for these people and they began complaining to their leaders. They felt that if the people at Short Creek could not even pay their own taxes there was not much use to support such a place.

The Priesthood Council met and after much deliberation concluded that they would sell the property off, leaving those living there to make their own way as best they could. There was one member of the Council that did not want to give up Short Creek. That member was J. Marion Hammon.

Marion Hammon had been sent to Short Creek in the early 1940s by Joseph Musser to be the general manager of the United Effort Plan. He felt that he was still under that calling, to see that the United Effort at Short Creek would succeed. He asked the other Brethren of the Council if they would allow him the opportunity to go back there and try to do something to redeem the place. The other Council members agreed to allow him to do so. He asked that they give him free reign and not interfere with how he would run things there. They agreed, thinking there was not enough spirit left at Short Creek to accomplish any great measure of success.

Marion Hammon, having been given the permission to go to Short Creek and redeem what he could there, accepted this challenge with determination and set out with a vigor that was unparalleled by any efforts made at Short Creek up to this time.

Note 1: The special school fund is that portion of the local school costs above the amount received from state equalization funds. This special school levy is raised by exclusive taxation within the local district. In 1953, Arizona had 255 small districts, all of which had to raise some of their school costs through a special levy.

The Short Creek School District was a small district in terms of area. The amount of property in assessed valuation per child was less than one fifth as much as the Mohave County average and only one fiftieth the amount per child as the highest district in the County. It was the lowest in valuation per student within the County and nearly the lowest in the entire State. It would require a tax rate fifty times higher in the Short Creek District to raise one dollar per student as it would in the wealthiest district of the County.

Note 2: On the morning of July 26, 1953, Arizona Governor, Howard Pyle, gave a lengthy radio speech on *KTAR* Radio, Phoenix, Arizona. It was printed the following day in the *Arizona Republic*, July 27, 1953. The entire speech follows.

"Before dawn today the State of Arizona began, and now has substantially concluded, a momentous police action against the insurrection within our own borders.

"Arizona has mobilized and used its total police power to protect the lives and future of 263 children. They are the product and the victims of the foulest conspiracy you could imagine.

"More than 100 peace officers moved into Short Creek, in Mohave County, at 4:00 o'clock this morning. They have arrested almost the entire population of a community dedicated to the production of white slaves, who are without hope of escaping this degrading slavery from the moment of their birth.

"Highly competent investigators have been unable to find a single instance in the last decade of a girl child reaching the age of 15 without having been forced into a shameful mockery of marriage.

"The State of Arizona is fulfilling today one of every state's deepest obligations, to protect and defend the helpless.

"The State is moving at once to seek, through the courts, the custody of these 263 children, all under the age of 18. They are innocent chattels of a lawless commercial undertaking of wicked design and ruthlessly exercised power. This in turn is the cooperative enterprise of five or six coldly calculating men who direct all of the operations and reap all of the profits, and are the evil heart of the insurrection itself. It is no surprise that some of these vicious conspirators are former convicts.

"Warrants were carried into Short Creek this morning for 36 men, many of them related, who include not only a hard core of plotters but a wider circle of fawning beneficiaries of this conspiracy, that the State of Arizona is determined to end right now and completely.

"As the highest authority in Arizona, on whom is laid the constitutional injunction to 'take care that the laws be faithfully executed', I have taken the ultimate responsibility for setting into motion the actions that will end this insurrection.

"It should be clearly understood at this time that so complicated an operation has required and has received the co-operation of many elements of our government – and has been undertaken only as a last desperate resort

"In many situations of the last few years I have reminded the people of Arizona that law enforcement is primarily a county problem – until such time as the counties themselves declare or by their actions prove that they are able no longer to fulfill their function.

"Mohave County appealed for state intervention to end this insurrection. The county's plea came to your governor from the Honorable J. W. Faulkner, Mohave County's highest legal authority as judge of the superior court there, in March of 1951, when I had been on duty only two months.

"Judge Faulkner recited the almost incredible details of this conspiracy – details almost revoltingly incomprehensible at this midpoint of the 20th Century. The sheer magnitude of the situation demanded immediate action, but even more urgently, required proof beyond any possible doubt.

"Hence it is that 26 months have passed since Judge Faulkner's first letter came to me. The investigation has been most thorough. Two attorneys general have participated. Appalled successive legislatures have approved funds for every phase of the investigation – and it has been from the very beginning a disturbing undertaking.

"It has been, frankly, the one and only real sorrow of my administration, intruding as it has on a hundred other problems on our state, and occupying the time and energy of scores of men and women. There had to be absolute certainty that in the end the innocent should be as securely protected as the guilty were severely punished.

"Before a single complaint was drawn, or a single warrant prepared, or the first preliminary order for today's action issued, we had to be certain beyond the last shadow of doubt.

"All doubt is erased when it is realized that in the evidence accumulated there are multiple instances of statutory rape, adultery, bigamy, open and notorious cohabitation, contributing to the delinquency of minors, marrying the spouse of another, and an all-embracing conspiracy to commit all of these crimes, along with the various instances of income tax evasion, failure to comply with Arizona's corporation laws, misappropriation of the school funds, improper use of school facilities, and falsification of public records.

"The leaders of this mass violation of so many of our laws have boasted directly to Mohave County officers that their operations have grown so great that the state of Arizona was powerless to interfere.

"They have been shielded, as you know, by the geographic circumstances of Arizona's northern most territory – the region beyond the Grand Canyon that is best known as The Strip.

"The community of Short Creek is 400 miles by the shortest road from the Mohave County seat of Kingman. Short Creek is unique among Arizona communities in that some of its dwellings actually are in another state.

"All the residents of Short Creek who live in Utah have been charged with the crimes they have committed in Arizona. We have neither enlisted nor encouraged the State of Utah to take action simultaneous with or parallel to our own, for it is a mass insurrection against the State of Arizona that we seek to suppress.

"To the best of our knowledge and information, there are only five residents of Short Creek who are in no way involved in the situation. They are Mr. and Mrs. Jonreed Lauritzen, Mr. and Mrs. Alfonzo Nyborg, and Don Covington. They are old residents of a colorful part of Arizona who have found themselves surrounded by this conspiracy, and have given invaluable help in the elimination we have now undertaken.

"Massive cliffs rearing north of Short Creek's little central street provide a natural rock barrier to the north. To the east and west are the sweeping expanses of dry and almost barren plateaus before the forests begin. To the south there is the Grand Canyon.

"It is in this most isolated of all Arizona communities that this foulest of conspiracies has flourished and expanded in a terrifying geometric progression. Here has been a community entirely dedicated to the warped philosophy that a small handful of greedy and licentious men should have the right and the power to control the destiny of every human soul in the community.

"Here is a community – many of the women, sadly, right along with the men – unalterably dedicated to the wicked theory that every maturing girl child should be forced into the bondage of multiple wifehood with men of all ages for the sole purpose of producing more children to be reared to become more chattels of this totally lawless enterprise. Some of the boys have escaped this dreadful and dreary life. But the girls – no.

"The very institutions such as school, upon which we all depend for the cultivation of the ideals that have made the nation great and Arizona great, have been perverted to the inculcation in our young of a devotion to this rank and fetid distortion of all of our basic rights and ideals.

"The very operations of this insurrectional conspiracy, with its complete disregard of all decency and of all law, have served to expand the population of Short Creek until it is probably the second largest community in Mohave County.

"Sixteen years ago it was nothing. You may recall that at that time two individuals, who were almost all of the male population of Short Creek, were sent to the Arizona State Prison to serve terms for flagrant violations of the state's moral laws. They had a half dozen wives or so.

"But their prison terms ended – they returned to Short Creek – and now the two have expanded to the 36 men named in warrants today – and their wives have increased from half a dozen to 86.

"The criminally deadly part is that their children under legal age now number the 263 mentioned.

"It is easy to see from this rapid expansion that in another 10 years the population of Short Creek would be in the thousands, and an army would not be sufficient to end the greater insurrection and defiance of all that is right.

"Of the 122 persons named in warrants as being involved in this ever-growing conspiracy, 85 have their principle homes in Arizona. The rest base their operations in Utah, although a number of these have additional homes in Arizona.

"Not all of the men for whom warrants have been issued have been arrested as yet, but it is fully anticipated that they will be. Those who have crossed, or subsequently cross, the state line into Arizona during the course of the police operations will be jailed on the

106

Arizona warrants. Those who elect to remain in Utah will be sought on warrants of extradition. This may take days or weeks, but it will be done.

"It is regrettable that this action had to be undertaken on a Sunday, but there were a number of vital considerations. There has been a community entertainment the last day or two in Short Creek that has attracted the maximum number of those named in the warrants. Today the maximum number of police officers have been free from other duties.

"It should be emphasized here that we have gone to almost unbelievable lengths to insure that the rights of no one are violated or even jeopardized in this action.

"Moving into Short Creek right behind the officers with their warrants have been the courts. Superior Judge J. Smith Gibbons, of Apache County, has been acting as committing magistrate, and has observed every legal propriety in holding the principal defendants to answer for trial in superior court as he also ordered these principal defendants to jail in Kingman, the county seat.

"The defendants are being transported right now to Kingman to await release on bail for those who are able to provide it, or who have it provided for them. These are the men and some of the women.

"In the case of the unwilling wives and the children, the action has been parallel by endaural different. Juvenile judges have gone along with the other superior court judges.

"Judge Lorna Lockwood of Maricopa County, whose understanding in juvenile matters is widely recognized, and Judge Faulkner himself, have started, and for some time will continue, a series of juvenile court actions through which the State of Arizona expects to be able to provide protection for the 263 children.

"This protection is very inclusive. It is calculated, under Arizona's laws, to give these children every possible garment of secrecy so that in years to come, the action in which they are now involved cannot appear anywhere as a matter of public record.

"Right along with the courts have gone trained social workers. A full staff from the state department of public welfare had gone along with the officers and the courts to take immediate custody of those children the courts decide should be brought under the protection of the State of Arizona.

"There hasn't been and there won't be any hardship in all of this. Facilities, equipment, and supplies have been sent into the area to be prepared to feed every defendant and every innocent victim, and every officer and participating state official, as long as may be necessary.

"There is a medical staff to guard against any health contingency and facilities are provided to care for everyone. There has been and there will be, no invasion of homes for quarters, for our people have with them a complete miniature tent city which, by now, has been erected in unused community space, and will house the state's personnel for as long as such housing is necessary.

"Representing the state department of law in the filing of complaints, the issuance of warrants and the general direction of all legal phases of this operation, is the attorney general himself, Ross Jones.

"He has with him three of his assistants, John Eversole, Paul La Prade and Kent Blake. LaPrade and Blake are the men who have conducted the preparation of all of the cases designed to shatter for all time, this insurrection and the conspiracy that supports it.

"To climax their work and beginning the conclusive phase of this operation, I signed an official proclamation on July 1, declaring a state of insurrection to exist in Mohave County and in the community of Short Creek

"Secretary of State, Wesley Bolin, and State Auditor, Jewell Jordan, have co-operated fully in handling the transfer of funds, especially appropriated to the governor's office for this purpose, to the office of the attorney general – and in the proper and orderly expenditure of sums from that appropriation.

"As your governor, I have been at my desk since early this morning, ready to issue any order or authorization to meet changing plans or unforeseen circumstances. I have been in complete and almost instantaneous contact with the operation from its beginning, through my administrative assistant who is at the scene.

"To the eternal credit of the press and radio of Arizona, none of this complex operation has been publicized in advance in any way, although representatives of all media have been fully appraised of every development during the entire 26 months of preparation. The whole purpose of this operation would have been destroyed had any part of it been known generally in advance.

"Now this most necessary cloak of secrecy is removed. From here on out and for some time to come, you will be hearing directly from press and radio correspondents, whose names you know well and in whom you have implicit faith.

"They have gone right along with the courts, to observe and report everything.

"While we leave the remainder of the details of this fantastic insurrection and its ending in their hands, it must be reiterated that the State of Arizona is unalterably pledged and determined to stop this monstrous and evil growth before it becomes a cancer of a sort that is beyond hope of human repair.

"Even if the letter of the law didn't exist as it does – common decency demands this.

"The right to life, liberty and the pursuit of happiness – and as so often been emphasized since, happiness of their own choosing.

"The State of Arizona is determined to insure that they have those rights for the remainder of their lives.

"We could do no less than this."

Note 3: One thing needs explanation. This book called Joseph W. Musser Journal was compiled by him, using notes from his day to day journal and written some years later. It was published by his family sometime after 1952. This is not to be confused with his journal, which is a day to day account of his life and is quoted in earlier chapters. From this book, on page 11, we quote:

"In the year 1915 an Apostle conferred upon me the sealing power of Elijah, with instructions to see that plural marriage shall not die out. President Snow had said I must not only enter the law, but must help keep it alive. This then, was the next step in enabling me to help keep it alive. I have tried to be faithful to my trust.

"May 14, 1929, I was ordained a High Priest Apostle and a Patriarch to all the world, by a High Priest Apostle (Lorin Woolley), and I was instructed to see that never a year passed that children were not born in the covenant of plural marriage. I was instructed to give patriarchal blessings to those applying for same and who were denied access to real patriarchs in the Church."

Then we find on page 20 of this same book;

108

"When I was ordained a High Priest Apostle in May 1929, it was done in response to a revelation of the Lord to the President of the Priesthood (Lorin Woolley). Previous to this, however, I was given the Priesthood of Elijah with instructions, as I was informed from President Joseph F. Smith, to seal couples in celestial marriage (1915)."

In his day to day journal, in his own handwriting is the following;

"Tuesday 14 (May, 1929), Received most wonderful blessing from Brother Lorin C. Woolley. Spent 2 ½ hours with him listening to his past experiences. I rejoice greatly (not legible)." Between the margins, someone (likely Joseph himself) has penciled in sometime later, these words: "Ordained High Priest Apostle."

Note 4: The following is taken from a book written by Jenna Vee Morrison Hammon, a plural wife of Marion Hammon, titled "THE BETRAYAL, of the Godhead, Priesthood Work, and Priesthood People," published in 1991, p 40.

"Leroy Johnson went to Louis Kelsch and asked Louis Kelsch if he intended to pick up the reins and lead the people? Louis Kelsch asked Leroy Johnson if they received revelation in their Priesthood Meetings and in their activities? Leroy Johnson replied, 'No, they did not'. Louis Kelsch said, 'Well, how do you expect to lead the people in the way that the Lord wants them to go, IF YOU DON'T HAVE REVELATION?'

"Louis Kelsch also told Leroy Johnson that if he (Johnson) had, what he thought he had in a Priesthood Way, that he wouldn't have to ask anybody's permission to do what he was doing.

"Leroy Johnson went back to his place of operation and in a Sunday meeting told the people that Louis Kelsch had told him to go right ahead and pick up the reins and start acting in that capacity.

"Being in the meeting and hearing this statement from Leroy Johnson, I was amazed, so I checked back with Louis Kelsch on this statement, and he said: HE DID NOT TELL LEROY JOHNSON ANYTHING OF THE KIND. HE ONLY TOLD HIM THAT 'IF HE HAD, REALLY HAD, WHAT HE THOUGHT HE HAD, HE WOULDN'T HAVE TO ASK ANYBODY'S PERMISSION'."

The United Effort Plan Revitalized

Before Lorin Woolley died in 1934, he called together the men whom he had set apart to keep polygamy alive and spent several months giving them instruction as to what their duty and calling was to be (see Note 3, Chapter 1).

He instructed them not to hold meetings, only allowing them to hold cottage meetings in the private homes of those interested in following their teachings. They were not to proselyte and not collect tithing from any of their followers. He also taught them that they were not to implement any kind of a United Order, that the Lord would not require such to be lived until he came and set the Church in order, allotting to the Saints their inheritance in Zion (see Note 2 and 8, Chapter Two).

Joseph Musser confirmed these instructions a few years later. Speaking to a group of men in a Priesthood Meeting at Short Creek on November 13, 1936, he told them: "The special mission and labors of the priesthood group was to keep plural marriage alive; that we were not called upon to colonize only as the Lord might dictate such a move; ...that the time had not come for the establishing of the United Order. The brethren should seek to live the spirit of the U.O. in their families, extending that spirit out among the Saints, thus preparing themselves to accept the great principle when the One Mighty and Strong comes to allot to them their inheritances."

Charles Zitting tells us a little about these meetings in the journal he wrote while in prison in the late 1940s (see Note 3, Chapter 1). "We (the Priesthood Council) met once a week, Thursday evenings. About two months before we completed our work, a messenger from heaven visited Brother Woolley and told him the time was short and we would have to meet twice a week in order to complete our work.... Therefore, we met twice a week and I remember well the night we finished our work, it was a very solemn occasion.... Brother Lorin C. Woolley arose and said to Brother J. Leslie Broadbent, who was next in seniority in this Priesthood Council, 'Brother Leslie, you are to me as Oliver Cowdery was to the Prophet Joseph Smith, before (he) apostatized. You are second elder to me and you are now to take charge until I come.'"

Soon after giving these men their instructions, Lorin Woolley had a stroke and was confined to his home in Centerville. This stroke left him incapacitated, rendering him unable to communicate to them any longer. He died a few months later, leaving Leslie Broadbent, the next man in seniority, in charge of the Group.

In teaching them, he had not been too specific as to just exactly what their duties and callings were, other than keeping plural marriage alive. One thing he did tell them: "Your callings into the Council of Friends (Priesthood Council) will have to be confirmed by God himself, Christ will have to lay his hands on your head himself and confirm your calling."

While Lorin Woolley lay in his sick bed at Centerville, the men of this group began to speculate as to what their duties were. They also desired that they receive the confirmation of their callings as Lorin Woolley had instructed them. They decided to go into the mountains and spend ten days of fasting and praying, asking that a messenger from heaven be sent to them to instruct them as to their duties and give them the confirmation Lorin Woolley had told them they needed.

On April 15, 1934, Leslie Broadbent, John Barlow, and Joseph Musser left Salt Lake City, going east into the mountains to begin their quest. The events of this venture are recorded in Joseph Musser's journal. He writes under date of April 15, 1934: "Preparing to leave for God's Temple in the morning with Jno. Y. Barlow and Prest. Broadbent...the Mountains...to make inquiry of the Lord regarding his will concerning us...."

"Saturday 23: "In our camp in Lamb's Canyon where we have been sojourning for the past week, seeking the will of the Lord concerning us and his people who are looking to the Priesthood for divine guidance, we have been fasting and praying and studying for a week, having finished our notes on the "Supplement to the New and Everlasting Covenant of Marriage" (a pamphlet they later published) which has been prepared with the collaboration of Elder J. L. Broadbent." These men all had dreams during their week of fasting and praying. These dreams were interpreted by them as being instruction from God that their duty was to tell their message to any who would listen, using those who believed in them to carry on the law of polygamy.

Quoting further from Musser's journal: "This morning at our altar, the sacred spot among the quaking asps on the ridge above our tent, which we have dedicated for the purpose, we having observed our fast since Thursday evening, we were blessed with the spirit of prayer and of prophecy. Bro. Barlow first prophesied that the prediction made by Brigham Young to the effect that men of his order of the Priesthood we hold would be walking along and be met by strangers from beyond who would converse with us about Celestial Marriage and other principles.

"Also in the Temple men would meet us and be given names to work for, some now being called to go in the temples and remain there night and day directing the work, etc, is soon to be fulfilled.

"Bro. Broadbent, being clothed upon by the Holy Ghost, prophesied that the purpose of our mission to this spot would be realized soon...that is, the confirmation of our calling.

"I was moved to prophesy with reference to the leadership of Bro. Broadbent, that the channel of revelation would be opened up; that the gift of leadership would be upon him, and the power of his Priesthood would be so manifest that the earth would tremble at his word; he would rebuke the nations with boldness and power from afar. The present Church authorities would be made to tremble at his word. He would have the power of Enoch.

"At our meeting tomorrow we would be able to feed the brethren who would become a power in sustaining us." (The brethren referred to here are the men of the Group that were following them in their teachings of living polygamy.)

Sunday 24: "Last night the Powers of darkness sought to overcome us. We could not sleep but very little. It affected all three of us. Bro. Barlow said three evil spirits had bothered him.

"Sunday opened up by a heaven rain storm. It continued until nearly noon, when we decided it unwise to try and hold a meeting in the grove, and having to go to the City anyway, we adjourned to Bro. Boss' home at 4 o'clock. About 25 of the Brethren had come to the canyon. It seemed impossible for my prophecy of the previous day to be fulfilled. However, when we did meet, the Lord was with us abundantly and the outpouring of his Spirit was marvelous (Note 1)."

Lorin Woolley died on September 18, 1934, never having recovered from the stroke that had rendered him incapacitated. Leslie Broadbent, the next recognized leader of the Group, died soon after (March 19, 1935), leaving John Barlow (next in seniority) to assume the leadership position. Before his death, Lorin Woolley had designated Leslie Broadbent as his successor, but Broadbent had failed to designate any leader to follow him. (The Kingston Group claims that Broadbent designated Eldon Kingston as Second Elder, as did Woolley with Broadbent. This claim cannot be substantiated outside the Kingston Group). Barlow became the leader on the premise of him being the senior (by ordination) member of the Group.

Joseph Musser writes in his journal under the date of March 16, 1935: "Brother Joseph Leslie Broadbent has passed on! …The brethren of the Priesthood attended him faithfully and pled mightily with the Lord for his restoration, but without avail…. The spirit of leadership is resting upon Jno. Y. Barlow and he will 'carry on' under the direction of heaven."

Throughout these events, these men had received no confirmation as to what their calling was. No messenger from heaven had appeared to any of them (some dreams had been interpreted as revelation), outlining what their course should be. It was at this juncture of events that John Barlow purposed to establish a United Order among the Group.

The first effort of living United Order at Short Creek (The United Trust) failed in the first year. Another attempt at the United Order was initiated in 1942. The United Effort Plan was organized on November 9, 1942. The Trust Document was filed in the Mohave County Court House at Kingman, Arizona, on August 8, 1944.

The organizers of the United Effort Plan left no doubt as to whether or not they were claiming to establish the United Order. In a letter from the Brethren to the people at Short Creek, written in 1948, they make this point clear (See Note 8, Chapter Two). The letter states in part: "Let us get this one fact in mind. We are not living the United Order, nor have we been living it. We are living toward it. The United Effort Plan was organized to protect our operations legally, looking to eventually entering into the United Order; and our community plan is calculated to prepare us for this great order. It is true some of the Saints are living the Order in spirit, but the Saints in general are not yet prepared to live it in fact."

It is true that the United Effort Plan was set up by men claiming ecclesiastical authority. They never did claim to establish a United Order, only an umbrella under which polygamy could be lived, thereby fulfilling the responsibility placed upon them by Lorin Woolley. Only by pooling the resources of the Group would it be possible to support the large families resulting from its (polygamy) practice. It was acknowledged by the United Effort Plan organizers that they acted on their own initiative in the forming of the Plan, not operating under Divine guidance in relation to its establishment. Acting in this capacity they contemplated some of the following principles, and attempted to incorporate them into Their Plan:

> Next to the gift of life, the gifts of freedom and virtue are man's most sacred possessions. Only by the influence of divine truth can social authority be established without infringing upon individual freedom. A balance of power is a necessary component of every social process. Social authority can neither arise nor be preserved without such balance of power. The United Effort Plan will allow freedom, develop brotherhood and maintain social authority under the Gospel Plan. The hope being, to establish a social order that will be an ensign of social, economic and political truth to the world. To accomplish these goals, it is necessary to hold fast to the fundamental principles of freedom that are guaranteed in the Constitution of the United States. It is also acknowledged that, within this framework of freedom and justice, this free and united society must be governed by the rules and doctrines as explained in the Doctrine & Covenants (undisputed law book of the Polygamists). Without this acknowledgment, the freedom and dignity of the members will be sacrificed. No matter how

philanthropic, humanitarian or benevolent they might claim to be,
it will only fail and will never stand the test of time.

The hard truth is that the high ideals of these original intentions have not prevailed throughout the history of the United Effort Plan. Later generations have departed from these principals and in a shortcut to achieve security, they denied the principles of freedom and the guidelines provided in the Doctrine & Covenants.

By the late 1950s the United Effort Plan had almost completely failed to achieve any of the purposes of which its organizers had envisioned. Those living on the property at Short Creek were so poor in spirit, as well as material things, and had sunk to so low an economic level as to render themselves unable to even pay the taxes on the property. Leroy Johnson, the head of the Priesthood Council, was no longer living there. The other Council Members had also more or less abandoned the idea of the United Effort Plan ever being of any value to the Priesthood Work. The only Council Members still at Short Creek were Richard Jessop and Carl Holm. These two Brethren, along with Fred Jessop (who still controlled the Store House), were struggling for survival, trying to keep the UEP alive.

About the only income to the UEP were the government checks received by the few widows living in the community, who turned their money over to the Store House. Those in the leadership positions were unable, either by choice or circumstance, to provide any income to the coterie. It was for this reason (Note 2) no doubt, that the Council decided to sell off the property and force the people there to provide for themselves. This then, was the circumstances surrounding the people living at Short Creek when Marion Hammon decided to Revitalize the United Effort Plan.

In the summer of 1958 Marion Hammon returned to Short Creek. He showed up at a Priesthood meeting that was held at the new meeting house just recently completed behind the home of Fred Jessop (the old chicken coops that had been converted for use as a meeting house and also leased to the Washington County School Board as a school building for the Utah children). Priesthood meetings had been appointed to be held on the first Monday of each month, beginning at 7:30 p.m. The brethren who were responsible for holding these meetings were Richard Jessop and Carl Holm. Neither of them were ever there on time. Most of the lay members soon learned that it was of no avail to come to the meetings at the appointed time, for they would just have to sit and wait an hour for one of the leaders to get there. Consequently all the men would show up late.

Marion Hammon came to the meeting on time. There was no one there. As he waited for the men to show up, he became perturbed. Finally, after about an hour of waiting, one of the Council members (Richard Jessop) came in. Marion Hammon, who was now in a very bad mood, stood up and opened the meeting an hour late. In scorching tones, he began to scold everyone there, including Richard Jessop (Carl Holm had not yet arrived). He told them that he would not tolerate tardiness in any degree. He was here to change things at Short Creek and he was going to start by demanding obedience and respect. He harangued the men for over an hour, but they didn't seem to mind. The feeling of the group was one of relief rather than of sorrow. They were pleased that someone seemed to care enough about them to try and help improve things in the community and the general spirit of the place. Marion Hammon was the right man to do just that.

He began first to hold meetings on time, general Sunday meetings as well as the Priesthood meetings. He did not dwell too much on spiritual doctrine in his Sunday talks, but talked more about how to improve things in the daily temporal lives of the people in their community.

The living conditions of the people was deplorable. There were only a few houses in the community that had running water (these were the houses on the old CCC line). None had inside bathrooms. The only electrical power in town was a small gasoline power plant at Fred Jessop's place and an old Cat diesel power plant on the Arizona side of the town that served about ten houses and was only run at night from dark until about 10:00 o'clock.

There was no real telephone service in town. A few homes had some of the old crank type phones where a system of long and short rings was used to signal which person or phone was being called, since all were on a party line. This phone line was only a local system without any outside connection. There was no high school in the community. There were no paved roads, either in the community or leading there from outside. The nearest town was Hurricane, Utah, about 30 miles of dirt road away.

The people, being very poor, were living in squalid conditions. They were proud, however, and resented the implications from Brother Hammon that they were poor in class as well as in material things. Getting them to change would be a challenge, making his job even harder than it would have been otherwise.

To add to these problems, the United Effort Plan (UEP) was in debt to several businesses, fruit growers and the like in the surrounding communities. This was what Marion Hammon faced when he came back to Short Creek in 1958. Realizing he needed some competent help to accomplish his task, he turned to members of the Group in Salt Lake City that had both the experience and the ability to help him build his city. He would go to these men for the help he needed.

In order to change the image of the UEP, the debts had to be paid. The people in Salt Lake City could help him raise the money he needed to accomplish this task. He set his mind on solving this problem first. He began by asking the men (heads of families) in both Salt Lake and Short Creek, to raise thirty dollars a head for each member in their respective households. This money was to be used for paying off the old UEP debts. Each family head responded both willingly and generously, some members contributing more than what was asked for. In just thirty days the effort had raised several thousand dollars. With this money, he then went to those the money was owed to and paid them off, thus creating good feelings and a new respect towards the UEP and the people at Short Creek from their outside neighbors.

This first effort of Marion Hammon to redeem Short Creek was very successful. It not only paid off the old lingering debts, but it also gave the people a renewed spirit and determination to move forward and do something to improve their circumstances.

He next established workdays. He would set aside a day, or days, when people would report to work on projects in the community. These days were every Saturday and any holiday that people could get off their regular work. This included not only the people at Short Creek but also the people from Salt Lake. The latter would leave Salt Lake on Friday nights and drive to Short Creek (referring to it as "going down south"), arriving there in the early morning hours. They would often get only a few hours sleep before showing up for work.

The projects at first included general cleanup work throughout the community: old eyesores such as abandoned vehicles and old farm equipment, old sheds and buildings that were no longer in use. These would be moved or torn down. The fences throughout the area were repaired and new ones built as needed. These were worthwhile projects that were necessary, but there were other things that were also necessary.

The necessity of building houses was one of the most pressing. He went to people in Salt Lake who either owned their homes there or at least were buying their houses and had some equity. These people were asked to sell their houses, collect what equity they had and then go to Short Creek, using the money to build a new home there. They were promised by not only Hammon, but all of the Priesthood Council (including Leroy Johnson), that if they would do this, they would be given a lot to build on. The title to the property would remain in the name of the United Effort Plan. The purpose of the UEP Trust was explained to them in somewhat the following generalities:

> The Brethren in the 1940s had set up the trust to hold title to the property for the security of their homes. Those building on the property would never receive a deed, the title remaining in the name of the trust. Anyone building homes would be allowed to live in them for so long as they chose, never being asked to leave them, understanding, however, that if they ever decided of their own accord to abandon their house, they would forfeit any claim of ownership.

The main purpose of the trust was to protect the homes and property from ever being taken for any reason. The people (not only from Salt Lake but also those from Short Creek) who would build homes, were told that they could rely on the Trust for all their security needs, such as life insurance, medical expenses, and also old age retirement benefits, that by contributing either time, money or property to the trust, they would be members of the United Effort Plan, becoming *co-owners in all the assets of the trust.*

The Brethren preached from the pulpit in the religious meetings that the policy of the UEP was not to force anyone out, but that the promises of the men who established the gathering place at Short Creek was that "any who was not in harmony with the Priesthood would get discouraged and move out."

Sam Barlow, speaking in a meeting held at Hildale, Utah, on October 25, 1964, said, "You cannot recognize your enemy until it's too late. One of the promises he (Joseph Musser) promised upon this place was that anyone that wouldn't come under the direction of the Priesthood would get tired and leave. This was a great promise. And I know it will stand. I'm sure it will stand regardless of who the person is, or who they're related to or what they may have done in the past."

Leroy Johnson said about the same thing a couple of years later. In a General Meeting in Colorado City on April 24, 1966, he told the people: "The presence of God came here – with a body of men (1940s), President (Joseph) Musser made great pronouncements and blessings upon this land. Among them was a statement something like this: 'Those who gather here will keep the commandments of God, or they will get dissatisfied and move away'."

The members of the Short Creek group (those coming from Salt Lake as well as those already living there) looked to the United Effort Plan as a social order to assist them to achieve three major goals:

The first, to protect them against their enemies being able to confiscate their property (a threat made by Governor Pyle at the time of the 1953 Raid).

The second, to safeguard the property from any mortgage foreclosure.

The third, to help build up and revitalize the community.

They had full trust in their leaders, believing them to be honorable men, having no reason to suspect they would ever change the rules of the UEP as was explained to them at this time.

There was only one small warning signal that would have caused any of them to doubt the honesty and integrity of these men.

A few of the people, who were asked to sell their houses in Salt Lake and move down south, wanted to see the trust document. They were reprimanded severely for showing distrust in the leaders. It was intimated to them that the document was somewhat sacred and anyone wanting to see it was on the road to apostasy for mistrusting their word about what was in it.

118

Although the Trust document was filed in the county courthouses of both Mohave County at Kingman, Arizona, and Washington County at St. George, Utah, this information was not revealed to any of the members coming to Short Creek, so in their ignorance, these trusting people put the matter aside. Their eagerness to establish a place of refuge, where they, with their families, could live in peace until the millennium, far outweighed any omen of trouble that should have been foreseen.

This reasoning, along with the promises made over the pulpit, dispelled any doubts that may have foreshadowed their confidence in the venture. Having overcome these obstacles, the momentum of the work began to move forward with surprising success. The members moving to Short Creek thus felt confident they would forever be secure in the homes they were building there.

The United Effort Plan was never claimed to be an ecclesiastical organization. There is no mention in the Trust Document of it being any kind of a religious Trust. The document specifically names the association as A Common Law Trust, leaving no doubt as to what the organizers intended.

The only reference to any ecclesiastical organization at Short Creek was referred to as: The Priesthood Work. The Priesthood Work was never known by any church name. It was explained to the people in their religious meetings (from Leroy Johnson down through all the Council members) that "we are members of The Church of Jesus Christ of Latter Day Saints." All who joined the Fundamentalists, either as new members coming from the Mormon Church, or as children being baptized when turning eight years old (as is the Mormon custom), were all confirmed members of The Church of Jesus Christ of Latter Day Saints (the LDS Church did not recognize any of these confirmations and none of these people were ever placed on the LDS membership roles). Any members of the LDS Church moving to Short Creek would be called to a Church Court, tried for their membership and, if they would not denounce the Fundamentalists, would most certainly be excommunicated.

The Priesthood Council taught that the LDS Church was God's Church. God had not rejected it nor would He ever reject it. The Church was out of order (because of giving up polygamy in 1890), but the time would come when "One Mighty and Strong" (D&C 85:7) would come and set the Church in order. (This One Mighty and Strong was to be Joseph Smith (Note 3). At such time as these events were to happen, the LDS Church leadership would be turned over to the Priesthood Council and the entire LDS Church would come under their jurisdiction.

The UEP or the Priesthood were not to build any church houses. They would get by just using the school houses for their religious meetings. The coming of these events were in the "near future" and there was no need to build any church houses because there would be plenty when the LDS Church was restored to the true Priesthood. They also taught that for these same reasons, there was no need to build Temples.

They made no effort to go to any of the present day Temples of the LDS Church for they believed the Church did not have the true priesthood. The work being done in the Temples was invalid and would all have to be done over. The only sealing work they performed was the marriage covenant and they claimed that a Temple was not necessary for performing this Ordinance: "It is the authority that validates the Ordinance, not the place." They not only claimed to be the only ones on earth having the authority to seal for time and all eternity, they also claimed to have the power to dictate who every girl was to marry.

This doctrine of placing men and women together was first preached to the people in the late 1950s, about the same time Marion Hammon came back to Short Creek to begin his work of building up the community. Up until this time, the policy of the Polygamists had been to go to one of the Brethren for permission to court and marry a girl for a new wife, the men having pretty much been allowed free rein to court whomever they chose.

By the mid-1950s this policy had become a major concern to the Priesthood Council. It created two problems. Any girl after reaching about 13 years-old would have a great number of suitors coming to her, all claiming to have had a revelation that she was to marry him, greatly confusing her young and tender mind. The other (and no doubt greater) problem was that the girls would invariably choose the younger men, making it almost impossible for the older Brethren to get new wives. The people were taught that only a member of the Priesthood Council could get revelation as to who a girl "belonged to" (should marry).

This situation brought the old clique factor into play. Each member of the Priesthood Council claimed to have the same authority, only recognizing Leroy Johnson to be the senior member, acting as President of the Council, taking charge in meetings, etc. to maintain order. Each Council member would "place" the girls *within his clique* when they came of marriageable age, telling them who to marry.

If a man wanted to get a wife, he had to align himself with one of the Priesthood Council members, supporting him in his clique. This condition allowed the factor of nepotism to rule in the matter of who would get a wife and when (at what age) they would get married. A natural circumstance developed wherein the sons of the Council members would not only be the first (youngest) to be married, but also the ones judged worthy to become polygamists. In most cases they were the least qualified for the choice, creating many problems in their later lives when their fathers would die, leaving them to their own abilities to cope with the problems of the big families these polygamist marriages produced.

120

The Polygamists teach that love is not necessary before marriage. Women are inferior to men and must learn to school their feelings, yielding to the desires of their husband. The girls of the Colorado City Polygamists are considered as chattel, to be used by the leaders to reward the faithful men of the Group for their support of the Priesthood Work.

Very few of them ever achieve any more than bearing as many children as possible, usually between the number of 15 or 20. Most are expected to work, turning what money they earn over to their husband to use as he sees fit. A few become school teachers to work in the public schools, while others become nurses to work in the hospitals of the nearby communities. None are ever allowed to become professors, doctors, lawyers, or achieve other professional goals. Mostly they work at whatever unskilled jobs are available in the area. "In order to control them, we must keep them pregnant and uneducated," seems to be the philosophy of the Polygamists.

About the same time this doctrine of placing girls in marriage was being taught by the Priesthood Council, Marion Hammon set about to organize a missionary program. This program worked as follows: Any young man just out of high school, or in that age group, was called on a Work Mission. These young men were asked to give two years of their time to the building up of the United Effort Plan. In return for this service, they were told that after putting in their two years, they would be "given a wife and a lot on which they could build a house." The policy of the UEP on building houses on these lots was explained to them the same as had been outlined to the people that were asked to come to Short Creek from other places.

These missionaries would either be assigned to work on Priesthood projects or would be asked to seek paying jobs in the outside communities, turning their entire paychecks over to Marion Hammon. The missionaries were not allowed to keep any of their earnings for their own support, but rather it was required of their respective parents to support them. This missionary program was successful and was responsible for much of the progress that was accomplished in building up the Short Creek area.

The main flaws were that of putting such a burden on the poor parents, requiring them to support their young sons, having four or five boys serving at once in some cases. Once these young men were in the program, they would not be released in some instances for up to five years, causing them to become discouraged, not knowing when they would ever be released, which usually came when they were given a wife.

The sons of the Priesthood leaders would get married before the boys from less prominent families. Such nepotism caused hard and bitter feelings among the boys and their parents. Any complaint made about this discrimination was met with harsh reaction from Hammon. He would publicly condemn and chastise the miscreants, thus discouraging any who dare question his actions.

One of the first projects Hammon chose for the missionaries to work on was to get electrical power into the community. Garkane Power Company had recently installed a new hydroelectric generating plant at Boulder, Utah. Garkane was a small company and was looking for new customers because it was planning to expand its area of operation, anticipating acquiring a portion of the Government power that would be available when the Glen Canyon Dam would be completed. Hammon went to this company and negotiated a deal with them to get a power line into the community. Grakane Power had recently rebuilt a power line in Wayne County, salvaging the old material that had been replaced with new poles and wire. The company agreed that if Hammon would furnish the manpower to build a power line, they would supply the material, using the salvaged poles and wire from the Wayne County project. This newly formed missionary program was used to supply the laborers needed to construct the new power line. The building of the power line was completed in 1959. This improvement to the community enhanced the lifestyle of the people living there. Having electrical power in their homes greatly encouraged them, especially easing the burdens of the women.

At the same time the power line was being built, work was started on a pipe line to bring culinary water to the community from springs in Maxwell Canyon. The water rights to these springs were owned by the irrigation company that had been formed by the Lauritzens thirty or forty years earlier. Most of the Lauritzen families had moved by 1959, having sold their property to the UEP or people who had moved into the community and joined with the polygamists. For these reasons, it was a relatively easy task to get the water rights. The next step in building the pipe line was to raise the money to buy the pipe.

Marion Hammon believed that the people should pay for improvements with their own money, not asking for government help, either in the form of loans or grants. He would often say from the pulpit: "There is nobody here but us chickens," meaning that it is our community and it is up to us to build it. He was afraid that if the Government were to help finance these civic projects they would be able to dictate and control the town.

He asked every head of household to again come up with more money. The people had not entirely paid off the last assessment, but this did not deter him from requesting more donations. The amount needed this time was $200.00 each. The money was raised, albeit a great hardship was put on the people to meet the assessment because the people were not very affluent, living just a little above the poverty level.

Even though meeting these requests for donations would put their families in hard straits, causing them to suffer, they felt they must meet any requirement placed upon them by the Priesthood. This was probably one of Marion Hammon's greatest faults, not knowing the true condition of the common people. He had no true comprehension of how poor the people really were. He always lived a much higher lifestyle than any of the lay members could even dream of, oft times chastising them in public meetings for their poverty, never realizing what the real problem was.

An example is one of his Sunday Sermons where he scolded the people for not buying the high priced steak that was for sale at the community store. The steak had to be ground up into hamburger before the people would buy it. In this sermon he said, "You people can't even appreciate a good cut of meat. We have to make hamburger out of it before you'll buy it." He never realized that they just couldn't afford to eat "a good cut of meat." They could barely afford to buy a little hamburger to use in soups and gravy.

The assessment for the pipe was also put on the Salt Lake members and, with their help, the money to buy the pipe and build a water tank was successfully raised. The pipe was brought into town and work on the project was begun. Most of the work on the pipeline was performed on work days; however, there were a few men that spent their full time on these projects, their temporal needs being supplied from the store house.

Two such men were Joe and Dan Jessop. These two brothers were very dedicated to The Work and have consecrated their entire lives to the upbuilding of the United Effort Plan. Without their dedication, Marion Hammon's job would have been much more difficult. Had it not been for such men, these and others, the Priesthood could never have accomplished what has been achieved among its followers. Any success claimed by the leaders in their temporal advancements must recognize the consecrations made by such men as these. Their families have suffered poverty and privation to satisfy the callings the Priesthood placed on them. The doctrine of the Priesthood is just such as this: "You must be willing to sacrifice everything you have, including your wives and family, to the up-building of the Work." Men like these deserve the highest credit that can be given for such dedication.

Work on the pipeline moved along and was soon completed to a location just north of the town, a distance just a little over a mile. The water storage tank was erected there. The task of putting in distribution lines was begun. This was a never ending project, but for the first time, running water would be available to every home in the valley. This, along with getting electricity into the community, was a real accomplishment for Marion Hammon toward redeeming Short Creek.

When Marion Hammon assumed the leading role of directing the affairs of the United Effort Plan at Short Creek, he displaced Fred Jessop, who had pretty much been in control of running the community. Not only was Fred no longer allowed to make the daily trips to town, but his role of being the entertainment and activities director, along with controlling the work projects of the Group, were taken from him.

In a sense, his wings were clipped. He was still used as a messenger boy, but this was a hard blow to his ego. For the first time in his adult life, he went out and got a job. Joining the Labor Union, he went to work on the Glen Canyon Dam construction site, hiring on as a laborer. His job consisted of riding around the dam site in a pick-up truck driven by a Teamster, to load or unload small items that were needed on the project. According to the Union contracts, a Laborer could not drive on the site, as likewise a Teamster could not load or unload the small items. Most of his working day was spent just sitting in the dispatch shack, waiting to be called out.

While working on the dam project, he was able to win the favor of the Union Stewards and was instrumental in getting many of the men from Short Creek working there, taking advantage of earning the high wages that were being paid at the remote project site. This was very helpful and his influence contributed much toward bringing in a lot of the money that built the community. He did, however, resent Marion taking his job from him. There would be bitter conflicts resulting from these resentments, especially along the lines of controlling the social affairs of the community.

The conflict between Marion and Fred intensified when Marion proceeded to establish a high school in the community; this high school would ultimately dominate the social aspects of the whole Group.

In 1959, Arizona law did not require students to have a high school education. Mohave County had never provided any schooling above the eighth grade at Short Creek. In the early 1950s, there was an attempt made to establish correspondence courses through Phoenix Union High School for those wishing to acquire a high school diploma. These courses were limited at best, only the more tenacious and studious participants were able to archive any success under this program. The Short Creek Raid of 1953 put a stop to even this token effort.

Marion felt concern over the attitude the Group Members had toward formal education. Few of them showed any concern about the lack of their children's high school education. When a girl graduated from the eighth grade, she was considered old enough to get married and was fair game for the men (or boys) to begin to court her (it was not uncommon for girls to get married at thirteen years of age). So, the only education a girl needed was how to be a good housekeeper and mother (wife). The boys coming out of grade school were expected to help on the UEP projects, or go to work earning money to support Fred Jessop's store house. The exception was that a few were picked to get their teaching certificates, with the view in mind of providing group members qualified to teach in the public school.

124

Marion concluded that a High School must be built and this became another of his priorities. He reasoned that by having a private school, the students could be taught the doctrines of the Priesthood along with academics. He proposed establishing the school as soon as possible. There was no available building in the community that could be used for the school, one must be built. Construction on the school building was begun in the spring of 1960.

The first obstacle to overcome was the question of building material. Hammon knew he could not ask the members of the group to donate more money. They had been pretty well bled out so far as raising money for another project was concerned. He devised a way to construct the building from "out of the ground" so to speak. He sent work crews (missionaries, as well as the crews on work days) to the rock quarries in the foothills. Here sandstone building blocks, to be used for the foundation, were hauled to the site picked for the new high school, about 100 yards from where the old CCC camp had been east of the town. Other crews were put to work building adobes from the natural soil of the area, which was ideal for adobe construction. The adobe-making crews were made up primarily of the young people, future students of the school.

These young folks deserve much praise for their dedication and efforts, for by working long and hard hours, they accomplished the task put upon them and the adobes were built. Lumber for the roof was the next major hurdle to conquer. Marion was also able to meet this challenge.

In the early 1950s, the UEP had purchased a small sawmill, setting it up just east of town, where the old CCC Camp had been. This was not the same sawmill the UEP had owned and operated in the 1940s. That sawmill had been moved from Widstoe to the Kaibab Forest near Jacob Lake in 1947. The UEP sold it to Whitting Brothers in 1948, and they then moved the mill to a site near the Big Springs Ranger Station. It had only been in operation at the new location for two weeks when it burned down, resulting in a great loss to the new owners.

The new mill was acquired with the intention of obtaining timber from Mt. Trumbull, about fifty miles directly south of Short Creek. What logs were sawed on this mill in the early fifties, however, were hauled from the area east of Zion National Park. By the time of the 1953 Raid, very little lumber had been produced by this sawmill and it was not used for the next few years. There was lumber produced by the UEP, however, but it was sawed on a mill near Bryce Canyon that belonged to Orlin Colvin, a son of Elizabeth Colvin, one of the first settlers at Short Creek. Orlin Colvin lived at Tropic, Utah, and was never a member of the UEP, but he did lease his mill to them in the mid-1950s. It was from this mill that lumber was produced to build the meeting house behind Fred Jessop's home. After the return of the women and children in early 1955, the sawmill at Short Creek was moved to a site just west of Mount Carmel, Utah, on the Muddy Creek. The timber was purchased from private land owners and lumber was sold to Whiting Brothers at Fredonia, Arizona (Kaibab Industries). This did not turn out to be very profitable, and the project was soon abandoned.

The sawmill was moved back to Short Creek in 1955, where it was again set up on the site at the old CCC Camp. A timber sale of almost a million board feet was purchased on Mt. Trumbull. Again the lumber from this venture was sold to Whitting Brothers at Fredonia. After this timber sale was logged out, the sawmill had just sat idle, not much hope of it being used again in the near future. It was this sawmill that Marion Hammon was to activate to obtain the lumber needed to build the new high school.

The first timber he obtained was from a small salvage sale on the Buckskin Mountain (Kaibab Forest). These logs were hauled to Short Creek, using the missionaries for the work force. By utilizing the young men of the missionary crew, the sawmill was put into operation. One particular missionary, Andrew Bistline, a young man greatly talented along both technical and mechanical lines, was very dedicated to the Priesthood Work, somewhat the same as the Jessop Brothers, Joe and Dan. Without his expertise and determination, the renovation of the sawmill would never have been successful. He spent long and hard hours putting the sawmill in operation. He dedicated his time and talents toward producing the lumber needed to build the high school building. His faithfulness to the Priesthood and his service to the UEP is especially noted here, because of the unjust treatment he received from the hands of the UEP leaders in later years.

Another person who dedicated much of his time and talents to finishing the building of the high school, which step-by-step process took almost ten years to complete, was a man by the name of Harold Blackmore. He was asked by Hammon to move to Short Creek in 1963 to help in the renovation of the community. He was living in Canada, associated with a group of Polygamists who followed the Priesthood Council at Colorado City. Because of his many talents in the building trade and his ability to procure building material, it was decided he would be an asset to the Priesthood Work. Much the same as Andrew Bistline, he later received unjust treatment from those who benefitted most from his labor and talents (Note 4).

Due to the dedication and hard work of such men as Andrew Bistline, Harold Blackmore, Edson Jessop, and the missionaries, enough of the school building was completed to enable classes to be started by the fall of 1960. The name chosen for the high school was The Colorado City Academy and this institution grew to become the pride of the valley.

When Marion Hammon returned to Short Creek in 1958, Fred Jessop was able to perceive the effect his return would have on his (Fred's) managing position there. In an effort to maintain a measure of control in the community (and over the people), he devised a plan to maintain his power role. He would establish a new community on the Utah side of the valley, splitting Short Creek at the state line. He named his new town Hildale and began the process of incorporation. He would always dictate who would be on the Hildale Town Council, thus assuring that none of Marion's clique would have any role of managing His Town. Fred was able to do this because of the influence he had with Leroy Johnson.

By lobbying Leroy, convincing him it was necessary for the good of the Work, Fred was able to do just about anything he decided to do at Short Creek. At the outset of Marion's arrival in the community, Fred immediately gathered his supporters around him and began the process of undermining Marion's reputation and influence. This was not only done in defiance of the promise made to Marion by Leroy (to let Marion run the affairs at Short Creek how he wanted, without interference from anyone), but also in direct opposition to covenants made between Fred Jessop and Marion Hammon (Note 5).

Fred's most prominent supporters were his nephews, the sons of John Y. and Martha Jessop (Fred's sister) Barlow. In the first year of Marion's return, Fred Jessop, with the help of the Barlows, caused Leroy to thus break his promise to Marion, that of allowing him to revitalize the UEP without interference.

For the next twenty years or so, Marion would continue to struggle to combat the efforts of these Big Elders, who were determined to destroy him and his position of authority in the UEP, without him ever fully realizing that such a cabal even existed.

With Fred Jessop establishing a new name for the Utah side of the town, Marion Hammon concluded it would be wise to change the name of the Arizona side as well. Short Creek was changed to Colorado City (1961) soon after the high school was opened. He concluded that because of polygamy and the recent notoriety of the 1953 Raid, the name Short Creek was a stigma that the community suffered under. He supposed that if the name was changed, the feelings of the people from the outside communities would change towards the polygamists.

These feelings did change over the next few years, but it was more because of the changes made by the people in Colorado City, rather than the changing of the name itself. The polygamists earned a reputation of being a hardworking and honest people, and the neighboring communities came to respect their ability to perform in their contracts made with them and the quality of the work on these completed projects. The young men that came from the community, and especially from The Colorado City Academy, were always in demand by outside employers. The reputation these young men established was known for miles around. This is what changed the stigma of Short Creek from one of disrepute to Colorado City's reputation of being an honorable one.

Marion Hammon was responsible for other civic improvements in the community. He established a new dairy, building a new barn with modern equipment such as milking machines and sanitary facilities to properly handle and take care of the milk. The old barn, one that had been built in the early 1930s by Isaac Carling, was an eyesore in the center of town. This was one of the first buildings torn down when the renovation of the community was begun.

A new paved highway was constructed from Hurricane to Colorado City, completed in 1962. The highway was not completed on to Fredonia until 1965, but having a paved road into the community made a tremendous impact on the people living there. The completion of the new road was not because of anything Marion Hammon especially did, it would have been built anyway because the need of another traffic route through the area was fast becoming a necessity.

Another improvement Marion Hammon was responsible for was getting telephone service into the community. Louis Barlow was largely the person who did the negotiation and ground work to accomplish this achievement, but he was acting under Hammon's directive to do so. He had attempted to bring telephones to town earlier, but had been unsuccessful. Without Hammon's support, it surely would have been even a few years longer.

South Central Utah Telephone Association, a user-owned cooperative with the main office based at Escalante, Utah, agreed to provide telephone service to Colorado City if enough subscribers would join the association. There was no problem getting the number of potential users to sign the membership pledge. The membership initiation dues were forty dollars per member, to be paid at the rate of five dollars a month, added to the phone bill after hookup service. This made it relatively easy for the users to obtain telephone service. A telephone line was built from Hurricane to Colorado City and the first telephone, a single toll station in front of Louis Barlow's house, was put into operation in April of 1964. An automated telephone exchange building was constructed on the south side of the Creek and work began on running underground lines to all the homes in the community.

Telephones were a real luxury to the people of Colorado City. They had not missed them before having them, but one thing the polygamists are notorious for is their gift of gab. Having telephones enabled them to exploit this talent to the fullest. In the first few years after telephone service was available to them, a high percentage would have their service disconnected due to unpaid bills. This was a discipline problem that was hard for them to cope with. Such Big Elders as Orvil Johnson (Leroy's son) were the worst of the offenders. Any small excuse to talk long distance would, in their own minds, boost their ego of importance, convincing themselves that it was all for the good of the Work.

The telephone company did not feel that their intentions of helping the Work was reason enough to excuse them from having to pay their bill. When their phones were cut off, these important people, never having been responsible for paying their own way in the past, having been used to riding on the backs of the more conscientious UEP members, would become very indignant when expected to pay their own bills. Nevertheless, the telephone company was no respecter of the importance of these persons and, if the bill was not paid, the service was discontinued.

The polygamists have learned that any outside controlled utilities such as telephone and electrical service must be paid for, or they will be disconnected. The same is not true for utilities controlled by the companies of the community. Such services as water, sewer, and garbage collection are not paid for as conscientiously, because they know these services will not be cut as quickly. The ones most guilty of not paying these bills are the ones who claim to be the most righteous of the society. Water bills into the thousands of dollars are never paid by some of these high ranking members and service is never discontinued to them, putting the burden on the lay members to carry them. Members who do not pay their bills are the elite of the society. They are the ones going on trips and tours to exotic lands and places. Sam Barlow (son of John Y. Barlow) was one such person. He learned at an early age how to play the game of riding on the backs of other members of the society, working his way into cushy positions and becoming a leach on the producing element in the UEP.

Marion Hammon advocated that the polygamists establish as much home industry as possible. The first place to begin was to bring the farm lands of the community into production. The biggest drawback to accomplish this was the lack of irrigation water for the fields that lay barren. There was the small irrigation ditch that the Lauritzens had brought from Water Canyon in the 1920s, and by the1960s most of the water rights to this ditch were under the control of the UEP. The ditch, however, was inadequate to deliver all of the available water to the farm land; much of it would be lost due to seepage and evaporation. Hammon reasoned that if the water could be put in a pipeline, it would not only irrigate more farmland but could also be pressurized to utilize a sprinkler system, thus becoming more efficient. The first step to accomplish this undertaking would be to obtain pipe for the project. In the fall of 1964, he stood before the people in a meeting at Hildale and asked for a donation of $500.00 from "Every man in this Group," to pay for the pipe (Note 6). Most of those who were asked to contribute responded to the request and again the money was raised.

The Mercury Project, where the testing by the Atomic Energy Commission was carried out near Las Vegas, Nevada, was closing down. There were several miles of 10" steel pipe that had been used as gas lines in this project. The government put the pipe up for bid at a salvage sale and Marion was the successful bidder. It was all underground and had to be dug up, cut into forty foot lengths, and hauled from the area.

This task fell to Joe Jessop and a crew of missionaries. The work of salvaging this pipe, moving it to Colorado City, digging the trench from Water Canyon, welding the pipe together and burying the pipe, was a major undertaking. Joe was capable to the challenge and in just a little over a year, the job was completed. This successful herculean project of Marion Hammon is further evidence of the dedication and willingness he was able to inspire in the people who honored him in his calling of building a community where they could enjoy security and self-sufficiency.

After the pipeline from Water Canyon was completed, work was begun on the construction of two large reservoirs east of Colorado City, near the mountain. These reservoirs were built under the supervision of the Soil Conservation Service, the costs being reimbursed by the Government when the projects were completed. Marion Hammon was against taking money from the Government to pay for any UEP improvements. Leroy Johnson felt the same as Marion did at this time. Fred Jessop did not feel the same way, however. His philosophy was "We are entitled to all the Government will give us, for they owe it to us."

Fred reported to the men in Priesthood meeting one morning that the Government was going to give him money to build a new road from the highway (U-59) into Hildale (Utah Avenue). Leroy got up after he finished and told the men, "If we take money from the Government, we will lose control of the town. If the Government puts money into a community or project, then they can come in and dictate how the community is run (Note 7)." Fred was not willing to follow the counsel of either Leroy or Marion on this issue. He took the Government money and built the new road. This was the beginning of the Polygamists' abuse of the Government help systems that in time reached scandalous heights.

Once the irrigation system was completed, the next step was to bring the farm lands into worthwhile production. Out of all the Polygamists at Short Creek, about the only person who had been successful at farming in any degree was Bill Cooke, when he had been raising chickens to make the payments on the Don Lauritzen property the UEP had purchased. Because of Priesthood politics, he had been shut down from even this modest achievement. By the mid-1960s his age pretty much ruled him out as being the person to manage the farming project. It was necessary to go outside the community to find someone with the experience to make a success of the endeavor. In Hammon's search among the Priesthood's followers for a manager, he settled on Parley Harker.

In 1950 the Federal Government had opened up the Escalante Desert, just west of Cedar City, for Desert Entry (Desert Entry was an act that allowed farmers to Homestead designated areas, bringing the land into production). Parley Harker moved from Lewisville, Idaho, about this time, taking out a claim on a parcel of the land offered in the Escalante Valley. He was a brother in-law to Newel Steed and after a few years of his moving to Southern Utah, he became converted to

130

polygamy. Parley Harker was a very successful farmer. In the ten years or so since leaving Idaho, he became quite prosperous and was well respected in the Beryl area. It did not take Hammon long to decide on him as the man he needed to help with the farming at Colorado City, and the farming operation was turned over to Parley in 1963. He spent much of his time (and his own money) establishing a successful farming operation there, leaving his own farm at Beryl to the management of his oldest son Merril, who, because of his training, was able to do a very good job of running the place.

Hammon did something that was out of character for him, he turned the project over to Parley to manage as he decided. This was the one thing that made it possible for Parley to succeed in his efforts, being able to make the decisions necessary to run the operation (The biggest mistake made by the leaders of the Polygamists is this one fault, that of not allowing their followers the free agency necessary to run the stewardships that are placed upon them. The leaders always want to make the decisions, using the excuse that only they can get the revelation necessary to make the projects successful). Parley had the equipment and the expertise necessary to put the farm lands at Colorado City into successful production, but the soil was run down and needed much fertilizer to build it back up. When he went to Hammon with the problem of where to obtain inexpensive fertilizer to accomplish this task, Hammon again met the challenge – he would use chicken manure.

There was a chicken farm in La Verkin (near Hurricane) owned by a Mr. E. J. Graff. On this farm was a huge pile of chicken manure that had accumulated over the years. Hammon negotiated a deal with Mr. Graff to not only buy the manure pile, but to clean the coops in the next several years to come, hauling it to Colorado City and spreading it on the fields. This turned out to be a successful and worthwhile project, building up the soil sufficient to produce abundant crops. For the first time in the history of the United Effort Plan, crops were successfully grown in Short Creek, one of its main goals since its inception.

It should be noted here that this became possible for two main reasons: Hammon's missionary program produced the money and the labor necessary to carry out the program, and he turned the project over to the competent management of Parley Harker to run the operation as he saw fit.

For the first time in the history of the Polygamists and the United Effort Plan, things were looking up. Towards the end of the 1960s, the dreams of their founders were finally being realized. A united effort among the members was proving a success. Several new and modern homes had been built, including one for Leroy Johnson, and electrical power and telephone service had been brought into the community. A new paved highway was completed from Hurricane. A culinary water system was in operation. A modern dairy was established. The farming projects were economically producing crops, both for the community and even such produce as hay was being sold outside of the town. These improvements had all been accomplished by using only the money contributed by the UEP members (both in and out of the missionary program), not from any government financial help. This fact was the greatest achievement of all. And the credit for this achievement goes only to Marion Hammon. The credit for the building of Colorado City and the UEP must be given to him.

Through the efforts of Alma Timpson (a Council Member), a movement was started to bring a sewing plant into the community in the late 1960s. This sewing plant was to be established through negotiations with Barco Inc. in Southern California, and would supply employment for about 80 people in town. Providing employment for their members was something the leaders had dreamed about for years and this seemed to be an opportunity to take advantage of, but not without some problems.

As is the case in most societies, there is always an element that will spring up and attempt to seize power and control of any successful enterprises that are built either by individual or group effort. The Polygamist Society is no different in this respect. As soon as it was realized that a money making institution was to be established in their midst, the sons of John Y. Barlow began scheming how they could get control of it. Thus began the first undercurrents to breakup and destroy the United Effort Plan (Note 8).

Note 1: Guy H. Musser, son of Joseph Musser, in a discourse delivered in a General Meeting held on Sunday, March 21, 1972, in Salt Lake City, Utah, makes the following statement:

"Leslie Broadbent was the next man in order (after Lorin Woolley died); he had the senior ordination. I have the material that the clerk wrote. Louis Kelsch was the clerk and he wrote everything that they said in their meetings for the next six months. Father told Louis to turn that over to me for safe keeping, and I've read it all. So they talked about what we are talking about and they were very frank with each other. They also went on a private trip to Lamb's Canyon for two weeks to fast and pray and to try to find out if the Lord wouldn't give them additional information – see if He wouldn't make their calling and election sure. They didn't report that to me; that was their business and not mine. But they did report to me that the Messengers appeared and certified the material they had already written. Brother Broadbent had written a little book, and he and Father had written 'The Supplement to the New and Everlasting Covenant,' and they had this affidavit of Lorin Woolley's. And the Messengers certified that it was correct. In fact when Lorin – it took several days to get that written up, to correct it, to use the right words, to make it definite so that no one could make a mistake about it – Lorin read it, or they read it to him, and he said; 'Before I'll sign it and accept it I'll have to take it up with the Lord.' So he took it away for a couple of days and he came back and said that it had been certified by the Lord."

These statements of Guy Musser leaves questions as to what the truth is in regards to what happened in Lamb's Canyon in 1934. The account of the incident in his father's journal is in direct contrast to what is said in this sermon. According to Joseph Musser, no messenger ever came to them while in Lamb's Canyon. He conveys a message of disappointment that no messenger came to them, that their prophecies were not fulfilled and that they did not receive their confirmation from the Savior. Reason tells us we must choose what is in his father's journal against what he is saying here. This puts Guy Musser in suspect as to telling the truth. It puts a cloud on his credibility, leaving the reader to question everything he relates regarding the history of the Polygamists.

Note 2: In the mid-1950s, advancement of any kind had almost come to a standstill at Short Creek. Richard Jessop was the recognized Leader, but Carl Holm was the General Manager of the United Effort Plan. Fred Jessop, however, was the one man who was pretty well running affairs there. There were a few people, mostly young men, who were working out of town, bringing in a little money. Due to the recent policy of the Priesthood for all to support themselves, these men, after paying their tithing, would have very little money they could turn in, to help support any improvements sponsored by the leaders. This left only the Welfare and Social Security Checks that were coming to the women (widows and divorcees) of the community, to finance these leaders in their building up of The Kingdom.

A typical day in the life of the men living there would begin at about 10:00 a.m. in the morning, when Fred Jessop, Carl Holm, and Richard Jessop would gather at one of their homes to discuss the activities of the day. If there were any projects to work on these would be discussed first so that those working on them could leave by at least noon (more times than not it would be closer to 2:00 p.m. to be on their way). These projects would consist of such activities as: cutting posts, building fences for the neighboring ranchers, picking fruit in Hurricane, pruning fruit trees for the fruit growers (usually to pay for fruit bought the summer before) in Hurricane and whatever other work could be contracted from people in the surrounding area. Richard Jessop would go with the crews on these projects, usually getting home about midnight. Carl Holm would have his duties aside from these projects, he being the one running the farming and ranching projects at such places as Hatch, Alton, and Beryl, Utah. He was also in charge of selling the Cedar Posts that were cut, and collecting any money that was earned from any of the other projects.

Fred Jessop's job was the one activity that brought in no income whatsoever; in fact, had it not been for his "occupation," there may have been enough money earned on the other work related endeavors that the people there could have paid their taxes and not allowed this burden to fall on the Salt Lake people. It was his responsibility to go to town (every day) and bring back groceries for the store house, to supply those still depending on it for their sustenance.

A home in Hurricane was rented by the UEP where one of Richard Jessop's families lived. One of the purposes of renting this home was to provide a place were those children from Short Creek who desired to attend high school could do so in Hurricane. Fred Jessop, who was already a polygamist (three wives), had become romantically attracted to one of the teenage female students. Because of the results of a childhood disease, he had never been able to father children. In trying to win over the heart of the young girl (who will not be named here), one of his arguments to convince her to marry him was that if he could mate with a younger wife it may help him produce the faith necessary to father children (why this same reasoning had not worked when his other wives were younger did not seem to occur to him). The girl, although flattered by his attentions, was not ready to commit herself to a marriage without children. She did not want to get married until she had finished high school and besides, her mother was against her marrying Fred Jessop, who was 30 years older than her teenage daughter. These reasons did nothing to stop Fred in his quest.

Fred Jessop did not have a truck or pickup to haul the groceries home from town for his store house. All that was available for his use was a two-door sports car that one of the young men had turned in to the UEP. It was necessary for him to use this car to bring the supplies home. He made the trip to town (Cedar City) every day, always getting back to the home in Hurricane at about the time the school children came home. He and the girl would go upstairs to her private bedroom and stay there until well after dark, usually not coming down until about midnight. He would come downstairs in a big hustle, urging those who were going home with him (there would always be a car full of people riding with him) to hurry, although they had been waiting for several hours for him to finish his amorous duties. The people would fill the seats of the car, leaving only the trunk space to haul the commodities. Sometimes it was necessary to pile such things as sacks of flour on the lid of the trunk. It was a humorous sight indeed to see the small sports car, the seats full of people, with packages and sacks piled on the trunk, leaving Hurricane in the middle of the night, climbing the steep hill out of the valley, to make its way over the rough and sometimes muddy, dirt road to Short Creek. This same procedure would be again repeated the next day, and every other day of the week except Sunday. This was pretty much Fred Jessop's routine and his occupation at the time that Marion Hammon came back to Short Creek to revitalize the United Effort Plan.

Note 3: It is interesting to note that throughout Mormon History there have always been people coming forward claiming to have special power, or priesthood, that puts them ahead of the Church Leaders (this began happening even before the Prophet Joseph Smith was assassinated at Carthage Jail). These people (usually one man) will claim that the Church Leaders are out of order and are leading the people astray and that through some special calling, they have been chosen by God to set the Church in order. In the early 1930s there were men claiming to be this One Mighty and Strong, spoken of in D&C 85. The polygamist leaders have taught since the mid-1930s that this man spoken of in the Doctrine & Covenants was to be Joseph Smith. This doctrine came about because of a dream that Joseph Musser had in 1936.

From Joseph Musser's journal: September 16, 1936:
"On 16th. I dreamed I was telling the Saints that Joseph Smith was the One Mighty and Strong and that he has already come – and is among us now, preparing and getting things ready for the necessary changes. I awoke with conviction in my soul."
Much of the Doctrine taught by the Polygamists have come about because of dreams of the leaders. As new leaders take over and they have new dreams, the doctrine changes. As one of the new leaders of the fledgling Fundamentalist movement, Musser was one of the prime persons responsible for establishing what the doctrine was, but his teachings have been changed by some factions of the Polygamists today.
A case in point is that of Joseph Musser choosing Joseph Smith as the One Mighty and Strong in 1936. In 1929, a man by the name of John T. Clark was proclaiming to be this One Mighty and Strong.

From Musser's journal, March 3, 1929:
"John (T. Clark) spoke very positively of his being chosen by the Lord to set the Church in order as outlined in the 85 sec. of the D&C While he appears to have unusual faith and powers and is absolutely clean, I am yet unconvinced of his exact mission and am trying to keep an open mind on the subject. If the Lord has chosen him, he shall have my full support."
Lorin Woolley told Musser in 1930 that Clark was not the One Mighty and Strong.

From Musser's journal we read:
March 31, 1930: "He (Woolley) spoke of my friend Jno. T. Clark as in error in supposing he is the One Mighty and Strong, like unto Moses, etc."
Musser is still listening to Clark after this. On May 6, 1930 he writes (quoting Clark):

"Pres. Grant will make the announcement that he (Clark) is to succeed him as leader and is the one Mighty & Strong to lead the Church out of bondage spoken of in 85th. sec. D.& C. And that the records are about to come forth through. him, where these records are, is at Alpine, Utah County, where he took me to view the hiding place."

On July 15, 1931, Musser is still troubled over who John T. Clark is. He writes:
"Last night I awoke – could not sleep – arose and bowed to the Lord asking him about Diamond Well, also as to just who Jno.T. Clark was, who is making so many claims. Today Bro. (Pete) Westman came to office, introduced himself and without any preliminary proceeded to testify that Jno. T. Clark is the One Mighty and Strong 'spoken of in the D&C, and he will begin his work shortly'. Also it has been known to him we will succeed in our Diamond Fork undertaking. He was very definite and had a marvelous spirit. Perhaps it was the Lord's answer to my prayer. With your help Father, I will do thy will forever and I rejoice in thy mercies" (the Diamond Fork well referred to here never was successful).

Musser writes again of John T. Clark. Under the date, July 23,1931:
"Brother Westman gave Jno. T. Clark a blessing in my office, proclaiming him the One Mighty and Strong. I am still unconvinced, but believe Bro. Jno. T. has an important work to preform.
Bro. Jno. T. Clark later expressed disappointment of Westman's blessing setting him apart etc. as he (Westman) had no such authority."

A little over a year after this, John T. Clark died. Again from Musser's journal:
September 16, 1932: "At about 12:30 A.M. Jno. T. Clark died at Reno. He was under medical attention. He had claimed to be the One Mighty and Strong, the one like unto Moses and the Indian Prophet and had created quite a stir. He was clean and apparently sincere, but it appears he was mislead by the spirit he followed. There are among his followers now who claim he will come back to do his work of setting the Church in order, that he has just gone over to get instructions."
Musser was "ordained a High Priest Apostle," May 14, 1929. The calling he was given must not have been too plain to him at the time or he would not have even been concerned about "who John T. Clark was." Also, on March 31, 1930, Lorin Woolley told him "that his mission (Woolley's) was not to set the Church in order, but to do what he was set apart to do (keep plural marriage alive)." It was after Woolley's death in 1934 that Musser had the dream about Joseph Smith being this One Mighty and Strong. We must assume that it is not Woolley's doctrine.

Note 4: In the latter part of the 1950s, a group of polygamists in Canada joined the Fundamentalist group led by Leroy Johnson. Harold Blackmore was one of these polygamists living in Canada at the time. Harold was a man of many talents. He was very thrifty and was a man of capability. Marion Hammon asked him to move to Short Creek in 1963 to help with the building of homes for the people there. Harold had many good ideas, not only of providing homes for the people, but also of them becoming self-sustaining, free from the money system of the rest of the country. Hammon allowed him to implement some of his ideas, but he soon became threatened by Blackmore because of his ability to manage businesses and make money. Hammon would allow him to go just so far, then he would either stop him or put someone else in charge of the project, someone Hammon could control. Hammon told Blackmore one time: "If I'm not careful, you'll own this town someday." These actions of Hammon's eventually led to Blackmore's apostasy.

Harold Blackmore is a controversial person in the development of Colorado City. He only lived there a short time, but of all the apostates who have lived there and left, he has probably had more of an impact on the community and the Cult than any other person. More will be told about him in a later chapter.

Note 5: In about 1960, the Priesthood Council established a "Special" Class to be held at Colorado City once a month. This Class was called "The Junior School of The Prophets" and was held in the home of Marion Hammon in the evening of the second Saturday of every month. This was a very exclusive Class and only the most favored men were invited into it. There were three conditions required of every member coming into the Class and the new member would raise his hand and swear, under covenant, to accept these rules and conditions. These were as follows: He must accept the Priesthood Council as constituted; accept the Adam God Doctrine (Adam being God the Creator, more will be told about this doctrine later); and accept the Oath and Covenant of the Priesthood. This Oath and Covenant is as follows:

"I will now covenant with you before God, that I will not listen to nor credit any derogatory report against any of you, nor condemn you upon any testimony beneath the heavens, short of that testimony which is infallible, until I can see you face to face and know of a surety; and I do place unremitted confidence in your word for I BELIEVE YOU TO BE MEN OF TRUTH!"

"And I further consecrate unto the Lord, under the direction of His established Priesthood, my life, property, talents, wives and children."

At the close of the meeting the men would stand in concert circle prayer. These prayers were led by one of the Class members, who followed guidelines set up by Joseph Musser in 1939. These guidelines or as follows:

SUGGESTIONS FOR PRAYER AS GIVEN BY PRESIDENT JOSEPH W. MUSSER IN THE JUNIOR SCHOOL OF THE PROPHETS IN 1939.

1. Express gratitude for all blessings.
2. Seek forgiveness of sins as we are willing to forgive others.
3. Pray for unity among, and divine guidance, for the priesthood and circle groups, including those specially appointed to labor in the Americas, on the Eastern continent, and among the ten tribes; For the early setting in order of the House of God, and the imparting to the worthy saints of their temple blessings.
4. For the spiritual and economic advancement of the saints, opening the way for those desiring and qualifying to enter the patriarchal order.
5. For the Church leaders, that they either repent and do the will of the Lord, or be removed from power and cease to be stumbling blocks to the saints.

6. For the confounding of the enemy, the complete operation of the DIVINE LAW OF RETRIBUTION, the early dissolution of the government of the U.S.A. with all world governments, and the setting up of the Kingdom of God.

7. For the gifts of the spirit, with particular reference to the gift of healing and of the discernment of spirits.

Most of those who attended this Class pretty well lived up to these conditions. The exceptions were those who felt themselves above the law. Such examples were Fred Jessop and the Barlows, who expected the others to honor these covenants, but had no intentions to do so themselves.

Note 6: In a meeting at Hildale, on November 15, 1964, Marion Hammon made this statement.

"We have borrowed over forty thousand dollars to buy pipe and lay it into the community to bring the water from Water Canyon.... Now this is going to call for the neighborhood of five hundred dollars from every man in this group. A man might have three or four sons, and that's going to mean four or five thousand dollars, but I think we're equal to it....We need a thousand dollars by the fourteenth of July, if any of you feel the Spirit of God moving on you, that you have it, I recommend that you come forward and turn it in."

Note 7: On September 25, 1966, in a meeting at Colorado City, Leroy Johnson said, "I believe it is within the power of this people to continue to build up and establish the Kingdom of God and come under no other covenant or government.... I am more determined today than ever before to turn down that enticing element to accept of government aid, because the minute we accept government aid we come under their power."

Note 8: The Barco plant at Colorado City did not go into production until September 28, 1970, but the planing, construction of a building, etc., began in about 1968.

Colorado City & Hildale

In the early 1960s Marion Hammon organized what he called the Planning Board Committee. This committee was supposed to meet with him once a week and help with the decision making of running the community and the UEP. The people he chose were either "Yes Men" (people who would only echo his decisions), or he would soon get rid of them, replacing them with someone who would agree with him.

He also organized an entity he named The Colorado City Area Development Association. He began to use this Association to conduct the business of what should have been business of the United Effort Plan. By using the CCADA to do business under, he was able to make decisions without consulting other UEP Trustees. For example, he negotiated a purchase contract on what was called The Hirschi Property, several hundred acres of land about six miles west of Colorado City. He called for donations of money from the people to make the payments ($10,000.00 a year), telling them it was United Effort Plan property, but in truth, the property was never part of the Trust. He was able to raise the money for the payments and in the few years that he had the property, he built considerable equity there for himself.

The personnel on the Board of Directors of these two organizations (the Planning Board committee and the Colorado City Area Development Association) were mostly the same people, and were people who would agree with whatever Hammon wanted, thus only acting as puppets for him. It was through these two organizations that all the decisions of running the community were made. This became a sore spot for some of the men who had been making these decisions and some would not fully accept Hammon's control, Fred Jessop being one of the most prominent among this group. He would appear to follow Hammon's direction when in his presence, but then would go about undermining what he did not agree with, always going through Leroy Johnson so as to move with credibility. One such action of Fred's was the incorporation of Hildale.

It was in 1958 when Fred first established that the north side of Short Creek would be called Hildale. He began the process of incorporation a short time later. This required that the Washington County Commissioners approve of the incorporation, which, along with the slow pace of Fred's administrative ability, put the actual incorporation at about 1968. He did not wait for the incorporation to be completed before he began operating as a town.

He organized a Town Council, complete with a Mayor. He was not on the Council himself, but rather appointed himself the Town Clerk. As the Town Clerk, he made all the decisions in the meetings, having the Council vote unanimous on each measure he would put before them. He would only allow members on the Council that would support him. To insure this support all he would have to do was tell them he had talked with Uncle Roy and "this is what he wants."

It is true the Town Council members were elected by the town citizens, but there was never more than one candidate for each position on the ballot. He would pass the word around that this person was the one Uncle Roy wanted in the position. It was through the entity of the town of Hildale that Fred was able to continue on in a lot of his activities.

With the organization of the Colorado City Academy, Marion Hammon through its auspices was pretty much in control of all the social activities of the community. This had been one of Fred's responsibilities before Hammon took over the management of the UEP. Before the establishment of the Academy, these social activities had consisted primarily of a dance every other Friday night, a movie on the alternate Fridays and a celebration on the 4th and 24th of July each year. Fred would usually stage a play production about every year or so, using the same scripts over and over. There were only two scripts that he would approve of to use in the community, not only in his productions but also in the public schools. These were "Windmills of Holland" and "Little Women." The people were getting a little tired of these two plays to say the least. The socials of the Academy were a welcomed relief to most of the community members.

Every fall the Academy students would go to the Harker Farm near Beryl, Utah, and help in the potato harvest in the Escalante Valley. The money they earned would go toward the running of the Academy. These harvest projects would last for two weeks. When the students returned home, Marion would have a Harvest Ball. The whole community would participate in these celebrations and they were the highlight of the summer's end. Fred was not happy with the Academy (Marion) taking control of the social activities in the community. He used the authority of Hildale Town to carry on in competition with Marion and the Academy.

In order to diminish the impact of the Harvest Ball, Fred began having a Hildale Town Fair every fall. The Fair would be staged just a week or so before the Harvest Ball of the Academy. These Fairs would last about three days and were lavishly staged, using local talent to provide much entertainment for the citizens. They were well supported by the people and did indeed diminish the impact of the Harvest Ball, thus accomplishing Fred's designs. The Hildale/Colorado City Fair was put on every year for the next fifteen or twenty years, becoming quite popular among the entertainment starved Polygamists, especially the younger people.

One of the biggest mistakes the Polygamist Leaders make is neglecting to provide activities and entertainment for the young people of the society. The policy of the Priesthood is to separate the boys and girls and this is the main reason that very few social activities are allowed. This policy has been the cause of many problems for the young people, especially the boys at Colorado City. Since this mating policy of the Priesthood (that of placing the girls with their marriage partners) created problems for the young boys and girls who become attracted to each other, it became necessary to establish a monitoring system to protect the girls from becoming attached to the wrong boy. In the 1960s the leaders became so concerned in regard to this issue that it was necessary for them to take steps to curb any out of line associations between the young people. Their first line of defense was to place a peace officer in charge of keeping the problem in check.

In the late 1950s, after the families of the Polygamists had been returned to their homes following the 1953 Raid, the County Officials at Kingman deemed it no longer necessary to keep a County Deputy Sheriff on the Arizona Strip. This meant there was no civil law enforcement authority in Colorado City. The Priesthood, however, concluded it was necessary to establish some kind of Peace Officer status. To accomplish this they created a fictitious entity called The Colorado City Law Enforcement Agency. This agency had no recognized civil authority whatsoever and was only established so the Polygamist leaders could better control their young members. Sam Barlow (son of John Y. Barlow) was picked to be the enforcement officer of this agency. He was supplied with a badge to give the illusion that he had peace officer status, when in reality, he had no authority at all until about eight years later, when in 1968, he was designated a "Range Deputy" by the Mohave County Sheriff. As a Range Deputy, he worked without pay and could only make arrests, give tickets, etc., at the specific direction of the County Sheriff, this being determined on a case by case basis.

Leroy Johnson, speaking about the appointment of Sam Barlow to this position in a public meeting said: "For many years we were under the direction or the management of outsiders. We had to be governed by the laws of the State of Arizona…. We had to take what the County Commissioners dealt out to us as Peace Officers, until the Lord opened up an opportunity to us to get a peace officer of our own. We accepted the offer and put it into process…. I want to call your attention to the fact that you are not altogether displeasing me or Sam Barlow, but you are throwing out a challenge to God to see whether He will do what He said He would do, Punish the wicked or the disobedient…. Whenever you do anything wrong in this community, you are not only breaking the laws of the land but you are breaking the laws of God. We have had a certain clique of boys here ever since the blessing (placing partners in marriage) was given…we have had a certain body of young men that have been determined in their minds to run the place their way and not be governed by our peace officer…. You young men can go a long way in bringing to pass the blessings that the Lord has placed upon this place by ceasing to antagonize the man that the priesthood has set as a peace officer in this place (Note 1)."

Sam's paramount duty as a Peace Officer was to make sure that the boys would not associate with the girls. At his discretion, he would run the undesirable boys out of town, forcing them to go to the neighboring communities to fend for themselves as best they could. He was encouraged and supported by Leroy in this action. Addressing the people in their meeting Leroy said: "We have young men that are determined to have their own way. They are slow to listen to counsel.... You young girls and you young men, when you come to the age of accountability and want to be added upon (get married), you are put on trial. The Lord is trying you to see what you will do with the blessings He has heaped upon you.... Many of our boys have been led by the enticings of young women. Many young women have been enticed by the enticings of young men. Through this the Lord is displeased, because He had said that this law cannot be trampled underfoot. It cannot be dishonored in the minds of men or women. It is a Celestial Law. Zion cannot be redeemed only upon the principles of the Celestial Kingdom....When a young man will take the advantage of a young woman, he severs himself from the presence of God, for God has said it....This goes for the young lady, too. If she steps out of the way and seeks for companionship before it is her right to do so, the Spirit of God leaves her, and she is left on her own. She has no power to combat the evil that comes her way.... We have had to invite men out of this town because they wouldn't leave our girls alone.... This is a vexation in the sight of God, and it is a vexation to the Priesthood.... It is a vexation in the ears of the servants of God (Note 2)."

The birth ratio of boys to girls among the Polygamists is the same as it is anywhere else in the world, pretty much one boy to one girl. If one man has even two wives, then some boy in the society must not get married. The doctrine of the Polygamists is that a man must have at least three wives to reach the highest degree of heaven. The perceived importance of a man goes up by the number of wives he has, thus the ratio of wives to a man is important; those in leadership positions have wives numbering into the tens. This causes a dilemma for the Polygamist Leaders, what to do with the surplus of boys. It is only natural for young boys and girls to be attracted to each other. Most girls relate more to boys near their own age, rather than a man ten to thirty years older (the extreme is a seventeen-year-old girl marrying a ninety-five-year-old man). In later years these young people have learned how to beat the system. If a boy and a girl decide they want to get married, they simply have sex with each other, then go to the Prophet and confess their sin. He tells them to have a civil marriage, wait a year, come back to see him and if he feels they have repented, they can get rebaptized and he will seal them to each other.

It becomes paramount then to keep the boys and girls separated at all costs; only under very strict supervision are they allowed to associate with each other. Since this is not always possible, it became necessary to establish a "Teenage Chastity Patrol," with Sam Barlow at its head. His primary police duties in the next fifteen to twenty years evolved to that of running the surplus boys out of town, making it possible for the "worthy" men to live the Law of Celestial Marriage by adding more wives.

He was able to do this by trumping up some criminal charge against the boy he would select to eliminate from the society. He would then harass the offender (under his peace officer status) until finally he would leave (some of these young boys were as young as thirteen years old). The reader no doubt questions how a father would allow his sons to be criminalized by such an immoral system, passively standing by while such treatment was meted out.

This high handed and immoral conduct of Sam Barlow and the Polygamist Leaders was not so prevalent in the 1960s era, but rather reached its peak in the late 1970s and 1980s. How Sam Barlow was able to worm his way into such a position as to be the Judge, Jury and Executioner is worthy of explanation.

Sam Barlow

Samuel Stevens Barlow was born at Short Creek, Utah, February 18, 1937. He was the sixth living son of John Y. Barlow and Martha Jessop (his fourth wife). Sam's mother died when he was only six years old. His father had recently married a new wife (a fifteen-year-old girl whose widowed mother had just moved from Idaho after joining the Work) and the responsibility of taking care of Sam and his eleven siblings (of which three were older than she was) fell on the shoulders of this new wife. At about this time in Sam's life his father took him on his knee one day and told him, "You were named after Samuel of old (Biblical Prophet) and the day will come when you will be a great Prophet like him."

This event was a significant occurrence in Sam's life and he would reiterate it to his associates throughout his life. In his adolescent years he would attempt to rule over his peers, causing much resentment among these childhood associates. This only resulted in him becoming despised by his contemporaries, none of them placing any trust in him, consequently causing him to become a loner. He resorted to becoming a "Snitch," always sneaking around, trying to get the goods on his friends, so he could run to one of the Brethren and report what evils he had uncovered. This, of course, only lessened his credibility with those he associated with.

Sam's first role as a policeman was while he was in the 7th grade of the Short Creek School, where his older brother Louis was the principal. Louis Barlow was hired as the Principal of the Short Creek School in 1949 and taught the 7th and 8th grades. He told the students one morning that he did not want a School

Policeman, because he didn't like the idea of having to have a Policeman bully the kids. He did, however, think it was necessary to have some kind of Police presence on the school grounds, not to bully the kids, but rather to protect them. He chose his younger brother, Sam, to be this Policeman and called him the Chief Protector.

As the Chief Protector, Sam was really in his element. The very thing that Louis had warned against, a Police Bully, was what he turned out to be. He was too big a coward to physically confront any of the other students he felt were in violation of the rules, but rather would just go to Louis with exaggerated stories of wrongdoing by the students he had singled out for breaking the rules.

By this manner he would punish those who refused to show him the proper respect he felt he was entitled to. He learned at this young age how to take some small fact of truth and weave into it so much conjecture, embellishing the story with supposition of his own imagination as to convince Louis that some great crime had been committed by the poor unsuspecting victim of his scheme. He also learned to use religion to accomplish his designs, convincing Louis that the boy he was reporting on was guilty of some immoral conduct such as masturbation, a most grievous sin among the Polygamists, or worse yet "looking on some girl, to lust after her," thus being guilty of lewdness. Some of Sam's accusations toward these other boys during this period of time, have followed them throughout their lives, making it very hard for them to gain the confidence of the Polygamist Leaders.

After leaving school and as he grew older, Sam carried on in this role of being the Chief Protector of the community and the Polygamist Society at Colorado City. Instead of reporting to Louis though, he would report to such of the Brethren that would listen to him, these being primarily Leroy Johnson, Richard Jessop, Carl Holm, and in the 1960s, Marion Hammon. None of his peers ever took him seriously, never suspecting that he had any more credibility with the Brethren than he had among them. It was a big surprise to many of his victims, when out of the blue, they would be severally scolded by one of the leaders for some infraction of conduct that they, in most cases, knew nothing about.

It was this man Sam Barlow who was chosen by the Priesthood to be the Peace Officer in the polygamist society in the early 1960s. More about Sam Barlow and his role of enforcer for the Priesthood will be elaborated on in a later chapter, where it will be explained how he was able to acquire the power he had over the members of the Group and how he could accomplish his skulduggery.

Bountiful, Canada

In the 1960s there was a group of Polygamists living in Western Canada that aligned themselves with the Group at Colorado City. The leadership of the Canadian Group was assigned to Ray Blackmore, a man the Priesthood Council

144

had confidence in. His nephew Harold Blackmore was actually more competent than was Ray, when it came to making crucial decisions. This caused a severe controversy among the Saints at Canada. It became so bad that the Brethren determined to do something to solve the problem.

Harold, an industrious person, owned a nice tract of land near Lister, B.C. that was much coveted by the United Effort Plan Leaders. A scheme was devised to get Harold out of Canada and at the same time get his property. In discussing the situation with Louis Barlow, Leroy Johnson (Polygamist Prophet) asked him about acquiring Harold's Property for the UEP. Louis thought this would be possible and was told, "If there is any way you can get the property, I want you to do it, no matter what you have to do." To accomplish this, Louis solicited the help of Jack Knudson.

In the mid-1950s Jack Knudson was working as a stockbroker in Salt Lake City. He had learned how to manipulate the stock market by acquiring stock certificates of new companies while in their infancies, then promoting the stocks of these companies to his clients. This would cause an artificial inflation in the stocks of the company and he would then sell his own shares, flooding the market, which would then cause the stocks to fall. He reasoned that he could start his own companies for the soul purpose of promoting the stocks, not really intending that the company itself make money. (He was eventually caught by the Securities Commission and his Broker's license temporarily suspended.)

One of the companies he had formed for this purpose was a real estate company named National Land Corporation. The company was formed with a stock value of $1.00 per share. It took him about three years to pump the value up to $12.00 a share, at which time he began dumping his stock. The company soon became almost non-existent due to this stock maneuver. Jack Knudson formed a new company, using the assets of National Land, and converted the National Land stock to stock in the new company, thus eliminating National Land altogether.

Louis Barlow was involved with Knudson in the National Land scheme and profited greatly financially. It was soon after the National Land Fiasco that Jack Knudson's stockbroker's license was suspended. Along with this suspension, Knudson was put on a five year probation, prohibiting him from dealing in any kind of stock transaction. He moved from Salt Lake to Colorado City and began teaching in the newly formed Colorado City Academy. It was soon after Knudson began teaching that Leroy Johnson directed Louis Barlow to get the Blackmore property for the UEP. Louis and Jack came up with the following plan.

Louis would convince Harold to put his property into a land development corporation, they would then sell stock in the company to raise the money to build a hunting lodge that Harold would manage, providing employment for a few of the polygamists in Canada. The Priesthood would then ask Harold to go down to Colorado City to help with building homes for the people there. While Harold was in Colorado City, Louis and Jack would convey the property to the UEP, moving some faithful members onto the place, thereby preventing Harold from moving back on the property.

It was at this time (about 1963) that Marion Hammon approached Harold Blackmore and asked if he would go to Colorado City and help with the building of homes there for the people. Harold tells about his moving to Colorado City in a deposition taken in July of 1988:

Questions by Mr. Smith, attorney for the Trustees of the United Effort Plan:

Answers by Harold Blackmore

Q. How did it come to pass that you went down to Colorado City in the first place? Explain that to me.

A. Because Marion Hammon came to me and said that the Council has "asked me to have you come down to Colorado City and help us with our deplorable housing situation." Those are his exact words.

Q. Did he say that orally or in a letter.

A. Orally. Immediately after a meeting.

Florence Blackmore: And the academy. And the academy.

The Witness: Yeah, and…and help teach in the academy. Teach building trades to the boys, things like this. I said, "Now, look. I can't go at this time." This is in the summer.

Mr. Smith:

Q. Of what year?

A. 1963. I said, "Look, this is the only time I can make a living. But when it freezes up here and I can't work any longer, I'll come down and help you." And that was all the understanding. And I disliked the idea of going down there very strongly because the looks of that desert just did things to me after what I was used to. I don't see how anyone could live in that environment. And I had no desire to go down there. In fact, I was quite upset to be asked to go down.

Q. Why did you go down?

A. Because I was asked to help them.

Soon after Harold came to Colorado City, Louis Barlow approached him and began promoting the idea of forming a land development company, using his property in Canada as the base of the venture. In the same deposition Harold describes what happened:

Mr. Smith: Okay. Let's just continue.

Q. You lived in Lister, B.C., between the years of 1947 and 1964, right?

A. 1963.

Q. 1963?

146

A. Well, the latter part of 1963. You can say 64.

Q. Did you live any place between moving from B.C. and your residence in Colorado City?

Q. At some point you conveyed your land in B.C. to National Land Corporation, right?

A. That was in Colorado City.

Q. Your family (was) in Canada, did they live with Ray?

A. No, sir. They lived on my property. Until it was confiscated.

Q. Well, you conveyed it, didn't you?

A. Not to the UEP.

Q. Well, you conveyed it to National Land Corporation, did you not?

A. Exactly.

Q. And that was 1964?

A. That is correct.

Q. And at the time of that conveyance, is that when your family moved off?

A. No. They were there for a while later, but they were being harassed and bothered. Until I could bring them down. I want to definitely…

Q. Well, tell me how they were harassed, Mr.Blackmore.

A. As soon as…

Q. Let me ask first: Who was up there?

A. My daughter…the one I left in charge until we came back.

Q. (Your daughter) was in charge and your two wives were down in Colorado City with you?

Florence Blackmore: No. I came down in June to go to school.

The Witness: Yes. Well, she came down. She was there until…in order to…she wanted to go to school and she had to come down when the college started.

Mr. Smith:

Q. What college?

A. She went to college in Cedar, too.

Q. That's Florence?

A. Yes. To reinstate her teaching certificate.

Q. Okay. So Florence was in Cedar City going to college.

A. She came down to (do) that.

Q. And that was also in 1963?

A. No, 1964.

Q. 1964.

A. None of us…I didn't go down till the latter part of 1963.

Q. Okay.

A. And I want it understood that I had no intention of staying there when I went down. I went down to help them. I was trapped there. I intended to go back.

Q. Well, where were you going to live back in Canada, Mr. Blackmore?

A. At the time when they finally took over the place I was trapped there.

Q. Well, when did you convey your property to National Land Corporation? May of 1964?

A. Um-hum (affirmatively). And you had been down in Colorado City...or Hildale for several months prior to that, correct?

A. Yes. Helping them with their deplorable housing situation.

Q. Well, now, Mr. Blackmore, if you conveyed that property...and you did it voluntarily, did you not, to National Land Corporation?

A. I was approached by Louis Barlow about working together forming a new corporation in conjunction with Jack Knudson for real estate development.

Q. Okay. We'll get to that, Mr. Blackmore. But the point is that you conveyed that property to a corporation, correct?

A. Yes. That was being formed as a new corporation and the three of us were the only persons in it, according to what I was told.

Q. And you got stock in exchange for the...

A. I never got one share of stock ever.

Q. Were you ever shown as a shareholder?

A. I never ever received a stock certificate.

Q. Did you understand yourself to be the owner of shares?

A. I'm the one that was supposed to receive shares in return for my property. I have never seen a stock certificate to this day. I never endorsed one to this day.

Q. How many shares did you understand you owned, even though you didn't get a stock certificate?

A. They persuaded me...

Q. Who's "they?"

A Louis Barlow and Jack Knudson. To go in and form a company, for real estate development, and that they had not seen my property in Canada.

Q. Weren't you trying to sell your property in Canada. Mr. Blackmore, hadn't you listed your property?

A. No, I never listed my property.

Q. Were you trying to sell it?

A. No.

Q. Did you ever try to sell it?

A. I would have sold it if I found I wanted to stay down there. It was that kind of situation.

Q. Did you ever enter into a sales agreement with anyone to sell it?

A. I never.

Q. Did you ever post the property...

A. Never.

Q. ...for sale?

A. Never.

Q. After you lived in Colorado City for about...you said you went down at the end of 1963. You conveyed this property in April of 1964.

A. No, in May.

Q. In May of 1964?

A. Maybe I'm wrong. It was April, I'm sorry.

Q. Okay.

A. I made a misstatement. It was in April. About April the 25th of 1964.

Q. Okay. You conveyed that property, and your family eventually moved off, correct?

A. Yes.

Q. And you made the determination to live in Colorado City or Hildale, did you not?

A. When I found that they had taken the property and given it to the UEP, I had nowhere to go.

Q. Well, Mr. Blackmore, hadn't you already conveyed that property away? Did you figure you still could live on the property after you'd conveyed it?

A. Yes, because the approach made to me.... "You have a nice place, I understand, up there and it would make a fine hunting guest ranch. Why don't we go into a joint venture."

Q. Who said that?

A. Louis Barlow. And, "Why don't we go form a corporation and develop that into a guest ranch and you can go up and prepare it." We discussed it numerous times.

Q. You and Louis?

A. Yes, sir. And he even took me to see a woman that was in that kind of business....

A. And we sat in the car with her and she told us...we asked questions about operating that type of a business. She says, "It's a very good business." And she recommended that such a thing be done. And they convinced me that this would be a good thing. And I thought, "Well, now, this is a source of employment for me and we can run this type of a business." And so I thought, "Well, I'll go along with that." And Louis took me to meet Jack Knudson and told me that he was a specialist in corporate matters, bookkeeping and things of this nature, and that he could form the company. And that my property was to be the incorporating capital.

They said, "We don't have any money. We can't put anything in it except our services. But we'll each take a third. With our two-thirds we will sell stock and turn over $100,000 to you to develop that property and develop a subdivision and we will carry on this joint venture." Some time passed after that. I said, "Well, all right." They said, "We'll let you know when we want to receive it." And at the time Louis brought me…that, they were ready to form the corporation. But to do so they had to have my deed. So I went there. And they decided to call it the National Land Corporation. That was all right with me. This property was to be the basis for the stock issued. I deeded it. With this understanding: It was (to be) stock for (me). There was no other consideration discussed.

Q. You were to get stock for the deed?

A. The stock was to be issued for the entire value of this property. I didn't hear anything in quite a while. They never came to me with any report. Anything. I started getting letters from Canada that my place was being occupied.

Q. Did you produce any of those letters, Mr. Blackmore?

A. Oh, you bet. My attorney…

Q. Are they among the letters that you produced to counsel?

A. My attorney has them. (nodding head affirmatively).

Q. All right. Can you tell me who wrote you from Canada?

A. …(Deleted)… She was greatly disturbed over what was going on.

Florence Blackmore: And…(Our daughter)

The Witness: Oh, yes,…My daughter. Wrote some very distressing letters.

Mr. Smith:

Q. Did you provide those letters?

A. No, I didn't keep them. But they were ordering her to get rid of our goats. Put "No Trespassing" signs all over the place, and harassed her. Well, I…

Q. When was she being harassed, Mr. Blackmore?

A. Pardon?

Q. When was…(Your daughter)…being harassed?

A. Well, it started when Louis Barlow and Rulon Jeffs went up there and they formally turned that property over to Ray Blackmore to administer. The first suspicious rumor I got, I was told that Johnson went up two weeks after I deeded it to National Land and told the people there that Blackmore had no more to do with this property. "We own it."

Q. When was that?

A. That was in the first week of May. Immediately after. And…

Q. May 1964?

A. That's right.

Q. When did you hear that it had been turned over to the UEP?

A. When this letter from…came in the first part of June.

Q. Of 1964?

A. 1964. Telling me what they had done and, what was going on here. It didn't agree with what I had understood. And subsequent to this, when I got this information down from these people, I went to Louis and Jack and said, "What's going on? How come this property is being turned over to those people?"

150

Q. Is it your testimony, Mr. Blackmore, that you never directed the property to be sold?

A. I never did.

Q. And you're stating that under oath?

A. The listing with the real estate outfit or something?

Q. I'm talking about directing anyone to sell the property.

A. (Pause) Selling it?

Q. Yes. I'm asking whether you participated in any decision to sell that property.

A. I solely put it in…

Q. Is the answer, "No," or, "Yes"?

A. Not that I'm aware of.

This was a maneuver to get Harold's property. It is explained further in the deposition.

Q. September of 1965 it was deeded to the UEP?

A. Yes. But they told me that they had already done it at that time. And that it couldn't…I couldn't do a thing about it. They told me that they had acted under (the) direction…

Q. Now, who's "they"?

A. These two men right here. (indicating) Louis Barlow and Jack Knudson. And in defense of their …this betrayal they told me that they had been called into a meeting of the Priesthood Council and had been instructed to get my property for them any way they could.

Q. Who said that, specifically?

A. Well, they both participated in the discussion.

Q. And when did they tell you this?

A. When I accosted them after being told that it had been formally turned over to the people up there. And I went to them for an accounting of how in the world this could possibly be.

Q. This, you testified, was in the month after you deeded it to National Land Corporation?

A. It was a…no, that is not correct. Johnson had told the people up there that I had nothing to do with that property any more, that they owned it. People wrote down and told me this.

At the time that Louis Barlow and Jack Knudson were working out this charade with Harold Blackmore, National Land Corporation was a non-existent company. Jack had converted its assets to another company (Dynamic American). What they told Harold about forming a company to develop his property was nothing more

151

than a scam to get his property into the UEP. It was about three years before Harold realized this had happened. In that three years time he had met with other problems in dealing with the Polygamists.

He had been asked to help build houses for the people of the Group. He devised a plan to finance the building of these houses. He discussed the plan with Marion Hammon and received, somewhat, his approval. The plan was to work as follows: Twenty-four men (families) were to begin paying $200.00 a month into a fund to build a house for each of them. Harold, by using the high school boys and a few of the missionaries, would construct these houses at the rate of one per month. It would be determined by lot who would get the houses in the order that they where finished. One man would get his at the end of the first month, while the last man would get his at the end of the two years. At the end of the two years, after paying the $200.00 per month, each man would have a home built and paid for. This plan seemed all right to Hammon, except he decided that he would be the one to collect the money. Needless to say, the plan was a total failure.

Only one man (Dan Barlow) paid his $200.00 for the two years. At the end of the two years, Dan Barlow went to Hammon and asked, "Where's my house?" Though Hammon had collected Dan's $200.00 every month for the last two years, there was no house built nor did Hammon have any of the money Dan had paid him. Hammon got up in Sunday Meeting and told the people that they had to build a house for Dan Barlow. Enough of them responded that a house was built for Dan, but due to Hammon's management of the money collected for this enterprise, the plan was a failure and turned out to be just one of many bitter disappointments for Harold.

When Harold came to Colorado City, he had several good ideas to help the people there to improve their circumstances, but he met resistance from Hammon on almost every thing he tried to do. Hammon was reluctant to allow anybody free reign in the community. He would have to pass final judgement on any and everything that Harold wanted to do. At the end of the three year period Harold was so distraught that he began to study the scriptures to determine just what allegiance he owed to this Priesthood Council. It didn't take long for him to convince himself that it was not a Priesthood Council ordained by God, but rather it was Priestcraft. He determined he would be better off to leave the Group.

In the three years that he was in Colorado City, Harold had built a house for himself. He went to Hammon and offered that if he could get $6,000.00 for this house he would move out of the Polygamist Community. Hammon accepted his offer. The money was raised and Harold moved to La Verkin, Utah, where in the years to follow, he became very successful in the building trade, becoming quite wealthy. The Priesthood thought they were rid of him, but he was to cause them trouble again in the mid-1970s when Leroy Johnson, president of the UEP, stole the house of James Blackmore (Harold's son). More will be told about this in a later chapter.

In about 1964 the elementary (public) school in Colorado City was relocated. It was moved to a location that would be better suited for expansion. The UEP donated the property and by moving one of the buildings from the old location, the county allowed the site to be used for the school. Over the next few years, with the help of the students and with the UEP donating some material, a new building was built. This building was also built of adobe, with Alvin Barlow supervising the adobe building in the summer months. The lumber for the roof was again sawed on the sawmill, with Andrew Bistline donating most of his time to the project.

In 1968 the public school in Hildale closed, and combined with the school in Colorado City. One of the reasons for combining the schools was to free the building at Hildale for other uses of the UEP. It turned out that one of these uses would be to temporally house a sewing plant that was being moved into the community to provide employment for some of the Polygamist women. Negotiations with a company in California (Barco Inc.), were begun in 1969, to establish this sewing plant in Colorado City.

Alma Timpson, a Priesthood Council member, had been contacted by a representative from the Barco Sewing Co. of California. The owners of the Barco Co. were interested in establishing a sewing plant in Colorado City if the United Effort Plan would furnish a building for them. They were willing to pay rent for the use of a building, but didn't want to invest any money toward its construction. Timpson reported this to the Priesthood Council and the other members were in favor of accepting Barco's offer. Since Marion Hammon was the Manager of the UEP projects at Colorado City, he began speculating on how to raise the money to construct the needed building. He first proposed setting aside an acre or so from the trust property that could be mortgaged to a bank, thus borrowing the money for the building. He presented this idea in a General Priesthood Meeting to all members one Sunday morning. When Fred Jessop heard this, he immediately opposed the idea. He did not oppose building a building for the sewing plant, but rather opposed mortgaging the property. (It turned out that he was not so much against mortgaging the property as he was of Hammon having control of the sewing plant.)

Fred Jessop, along with some of his Barlow nephews (Louis, Joe, and Dan Barlow), gathered at Leroy's place immediately after this meeting. These conspirators pointed out to Leroy that mortgaging the property was not the thing to do. They asked him to let them come up with a way to raise the money to construct the building, thus allowing them control of operating the sewing plant. It was not hard convincing the Polygamist Prophet to let them do what they wanted in the matter.

An association was formed by the conspirators to expedite the project. They named it the Colorado City Improvement Association (Note 3).

Among the board members of this association were Fred Jessop, Merril Jessop, Truman Barlow, Dan Barlow, and Bill (William) Shapley. The United Effort Plan leased a small tract of land (about five acres) to the Colorado City Improvement Association (CCIA). This lease was granted by Leroy Johnson, who acted solely on his own initiative, never bringing the issue up in any UEP Board Meetings (Note 4). By not conferring with any of the other UEP Trustees on the matter, he violated the rules governing the Trust.

With the twenty year lease, Fred Jessop (CCIA) went to the Bank in Cedar City and asked for a construction loan to put up the building. The Bank granted the loan, accepting the lease as collateral. When Leroy informed Marion of these developments, he and Alma Timpson made no objections to what had happened. They were both naive enough to believe that it didn't matter whether they or Fred built the building, so long as the employment for the people was provided. Marion felt a little rebuffed that Leroy had not bothered to include him in the decision making of such a major transaction, but by this time he was getting used to such treatment. If Leroy didn't like the way Hammon was managing the affairs of the polygamist community, he would never go to him directly and discuss his disagreements, but would rather work around behind his back, using his influence to undermine him. An outstanding example to support this characterization of Leroy involves a school lunch program that Hammon attempted to establish for the elementary school students. This incident happened as follows:

When the Colorado City Academy opened, a homemaking class was part of the curriculum. Part of the homemaking class included teaching the girls to cook. Marion Hammon thought it would be a good idea to have the high school girls at the Academy prepare a noon meal for the elementary school students as part of this class. The meals were prepared at the Academy (these meals usually consisted of a serving of soup or stew with the students providing their own eating utensils and a slice of bread from home), then at noon the kettles were taken down to the elementary school where it was served to the students in their classrooms. This procedure worked pretty well, the only real problem was that some of the parents would have preferred their children come home for lunch, especially those living close to the school.

Hammon would not allow the parents this option, but rather decreed that all children must remain at school to eat the lunch prepared by the Academy students. After this program had been in effect for three or four years, Hammon decided to also provide breakfast for the school children. He was concerned that a number of the Polygamist children were not getting proper nourishment because so many of their mothers would not get up in the morning in time to prepare a proper breakfast for their children before they left for school. Hammon's assessment of this situation was correct. The parents of the Polygamist children were very remiss in providing enough for the youngsters to eat. It was not with malice that he wanted to feed the children, but rather out of pity for the children themselves, to assure them good health in this regards. He planned to go ahead with this program in about 1969.

Marion Hammon got up in a General Priesthood meeting one Sunday morning and announced his intention of implementing breakfast into his School Lunch Program. After spending about thirty minutes of time, telling the men all the benefits of this lunch program, he sat down, turning the time to Leroy to address the people as was the custom (each of the Leading Brethren present at the meetings were given an opportunity to talk to the men in these meetings before they would separate to their respective classes). Leroy got up and immediately began to criticize Hammon's plan. He told the men "this thing of furnishing meals for the children at school is a trick of the Devil." He told them that the children should not only eat their breakfast at home but should also go home for lunch. He was unmerciful to Hammon, heaping all kinds of evils upon the community because he wanted to provide the kids with decent meals. He completely discredited Hammon in the minds of most all the men in the building and consequently the school lunch program was discontinued. Alvin Barlow, who was the Principal of the elementary school, chose to go along with Leroy completely.

The school lunch break was extended from one hour to one and a half each day. School buses were provided, not only to pick the children up in the morning, but also take them home for lunch at noon. Alvin required that all children ride the buses home to lunch, even if they lived only a block from the school. Not only was it necessary to hire more bus drivers, but also more buses were purchased by the small school district. This greatly increased the cost of this program, resulting in a waste of money that under Hammon's program could have been put to a much better use, such as paying the teachers a wage comparable to other schools in the area. This program of no school lunches in the Colorado City Schools was still in effect, until they were all compelled to be home schooled.

It was decided to temporally house the sewing plant in the building behind Fred Jessop's house that was at the time being used for the Hildale School. This same building was where the Polygamists held their religious meetings. Before the sewing plant could be established there, it was necessary to make different arrangements for these other uses. A new assembly hall was constructed at the Colorado City School house on the Arizona side of the community. This was allowed by the local School Board to be used for the religious meetings, no rent ever being charged for its use. The Hildale School was closed on May 1, 1968,

155

combining it with the Colorado City School. This opened the way for the building to be turned into a sewing plant.

The Barco sewing plant at Colorado City opened in the fall of 1970, in the Hildale Meeting / School House behind Fred Jessop's home. Dan Barlow was appointed manager of the plant. This opportunity for some of the women of the community to work at home was a welcome thing indeed. Up until this time there was very little employment in the area for the Polygamists to support themselves. There were a few attempts made before Barco came in, but few of them had achieved any success. There was only one of these ventures that had realized any measurable achievement.

Merril Jessop had established a Door Core manufacturing mill that was employing about twenty people at the time the Barco Sewing Plant opened in Hildale. It had been a real struggle for Merril to get this Door Mill into profitable production and the story behind it deserves telling.

When the United Effort Plan bought the sawmill in the early 1950s, Leroy Johnson made the statement that the Lord had put timber on Mt. Trumbull for the Saints at Short Creek to build homes with (Mt. Trumbull has a small stand of timber and is about fifty miles south of Colorado City). In the 1950s Mt. Trumbull was part of the Kaibab Forest, controlled by the Forest Service Ranger Station in Fredonia, Arizona. In the late 1970s it was turned over to the Arizona Strip District of the Bureau of Land Management, with the District office in St. George, Utah. It has since been turned into a Wilderness Study area and no timber harvesting is allowed.

Soon after the Colorado City Academy was completed Merril Jessop (under Leroy's direction) took over the operation of the sawmill. Leroy instructed him that "the sawmill must run," no matter what it took to do so. The main purpose for Leroy wanting the sawmill to run was to provide lumber for homes of the Polygamists. Merril soon found that to do this, the sawmill must be heavily subsidized from the other UEP owned businesses that he was operating (these other businesses included the General Store and the J & B Service Station). He was able to negotiate a salvage timber sale with the Chief Ranger at Fredonia for timber on Mt. Trumbull and began a modest logging and lumber effort. By not paying those working for him a substantial wage, he was able to achieve a small measure of success in the operation. He was given missionaries for most of the labor force, but it was necessary that he have some management personnel.

Two men in this regard were his brother Ray Jessop and Andrew Bistline. These two men worked many long and faithful hours for starvation wages just to help out the Work. Ray, with the help of one or two of the missionaries, would drive his logging truck to Trumbull every day. He would load the truck, hauling from four to five thousand board feet of logs, return home and repeat the routine the next day. Although he received very little wages for his efforts, he was very consistent in this endeavor, faithfully hauling logs for the sawmill for a number of

156

years. When there was a pile of logs on the sawmill yard, Andrew, with the help of a few missionaries, would crank up the mill and spend a few days, or weeks as the case may be, and saw them up into lumber.

Andrew Bistline had been one of the missionaries in 1958/59 and was one of the main crew that worked on the power line to get electricity into the community. He had faithfully served his mission, had been given a wife and a building lot to build a house on as was the promise of the Priesthood to those that were called on these missions. He had been appointed by Marion Hammon to renovate the sawmill to produce the lumber for the building of the Colorado City Academy. When Merril took over the sawmill he asked Leroy if he could keep Andrew to run it. He promised to pay him a small wage, but there were many times he could not, or would not, meet this promise. Andrew felt that once Leroy had asked him to help Merril, he was religiously bound to "Stand at the Rack, hay or no hay." He spent several years of his younger life working under these conditions before he finally abandoned Merril and decided to take care of his family.

Even though Merril subsidized the sawmill with funds earned from the other UEP projects and paid no wages of any consequence to the workers, it was still a failure. The door mill (cores for solid core doors were being manufactured and shipped to a door factory in the southeastern part of the United States) was finally brought into successful production. The wood for the door cores was not obtained from the sawmill, however, but rather number five lumber (poorest grade of all lumber) was purchased from the Kaibab Industries sawmill at Fredonia. The number five lumber was cut into strips of wood about two inches square. The knots and other bad parts of these 2x2's were then cut from the strips. The good blocks were glued together to form a door core. These door cores were cooked in a steam chamber to cure the glue to complete the process. There were about twenty people working in the door mill by the first of 1971 and it looked like the venture was going to be a success.

The Fates would have their due, however, for on the night of April 9, 1971, the door mill burned to the ground, resulting in an estimated loss of one million dollars in equipment and material. This was a terrible catastrophe for Merril Jessop; it would be for anybody. There was no insurance of any kind on the building or business, everything was a total loss. The door mill was never put back into production and consequently the sawmill was never used again at Colorado City. Merril, much to his credit, pulled himself up by his bootstraps. Turning his efforts toward the rock, sand, and concrete business, he was able to overcome the tragedy and in a few years became very successful in this field of work.

At the time of this catastrophe, the Barco Sewing Plant had been brought into successful production. The new building (on the Arizona side of town) to house the plant was soon completed and eventually about eighty people, mostly women, were gainfully employed there. To pay for the construction of the building, Fred Jessop, as has been already referred to, borrowed the money from a bank. The payments on this loan were $800.00 per month. The rent received from Barco, however, was only $400.00 per month. This left a deficit of $400.00 that Fred needed to make up every month.

He went to the women who were working in the sewing plant and after explaining his dilemma to them asked if they would contribute part of their wages to him to make these payments. Almost all of the women were willing to help out with the cost of constructing the building and the average amount each gave Fred was $4.00 per week. This was subsidy enough for him to make the payments.

An interesting historical anecdote here is that none of the money paid to Fred by these employees was ever accounted for. They were never reimbursed for it nor were they given any credit for it on the books of the UEP, the equity of their sweat going into the Colorado City Improvement Association, which is owned and controlled by Fred Jessop. It is not even recognized by Fred Jessop that the equity belongs to the United Effort Plan Trust (of which most of these workers were beneficiaries), the registered property owner of the land on which the building is standing. Barco continued to pay the $400.00 rent for many years after the building was paid for, but this money went into Fred Jessop's pockets, none of it was ever given back to the working women who helped pay for the building.

In the late 1960s the sons of John Barlow began an underground movement to discredit Marion Hammon's reputation and good standing in the minds of the members of the Polygamists community. There has always been enmity between the sons of John Barlow and Marion Hammon (this enmity has carried over to following generation as well). This enmity no doubt exists because of the disagreements between John Barlow and Joseph Musser (Marion was a protege of Musser), the greatest of these being the One Man Doctrine promoted by Barlow.

Barlow taught that the senior member of the Priesthood Council was the only man on earth that held the keys of the Priesthood and, since he was that senior member, he alone held these keys. Musser and the rest of the Council claimed that Lorin Woolley taught them in the 1930s that all of the Council members held the same priesthood keys (the only authority they had been given was to keep polygamy alive because the Church had abandoned its practice).

In a General Meeting held by the Group in Salt Lake City on March 9, 1941, this controversy is born out. Charles Zitting said: "The Priesthood is on earth today to give you the higher blessings. So, do you know where to go to receive these blessings? I know of only one place. It takes a High Priest Apostle who is ordained through God to perform these duties. There are others who work under the High Priest Apostle to help with the work. If we can receive all the blessings of the Gospel without that higher authority, then why the higher authority? The Lord places it here for a purpose. You cannot receive your higher blessings without it. I remember Bro. Lorin (Woolley) in conferring the Priesthood upon us said 'I confer upon you all the keys, power and authority that I myself hold and there is no other power or authority on earth (to perform Plural Marriage), but I am your senior because I have been in this longer than you have. President Taylor said that (also) when he conferred the keys upon us in the same manner.' The same words were used to set President Taylor apart, and others before him received it the same way. The senior presides BUT THEY ALL HOLD THE SAME POWER AND AUTHORITY."

When Charles Zitting finished with this sermon, John Barlow got up right after and said: "My brothers and sisters, I can say that I am glad to be with you. While I can say with Bro. Charles that HE IS RIGHT, some things he misunderstood a little bit. I know the Gospel is true. I know these brethren (in the council) were called of God as was Aaron through a prophet of God and I know that their work will go on. I know we can live the Gospel as it is laid down. Whenever a man turns from the Gospel plan as IT WAS LAID DOWN BY THE PROPHET JOSEPH SMITH, HE IS ON THE WRONG ROAD (Note 5).

"The keys that Joseph laid down will get us through the highest kingdom. The keys of the kingdom of God are committed unto man on the earth, and from thence shall the gospel roll forth unto the ends of the earth, as the stone which is cut out of the mountain without hands shall roll forth, until it has filled the whole earth. Pray to the Lord that the Kingdom of God may go forth, that the Kingdom of Heaven may come where the Kingdom of God is set upon the earth."

Barlow did not attempt to set Zitting straight as to what "things he misunderstood a little bit." At this late date we can only speculate that he was referring to Zitting's statement as to what Woolley had taught them, namely that "They all hold the same power and authority." The question is: who is right on the matter, Lorin Woolley or John Barlow? Marion Hammon chose to accept the teachings of Lorin Woolley over those of John Barlow, thus the controversy between him and the Barlow Boys in these later years.

By 1968, these Barlow Boys were beginning to feel a little uneasy over the situation of Hammon being the next man in the line of seniority of the Priesthood Council after Leroy Johnson. Leroy in 1968 was 80 years old and was more than 20 years older than Marion; it was only natural to assume that he would die before Marion. This became a matter of concern for the Barlow Boys. If Marion was allowed to take over the UEP it would put them in great straits. They knew that as long as Leroy controlled the Trust, they could be assured they would never lose the silver spoon (soft life) of which they were accustomed. They also knew that if Marion became President of the Trust, he would expect them to earn their own way in life, the same as the other UEP members were doing.

This concern of theirs reached a crisis level in their minds and in their secret meetings they began plotting how they could keep Marion from ever gaining control of the UEP. They planned to discredit Marion's reputation among the Group members, somehow destroying the confidence between him and Leroy Johnson. If they could destroy the bond that held the Priesthood Council together, then they could come between Leroy and Marion, and from there it would only be a matter of time until Marion would be out of the picture, thus making it possible for them to gain control of the United Effort Plan themselves.

One of their first bold efforts of implementing their plan was when they took control of the Barco sewing venture. By keeping this money making industry out of the United Effort Plan, thus out of reach of Marion Hammon's control, they were able to exercise control over who not only worked at the sewing plant, but where the money went that was earned there. They also knew that in order to accomplish their goals, their maternal uncle, Fred Jessop, would have to be included in the conspiracy. Fred had been in the Work from its inception and was one person that Leroy had confidence in. If the time ever came that Leroy would have to make a choice between placing his loyalty with Marion Hammon or Fred Jessop, they knew that he would choose Fred. It would take time for the plan to work out, but they were willing to spend whatever time it took to save the Work.

At the end of the decade (1969) Marion Hammon knew he had problems with the Barlow Boys, but he believed that the bond between himself and Leroy and the covenants they had made in their Council Meetings would be stronger than any seeds of discord the Barlows could sow between them. There were more members of the Council who believed the same as Marion did in relation to doctrine, than believed in what the Barlows advocated; sadly though, Leroy was in agreement with the Barlow philosophy, because it was what John Barlow had taught him back in the early days of the Work.

Marion Hammon never thought he could lose his position in the Priesthood Council, so never worried too much about the undercurrent of unrest that the Barlows were stirring up among the Group members concerning him. He just went on with his work of building up the City and the Kingdom for the Priesthood. He was being called "a sick old guy" by Louis Barlow, and Joe Barlow was telling people that Uncle Marion "has always been a problem child of the Priesthood." With these little fiery darts, the work of destroying a man's character was begun by the Barlows.

This chapter will close by quoting from Proverbs 6:16-19.
16. These six things doth the Lord hate: yea, seven are an abomination unto him.
17. A proud look, a lying tongue, and hands that shed innocent blood.
18. An heart that deviseth wicked imaginations, feet that be swift in running to mischief.
19. A false witness that speaketh lies, and he that soweth discord among brethren.

Note 1: See Leroy Johnson's Sermons, p. 845

Note 2: See Leroy Johnson's Sermons, p. 921

Note 3: The Colorado City Improvement Association was organized in opposition to Marion Hammon's Colorado City Area Development Association. Marion was doing things outside of the United Effort Plan, using Trust assets to fund his projects. He had transferred such things as the UEP Cattle herd to his association. He was buying the Hirschi property down in the Gap with UEP assets (donations of the people, thinking they were donating to the UEP). The farming projects at Hatch, Alton, and Beryl (UEP farms) were being operated under the CCADA. The organization of the Colorado City Improvement Association was probably a defensive measure in the minds of its organizers, no doubt thinking that something must be done to protect the assets of the UEP, at least this is what was put to the people to defend their actions. More the truth is that the ones involved in this conspiracy were moving toward an effort of "takeover" themselves. This was the first major act of defiance by this Take Over Conspiracy toward Marion Hammon.

Note 4: There were no United Effort Plan Board meetings held between 1946 and 1984. Since all of the Priesthood Council members were Trustees of the UEP, all UEP business was handled in the Council meetings (The Priesthood Council held a meeting once a month on the third Saturday where UEP business was discussed. They then held a meeting the next day, Sunday, where spiritual matters were discussed). Although the rules governing the management of the trust, as set forth in the Trust Document, specifically states that all actions of the President of the trust must be voted on and made by a declaration of the board of trustees, Leroy Johnson would always make whatever decisions he wanted, knowing that the other board members would never call him to an accounting.

Note 5: The two passages of scripture that the Barlows quote most often to support their One Man Doctrine is Sec. 132 of the Doctrine & Covenants, and *History of the Church*, 6:46. When John Barlow professes to be operating under the rules as set forth by Joseph Smith, he is relying on these two scriptures to substantiate his doctrine of "The One Man Authority." These two scriptures must be examined to establish their credibility.

In the *Truth* Magazine (vol. 10. p. 209), Joseph Musser explains a little about Section 132:. "Much is being said of and much is claimed for the interpolation contained in verse 7, Sect. 132 of the Doctrine and Covenants, viz: 'And I have appointed unto my servant Joseph to hold this power in the last days, and there is never but one on the earth at a time on whom this power and the keys of this Priesthood are conferred.' The statement is a self-evident truth, though the interpretation given it by many is far afield of the facts.

"Certainly the Celestial order of marriage, which to be complete comprehends plural marriage, is a law of the Priesthood. And he who rightfully holds the keys to Priesthood is the one man through whom this blessing from the Lord is expressed to the Saints. It could not be otherwise. There can be only one Commander-in-Chief of the army of the nation. Were there two or more Commanders-in-Chief one can easily understand how clashes in authority would occur resulting in complete chaos.

"When Joseph Smith dictated the revelation to William Clayton he was inspired to include that interpolation doubtless in order to correct an impression, then growing, to the effect that all men holding the Melchizedek Priesthood possessed equal authority. In fact this thought was given some justification in the language recorded by the Prophet in setting apart his counselors, Sidney Rigdon and Frederick G. Williams, in the First Presidency. We quote from History of the Church, 1:334:

"'March 18,1833: Doctor Hurlburt was ordained an Elder, after which Elder Rigdon expressed a desire that himself and Brother Frederick G. Williams should be ordained to the offices to which they had been called, viz: those of Presidents of the High Priesthood, and to be equal in holding the keys of the Kingdom with Brother Joseph Smith, Jun., according to the revelation given on the 8th of March, 1833. Accordingly I laid my hands on Brothers Sidney and Frederick, and ordained them to take part with me in holding the keys of this last kingdom, and to assist in the Presidency of the High Priesthood, as my counselors.'

"From this language it may be inferred that Joseph's counselors considered themselves possessed of the same authority held by Joseph and could act separately from and independently of him. No such a thought could have been in Joseph's mind, however. These brethren were his counselors and were set apart to 'take part with him (not independent of him) in holding the keys of this last kingdom, and to assist (not direct) in the Presidency of the High Priesthood, as his counselors.'

"Sidney Rigdon, according to all accounts, assumed too much and it was because of this assumption, based upon lack of understanding and upon ambition, that caused the Prophet to be impressed to add the interpolation mentioned.

"True, in the revelation of 1880 to Wilford Woodruff, the Lord said;

" 'And while my servant John Taylor is your President, I wish to ask the rest of my servants of the Apostles the question. Although you have one to preside over your Quorum, which is the order of God in all generations, do you not all of you, hold the Apostleship, which is the highest authority ever given to men on the earth? You do. Therefore you hold in common the keys of the kingdom of God in all the world. You, each of you have the power to unlock the veil of eternity and hold converse with God the Father and his son Jesus Christ, and to have the ministration of angels.'

"In regarding this statement from the Lord it must be remembered that these brethren had received the higher order of Priesthood, they were High Priest Apostles, the same as Joseph was. Yet while they all held equal authority John Taylor was their head and spokesman as Joseph had been before him."

According to Musser's teachings (as was also Lorin Woolley's teachings) all members of the Priesthood Council held the same authority. It is true that the term High Priest Apostle does not show up in any of the Polygamist's history until about 1935, after Lorin Woolley died, but the Priesthood Council all claimed to hold that office up to and in the 1960s. As a High Priest Apostle they claimed they held the highest priesthood authority ever given to man on the earth.

The other scripture often quoted by the Barlows is in Church History, vol. 6:46, and reads: "Gave instructions to try those persons who were preaching, teaching, or practicing the doctrine of plurality of wives; for, according to the law, I hold the keys of this power in the last days; for there is never but one on earth at a time on whom the power and its keys are conferred; and I have constantly said 'No man shall have but one wife at a time, unless the Lord directs otherwise.'"

When incorporating Joseph Smith's journal into the *History of the Church*, Apostle George A, Smith, a cousin, altered the above passage to reflect later Mormon thinking: It is not a direct quote of Joseph Smith. Willard Richards, keeper of Joseph Smith's personal journal, recorded on October 5, 1843: "Gave instruction to try those who were preaching teaching or (crossed out: practicing) the doctrine of plurality of wives. On this Law, Joseph forbids it and the practice thereof. No man shall have but one wife." (Joseph Smith's personal journal.) It is interesting that nothing is said in Joseph Smith's journal about only One Man holding the keys.

The Barlow Conspiracy

On April 27, 1972, Carl Holm died in Salt Lake City of congestive heart failure at age 55. Carl Holm was the next to last member that John Barlow had called to his priesthood council. His passing came as a shock to the Polygamists because he was the youngest member of the Council and it was expected that he would some day be the Priesthood President. At his funeral, Marion Hammon said that he had supposed all members of the Council were invulnerable and it was a great shock to him that any of them would die.

Carl Holm was born in Ammon, Idaho, on May 14, 1917. He married Marjory Morrison on July 5, 1940, at Salt Lake City, Utah. Carl had inherited a large farm from his father in Ammon, Idaho. In the 1940s he "turned it in" (donated it) to the United Effort Plan and moved to Short Creek. John Barlow called him into the Priesthood Council in June of 1946 and by the 1950s he was the UEP General Manager. He was loyal to the Polygamist Priesthood leaders and at the time of his dying, was choosing to side with the Barlows on the One Man Doctrine. With his passing, however, the Barlows lost their edge in the balance of power in the Priesthood Council. His leaving left the Council with three members against the One Man Doctrine, two in favor and one undecided. The undecided member was Rulon Jeffs.

Rulon Jeffs had been a protege of Joseph Musser in his early days in the Group. His sermons to the people were along the line of Joseph Musser's teachings, that all members of the Council held the same authority. Jeffs was not called into the Priesthood Council until 1943, but his sermons before this time, as well as after his calling, although usually short, were received with much credence from his peers.

In a sermon he gave in Salt Lake City, at 2157 Lincoln Street, on May 31, 1942, he states: "What is the (Priesthood) situation today? It has come down in regular succession from Joseph Smith to the present day. I want to testify to you as a servant of God that these men in the Council hold the keys today. If you haven't a testimony of that you should not be here today. I want to read this by Joseph Smith: 'O ye Twelve! And all Saints! Profit by this important Key – that in all your trials, troubles, testations, afflictions, bonds, imprisonments and death, see to it, that you do not betray heaven; that you do not betray Jesus Christ; that you do not betray the brethren; that you do not betray the revelations of God, whether in

Bible, Book of Mormon, or Doctrine and Covenants, or that which is to come. Yea, in all your kicking and flounderings, see to it that you do not this thing, lest innocent blood be found upon your skirts and you go down to hell. All other sins are not to be compared to sinning against the Holy Ghost and proving a traitor to the brethren.'

"Look back over the history of the Church, the apostasy and traitorship of the brethren and heads of God's Church. We kick and flounder God's anointed. I say we had better cease it or we will be damned. I have been dubbed a yes man as far as the things that the Priesthood have given me to do. I want to serve the servants of God! This is a Priesthood issue."

Because of these instructions from Joseph Smith, of not turning against those whom the Lord has chosen, and of his early teachings from Joseph Musser, it was a real trial for Rulon when Leroy Johnson began supporting the Barlows in their claims of the One Man Doctrine. In 1972 Rulon was very close to Guy Musser (Joseph's son), also a member of the Council and very much against the Barlow doctrine. When the Barlows began the campaign to destroy Marion Hammon's credibility among the Polygamists, Guy came to his defense with much public support. This put him in the Barlow line of fire just like Marion Hammon. Jeffs began to understand the dilemma he was facing; he could go with his teachings and conscience, or he could choose the political course and be safe.

Rulon Jeffs made his first trip to Short Creek (Colorado City) in January of 1942. He was very impressed by the dedication and sincerity of the people. He was able to see a great potential there to help establish a united order. He was one of a group of men that went down in October 1942 to help set up the United Effort Plan. He felt to support the movement there and wanted to see it succeed. In 1972, the One Man Doctrine was new to him and the choice he must make was a hard one, whether to go with his conscience or with the Barlow claim that President Leroy Johnson was the only man holding the keys. (Note 1).

Leroy Johnson was a leader loved and respected by the people who followed him. He had never claimed to be a prophet, but spoke with authority and conviction. One time in Priesthood Meeting he said: "You have heard other men call me a prophet, but you have never heard me make that claim (Note 2)." His sermons to the people were pretty much repeats of what he had said sometime before, never giving much specific instruction.

There were, however, times when Leroy would make prophetic statements that would sooner or later turn out pretty much as he predicted. The interesting thing about these fulfilled predictions was that it was not those who proclaimed themselves to be in righteous positions that were passed by, but rather, in most cases, they would turn out to be the ones he was warning the people against. In a sermon he gave at Short Creek, Arizona, in 1952, he made this prediction: "It is my opinion that our greatest persecution, our greatest test rather, will not be from the outside people prosecuting or persecuting us, but our great test will come from within our own ranks....

"The greatest persecution and the greatest test that will come to this people will be from those who have drawn away from the true line of Priesthood and accepted the priesthood of Satan as their guide and companion. Now, we will be tested beyond all comprehension. At the present time our minds cannot conceive of the delusion that will be brought to cloud our minds of the testimony which we have of the true way of living...(but) we are living in a time, my brothers and sisters, when the Lord is causing a great delusion to come upon the minds of the people. And those who have it in their hearts to do good and to bring about their eternal salvation must know for themselves the way that they should go, or be left.... The minds of those who will not follow the true line of Priesthood will be arrayed against those who do. And the time will come, my brothers and sisters, when we will wish that we had been more faithful in keeping the commandments of the Lord (Note 3)."

At the time of this sermon, February 1952, the people of Short Creek were doing just about as well spiritually as they have ever done, before or since then. Such a warning seemed to them to be absurd. The community was small, most everyone was congenial with their neighbors, and a spirit of harmony existed among them. Thus his warning was mostly forgotten.

Leroy Johnson always claimed that the Lord had not commanded the Priesthood to set up another church. He claimed that the Polygamists were members of The Church of Jesus Christ of Latter-day Saints. This Church (LDS) was set up by God and was still his Church. It was out of order, but the One Mighty and Strong was going to come and set it in order. "We (the Polygamists) are being prepared to be the people that He (the One Mighty and Strong) will use to do this great Work." He never referred to the Polygamists as the Fundamentalists until about 1978, when he obtained a minister's license to protect himself in a lawsuit that was filed against him (Note 4). His sermons were mostly telling the people that they must repent, not being too specific as to just what they needed to repent of. If there was some problem to address he would do so, but his talks were mostly about his experiences as a young man and the things he had learned from his Church Leaders in his early days.

He would make many references to the United Order, always claiming that God had not commanded the Polygamists to live such. His references to the United Effort Plan were mostly that it was only a step toward the United Order. In 1972, he said: "A week doesn't pass but what someone comes in and wants to know when we are going to organize the United Order. We are not ready for the United Order. Joseph Musser told me this when I first got acquainted with him. 'We are

167

not worthy of the United Order,' he said, 'but we will unite ourselves together and live at it, if we can.' How many of us are ready? We have tried it time and time again."

He taught that only those living polygamy could live the United Order. Again in 1972, he said:

"We are continually asked why we don't organize our people in the United Order.... We are trying everyday to set up the Order of Heaven in our midst. There is no other place on the face of the earth where the Celestial Law is being promulgated under the direction of men who have been called into this position. This has been told to you already today. In order for a man to be prepared for the United Order, he has to be added upon (living polygamy). When the United Order is set up, you won't find monogamy there.

"We administer the order of plurality to a man, and he immediately feels that he is ready for the United Order. But let me tell you something and draw your attention to conditions that existed before. Can you cite me a United Order that Brigham Young was connected with personally? I have been searching for this condition; but I am still searching. You know why he didn't? Simply because he couldn't prepare his own family.... I have been asked many times why we didn't set up the United Order in this place and live it.

"A lot of people think that when they are administered to with a plurality of wives that they are ready to go right into the United Order. It is the greatest confusion in the world to try to unite a people that are not more prepared than we are today. It would be nothing but confusion. We have tried it in this place. We have tried it in other places. They haven't been able to become united to a point where God could bless them.... When we can become united as a people, (then) we can be united in a United Order that the Lord can bless. When that time comes, there will be no monogamy in the United Order. There is no Monogamy in the Celestial Kingdom. We are trying to prepare a people for the Celestial Kingdom (Note 5)."

When he said: "Men called into this position," he was referring to those who have held the Keys to Priesthood from Joseph Smith down to his time. One of the delusions the Barlows were perpetrating through the 1970s and 1980s was the elimination of some of the past Priesthood Presidents from the history of the Polygamists' line of authority. They would not be able to succeed in this deceit until after Richard Jessop (a Priesthood Council member) died in 1978.

Richard Jessop was the only member of John Barlow's Council that had known Lorin Woolley in any degree of intimacy. In the early 1930s, during the years of the Great Depression, he had spent many hours visiting with Woolley. The only one of the other Council members that even knew him at all, probably even ever met him, was Guy Musser. Guy Musser was living in California during these years and didn't join with the Polygamist Group until 1935 (Note 6). For these reasons, he had not been tutored by Woolley, like Jessop had. Leroy met John Woolley (Lorin's father) only once and had never, even once, met Lorin Woolley (Note 7).

Richard Jessop would often tell about his experiences of being schooled under Lorin Woolley. In these sermons, he would always emphasize the Priesthood lineage in the order of seniority of the Presidents ("those who had held the keys to Priesthood") down through the Polygamists' history. Often, after Richard had finished his talks, Leroy would get up in the meetings and in agreement, confirm the truth of Jessop's statements.

Leroy never did tell the people in any of his public addresses that the Lineage of Priesthood was any different than the order that Jessop would explain it; in fact, he would name them the same. Two examples: On December 21, 1975, he said: "The Gospel is true. Joseph Smith was a Prophet of God. Brigham Young was his successor in the line of Priesthood. John Taylor and Wilford Woodruff, John W. Woolley, Lorin Woolley, Leslie Broadbent, John Barlow, Joseph White Musser, Charles F. Zitting, and the Council you see before you today are also successors in the line of Priesthood. So, let us go to and obey the counsel that we get from Sunday to Sunday and apply it to our lives."

And again Leroy said on August 27, 1978: "I have been called into this position by God, Almighty, and if He is willing to sustain me in this position, you ought to be willing to sustain me in this position. I am not boasting. I am not speaking out of turn. For the Lord has always had a mouthpiece to His people. And I have just as much right to give the word of the Lord to the people as Brigham Young, John Taylor, John W. Woolley, Lorin Woolley, Leslie Broadbent, John Y. Barlow, Joseph W. Musser and Charles F. Zitting. The Lord has sustained me here and I am not afraid to speak, remembering that one man and God is a majority. But I say it with all soberness of mind and I say it so that you can understand it (so there are people who had better sit up and take notice), that the Lord is, for the last time, trying to bring a people up that He can use in the Redemption of Zion (Note 8)."

In his chronology in this sermon, Leroy left out the names of Joseph Smith and Wilford Woodruff. This seems to be only a mistake of memory recall rather than any elimination of these men from their position.

Richard Jessop died just two months after this sermon of Leroy's. He was never challenged on his testimony of the Polygamist lineage of Priesthood authority (Note 9), either by Leroy or any of the Barlows. Soon after his death, however, there began a campaign to change the history of this line of authority. The Barlows, along with their maternal Uncle, Fred Jessop, took it upon themselves to *save* the UEP from falling into the hands of Marion Hammon. If Hammon was ever allowed to achieve the position of President of Priesthood (as he surely would according to the order of things set up by Lorin Woolley), he would also gain control of the United Effort Plan, and this would mark the end of power for any of the Barlows and especially for Fred Jessop. In order to achieve this, the people would have to be told things about the history that were untrue.

Fred Jessop and these nephews of his, the sons of John Y. Barlow, had always felt that Marion Hammon was an interloper in the Priesthood Work. The Work belonged to the "Chosen Seed," the lineage of John Y. Barlow. The Keys of the Priesthood must be protected from falling into the hands of any outsiders and Marion Hammon was definitely an outsider. Hammon's credibility must be destroyed among the Polygamists and this is what they conspired to do. They began whispering it about that Marion was not willing to do what Leroy asked him to do. They would hatch up incidences where it would appear that Hammon was not willing to support Leroy. Their biggest cannon was the controversy over the One Man Doctrine, which Hammon did not agree on. With little white lies (exaggerated incidents), they began their work of undermining his integrity in Leroy's mind.

Leroy was an old man (90 years old in 1978) and at the end of the 1970s decade he contracted the shingles, forcing him to his sick bed for five or six years. While in this condition, the Barlows were able to mold his mind and convince him to say and do things that he never would have done 20 years before.

Their first success of manipulating his mind was in regards to the elimination of the former Priesthood Leaders from their position of seniority in the Priesthood Council (Note 10). To eliminate Marion Hammon from the leadership position of the Priesthood Council, they would have to destroy the credibility of all of the Polygamist's Leaders that had contradicted John Barlow's claim of only one man holding the Keys.

The following is the Polygamist line of Priesthood authority. The names in parenthesis are those eliminated by the Barlows:

Joseph Smith, Brigham Young, John Taylor, (Wilford Woodruff) John Woolley, Lorin Woolley, (Leslie Broadbent), John Barlow, (Joseph Musser), (Charles Zitting), Leroy Johnson, (Marion Hammon) and Rulon Jeffs. (Alma Timpson came after Marion Hammon in the line of authority because Rulon Jeffs, through later betrayal of the Brethren, was not the "next Worthy Senior"). An interesting point here is that Wilford Woodruff was not eliminated by them because he had signed the Manifesto, but rather because he had copied a revelation (that he had received) into his journal that stated: "all of the men in the Council held the same authority" (Note 11).

Leslie Broadbent was eliminated because he acknowledged that Lorin Woolley had told the members of the Council before he died that they all held the same authority (The only keys Woolley gave to these men was to keep Patriarchal Marriage alive). Joseph Musser was eliminated because he had too much to say against the One Man Doctrine and the Barlows don't accept everything that is in the *Truth* Magazine.

Charles Zitting was eliminated because of the statements in his public sermons: "All of the Council members hold the same authority." The Barlows also claim that Zitting forfeited his position of seniority in the Council because he refused to sign the prison manifesto of 1945 when John Barlow did and remained in prison while most of the others came out.

If the Barlows were going to gain control of the assets of the United Effort Plan, they would have to promote Leroy as the only man who could make decisions in regards to the management of the Trust, effectively making him a king. And this is just what they set about to do. All they would have to do to get the people to believe their false doctrine would be to tell them that it was what Leroy was teaching. Few would go to Leroy and check it out.

Those who did, however, would find that Leroy had not been quoted correctly; in fact, Leroy would publicly warn the people against those who were trying to cause enmity between the people in the society. In a public sermon at Colorado City, on November 7, 1971, he said: "Here's a people that have been taught for many years. This body of young people here today have been brought up and reared under the direction of the Priesthood. Why the fathers and mothers of these children would allow conversations to go on in their homes criticizing the actions of others I don't know. I don't know why they do it.... They have no business to let a word drop to the ears of a child in their homes about the apostate conditions of any man. I don't who he is. If you will stop to listen or think just a moment, it puts you in a condition worse than the apostates are because you should be further down the road than they are. If you don't repent, you are going to find yourselves going the same road they are.... If we criticize our neighbor for his faults and failings, it places us in a worse condition than our neighbor is. We are guilty of the greater sin, so the Lord says.... Let us learn this one thing, that before we criticize someone else, let us look to ourselves and see whether we are worthy to criticize or not. Let's see if we are doing all things whatsoever the Lord has commanded us to do."

Leroy then, in this same sermon, gives some advice to the people on how to tell if things that are being taught them are true or not. He goes on to say: "I have been greatly distressed in my feelings over the actions of men who have come to see me lately, knowing that they know the Gospel is true, that Joseph Smith was a prophet of God and they've been tutored and trained in The Church of Jesus Christ of Latter-day Saints. They've had access to the doctrines of the holy Priesthood through the teachings of early leaders of this work and knowing that it is their privilege to apply the square to that which they hear, to see if it squares up with the revelations of God or not, yet they have by-passed the order of Priesthood that God has been trying to get before them, not only the *Truth* Magazine, but the *Journal of Discourses* so that they could be properly instructed."

Leroy could not have been more plain. He not only warns the people against those spreading criticism, but supports the validity of the *Truth* Magazine so far as proclaiming correct doctrine. He further admonishes them to accept the teachings of their former leaders and told them to go to "the *Truth* Magazine," and the *Journal of Discourses* to square up what they were being told.

He did not stop there; he said more about those who are spreading false doctrine among the people: "I have used pretty hard words to some of these people, because knowing that they know as much about the Gospel as I know, or they ought to, yet they by-pass us, and when they get into trouble or their minds are troubled and they don't know where to look, they come to us to get straightened out.... I told one man that he just as well quit asking the questions.... You have gone out and got yourself confused by every wind of doctrine that has been preached. Now you come back to the fountain of truth to find out what is the truth and you don't know the truth when you hear it (Note 12)."

These statements of Leroy did nothing to stop the Barlows in their efforts to destroy Marion's position in the Priesthood Council. In the late 1960s, they began a routine of meeting with Leroy at the Sugar Loaf Cafe in Cedar City every Monday to discuss and criticize the things that Marion Hammon and Alma Timpson had said in the meeting the day before. These meetings at the Sugar Loaf became legion, for it was here that the Doctrine of the One Man Authority was taught to those who were allowed to participate in the gatherings. There would be anywhere from ten to thirty people there, mostly all Barlow supporters because they were somehow able to screen out those who did not agree with them.

Leroy would always demand that he pay the bill for the meals, which would run into the hundreds of dollars. The Barlows were very aware of those in the entourage who would later slip up to Leroy and give him at least as much money as his portion of the bill. Those who were dilatory in paying their share, would be in danger of being whispered about sometime later.

It was in these meetings at the Sugar Loaf that the Barlows were able to do their greatest damage in manipulating the truth and destroying the Priesthood Work. Not only were they able to gain many converts to their doctrine, but they were also able to warp and mold the mind of the Polygamist Prophet, Leroy Johnson.

Marion Hammon was no fool; he could see what the Barlows were up to. As the animosity against him grew, he became hurt in his feelings over what was happening. He had genuinely put his all into the up-building of the Priesthood Work and now his name was being dragged through the dirt; respect for him was fading. He concluded that if the people (and this included Leroy) were going to resent him, he would move out of their way, allowing the Barlows to take over. He began looking for another place where he could go and continue living the principles of the Gospel. He supposed there were other people who could see what was happening and some of them would be happy to move on with him.

Marion had been farming and ranching, using UEP assets and his own sons to do so. He was using the UEP farm near Beryl, Utah, and a cattle ranch at Hatch, Utah, that was also a United Effort Plan asset. This cattle ranch, several hundred acres in size, was all on UEP privately owned property. These two properties were free and clear, having been paid for with time and money donated by UEP members. For some reason Marion was not satisfied with just operating these two enterprises, he wanted to go back to his home state of Idaho. One day in 1971, Leroy told the Boys gathered at the Sugar Loaf Cafe in Cedar City that "Brother Hammon came to me and demanded the deeds to the Hatch and Beryl properties. The Lord told me that if I gave him the deeds he would lose the property, but He (the Lord) told me to go ahead and give them to him (Note 13)."

Leroy did indeed give the deeds of these properties to Hammon. They were signed by himself, as UEP President, and Rulon Jeffs, as UEP Secretary. This transaction was executed by these two men without ever holding a United Effort Plan Board meeting and without a resolution by the Board of Trustees authorizing such a major transfer of UEP assets. As a matter of fact, the only Board members that even knew of the transaction were Leroy, Rulon, and Marion. This matter of doing business was in direct violation of the rules governing the Trust as set forth in the Trust Document. Such underhanded maneuvering has the earmarks of Leroy buying Marion out of the United Effort Plan, and some people have made this accusation.

As soon as Hammon had the deeds of these properties in his hands, he began looking for a place in Idaho where he could establish himself independent of any interference from the other members of the Priesthood Council. His hope was to have a place where he could demonstrate to the Polygamists how to live the United Order. He reasoned that by going back to Idaho, it would be easier to live a United Order because farming there would be more successful than in the semi-arid conditions of Southern Utah and Northern Arizona.

Hammon's success in Idaho would depend on two major things: finding a good farm and getting competent help to move there with him. To find the good farm, he went to Jack Knudson, the same man who had robbed Harold Blackmore of his property in Canada for the UEP.

It just so happened that Knudson had a farm that was for sale. In his land swapping deals, he had acquired a farm near Blackfoot, Idaho. He had been trying to sell it for some time before Hammon approached him, but had been unable to dump it up to this time. This seemed to be an opportunity for them both; Knudson could sell something he did not want and Hammon could get a farm.

The Blackfoot farm was not one of premium value. Having been reclaimed from the midst of a lava bed, there were almost as many acres of rock (islands in the portion that was being farmed) as there were acres of arable land. At the time of these events, prime farm land in the Blackfoot area was selling for about $400.00 per acre, but Knudson was not inclined to give Hammon any kind of a special deal. He had chosen the Barlow side in the politics of their One Man Doctrine controversy and had sided against Hammon on the issue. He decided to ask $800.00 for his inferior farm. There can be no dispute that he inflated the price for this reason. He probably expected he would have to negotiate the price down some, but knew he had a fish on the line and was going to get all he could at the time of the sale. There is no question that Hammon could have bought the farm for less than the asking price had he attempted a lower offer, but instead, he just agreed to pay the exorbitant amount.

Hammon gave Knudson the Hatch Ranch (which was probably worth more in actual value than the Blackfoot farm) and what equity there was in the Hirschi property at the Gap west of Colorado City (he was buying this property with donations from the people at Colorado City, they thinking it was a United Effort Plan project, when in reality it was in the name of the Colorado City Area Development Association), for a down payment on the farm in Idaho. Knudson would carry the contract, allowing Hammon to pay him off over a 20 year time period. Jack Knudson really cleaned up. He not only dumped the place in Blackfoot, but after selling the Hatch Ranch he made more money than he gave for the Idaho farm. He had the property in the Gap as a bonus. On the other hand, Marion Hammon's problems had just begun.

Marion Hammon began his exodus to Idaho in about 1972. This was a major undertaking in his life; he was selling everything he had in Southern Utah for below its real value. One example of this was when he sold the farm at Beryl, Utah. He sold it for about $60,000.00. Two weeks after he sold it, it was sold again for about $90,000.00. About two weeks after that it was sold again for about $120,000.00. He had no plans of ever coming back to Colorado City. He planned to move all of his family to Idaho just as soon as he could make arrangements up there for them to live. He felt an urgency to establish himself outside of the dominion of those who had betrayed him and was just getting what he could out of the Work to help him in his venture. He justified what he was doing, not because he thought he had anything coming for his services, but rather he believed that he was setting up a refuge where the faithful people could go after the Barlows had completely destroyed the United Effort Plan. His problems began when none of the Polygamists would see it the same way, most of them thought he was just getting out and taking what he could grab as he went. One who Marion surely hoped would go with him was Edson Jessop.

Edson Jessop had came to Short Creek with his father Lyman (a brother to Richard and Fred Jessop) in the early 1940s. He was a young man of about 22 years old at the time and was a very zealous supporter of the Priesthood work. He was the same caliber of person as were his cousins, Joe and Dan Jessop. Much of the success of building up Short Creek in the early years there can be attributed to Edson Jessop.

When Marion Hammon came back in 1958 to begin the revitalization of the United Effort Plan, he depended a great deal on Edson and his ability and trade as a carpenter. Edson became very close to Hammon, emanating many of his characteristics, becoming as a protege to him. For these reasons Marion felt certain that Edson would go with him to Idaho and help with his new United Order. When Edson was approached by Hammon and asked to go to Idaho, it became one of the biggest trials he had ever faced in his experience of supporting the Priesthood Work. It upset him greatly to think that the Priesthood would ask him to leave his beloved valley, which he had been taught for most of his adult life was where the Promised Land was to be established by the Priesthood of God.

He had been taught that all of the men in the Council held the same authority, that if any one of them asked you to do something it was the same as if God Himself was asking you. To refuse to do as Hammon was asking was the same as refusing to do what God would ask. He spent many sleepless nights, contemplating what he should do. He finally decided to go against all that he had ever been taught, to go to another one of the Brethren, explain his dilemma and seek different counsel.

He went to Leroy Johnson to either have him confirm what Marion was asking him to do, or to tell him he didn't have to go to Idaho. When going to Leroy, Edson was willing to do whatever was asked of him to do. He did, however, explain to him that he did not feel very good about leaving Colorado City and running off to Idaho to establish a new Order when he had been taught all his life that this (Colorado City) was the place to set up the Kingdom. He explained how he felt about living at Colorado City and that because of his love for the valley, the mountains and the goals of the former leaders that he had dedicated his life to support, he just did not feel very good about leaving. He was not aware of the split that was developing between the members of the Priesthood Council and supposed that Hammon had cleared everything he was doing with the other Council Members. Imagine his joy and surprise when Leroy told him he did not need to go to Idaho.

Edson Jessop's refusal to go to Idaho was a great blow to Marion Hammon. Of all the Polygamists, he supposed that Edson would be one he could count on; this was indeed very discouraging. Hammon was unable to convince even one adult member of the Colorado City Polygamists to move to Idaho and help him with his farm. For this reason, more than any other, his dream would result in failure.

Marion Hammon had never had any real experience in successful farming. All farming projects he had been involved in before his Idaho venture had been heavily subsidized by other sources of financial support, such as tithing or money from the missionary program that had been instigated at Colorado City. He had also been able to call on such people as Parley Harker for competent advice and even physical help when needed.

In Idaho, he had neither the subsidizing money nor the competent help. The only people he was able to take with him were some of his own sons, none of which had the ability to successfully run the farm. Some of these sons were able to obtain work in the nearby communities as drywall laborers, which did help to subsidize the project to a small extent, but even this venture brought sorrow to Marion Hammon and his family when one of his young sons was killed in an automobile accident on the way to work one morning near Blackfoot, Idaho. This was a terrible blow to Marion Hammon and from this point on things in Idaho went downhill for him. He leased part of the farm to a local farmer of Japanese decent, who was quite successful in raising potatoes. Hammon attempted to induce the man to come to work for him and manage the whole farm, but was unsuccessful.

After the third year of trying to run the farm in Idaho, Hammon could see that under the circumstances there was no chance that he would ever be successful. In dejection, he went to Leroy and offered to turn the farm into the United Effort Plan. He supposed that if the UEP owned the farm, then Leroy would send him both competent help and financial support to bail him out. Leroy refused to help him. He had supposed he was rid of Hammon when he had given him the UEP farms at Hatch and Beryl, then going off to Idaho. He simply told Marion that the UEP could not accept property that was not paid for. Leroy made up this rule on the spot so as not to have to bail Hammon out. The UEP had accepted property that was not paid for from its very beginning, this was only a polite way of telling Marion to go to hell. With this rejection Marion found that he was really in trouble with the project. This had been his last hope; all there was left for him to do would be to look for a way to dump the farm and move back to Colorado City, the only refuge he could see.

He put the farm up for sale and accepted the only offer made to him, which was to raise $20,000.00 dollars to put with the farm so a broker would take over the payments. In the three and a half years that he had made payments to Jack Knudson, along with the down payment made when he bought the farm, he still had to come up with $20,000.00 to be able to get out from under the contract with Knudson. This shows what the real value of the farm was when he bought it.

In about 1976 Marion Hammon returned to Colorado City expecting he would carry on there as he had before he left. He found, to his sad disappointment, that there were very few people there who still respected him; the Barlows had been very busy while he had been away.

176

It is a misnomer to say that he had "been away" because most of his family had remained at Colorado City for the four years he was trying to establish himself in Idaho. He would come back there on most Sundays, where he was still very active in preaching to the people in Sunday meetings. It is true that there was a lot of disrespect for him, making it harder for him to preach to the people. He was able to see what the Barlows were up to and tried to explain to the people that what they were telling them was not true. He was not very successful in convincing them of this, however, and due to the stress of the situation, he suffered a heart attack and underwent a five bypass operation. He would never fully recover from this operation, being mostly bedridden the rest of his life. He did, however, manage to outlive Leroy and was able to recuperate enough to come back to church in the early 1980s, when the controversy over the One Man Doctrine reached its height.

In 1976 Jim Blackmore filed a lawsuit against Leroy Johnson to regain the occupancy of a house he had built in the late 1960s at Colorado City. The house had been built on UEP property by Jim soon after he had completed a mission for the Priesthood. When his father Harold Blackmore moved to La Verkin, Jim had begun working with him there in the home construction business. Jim had built a home in La Verkin and had temporally moved there while helping his father build houses in the area.

His brother-in-law, Marcus Jessop (brother to Jim's wife) had moved from Salt Lake City to Colorado City and needed a place to live. Jim allowed him to live in his house in Colorado City since he was not using it. In 1976 Jim decided he wanted to move back to Colorado City so asked Marcus to vacate the house. Marcus had built himself a new home in the meantime and could easily move into his own house. Leroy told Marcus to stay in Jim's house and not let him have it back. This came as a very hard surprise for Jim because he had maintained good relations with the Polygamists at Colorado City. He had faithfully attended church there, paid his tithing to Leroy, and given allegiance to their religious teachings. When he went to Leroy to find out why he was out of favor, he was simply told that because he was Harold's son, he was no longer welcome there. In frustration he went to his father and they decided to file a lawsuit to see if Jim could regain occupancy of his house.

This lawsuit put a real scare into the polygamists. Leroy would get up in meetings and plead with the people for money to help fight it. He would always collect money because the people were told that if the UEP lost the lawsuit they would all lose their homes (a total misnomer). It did not take Harold and Jim Blackmore long to see that they would not get any justice from the courts unless they had thousands of dollars to pay the lawyers. They decided to drop the lawsuit. Before they dropped it, however, they had their attorney require that the UEP file a list of all its beneficiaries in the county court house in Kingman, Arizona, in accordance with a law that had recently been enacted by the Arizona Legislature. The law states in effect: "A trustee (of a blind trust) shall name the beneficiaries of such trust and their addresses; …and file the names in the public records in the court house of the county in which the property is located." This was accomplished. Fred Jessop made up the list of all members of the United Effort Plan who were living in Colorado City in 1976 and filed it in the Court House at Kingman, Arizona (Note 14).

Because of the threat of the Blackmore lawsuit, the UEP Trustees considered it necessary to implement a way to protect them from any such threats in the future. A document was drawn up and all UEP members were required to sign it. The purpose of the document, as seen by the Trustees, was to secure to the UEP that the members who signed it would be acknowledging that as members of the UEP, if they ever decided to move from their homes, they would not attempt to claim any equity in them, thus barring them from filing any more lawsuits. The members, in signing the document, looked at it quite differently. They read it as a guarantee to them that they could never be asked to leave their homes; but they would lose their equity if they decided, on their own initiative to leave these homes. At the time of these events, most all the UEP members were satisfied with the management of the UEP and could see no problems ahead if they signed the document; most all of them willing signed it.

The document is as follows:

Date: Place:

This is to certify that I, _____ understand the United Effort Plan, to which I do hereby subscribe myself, realizing that for the security of our homes, which cannot be mortgaged, sold or bartered away, that whatever improvement is made on the premises, which are allotted for our use, becomes part of and are to remain part of said premises, regardless of what course I may choose to take; and that I further agree to pay my allotted share of taxes levied against the property I occupy, of my own free will and choice, on the day and date above written.

(signature)_____

In the presence of (witnesses)

_____

_____

The taking of Jim Blackmore's house was the first atrocity of this kind (the act of stealing a man's house) to be perpetrated by the Polygamist leaders. It is true that farms, homes, and personal property had been sold and the money squandered by them in the past, but these properties had all been voluntarily turned in to the United Effort Plan. In the past, when one of these contributors had become dissatisfied because of the poor management of their assets, the Polygamist Leaders had made an effort to reconcile their feelings. In some cases deeds of property were given to the dissatisfied members, leases on property or equipment were granted, and none of these members were ever asked to give up the homes they had built. The policy of the Polygamist Leaders had always been "if someone apostatized, they would get discouraged and leave." This policy had worked pretty well because those who became dissatisfied had eventually done just that, picked up and moved (even some who had been given the deed to their place left and the property was later bought back).

When the UEP paid Harold Blackmore for his place in the 1960s, Leroy Johnson made the statement: "This will be the last time we will ever pay an apostate for his home." Leroy had decided to become a harsher leader than were his predecessors, making the decision to force the people in line rather than allowing them their free agency to choose their course of religious sentiments and to force any member out of the society if he believed that person was out of harmony with him in any degree. This was a dramatic change in the policy and purpose of what the United Effort Plan had been set up to be used for by its founders in 1942. From this time on, the feelings and the spirit of the Polygamist Society at Colorado City began to change from a carefree atmosphere of freedom and joy, to one of fear and oppression.

On October 23, 1978, Richard S. Jessop (Priesthood Council member) died. The death of Jessop gave the Barlows a free and open road towards their goal of taking over the UEP. Richard had been their biggest obstacle up to this time because they could not sway Leroy's mind on Priesthood history so long as Richard Jessop was alive; he was a living testimony of what the history was, having personally lived through it. At his funeral, Leroy Johnson spoke of Jessop's testimony: "His testimony is recorded and it is where we can get it and refer to it from time to time.... My great concern is not over Richard Seth Jessop or about him, but my great concern is for those who are left behind.... There isn't a man or woman that ever heard the man speak over the pulpit but what his words condemn them if they don't do what he told them to do... All of you that knew him will have to get a little slip of paper that says, 'This man is OK, or this women is OK, I knew them well'."

Richard S. Jessop's teachings of the Polygamists' lineage of Priesthood authority (Note 9) is the part of his testimony that condemns the Barlows' version of the Priesthood Line. If Leroy is to be believed, then the Barlows are wrong, it's that simple.

It did not take long for the Barlows to make their move after Richard Jessop's death. They were able to convince Leroy that the 1880 Revelation given to Wilford Woodruff was really two revelations. The first part was from The Lord; the second half was from Satan. Leroy presented this theory to the remaining (living) members of the Priesthood Council in one of their regular council meetings at Salt Lake City in the spring of 1979. These surviving members were as follows: Leroy Johnson, Marion Hammon, Guy Musser, Rulon Jeffs, and Alma Timpson.

After Leroy presented his astonishing interpretation of this revelation to the Council, Alma Timpson reached over to the table in the corner of the room, picking up the Three In One (a book containing the Book of Mormon, Doctrine and Covenants, and the Pearl of Great Price, the standard LDS scriptures) and he asked: "Can we discuss this, Brother Johnson?"

Leroy became very wroth, saying; "Do you want a sign, brother Timpson, like Korihor of old (Note 15)?"

Alma Timpson, folding the book closed, simply replied: "No, Brother Johnson, I don't need a sign."

This was one of the last times the Priesthood Council met in a regular Council meeting. Rulon Jeffs was the only one of the Council that accepted Leroy's philosophy regarding the 1880 revelation. This left the Council split as follows: Leroy Johnson and Rulon Jeffs in agreement with the Barlows' One Man Doctrine. Marion Hammon, Guy Musser, and Alma Timpson against it.

These latter men could not go against their earlier teachings; that all the Brethren in the Council held the same Authority. Rulon Jeffs, although it was against what he knew was the early teachings of the Polygamist Leaders, chose to side with Leroy and the Barlows. It appears that this was a political decision he chose rather than a doctrinal one. Shortly after the Council meeting wherein Leroy made his stand, Rulon, in a Junior School of The Prophets meeting at Colorado City, got up and, in a halting address to those attending the meeting, told them that the 1880 Revelation to Wilford Woodruff was from the Lower Regions (Note 16). This firmly assured his position with the Barlow Cabal on the issue. This was the last meeting of the Junior School of The Prophets among the Polygamists. This breach of the unity, which had been one of their trademarks for so many years, was now forever shattered.

Soon after these events, Leroy Johnson became very sick with the Shingles. He was not able to attend any of the meetings for the next three or four years. This left the conducting of the meetings and the affairs of the Polygamists in the hands of Marion Hammon as the next Senior member in line of authority in the Priesthood Council. These next few years became years of much turmoil among them. Hammon, along with Musser and Timpson, labored very hard to convince the people that because of Leroy's age (91 in 1979) and his sickness, he had been allowed to be swayed by unscrupulous men in their greed and desire for power.

The love the people had for Leroy blinded them to these warnings and their efforts were mostly unsuccessful. Because of his anxiety over the issue, Marion Hammon became very sick due to his heart condition and he too was unable to get out among the people for the next two or three years. This left Guy Musser the next senior member of the Council in charge for the time being.

Musser spent his time in Salt Lake City while Timpson was in charge at Colorado City. This arrangement was not at all satisfactory with the Barlows and they did everything they could to discredit what these two Brethren tried to teach the people through these tumultuous years. Consequently the Priesthood Split among the Polygamists became very evident and it was very few, if any of them, who were unable to see it. By 1980, this split was becoming very much recognized, with many hostile feelings being manifest in the community; manifest, not only in the day to day mingling of the people but more particular in their religious meetings. The teachings of those who would be called on to talk to the people almost became a debating issue rather than instructions to the members of the society.

These feelings of discord became worse as time went on, leaving the people in a state of confusion, causing many of them to quit attending these meetings rather than partake of the bitter disputes that occurred between the opposing factions. This condition of rebellion from the Barlow faction would ultimately result in the complete repudiation of the Priesthood authority of both Marion Hammon and Alma Timpson among most of the Polygamist Group.

Note 1: Jeffs was one of a group of men (John Barlow, Joseph Musser, Marion Hammon, Guy Musser and Rulon Jeffs) who had just returned from Short Creek. He had been called on to talk in a meeting at Salt Lake City after their return. It is in this sermon (on October 25, 1942 at 2157 Lincoln Street, Salt Lake City, Utah) where he tells of his first trip to Short Creek in January of 1942. It was this trip to Short Creek in October of 1942 that the United Effort Plan was created. The Trust Document was signed by the officers of the UEP on November 9, 1942. It was not filed in the County Court House at Kingman, AZ until August 8, 1944, almost two years later.

Note 2: This statement was made in about 1980. The author was in the meeting and heard Leroy make this statement. Those who compiled and published his sermons have left this one out of the collection. They did, however, let one of his statements get into the published sermons that backs up his not claiming to be a Prophet. It was given on February 13, 1972. It is in Volume Two, p. 414, and reads:

"A lot of people believe…that they don't have to take the word of the servants of God, that it is their privilege and their responsibility to have a personal knowledge and vision of God, the Eternal Father, and His son, Jesus Christ, or they don't have to believe. A lot of people have that testimony. We have had men come to us and say something like that. In fact, I have a letter somewhere in my possession from a man in Florida saying, 'Brother Johnson, I understand that you hold the keys of the Holy Priesthood – hold the same office and calling that the Prophet Joseph Smith held. Now, if you will put it in writing, in a letter, and send it to me with your name signed to it that you have had the visitation of the Savior and had His hands laid upon your head and confirmed you a prophet of God as was Joseph Smith, then I will believe that you hold the keys of the Holy Priesthood.'…. How many of us feel like we have the right to demand that God come out and reveal Himself to us before we are under the obligation of believing?"

The man who sent him the letter was not asking that the Lord appear to him, but rather was asking if the Lord had appeared to Leroy. It is interesting that Leroy would go on the defensive over this legitimate question. According to Lorin Woolley, before he could become a true member of the Council of Friends he would "have to be confirmed by God himself, Christ will have to lay his hands on your head himself, and confirm your calling (See Note 3, Chapter 1)." Leroy has never, in any of his sermons, claimed that this ever happened. Here was the perfect chance for him to make the claim if it was so. Because he never claimed it to be true, we must assume it was not. In the later years of his life there were people around him (the Barlows) who claimed that he was visited by spiritual beings, but he never made such a claim himself.

Note 3: See L. S. Johnson Sermons, vol. 1, p. 9. On p. 383 of this same volume Leroy said further on the subject: "Anything that is contrary to the revelations of God is the revelations of man or the devil to man. There are only two powers working – the power of Christ trying to bring people unto eternal life and exaltation in the Celestial World to enjoy eternal life – the other, trying to destroy the work of Christ. This is the handicap that we are working under. We are working under the handicap of delusion."

Note 4: In a sermon on December 11, 1977, Leroy gives Mark E. Petersen (one of the Twelve Apostles of the LDS Church) the credit of calling the Polygamists, "The Fundamentalists." "On p. 1491, volume four of his Sermons, he says: 'There is a missionary work going on under the direction of the Priesthood of God. It is not in modern doctrines of the Church, but it is the original doctrines of The Church of Jesus Christ of Latter-day Saints, the fundamental principles.' I was grateful when I heard that Mark E. Petersen branded us as Fundamentalists."

From L. S. Johnson Sermons, vol. 4, pp.1616 and 1618. "A lot of people want to know something about the Fundamentalist Division of The Church of Jesus Christ of Latter-day Saints, but when they find out the conditions under which they have to subject themselves in order to join up, they don't get very far. Yet, they claim they are trying to find out exactly how the Fundamentalists live."

It became necessary for Leroy to obtain some kind of religious entity to protect himself from the IRS. In 1978 he filed for a minister's license with this agency. From his sermons: "I happened to have a Minister's License signed by the Federal Tax Commission: 'Minister of the Fundamentalist Division of The Church of Jesus Christ of Latter-day Saints.' That is on record in the court.'"

Leroy never, in any of his recorded sermons, claimed to be the Fundamentalist Church of Jesus Christ of Latter Day Saints. The only times he used the term Fundamentalists as a designation to the Polygamists, it is either the "Fundamentalist Arm of the Latter-Day Saints (vol. 3:1092)" or the "Fundamentalist Division of The Church of Jesus Christ of Latter-day Saints." These terms are used as though the Polygamists were an appendage to The Church of Jesus Christ of Latter-day Saints; he certainly never claimed to be "THE" Church.

Note 5: See L. S. Johnson Sermons, vol. 2, pp. 427, 469, 470 and 471.

Note 6: The following is taken from Joseph Musser's Journal, dated May 27, 1935.
"Held meeting with Bros. Barlow and Kelsch this morning advising on matters South (Short Creek) and called special Priesthood meeting for this evening at 7:30. At meeting there were present Elders John Y. Barlow, Edwin and Burt Barlow, J.W. Musser, Louis A. Kelsch, James Athay, Buss and Art Halliday, Roy Pace, Morris Kunz, (Doc) Lindsay, Rich (Richard Jessop) and Moroni Jessop, Guy Musser, Harold Allred, George Woodruff, James Martin, Worth Kilgrow, Arnold Boss and Royal Madsen. The Spirit of the Lord was strongly manifested throughout the meeting. At the close of the meeting my son Guy came and confessed that my testimony was true and he was with me. We embraced and kissed and shed tears of gladness. I feel that at least one of my children is with me and through him others will become converted. I have placed all on the altar, withholding nothing; I want nothing but the Lord's will; nothing else is worth trying to possess. I rejoice in the truth and thank my God for the desire I have to serve

Him and fulfill every part of my earthly mission. Without His help I can only fail."

Guy had spent the last several years in California and had been on a mission for the LDS Church before that. Lorin Woolley had died in 1934, about one year before this conversion of Guy Musser. The many stories that Guy Musser would tell in the years to come (after he had been called into the Council) were only repeats of what his father had told him in regards to what Lorin Woolley taught.

Note 7: See L. S. Johnson Sermons, vol. 4, pp. 1370, 1504 and 1575.

On April 17, 1977: " I have been quite interested in President Musser's (Guy) sermon, and I want to say just a little about the men that he has spoken about. I was well acquainted with John Y. Barlow, worked with him for years; I knew Joseph Musser and Charles F. Zitting; and I shook hands once with John W. Woolley. Lorin Woolley, I don't remember ever meeting. I don't remember ever meeting Leslie Broadbent. But I did visit John W. Woolley in his home about a month before he passed away in 1928."

On June 3, 1978, he again confirms that he never met Lorin Woolley. "I was almost fifty years old before the Lord put His finger on me. He said He wanted me to get prepared for another work when He called me into the Apostleship. About four or five years before that, I visited Brother John W. Woolley who was then head of the Priesthood – God's chosen servant in the earth…. A few years later, a meeting was held at Brother Charley Owens' home. I heard Brother Zitting, Brother Kelsch, Brother Joseph Musser declare that John Y. Barlow held the keys of the Priesthood. I knew that Brother John W. Woolley had passed away, and that was all I had heard about it. I never saw Lorin Woolley. I never had the privilege of seeing Leslie Broadbent. Until that time, I had never met John Y. Barlow."

Note 8: In his sermons, Leroy would back up what Richard Jessop would say about the lineage of Priesthood. The following is taken from these sermons.

L. S. Johnson Sermons, vol. 3, p. 1039.

On April 13, 1975: "I have been really interested today in the remarks that have been made, especially about the calling of the Priesthood. couldn't help but reflect upon the fact that the Lord is mindful of His people. We don't need to worry about who the Lord calls to preside and to guide and direct His work here in the earth. We had a real fine rundown by President Jessop on the order of Priesthood. I couldn't help but reflect about those who are guiding this work today – those who were called since I joined up with this order of things.

"The first time I heard Brother Barlow talk, the Lord bore testimony to me that he was what he professed to be, or what his colleagues or council bore testimony that he was. The Lord told me that he was His servant, and if I did what he told me to do, I would gain my salvation. This, I believe yet. At that time, we had a completely different body of men leading us.

"These men were called and set apart by Lorin Woolley. Today, we have a governing body that was called and set apart by President Barlow, since I met up with this work. We don't need to worry about who is leading or whether the Lord is directing the work or not. I want to bear testimony to you that I am greatly pleased with and I greatly support those who the Lord has placed around me – President Hammon, President Musser, President Jeffs, President Jessop, President Timpson. These men were called by

184

revelation of the Lord and placed here to support this work. It is our duty to uphold and sustain them in the calling that they have. I want you to know that I sustain them with all my heart, might, mind and strength."

For Leroy's statements on the Priesthood lineage see Sermons of L. S. Johnson, vol. 3, p. 1153 and vol. 4, p.1612.

Note 9: On September 5, 1965, while speaking to a group of students at the Colorado City Academy, Richard Jessop said: "I have a burning testimony of the divine position to which these men who are sitting here behind me (The Priesthood Council) are called, and the succession of that office to which they are called, down through the last 40 years or more, which it has been my esteemed privilege, if you please, to be more or less in close personal contact with those men who have borne the keys of the eternal Priesthood. And through this office I have been given the appointment, about the time the Academy cleared its season's work, to furnish to the young people, particularly the young Academy students, a background and an understanding of the order of the Priesthood.... I want to say to you members of the Priesthood, you young men, going into the Academy, and going out of it, and all the rest of us, in the words of Joseph Leslie Broadbent, to a little group of people during that short duration of his presidency – the senior position in this order of Priesthood – that 'this body of men have got to learn to take direction and they'll take that direction from the Priesthood, or they'll take it from the Prince of Darkness'. That's where you stand today, my dear brethren. Every man under the sound of my voice, from the oldest to the youngest, you'll take direction from the hand of the Priesthood or you'll take it from the Prince of Darkness. Whether that Priesthood consists of any of these men or all of them or anybody else does not matter. You'll take your direction from the hands of the Priesthood or the adversary will direct you, whether you like it or not."

On March 12, 1978, in a Priesthood Meeting held at Colorado City, Richard Jessop talked on the perpetuation of priesthood from Joseph Smith to the present time. He named the men who were the Presidents as follows: Joseph Smith, Brigham Young, John Taylor, Wilford Woodruff, John Woolley, Lorin Woolley, Leslie Broadbent, John Barlow, Joseph Musser, Charles Zitting, and Leroy Johnson. At the time of this sermon (just a few months before he died) Jessop was beginning to suffer the pain of senility. When he was talking this morning he keep repeating himself, going over these names, in the above order. He must have named them at least ten times. There were some in the audience who were feeling sorry for him, supposing that in his senile state he did not realize that he was repeating himself. He surprised them by pausing after he named these men one more time and said: "I don't know why the Lord is having me repeat this line of Priesthood authority over and over, but I want you young men to hear what I'm saying and never forget it (from the journal of Ben Bistline)."

The evidence here is that Jessop realized what the Barlows were up to and was doing what he could to hinder them. Up until this time, Leroy Johnson had never publicly proclaimed his belief in the One Man Doctrine. Jessop had either never heard him say anything in its support, or else he was not in agreement with him on the matter. When confronting Fred Jessop and some of Richard Jessop's sons on the matter in the 1980s, their answer was: "Uncle Rich never really understood Priesthood."

Note 10: In the 1950s Guy Musser, who had taken over the publishing of the *Truth* Magazine, put together a collection of ten photographs depicting the Presidents of Priesthood according to the Polygamist's teachings. They were as follows: Joseph Smith, Brigham Young, John Taylor, Wilford Woodruff, John Woolley, Lorin Woolley, Leslie Broadbent, Joseph Musser, and Charles Zitting. All devout Polygamists purchased a set of these photographs and proudly displayed them on their living room walls.

By the end of the 1970s any of the Polygamists who were accepting the Barlows' One Man Doctrine, had removed from their display photographs the pictures of: Wilford Woodruff, Leslie Broadbent, Joseph Musser and Charles Zitting, posthumously striping these men of their Priesthood Authority.

Note 11: In 1880, Wilford Woodruff received a revelation while staying at a sheep camp near Sunset, Arizona Territory. The Barlows claim that since he was not the President of Priesthood at this time (John Taylor was the President), the revelation was from Satan. They must discredit this revelation because it destroys all support of the One Man Doctrine. The part of the revelation they don't like states:

"And while my servant John Taylor is your President, I wish to ask the rest of my servants of the Apostles the question, although you have one to preside over your Quorum, which is the order of God in all generations, do you not, all of you, hold the apostleship, which is the highest authority ever given to men on earth? You do. Therefore you hold in common the Keys of the Kingdom of God in all the world.

"You each of you have the power to unlock the veil of eternity and hold converse with God the Father, and His Son Jesus Christ and to have the ministrations of angels.

"It is your right, privilege and duty to inquire of the Lord as to His mind and will concerning yourselves and the inhabitants of Zion and their interests.

"And whenever any one of you receives the word of the Lord, let it be written and presented in your councils and whatever by united consent you deem wisdom to be presented by the President, my servant John Taylor, as the word of the Lord. In this way you will uphold him and strengthen his hands, as all the burden should not lie upon one man.

"For thus saith the Lord, all mine Apostles should be full of the Holy Ghost, of inspiration and revelation to know the mind and will of God and be prepared for that which is to come. Therefore let mine Apostles keep my commandments and obey my voice and the gates of hell shall not prevail against you.

"Fear not, for lo, I am with you until I come, and I come quickly. Even so, Amen (*Truth*, vol. 14:141)."

This revelation was accepted as the "word of the Lord" by John Taylor and the Quorum of the Twelve in April, 1880 (see *Improvement Era*, vol 1:874).

Note 12: See L. S. Johnson Sermons, vol. 7:203.

Note 13: The author was in the Sugar Loaf Cafe on the occasion referred to here and heard Leroy make the statement.

Note 14: This list of names was incorporated into an Affidavit of Disclosure. It was signed by all the Trustees of the United Effort Plan, their signatures being notarized by William

Shapley. The document, filed in the Mohave County Court House at Kingman, AZ in book 335 p. 818, is as follows:

AFFIDAVIT OF DISCLOSURE

Rulon Jeffs, Leroy S. Johnson, Guy Musser, Richard S. Jessop, Alma Timpson and J. Marion Hammon, each being first duly sworn, deposes and states as follows:

1) That pursuant to the provisions of Section 33-401 Arizona Revised Statutes, as amended, this affidavit is being executed and recorded in Mohave County, Arizona.

2) That each of the affiants is one of the Trustees of the United Effort Plan, A common law trust, as amended, which is established by a declaration of trust recorded in book 31 of Miscellaneous Records, at pages 597 through 600, Records of Mohave County, Arizona, and which is amended by certificate of amendments to the declaration of trust of the United Effort Plan, which is in book 33 of Miscellaneous Record, pages 150 through 151, Records of Mohave County, Arizona.

3) That the Trustees of the aforementioned trust hold title to the real property particularly described on Exhibit "A", attached hereto and by this reference made a part hereof.

4) That as of June 22, 1976, and as of the date that this affidavit is executed, the beneficiaries of the trust and their addresses are as set forth in Exhibit "B" attached hereto and by this reference made a part hereof.

5) This affidavit is made for the purpose of complying with the above referenced Arizona Revised Statute and for no other purpose.

Exhibit "B" is as follows:

(Names of the beneficiaries of the United Effort Plan, a Common Law Trust. Addresses in the document have been omitted here.) Richard J. Allred, Alma R. Barlow, Alvin S. Barlow, Arden M. Barlow, Authur L. Barlow, Daniel Barlow Jr., Dell J. Barlow, Donald N. Barlow, James L. Barlow, Joseph I. Barlow, Joseph I. Barlow Jr. Louis J. Barlow, Louis J. Barlow Jr., Millward Barlow, Nephi R. Barlow, Orval Fred Barlow, Samuel S. Barlow, Truman I. Barlow, Connel Bateman, David R. Bateman, Deloy Bateman, Jesse Beagley, Andrew P. Bistline, Benjamin G. Bistline, Francis Lee Bistline, Floyd Black, Francis I. Black, Isaac A. Black, Leonard Black, Martin Black, Orlin Black, Orson Black, Spencer L. Black, Vernon Black, Arthur Blackmore, Cyril Bradshaw, Constance Bradshaw (widow), Fawn Broadbent (widow), Viola Broadbent (widow), Alma Burnham, Mark Burnham, Claude T. Cawley, Helen Chatwin (widow), David Cook, John Cook, Charles Cooke, Donavan Cooke, Drue Cooke, Jack W. Cooke, Jack W. Cooke Jr., James Cooke, Joseph B. Cooke, Lynn Cooke, Rachel B. Cooke (widow), Richard Cooke, Donald B. Cox, Celesta Darger (widow), Lee Darger, Ronald Darger, Boyd Dockstader, David Dockstader, Harvey Dockstader, Leah Dockstader (widow), Bygnal Dutson, Hilda Dutson (widow), Marko Dutson, Erwin Fischer, Lorin Fischer, Mary Fischer (widow), P.O. Box 37, Richard Fischer, Vaughn Fischer, George Hammon, Heber Hammon, Jedd Hammon, J. Marion Hammon, Lloyd Hammon, Merril Harker, Parley Harker, Adaire Holm (widow), Berkley Holm, Con Holm, Edson Holm, Paul Holm, Rachel Holm (widow), Richard Holm, Terry Holm, Rulon T. Jeffs, Albert M. Jessop, Carlos S. Jessop, Dan C. Jessop, Dan M. Jessop, Dennis Jessop, Dwayne N. Jessop,

Edson P. Jessop, Frank R. Jessop, Fred M. Jessop, George M. Jessop, Glade R. Jessop, Jerry C. Jessop, John R. Jessop, Joseph L. Jessop, Joseph C. Jessop, Joseph S. Jessop,, Paul M. Jessop, Martin Hyrum Jessop, Merlin S. Jessop, F. Merril Jessop, Oscar K. Jessop, Ray L. Jessop, Richard S. Jessop, Sterling K. Jessop, Thomas S. Jessop, Val Jessop, Vergel Jessop, Charles Johnson, Eva Johnson (widow), Joseph Johnson, John B. Johnson, Christopher Kim Johnson, Lamar Johnson, Larry E. Johnson, LaVar Johnson, Leroy S. Johnson, Orval L. Johnson, Ralph Johnson, Ruth Johnson (widow), Rayo Spencer Johnson, Terrill C. Johnson, Warren E. Johnson, Charles B. Knudson, Jack Knudson, Robert Knudson, Edwin Lane, Clyde Mackert, Seth Mackert, William Howard Meldrum, Guy H. Musser, Frank Naylor, Laird P. Naylor, Calvin Neilson, Neil Nyborg, Harold Peine, James M. Pipkin, Leo Pledger, Barlow Quinton, Donald Richter, Melbourne O. Richter, Boyd Roundy, Samuel W. Roundy, William Roundy, William W. Shapley, Carling Steed, Gerald Steed, Lawrence Steed, Newel Steed, Walter Steed, John Stewart, David Stubbs, Lawrence Stubbs, Mayo Stubbs, Alma Thomas, Kenneth Thomas, Alma A. Timpson, John Timpson, Ray Timpson, Coy C. White, Richard White, Jerold R. Williams, Joel Williams, John Williams, Robert Williams, Rodger Williams, Thomas Williams, Clayne Wayman, Samuel Wilson, Elberta Wyler, Marvin Wyler, Dena Young (widow), James Zitting, Joseph Zitting, Lorin Zitting, Steven B. Barlow.

This document not only establishes who the trustees of the United Effort Plan were in 1976, but also names of the beneficiaries of the United Effort Plan as recognized by these trustees, in 1976. It was the teachings of the Priesthood Council that all members of the Priesthood Council were trustees of the United Effort Plan. This was acknowledged by every member of the Council in their public sermons from time to time and was commonly accepted by all members of the UEP to be fact. Although formal Board Meetings of the trustees of the UEP were seldom ever held, the business of the United Effort Plan was conducted in the regular monthly council meetings of the Priesthood Council and decisions concerning the UEP were made at these meetings.

Note 15: Leroy's reference here to "Korihor of old" no doubt was to intimidate Timpson. Korihor was a character in the Book of Mormon who asked for a sign from Alma (religious leader) and was struck dumb because he did not believe what was told him by this Alma (Book of Mormon, Alma 30: 43-50).

The implication is that if Timpson did not accept Leroy's doctrine on the 1880 Revelation, he too would be struck dumb.

Note 16: The following is from the journal of Ben Bistline: May 12, 1979.

"Tonight at Big Boys church (Jr. School of The Prophets) Rulon Jeffs got up to talk to us about the 1880 Revelation. He would not look us in the face, kept fumbling around with papers in his hands. He acted like he was embarrassed about something. He told us that the 1880 revelation is from the lower regions. This is a surprise to me that he is making this statement. I don't see what is wrong with the revelation, but Rulon was not comfortable with telling us what he did; I know he does not believe what he is saying and is lying; but why?"

The School of The Prophets was discontinued about this time.

Evicting the Faithful

Soon after the Colorado City Academy opened in the 1960s, the Mohave County Community College established a branch at Colorado City. Cyril Bradshaw, the principal of the Academy (high school), was chosen as the administrator for the College in Colorado City. The Community College, using the teachers in the local schools as instructors, offered much needed classes for the residents of the area. It provided a service for these residents to enroll in classes that most of them could never have obtained any other way. The courses most beneficial have been in the fields of education (school teachers) and nurse's training. The College did offer other classes in varied fields. One was a drama class taught by a young lady who had majored in that field and recently had moved to Colorado City to teach in the elementary school.

The young lady was an excellent teacher, but her ideas and training were markedly different than those of Fred Jessop, whose ideas were along very conservative lines. Fred had been used to having things his own way for twenty years or more and did not appreciate a young upstart (not only a female but one who was under the direction of the Academy) changing the status quo. She was ignorant of this situation, however, and threw herself into her work with the enthusiasm of youth.

The first play of any consequence put on at the Academy was not produced by the Community College, but rather by the Academy itself. This was the production of "Harvey." It was cast in the Round and without using any props, a very innovating thing for the Polygamists to do. The play was an unqualified success and was the first of many more productions (along with the Harvest Balls) to come, either sponsored by the Academy or the Community College, which became a real aggravation in the mind of Fred Jessop. In 1972, another play "Naughty Marietta" was produced that was not condoned by Fred Jessop. The rest of the Community enjoyed it very much and the last night it was presented, it received a standing ovation. Fred was very disgruntled over its reception by the community and left the building grumbling how such programs should not be allowed among the Saints.

Marion Hammon, who was the administrator of the Academy, had a little more tolerance for the innovating ideas of those producing these programs and several more of them were presented to the community, much to the joy of the people.

In the fall of 1977 Fred's Town Fair was probably the biggest and best that was produced up to that time. Fred had delegated other people to set up booths and provide something that could be sold to the people (he would receive all the money collected). Food, crafts and recreational programs were presented, where for a small fee ($1.00) people could sit and be entertained for a few minutes. One of these delegates, Howard Meldrum, asked Don Cox, a man gifted with musical talent, if he would take the responsibility of putting on one of these shows. Don agreed to help Howard and gathered together a very talented group of performers to assist him in the project. The theme of the music presented was Country and Western, with guitars and all. Now Fred Jessop does not like guitars, and he doesn't like Country and Western music, so Don would have trouble from the start. With the people of the community though, it was a different matter and this little sideshow was by far the most popular attraction of any others in the Fair. The Fair ran for three days. Don Cox's little string band and singing group were given one of the school auditoriums to perform in. The seats would all fill up for every performance, with people standing in the doorway and the hall to listen. Fred was very annoyed and he sent Howard in to turn the volume down. When the volume was turned down the people in the back of the room could not hear the music. When they complained, Don just turned it back up. Well, Fred would send Howard back in to turn it down again; Don would just turn it up again. Poor Howard was caught in the middle; he gingerly approached Don and explained to him the dilemma he was in. Don told Howard that if Fred didn't like the music he could tell them to go home, because he was not going to turn the volume down so low that the people could not hear it. If Fred wanted him to, he would give him his own personal concert after the Fair was over, but if he wanted him to play for the people he was going to do it so they could enjoy it. Howard reported to Fred and Fred left Don alone after that; however, due to his "rebellious attitude" Don was never asked to perform in any of Fred's Fairs again.

Later in this same year the Community College sponsored a Christmas program, which was a very big success among the recreation starved polygamists. It was called "Holiday Special" and included a segment copied after the "Hee Haw" television show. Fred Jessop had two criticisms against this program. The first problem was that the Polygamists don't believe in celebrating Christmas. The second problem was the type of music that was presented by the cast; it was too worldly (the Hee Haw segment made a satirical jab at Fred himself, a real no-no).

In 1978 the Community College put on the play "The Mikado." In the story of this play, an emperor of Japan was worshiped by the people as God. His very word must be obeyed as if God himself spoke. The moral of the play was that the Emperor was only human and was subject to making mistakes. When the people learned this, then they were able to prosper, not being held back by superstitions. This production was well presented and was very much enjoyed by the people of the community. Again Fred had a problem with the play. In his mind there was too much insinuation (though not intended) implied as to Fred being this "Lord High Pu-Ba." There were those in the community that compared him with the Mikado all right, but those producing the play had no such motives. Fred still took offence and vowed that such insinuating parodies must forever cease. The academy must be closed down. In order to accomplish this, Marion Hammon must be discredited in the eyes of the community. This became an obsession with Fred Jessop and his nephews, the sons of John Y. Barlow, and steps were taken to achieve this goal.

Due to his sickness Leroy Johnson was no longer able to attend any of the religious meetings. The Barlows would bring stories to him about what the other Council members were teaching the people. These stories were never the truth but rather were tales to discredit them, the intent being to poison Leroy's mind against their credibility. They did not stop with only sowing these seeds of untruths in his mind but were also busy spreading their doctrine to any of the other people in the community who had the courtesy to listen (Note 1). Anyone who would not agree with them, choosing instead to defend Hammon and Timpson, were also brought into the line of fire. The Barlows would start stories against them, stories of sexual improprieties and other sordid tales that were meant to damage moral turpitude. This became a real problem throughout the community and in order to address the situation, Marion Hammon attempted to bring the perpetrators of these deeds to an accounting of some sort.

On April 23, 1978, Marion Hammon gave a sermon in a public meeting at Colorado City telling the Barlows: "You cannot try me without a hearing. You are going around telling the people (and President Johnson) that I am teaching things that I am *not* teaching. If you have an accusation against me, then there is a proper way to handle it; call a High Council meeting and present the evidence and let it be handled the proper way (Note 2)."

When the Barlows carried their report of this meeting to Leroy, they told him that Marion had said in Church today, "nobody can call him to an accounting but he could call Leroy to an accounting if he so chose." Such was their accuracy in reporting things to Leroy, who of course believed them.

When Leroy was confined to his sick bed due to the Shingles, it became necessary to give him narcotic pain killing drugs to ease his suffering. At the height of his suffering he was receiving a shot of Demerol every two hours. While under the effect of these hallucinating drugs he began seeing "visions" and receiving "revelations." These manifestations were along the lines of the end of the world and the destruction of all the wicked people, especially those members of the Polygamists who were opposing him and his doctrines. There were many bizarre stories coming from him as to what was going to transpire in the world. These ranged from natural catastrophes to the slaughtering of the "wicked" people living in the community. Many of the Polygamists, because of their traditions and superstitions believed these weird "Prophecies" and began living in a state of fear. All of these Prophecies will not be covered here, but there are some that have affected the course of events in relation to the history of the Polygamist community that do require telling.

Sometime in 1980 Leroy received one of these "revelations." It seems that the Lord came to him and told him he had two years to "clean up the town." He gave Sam Barlow the commission of doing the "clean up" (Note 3). Sam began looking for "wickedness" he could clean up. His first "victim" was a widow with eight young children. Her name will not be used here due to propriety, but her story must be touched on.

The young woman had been a second wife to a man of questionable morals. His first wife had died due to a brain tumor and soon after her death, the husband was convicted of child molestation of his own minor daughters and was sentenced to serve time in the Arizona State Prison. A short time after this, the surviving wife became a target of Sam's cleanup campaign. He judged her immoral, accusing her of being involved in sexual activities with men of the community. There was never any direct accusations made to her, nor was there any kind of proof that such was the truth; this did not matter. Sam simply told Leroy that she was doing these immoral things. Leroy never called her in to confront her with the accusations, but told Sam she would have to leave the community.

Sam Barlow had enlisted a group of zealous supporters to assist him in his "duties" of policing the Polygamists. These men were organized into a vigilante type group of law enforcers that were nothing more than a "Goon Squad" to harass the young people and any who they felt were not living their lives according to the standards of the Priesthood. These Goons were becoming very bold in going throughout the community and beating up on the young boys they felt were not worthy to live there, forcing them to leave town. It was this Goon Squad that Sam used to force the young "widow" from her home and the community.

The "widow," due to her hard straits of supporting her children, had accepted an offer of employment from a sympathetic friend in Salt Lake City. She temporally moved there to take advantage of the offer. When the time came for her children to start school for the year, she went to Leroy Johnson and asked his advice on what she should do about enrolling her children in school. He told her to enroll them in a school in Salt Lake City because she was working there. She would travel to Colorado City about once a month to check on her house and keep her ties with the community. She fully intended to move back there once she had earned enough money to pay for some improvements on her home.

On October 22, 1982, after returning to Salt Lake from Colorado City, where the day before she had attended meetings there and paid Leroy her tithing for the month, she received a telephone call from a friend telling her that men had broken into her house and were taking possession of it, moving her belongings out, etc. She immediately left for Colorado City.

Arriving at her home just after midnight, she found the lock on the front door had been changed. Entering through the back, she stumbled upon several men in sleeping bags on the floor of the front room, which had been stripped of her belongings. She began screaming at them to get out of her house.

The men scrambled from their bedrolls and began calling for "backup" assistance on hand held two-way radios. They began to harass her as to what she was doing there.

She said, "I live here and I want you guys to get out."

Nephi Barlow, a brother of the deputy sheriff Sam Barlow, ordered her out of the house, informing her it was no longer hers. He told her she couldn't take any of the furnishings, nor could she go in or out of the house without his permission.

It became a standoff. The "widow" refused to leave and the intruders said they were waiting for Sam Barlow to come before they would leave. She went outside, bringing her children in to put them to bed, and discovered another shock; their bedrooms had been stripped of the beds. She went into her own bedroom and, discovering that her bed was still there, took the baby and went to bed. The other children huddled around the fireplace where they spent the remainder of the night. At one point, Jerry Jessop asked why she just didn't go home? She replied, "I am home."

Sam Barlow never showed up at the home. He realized that it would be a civil rights violation if he were to openly take Leroy's side in the issue. He did, however, act as a go-between for the "widow" and Leroy. The next day he told her she was being evicted because she was behind in paying his brother, Truman Barlow, taxes he had levied against her house (he would never tell her the real reason why she was being kicked out of her home and the town).

She went to Marion Hammon, seeking advice and help. When she informed him of the tax issue, he gave her $3,000.00 (the amount Sam told her was owing) to give to Truman. She gave the money to Truman, which he took, but she was not allowed to have her house back.

Two weeks after she had been kicked out on the street (she was allowed by some kind friends to stay with them) Sam Barlow officially (through the mail) gave her an "eviction notice." It told her she was to remove all her personal belongings within two weeks time and was never to enter the premises again. With her "Prophet," Leroy, against her, she felt she had no choice but to comply. She did indeed leave the community, enduring much trials and hardships, making her way in the world on her own. One of Truman Barlow's recently married sons (he had no children) was "given" the large house (that had been built and paid for by her husband before he was sent to prison and was valued at $150,000.00) for him and his one wife to live in.

This "charitable" act was carried out under the authority of Leroy alone. He never conferred with any of the other UEP Trustees or the other members of the Priesthood Council. This action was not only a violation of the Trust Document, but of other covenants that had been made among the "Brethren."

This was only the beginning of the evictions that were to come to those whom Sam Barlow felt were not worthy to live in the community. After this successful eviction, Sam Barlow began "searching" for others whose "immorality" would make them suitable candidates for the same treatment. He was "lucky," for it seems that a man by the name of Leo Pledger had molested one of his daughters several years before. Sam somehow discovered that "this crime" had taken place and he set about to remove the "blot" from the society of the Saints.

In order to have Leo arrested and convicted, Sam would need an injured party as a complainant. The alleged victim of Leo's incestuous conduct, his daughter, had grown to maturity and moved to Salt Lake City some ten years earlier. This did not deter Sam. He went to Salt Lake and began harassing the girl to sign a complaint against her father. She did not want anything to do with the matter. Sam was persistent. He convinced the girl that in order to help her father, she needed to sign the complaint so as to allow Sam to arrest him and get him into treatment for his own sake, to help him overcome his "problems."

The daughter reluctantly signed Sam's complaint. The fact that Sam Barlow was acting completely outside of his jurisdiction by going to the girl in Salt Lake City without working through the local law enforcement agencies there, did not even cross his mind. He was doing it for the "good of the work" and any actions on his part would be justified, regardless of the legal questions.

Armed with the complaint, Sam went back to Colorado City. He contacted Leo, who was working in the Las Vegas area at the time and convinced him to meet him near the Nevada/Arizona border in the Kingman vicinity. When Leo met him in Nevada, Sam convinced him to be arrested and taken on into Kingman, the Mohave County Seat, to the jail there.

Sam never had any intention of doing anything to "help" Leo as he had alleged to his daughter when persuading her to sign the complaint. He succeeded in having the bail set so high that it was impossible for Leo's family to bail him out. When his wives (of which he had two) went to Leroy for advice and help, he simply told them that Leo would not be bailed out and must be sent to the state prison. This was a real shock to them. They had known all along of Leo's conduct with his daughter but had been willing to overlook it, forgive him, and were going on with their lives. Now their world was crashing down around them.

Leo was never bailed out. After about ten days in the county jail he was brought before the judge for a preliminary hearing. In about five minutes time the judge learned that the "crime" was over seven years old, which was the statute of limitations on the offence. He scolded Sam severely and dismissed the case against Leo. Leo and his family were ecstatic; but little did they know that their real problems had just began. Sam was furious. He was not going to allow Leo or anyone else to make a fool of him.

Sam had arrested Leo in January of 1983. In March of 1983, Steve Baily, a newly hired deputy of the Mohave County Sheriff's department, delivered a Notice to Vacate to Leo's family, giving them thirty days to move.

Leo had built a home on UEP property as had all the members of the Polygamists in Colorado City. His home was one of the more expensive of the community. He had spent several thousands of dollars on the material alone and had never dreamed that he could ever be forced to give it up and move from the community that he had spent most of his life helping to build up. This was such a shock to his family that one of his wives suffered a nervous breakdown and was hospitalized, where she prematurely gave birth to a child she was carrying. She would never completely recover from the trauma of this experience and died a few years later from a brain tumor. Leo plead with Leroy about his situation, hoping he would relent on his decision to have him evicted. Leroy showed no mercy, telling Leo that he would have to move out but if he would change his ways he *might* be allowed to move back into the community sometime in the future. With a broken heart, a wife and premature baby in the hospital, Leo prepared to move. On the thirteenth of March 1983, he moved his large family to Phoenix, where he began the struggle of surviving under the hardships that Sam Barlow and Leroy Johnson had so "charitably" forced upon him and his family.

In the 1970s Ervil LeBaron of Mexico began making threats against any of the Mormon Break Off Groups that would not acknowledge him as the rightful successor of Joseph Smith, granting him their full allegiance. These threats reached their peak with the assassination of Rulon Allred, the leader of the Polygamist Group set up by Joseph Musser in 1952. Because of these threats, a "Night Patrol" was organized at Colorado City to guard against any suspicious intruders into the community and was fully justified at this time.

However, by 1983 it had degenerated into something much different, becoming sinister in nature. It was used by Sam Barlow as his "Teenage Chastity Patrol." The members of this Patrol were picked by him. They were mostly zealous young men who were willing to allow themselves to be used in any manner that was asked of them by the Priesthood. There were guards set up at the roads leading into town where everyone entering could be screened. The "intruders" would then be followed by one of these Patrol vehicles. If just being followed would not intimidate them enough that they would drive out of town in the next few minutes, they would then be stopped and checked out by these self-appointed "policemen."

This action was reserved just for the out-of-towners until the 1980s, when it began to be used by Sam in his effort to "clean up the town." It changed from a "Night Patrol" of guarding the leaders against any assassination attempts, to a "Goon Squad" that primarily harassed the young boys of the community that would not "fall into line."

A particular contingent of this Goon Squad was made up by a group of men who had taken it upon themselves to "stamp out iniquity" among the Saints. This group was headed by a man named Jerry Jessop. Some of his followers were among the most "self-righteous" young men of the community and included such names as: Stanley Jessop, Nephi Barlow, J. L. Jessop, Joe Timpson and any others who they would call upon from time to time as more were needed for backup. (It was primarily this group who were used by Sam in his eviction of the "widow" from her home in October of 1982).

This group of "Jerry-Joe-Harryites" became a fear and a scourge among the boys of the community. Without warning, they would gang up on any who they judged was "out of line," fiercely beating them up. The "offences" of the boys were such things as wearing long hair, talking to a girl on the street or just not "supporting" the Priesthood. The "Jerry-Joe-Harryites" became so bold as to storm into the homes of the boys (without invitation) in the middle of the night, pulling the boys from their beds and beating them up in front of their parents, who, in most cases were helpless to stop them (Note 4).

After the beating, some of these boys would be given warnings to leave the community with the threat that they would receive more of the same if they failed to do so. Along with the beatings, Jerry Jessop and his henchman began such dirty little tricks as slicing the tires on the cars and All Terrain Vehicles of any who they felt should be harassed out of town. This was not limited to only the young boys of the community, but was being carried out against adults who were judged as "apostates" by Sam and his Gestapo.

There were a few men (about five) in the community who decided to do something to oppose these atrocities being carried out in the name of Leroy Johnson. These were men who had come to the realization that Leroy's Priesthood Work was only a cult and the sooner the people could be brought to understand this, the sooner they would be free from the domination of such men as Sam Barlow.

In an effort to put a stop to the beatings of his "victims" they contacted the Mohave County Sheriff's Department at Kingman, asking for a representative of the Sheriff to meet with them to hear their complaints. Ironically, this request was made through Sam Barlow. In a confrontation with one of the five men (Ben Bistline), wherein he accused Sam Barlow (to his face) that he was running a

Gestapo, Sam, in righteous indignation, offered to set up an appointment with one of his superiors in the Sheriff's department.

On the morning of March 8, 1983, Sam called Ben Bistline and another one of the "five" men and said that a lieutenant from the sheriff's office was in his office and if they so desired, they could come over and talk with him. The two men went over to the office, where Sam, after making the introductions, excused himself, left the office secure in his mind that these men would feel too intimidated to reveal anything that would cause him loss of credibility. He was partially right. The second man he had called over was very nervous and after a few minutes of talking with the lieutenant, excused himself, saying he had something he needed to do and left. The other man (Ben Bistline) was not intimidated and proceeded to relate to Lieutenant Crouse some of the problems the polygamists were facing due to the policies of Sam Barlow. At first Lieutenant Crouse seemed uninterested in the problems, passing it off as only a personality clash between Ben and Sam, who had grown up together in the community since childhood.

When the beatings by the "Jerry-Joe-Harryites" were related to him, however, he began to take interest. After asking a few questions, he became somewhat animated, saying, "If such beatings are going on, then we will get them stopped." The beatings were indeed stopped.

Sam Barlow definitely had known that these beatings were going on, but when confronted by Lieutenant Crouse in the matter, he denied that he knew anything about them. Lieutenant Crouse pretty well rung him out on the issue, telling him that if they were not stopped there would be some intervention from Kingman on the matter.

Sam Barlow, right in character, blamed the whole matter on Jerry Jessop. He went to Leroy, explaining that he, Sam, had known nothing about the matter, putting the whole blame on Jerry, telling him about how the Sheriff's Office was going to get involved if the beatings were not stopped. This caused a panic for Leroy; if there was anything he didn't want, it was to have outside law enforcement elements in the community. He summoned Jerry to see him. He pretty well lowered the boom on the poor unsuspecting man. Jerry had supposed he was doing things that Leroy would be proud of him for doing. It was a real blow to be so reprimanded. He sorrowfully submitted to Leroy's rebuke, promising to do better. It was then Sam's turn to set Jerry straight. He picked him up one day, took him to St. George where he "treated" him to a steak dinner (at the expense of the UEP). He spent the time explaining to him that he had caused an embarrassing problem for the Priesthood and he, Sam, was not going to put up with any more of this kind of conduct. He told him that if Uncle Roy had told him to go around beating up on the boys, that he, Sam, would support him in it, but he didn't believe that Uncle Roy had given him that directive. This was after Leroy had told Jerry to stop the beatings, but Sam would later take the credit for getting them stopped.

About a month later Sam Barlow had an occasion to tell Ben Bistline about "clipping Jerry's wings." The following is from the journal of Ben Bistline: April 20, 1983:

"I have spent the last three weeks working in Idaho (grading roads).

"I talked with Sam in his office on Monday (18th). He told me about Jerry Jessop beating up on Robert Jessop. Told me he clipped Jerry's wings, said also that U. Roy clipped Jerry's wings. He also told me that he told Jerry that if U. Roy has told him to beat up on the kids in this town, that he, Sam, would support him in doing it, but he didn't believe U. Roy has told him to do it. He said that when he talked with U. Roy, that he said he had not sent Jerry to do it."

Sam's next victim to be evicted was Andrew Bistline. This is the same man that had spent so much of his younger life in dedication to the "up-building of the Kingdom." Andrew had spent 20 years working on projects for the "Priesthood Work" for which he had received little or no wages and very little thanks. He was the one who had renovated the sawmill to cut the lumber for the Academy building and many other buildings in the community. Also, he had spent many hours working for Merril Jessop to get the door mill working.

By 1983 Andrew was becoming disillusioned with how things were being conducted by the Priesthood leaders. He was dissatisfied with the inequity and partiality meted out by the leaders. He began studying the scriptures and came to the conclusion that their claims of authority and their changes in doctrine were a contradiction to what his conscience told him was correct. For these reasons he decided it was time to move from the polygamist community. He purchased a house (which was in very poor condition) in Fredonia, a neighboring community and began the task of renovating it so he could move his family of wife and ten children into it. He planned to take a year to make the necessary remodeling changes before the house would be suitable for habitation. In the meantime he had become subject to the enticements and comfort found in the drinking of alcohol. He spent much of his leisure time drinking with friends who had also become somewhat in the same frame of mind that he was. It was on one of these occasions, when he faced a confrontation with Sam, that would result in his eviction from his home in Colorado City.

On the evening of February 21, 1982, Andrew and another man were returning home from one of these drinking parties. They had been at the home of Mayo Stubbs, who had also become disillusioned with the actions of the Brethren. Due to their drinking, they were considerably intoxicated; however, the car was being driven by Mayo's Daughter, who due to her inexperience had slid off the road and become stuck in the snow. J. L. Jessop and his stepbrother, Stanley Jessop came up to where they were stuck, but when asked to help, they refused, only driving back and forth and harassing them, making sarcastic remarks, etc.

When Andrew got home he contacted Sam Barlow (Deputy Sheriff) and began complaining about the boys' harassment. Sam Barlow drove up by Andrew's house and stopped someone else for speeding. Andrew then went up to where he was, and asked him to do something about J. L. and Stanley's harassing him, which Sam refused to do. Andrew then called Sam "a chicken shit son-of-a-bitch," which only resulted in Sam giving Andrew a ticket, saying that nobody was going to get away with "insulting my mother." Andrew paid a $250.00 fine while nothing was ever done to J. L. and Stanley for their role in the incident. The fine levied against Andrew was not satisfactory punishment to please Sam. He decided that in order to properly discipline Andrew, he must have him banished from the community, thus fulfilling Leroy's directive to him of "cleaning up the town." He set about to find the excuse that would justify such action. He had to wait a little over a year for the opportunity to achieve his goal, but on the 24th of July 1983, he obtained the "evidence" he would need for this justification.

That year, 1983, Fred Jessop staged a "Pioneer" celebration at the Hildale Community Park in Maxwell Canyon. At this celebration a lady found an audio cassette tape lying in the parking lot at the park. She turned it over to Sam to "investigate" it for any possible information that would assist him in his "work" of eradicating the community of evil. The finding of this tape was an important discovery for Sam. It contained recordings of a camp-out party where some of Andrew's boys were present. There were some things said by his boys that were not very complimentary to Uncle Roy and even Sam himself was maligned in their recorded conversations.

After spending about two weeks "analyzing" the tape, which included "calling in" the brothers of Andrew (and several other people of the community) to listen to it, he went to Leroy to report his findings and interpretation of "what the tape really said." In his analysis of what the boys were saying, he put his own interpretation on things they said, such as: "cedar berries" to mean "marijuana," and "cactus" to mean hard drugs such as cocaine. With such imaginary evidence, he convinced Leroy that the boys were not only involved in using narcotic drugs, but also in the distribution of them. Since he had no real evidence that his accusation was fact, he could not arrest them. The only solution of ridding the town of the evil was to have their father, Andrew, evicted from his home. Leroy was convinced that Sam's solution was the way to settle the problem. He gave Sam the "go-ahead."

Sam Barlow contacted Steve Baily, the new Deputy of the Arizona Strip area, telling Baily to meet him in Kingman. There they went into the Sheriff's office where Sam presented a document to the clerk to be officially stamped by the sheriff's department. He then paid her $50.00 and gave the document to Steve Baily, telling him to serve it on Andrew Bistline in Colorado City.

Andrew Bistline was working at uranium mine on the Arizona Strip about fifty miles south of Colorado City. He would stay the week at the mine, only coming home on weekends, when he would go to Fredonia to do the renovation work on the home there he had purchased. On August 10, 1983, while he was at the mine Steve Baily, Mohave County Deputy Sheriff, served the "eviction notice" on his wife, Irene (Note 5).

Andrew and his family were able to move by the thirty day deadline albeit under severe hardship and circumstances. He moved into the house at Fredonia before it was completed, having plastic covering the windows, only a light grade of felt tar paper on the roof, and no electricity. The only conveniences were a water faucet in the front yard and an outhouse out back. Consider this "charitable" edict of the United Effort Plan in his behalf: driving him from a comfortable home that he himself had built with material he paid for, furnished with all of the modern conveniences that the home in Fredonia lacked, forcing such hardship upon not only him, but upon the tender heart of his wife and family. What "sin" had she committed to be so punished?

It should be noted here that these evictions were being authorized by *only two* of the four living UEP Trustees, Leroy Johnson and Rulon Jeffs. The other Trustees, Marion Hammon and Alma Timpson, were never informed by Johnson and Jeffs as to just what was going on. Because there were four Trustees and these were split as to what the UEP policy was, Johnson and Jeffs felt they could make whatever decisions they wanted to without consulting either Hammon or Timpson. This situation had only recently come about. A fifth Trustee, Guy Musser, had died on July 11, 1983, at Salt Lake City. He was on the same side of the issues as were Hammon and Timpson. He was senior to Jeffs in the pecking order of the Priesthood Council, and therefore took charge of all the Group Meetings in Salt Lake City. His feelings of animosity toward Jeffs were so fierce that even though these meetings were held in Rulon Jeffs' home, Guy Musser would never allow him to speak to the congregation. With Guy Musser's death, the Barlows felt bold enough to press their conspiracy because "the numbers were now two against two" in the Priesthood Council (Note 6).

There is evidence that soon after Andrew Bistline's eviction, Leroy was warned by his attorney that he was putting himself in legal jeopardy by evicting recognized beneficiaries (Note 7). Since Andrew Bistline was listed on an "Affidavit of Discloser," filed in the Mohave County Court House in Kingman, Arizona, in October of 1976 by the Trustees of the united Effort Plan, there was no question as to whether or not he was a beneficiary. Because of this warning, Leroy met with Fred Jessop and the Barlow Boys to discuss what they should do in regards to evicting beneficiaries.

It was concluded that a new list be drawn up, removing any and all of those members of the United Effort Plan who they felt might "need to be evicted" and filing it in the Court House to replace the list filed in 1976. This new list was filed in Kingman in November of 1983. One hundred and fifteen of the beneficiaries on the 1976 list were removed, while eighteen new names were added. Of the 16 new names added, six were Barlows, all sons of the sons of John Y. Barlow. Two of the names added were sons of a daughter of John Y. Barlow. Three of the names removed were of people who had been evicted. Fifteen of the names removed were of deceased members. And ten of the names removed were of women (widows). *The new list contained no names of women.*

This action of Leroy Johnson, Fred Jessop, and the Barlow Boys was conducted in total secret in so far as any of the beneficiaries were concerned. It was almost a year later before it was discovered.

Those who discovered it mailed an open letter to all of the disenfranchised members. The letter follows:

Colorado City, Arizona 86021
No man escapes when Freedom fails.
The Best Men rot in filthy jails.
And those who cried "Appease! Appease!"
Are hanged by those they tried to please.
Open Letter to the Former Beneficiaries of the United Effort Plan
Brethren (and Sisters?):

Many of us were invited into the community to help build this community and consecrated our time and talents toward that end, supposing that our efforts would be beneficial in helping establish the Kingdom of God. All that we brought with us was invested in the "United Effort," by improving the lot that was assigned to us, by furnishing materials and labor in the various public works projects that the Priesthood sponsored, etc.

Many of us consecrated lands and other valuable considerations to this same cause, fully considering that our consecration (which was expected by the trustees of the United Effort Plan) would resound to our good.

In 1976 a document was prepared and signed by six men, Rulon Jeffs, Leroy Johnson, Guy Musser, Richard Jessop, Alma Timpson, and J. Marion Hammon, all stating under oath that each and all of them were trustees of the United Effort Plan. Exhibit B of this Affidavit of Disclosure lists the Beneficiaries of the trust (as per paragraph 4). This was sworn to be true and signed by the above six men before William W. Shapley, Notary Public, on October 16, 1976. These designated beneficiaries appear in the left column of the included list.

An Amended Affidavit of Disclosure was prepared to set aside the original Affidavit. This document was signed before the same Notary Public, William W. Shapley, on November 12, 1983, by Leroy S. Johnson and Rulon Jeffs (without the knowledge and consent of the other trustees acknowledged under oath). This amended document also amends the list of beneficiaries. The right column on the list denotes these "updated" beneficiaries. Please note that over 115 of the original beneficiaries have been deleted from the original list, and some others added. To which camp have you been assigned?

UNITED EFFORT PLAN
BENEFICIARY LISTS
ORIGINAL - October 16, 1976
AMENDED - November 12, 1983

Original	Amended
Richard J. Allred	Richard J. Allred
Alma R. Barlow	Alma R. Barlow
Alvin S. Barlow	Alvin S. Barlow
Arden M. Barlow	.Arden M. Barlow
Arthur L. Barlow	Arthur L. Barlow
Daniel Barlow	Daniel Barlow
Daniel Barlow Jr.	
Dell J. Barlow	
Donald N. Barlow	
James L. Barlow	James L. Barlow
	Jacob L. Barlow
Joseph I. Barlow	Joseph I. Barlow
Joseph I. Barlow Jr.	Joseph I. BarlowJr.
	Jethro Barlow
	Kevin Barlow
Louis J. Barlow	Louis J. Barlow
Louis J. Barlow Jr	
	Moroni Barlow
Millward Barlow	
Nephi Barlow	Nephi Barlow
Orval Fred Barlow	Orval Fred Barlow
	Roland Barlow
Samuel S. Barlow	Samuel S. Barlow
	Samuel Y. Barlow
Steven B. Barlow	
Truman I. Barlow	Truman I. Barlow
Connel Bateman	
David R. Bateman	
Deloy Bateman	
Jesse Beagley	

Andrew P. Bistline (evicted)
Benjamin Bistline
Francis Lee Bistline   Francis Lee Bistline
Floyed Black
Francis I. Black
Isaac A. Black
Leonard Black (deceased)
Martin L. Black   Martin L. Black
Orlin Black
Orson W. Black   Orson W. Black
Spencer L. Black   Spencer L. Black
Vernon Black
Arthur R. Blackmore   Arthur R. Blackmore
Cyril Bradshaw
Constance Bradshaw (widow-deceased)

                                              David J. Broadbent

Fawn Broadbent (widow)
Alma Burnham
Mark Burnham
Claude T. Cawley
Helen Chatwin (widow)
David Cook
John Cook
Charles F. Cooke   Charles F. Cook
Donavan Cooke
Drue Cooke
Jack W. Cooke
Jack W. Cooke Jr.
James F. Cooke   James F. Cooke
Joseph B. Cooke
Lynn Cooke
Rachel B. Cooke (widow)
Richard Cooke
Donald B. Cox
Celeste Darger (widow)
Lee Darger (deceased)
Ronald Darger   Ronald Darger
Boyd Dockstader
David Dockstader
Harvey Dockstader
Leah Dockstader (widow)

Bygnal Dutson	Bygnal Dutson
Hilda Dutson (widow-deceased)	
Marko Dutson	
Erwin C. Fischer	Erwin C. Fischer
Lorin Fischer	Lorin Fischer
Mary Fischer (widow-deceased)	
Richard Fischer (wife evicted)	
Vaughn Fischer	Vaughn Fischer
George Hammon	
Heber Hammon	
Jedd Hammon	
J. Marion Hammon (UEP Trustee)	
Lloyd Hammon	
Merrill Harker	
Parley Harker	Parley Harker
Adaire Holm (widow)	
Berkley Holm	
Con Holm	
Edson Holm	Edson Holm
Paul Holm	
Rachel Holm (widow)	
Richard L. Holm	Richard L. Holm
Terry Holm	
Rulon T. Jeffs (UEP Trustee)	Rulon T. Jeffs
Albert M. Jessop	
	Arnold Jessop
Carlos Jessop	Carlos Jessop
Dan C. Jessop	Dan C. Jessop
Dan M. Jessop	
Dennis Jessop	Dennis Jessop
	Doran Jessop
Dowayne N. Jessop (deceased)	
Edson P. Jessop (deceased)	
	Edson Jessop Jr.
Frank R. Jessop	
Fred M. Jessop	Fred M. Jessop
George M. Jessop (deceased)	
Glade R. Jessop	Glade R. Jessop
Martin Hyrum Jessop	Martin Hyrum Jessop
	Jeffery P. Jessop
Jerry Jessop	Jerry Jessop

Frank Naylor
Laird P. Naylor
Calvin Nielson
Neil Nyborg
Harold Peine   Harold Peine
James M. Pipkin
Leo Pledger (evicted)
Barlow Quinton
Donald Richter   Donald Richter
Melbourne O. Richter (deceased)
Boyd Roundy
Samuel W. Roundy
William Roundy
William W. Shapley   William W. Shapley
Carling Steed   Carling Steed
Gerald Steed   Gerald Steed
Lawrence Steed   Lawrence Steed
Newel Steed   Newel Steed
Walter Steed   Walter Steed
John Stewart
David Stubbs
Lawrence Stubbs (deceased)
Mayo Stubbs
Alma Thomas
Kenneth Thomas
Alma A. Timpson (UEP Trustee)

                                              Dan Timpson
John Timpson
                                              Joseph Timpson

Ray Timpson
Coy C. White
Richard White
Jerold R. Williams
Joel Williams
John Williams
Robert Williams
Rodger Williams
Thomas Williams
Clayne Wayman
Samuel Wilson
Elberta Wyler (deceased)

Marvin Wyler
Dena Young (widow)
James Zitting   James Zitting
Joseph Zitting
Lorin Zitting
(end of open letter)

There was one more eviction by Sam Barlow in 1983. On or about December 1, 1983, Sam, without a search warrant, entered and searched the home of Dwight Nyborg looking for "evidence" against him.

Dwight was unmarried and living alone in a small two room house that he had built, paying for the material with his own money. He had served a two year mission for the UEP and was "given a building lot and a wife" in compensation for his faithfulness. The wife he was given did not choose to remain married to him and left the community a few days after the arranged marriage. Dwight remained, however, hoping to be able to receive another wife to replace the one that left. Sam Barlow decided Dwight was a "menace" to the community and began a witch hunt to find evidence to have him expelled. He found what he decided he needed while going through Dwight's personal property at his home. It was a body building magazine with pictures mostly of mens' bodies, but there was one picture that showed a woman's bare breast. This was all he needed.

Sam went to Leroy, telling him that Dwight was taking juveniles into his home and showing them lewd and pornographic material, showing him the Body Building magazine for proof. Leroy gave his permission to have Dwight evicted.

In Dwight's case there was no written eviction notice issued. Sam merely told him that "Uncle Roy wanted him to leave," which Dwight complied with, moving to Phoenix with a broken heart.

Along with these efforts to clean up the town by evicting the undesirables, the Barlows were busy at their work of poisoning the mind of Leroy Johnson against Hammon and Timpson. They were having so much success in their labors at this that it was causing much disunity in the Priesthood Council; in fact, it had pretty much broken it up. The Brethren no longer met in their Council Meetings. It was impossible for Hammon or Timpson to even meet with Leroy because the Barlow Boys would not allow anyone to meet with him unless one of them was there.

Due to his sickness, Leroy was not coming to public meetings and these meetings were still being conducted by Hammon and Timpson. Hammon, due to his heart condition, was suffering from ill health himself, so the meetings were mostly conducted by Timpson. He would try and tell the people in the meetings what was happening, that there was a certain group of men that were undercutting the Brethren and trying to break up the Priesthood Council.

In the late fall of 1983 Timpson was getting after the Barlows for wearing out Leroy. He accused them of pestering him so much that it was destroying his health. After haranguing them for some time, he said: "Keep your ungodly presence from Uncle Roy's midst." At this, Dan Barlow stood up and said: "That's a lie."

Such open defiance surprised Timpson. He stood speechless, staring at Dan. In an instant Truman Barlow stood up also, quietly staring at Timpson. Then almost everyone in the building stood up. In a few moments Timpson regained his composure, saying, "If that's the way you want it, then dismiss yourselves at home." He then walked out of the building.

The year 1983 ended on this note. The Barlows had broken up the Priesthood Council and Sam had successfully evicted four families from their homes and the community. They still had a long way to go before gaining control of the United Effort Plan, but they felt determined that this they could do. The next step toward reaching their goal would be to strip Marion Hammon of his "Priesthood" (Note 8). In order to do this they would need Leroy to come back to church and personally tell the people that Hammon and Timpson were out of line and that he was now going to take over and set things straight. Two months after the defiant "stand up" church experience, Leroy Johnson did indeed come back and stood in the pulpit to talk to the people.

On February 12, 1984, Leroy told the people that it had been six years since he had been able to talk to them, that he was not pleased with what the other Brethren had been teaching while he had been sick with the shingles. In this sermon, he says: "I was struck down in the early part of 1979. I had been called upon by some of my brethren to have the word of God changed in our Doctrine & Covenants, and this I objected to. Shortly after that, I was branded as a fallen prophet. I want to say a few words to these men who sit here on the stand today."

He turned to face J. Marion Hammon and Alma A. Timpson. "The Lord gave you men five and a half years to change your thinking on this principle of having one man holding the sealing powers in the earth at a time, and you have made a miserable mess of it by coming here and preaching over this pulpit that I was about to die because of my attitude towards the principle." Turning back to the audience he continued to speak.

"I know there are people here today who don't believe in me. They feel I have forfeited all my privileges to the Melchizedek Priesthood, (but) I am not afraid to speak. There is only one man at a time, and that is the way it has been throughout all the history of God's dealings with people, both in this world and the world before this one, and the world before that one. Only one man at a time holds the keys and power of the sealing power, and those who act during his administration are only acting under a delegated authority. That is what I told these men.

"I am coming back now. I am going to take my place, my position at the pulpit.... He (God) is going to come and visit this earth with great judgments. They have already started. He said 'In My house shall it begin.' It began with this council – six years ago this coming April. This Priesthood Council was broken up. Since then, we have suffered the death, first of Brother Richard Seth Jessop, and then Brother Guy H. Musser. So there are only four of us left. For about three and a half years, neither I nor Brother Rulon Jeffs were allowed to speak to the people. Why? Because I was stricken down and I couldn't speak, but I am speaking today. They (Hammon, Musser and Timpson) would not allow Brother Jeffs to speak because he sustained me.... From now on, there will be nobody in the Priesthood Council only those who sustain the words of the Prophet Joseph Smith. There is only one man at a time that holds the keys of the sealing power while he lives."

With this sermon, he dismissed Hammon and Timpson from the Priesthood Council and told them they could no longer sit on the stand and address the people. He said he could "no longer carry them on his back."

This was a sad day for many of the Polygamists, to see how their beloved "Uncle Roy" had been so badly deceived by a few men, including Fred Jessop and the Barlow Boys. They had supposed that God was at the helm and such a thing could never have happened. Hammon and Timpson were probably the most sad of all, to see their life's work go down the drain. To see the "Keys wrested from the Priesthood" was a sore trial for them, almost beyond bearing.

The Barlow Boys on the other hand were ecstatic. They were now in the position of power they had aspired to for so many years. They supposed that Hammon and Timpson would just humbly submit to this treatment by Leroy and offer no resistance to whatever was meted out to them. They were partially right. The defrocked leaders were not inclined to do anything more than just sit by and let things take their course.

But several of the people were not content to allow this to happen. They appealed to the men not to abandon those of the people who still wanted to be taught the truth of the Gospel, not some strange doctrine of worshiping a Man. In this they were successful and on May 13, 1984, the first Priesthood Meeting of what has come to be called the "Second Ward" was held at the home of Alma Timpson. This was the beginning of what has been referred to as the "Priesthood Split."

Note 1: Fred Jessop had built a Cafeteria he named: "The Early Bird Cafeteria" that was operated by one of his wives, Permellia, daughter of Leroy Johnson. This Cafeteria became the gathering place every morning for the coffee drinkers of the community, who, after making their show of appearance at their places of employment among the local business, such as the school, the service station, BARCO and any others of the Polygamist run enterprises, to gossip and "solve" any other of the world's great crises. It was at these "meetings" where Nephi Barlow, who was supposedly running the service station (J.&B. Service, a UEP owned enterprise) would spend hours "educating" any of the other patrons who would listen to him. These consisted mostly of the younger people of the community, and one of his favorite "doctrines" that he would attempt to impress on their minds was this: "The Gospel in a nutshell is Uncle Roy," explaining that whatever Uncle Roy said was the Gospel and could not be questioned. It was through his efforts of proselyting such damaging doctrines that would convince the members of the society that "Uncle Roy" had the power and authority to remove Marion Hammon and Alma Timpson from the "Priesthood Council."

Note 2: Taken from the journal of Ben Bistline. March…1978:

Bro. Hammon has made the statement in public meeting that the sentence in the 7th verse of sec. 132..D&C which says only one man has the authority, is a lie.

April 30, 1978:

Bro. Johnson has called Bro. Hammon on his statement about the 7th Verse in sec. 132..D&C (the part saying only one man has the keys) being a lie. Bro. Hammon gave a sermon last Sunday wherein he claimed "that no one can call a council and try him unless they hold the same priesthood he does. That means that he would have to be tried in the Priesthood Council; as an example, he could call a High Council and try Bro. Johnson."

Note 3: Taken from the journal of Ben Bistline. January 23, 1983:

Talked with Sam today. He told me he had put " L" in jail in Kingman. He also said U. Roy told him the Lord had given him two years to clean up this town (Short Creek). Sam also told me he was going to put men in jail who were in high places, meaning the Priesthood (Council), said he was going after one man that used drugs, I think he is talking about A.A. Timpson.

March 1, 1983:

Sam told me tonight that "L" was going to be asked to move. He told me that U. Roy has given him two years to clean up this town.

Note 4: The reason the parents of these boys were helpless to do anything about the actions of these vigilantes is a little complex and will be explained here.

To understand the power Sam and his "Goon Squad" had over the people of the community, several things must be explained. Any one of the factors involved might not seem like too much of a power grip, but when added up it then becomes clear how it worked.

The first control Sam had over the people was that the homes they had built were located on property that was titled in the name of the United Effort Plan, a Common Law Trust. Although all who had built these homes were listed beneficiaries of the Trust, some had been forced to abandon them and leave the community. This was becoming a real threat to some members of the community who were daring to stand up against the high-handed acts of Sam and his "Gestapo."

To take a stand against Sam was the same as taking a stand against Leroy Johnson, the Polygamist Prophet, who was fast coming into the position of having the power of a king. Sam had became his right-hand man in such matters and it was easy for Sam to get Leroy to endorse any decision he might make regarding what action should be taken. The Priesthood Council was fast approaching a split in their ranks and men of the group were choosing which side they were going to follow.

In order to stay in Leroy's good graces, any who were choosing to stay under his rule dare not displease Sam Barlow. In the event that one of their sons was singled out by Sam as one that should leave the community, the father was placed in a dilemma; he must believe Sam, standing against his own son (not even allowing the boy to tell his side of the story of whether or not he was guilty of any "crime"), allowing him to be driven from the society, or if he chose to side with his son (if he allowed him to tell his side of the story), then he was placing himself and his family in jeopardy of themselves being evicted from their homes and leaving the community. Most of these family heads were polygamists, with a very large family, making it almost impossible for them to go among any of the neighboring communities and completely start over. Most of them would just swallow their pride and allow their sons to be sacrificed, consoling themselves with the reasoning that whatever the "Prophet" asked of them was right.

Sam Barlow, a Mohave County Deputy Sheriff, was the only Law enforcement authority in the Colorado City area. Any complaints taken to him by the parents of the boys were simply "shelved" and the only action taken was against the boys themselves, if they refused to leave when they were warned by the vigilantes. Sam would build some kind of charges against the boys that would range from "Amorously enticing a girl" to throwing eggs at his "Night Patrol." The boys would always be the "offender," never would it be one of the real culprits.

Another factor governing the non-action of the parents was polygamy itself. All members of the Polygamists believe that in order to reach the highest degree of heaven, they must live polygamy. Whether a man would get additional wives depended upon whether or not one of the Council members would allow them to do so.

In most cases it was Leroy himself who reserved the right to decide who was "worthy" to be allowed to get wives. If a man was to offend him, it virtually cut off any chances of him ever becoming a polygamist. Since courting was not allowed, because all girls were "told" who they should marry, it was almost impossible for any man to go out and get a wife without Leroy's approval, thus denying him the blessing of ever entering the "Celestial Kingdom."

If any of the Polygamists were to give an honest answer as to why they desired to enter polygamy, it would not be to gain this highest degree in heaven, but rather it was to gain the "status" of being a polygamist. In Colorado City, those who are not polygamists are looked down on as though they are not quite as good as those who are. A non-polygamist cannot "preside" over a polygamist. This does not apply to ecclesiastical positions only, but is carried throughout all aspects of the society, whether it is in the work place, the schools, or in the town governments. The school principal, the town mayor, or even a foreman on a work project has to be a polygamist.

Another advantage for those who remain in Sam's favor are the benefits they receive from the "storehouse." If Fred Jessop, who controls the storehouse, judges a person "worthy," he not only gives to them commodities, but does not require them to pay their water bills, sewer bills, and health care bills. Also, Fred Jessop is in control of the person who is the County Representative for the Arizona State Medical Assistance Program in the Colorado City area. He decides who is "worthy" to receive these benefits. Hardly any of the polygamists have any kind of health care insurance, so this is a very significant factor.

Along with all these factors is the stigma of being castigated in the community if you are an "apostate." If you turn against the Priesthood the whole society turns against you, doing anything in their power to cause you to "get discouraged and leave." This stigma carries through from the parents to their children and it becomes very hard on the children of the "offenders" (apostates) in the schools where the other children will bring all kinds of persecution upon them.

The parents of these innocent children, when going to the school superintendent (Alvin Barlow), never get any justice from him. He will only do whatever is in his power to help discourage them from remaining in the community. These then are some of the reasons the parents are "helpless" to stop Jerry Jessop and his cohorts from doing their cowardly acts.

Note 5: A few years later Dan Barlow, Mayor of Colorado City, would tell news and television reporters: "There have been no evictions."

This was only a play on words on Mayor Barlow's part. The notice served on Andrew's wife by the Mohave County Sheriff's Deputy is as follows:

NOTICE TO VACATE TO ANDREW BISTLINE and all residents of the property known as 137 North Central, Colorado City, Arizona:

You are notified that the permission granted to you to occupy the property at the above address has been revoked. You are notified to vacate the premises within thirty (30) days from the date this letter is delivered to you, together with all of your movable personal property. In the event that any damage is done to the premises, you will be looked to for repayment. Any personal property remaining thirty (30) days after this notice is delivered to you will be deemed to have been abandoned and will be disposed of as may be appropriate. Dated this 2nd day of August, 1983.

> UNITED EFFORT PLAN
> By: (signed) Leroy Johnson
> Leroy S. Johnson; President
> Attest: (signed) Rulon T. Jeffs
> Rulon T. Jeffs; Secretary

This "eviction notice" was stamped by the Mohave County Sheriff's Office, number; A15132-D, dated 8/8/83, time: 4:35 PM. The charade of Mayor Barlow's, where he claims "there have been no evictions" is nothing more than a play on words and a bald-faced lie.

Note 6: The following is from the Journal of Ben Bistline. July 24, 1983:

Guy Musser died July 11, 1983 at Salt Lake City. (Sam Barlow told me soon after Guy Musser died that: "When he, Guy, was still alive, Leroy and Rulon Jeffs, could not do what they wanted to in the Priesthood Council Meetings because they were out voted so long as Marion, Guy and Dell (Alma Timpson) were still there, three against two; but now that Guy was dead, there was two against two and things were going to be different now."

Note 7: The following is from the Journal of Ben Bistline. November 8, 1983:

Sometime in the late fall of 1983, after Duff's (Andrew Bistline) eviction, Lee told me that U. Roy had told him that Sam wanted to evict me, but U. Roy told him to leave me alone. He also told me that he didn't think there would be any more evictions, indicating that an attorney had cautioned them against it (I deduced later that they would be in trouble for evicting beneficiaries.) (Added 3/23/87. It was about this same time that they changed the beneficiary list at Kingman.)

Note 8: A situation that should be touched on will be given a short synopsis here.

In Sam Barlow's "work" of "cleaning up the town," he began looking for sex offences in the lives of those he was trying to eradicate from the community. There were many rumors and accusations made against several men, these being those who would not support Sam in his "calling," and especially any who vocally disagreed with the actions of Leroy Johnson in his changes of the Polygamists' Doctrines.

These accusations even included Marion Hammon and Alma Timpson. Hammon was accused of incestuous acts with his own daughters. Timpson was accused of using narcotic drugs to increase the sexual passions of his wives. These accusations were entirely false, with no evidence of any kind ever shown. However, there were some men and boys who were guilty of some offences of sexual abuse. These would include men making sexual assaults on their own daughters, boys enticing and even forcing sexual intercourse on their younger sisters, and there were some instances of young unmarried men being involved in sexual conduct with young wives of older men (All of the Priesthood Council members had married young teenage girls).

Some of these girls were trapped in a dead-end situation with no hope of any fulfillment of life's joys. In such hopeless conditions, it was relatively easy for some young swashbuckler to come into their lives and take advantage of the situation.

Due to propriety, the names of the offenders will not be used here and only a brief account entered, but the situation must be covered to show the nature and character of Sam Barlow, the "Chief Protector" of the community.

Throughout the 1980s and into the 1990s there were about eight men of the Polygamist Community who Sam sent to prison on these sexual charges. These were men who were "out of harmony" with him and "Uncle Roy." These were vigorously pursued by Sam and in about half of the cases the men only plead guilty because they were unable to hire an attorney to properly defend them on charges that were highly exaggerated.

On the other side of the coin, there were over twice that many men (and boys, sons of the Barlows) who were guilty of the same offences (accused by their own daughters), who did no prison time at all except for the 2 or 3 days spent in a county jail waiting for bail to be raised. These were men who were either Barlows, the sons of Barlows, or relations to Leroy, or in some cases had given Leroy a large sum of money, some as much as $5,000.00. These men were provided with reputable attorneys (paid for by the UEP) and plea bargains with very light sentences were administered. There is evidence that Sam would even go into the Sheriff's offices of the county's involved and remove critical evidence such as reports he himself had filed, after Leroy would inform him that he was to get the particular person "off."

In some of these cases there were never any arrests made. One in particular involved a son of Sam Barlow himself. The young man had become sexually involved with a younger wife of one of the older men of the community. This affair went on for a while before it was "discovered." The girl was older than the man (who was not a minor) so Sam simply blamed the whole affair on her saying: "In all my experience of law enforcement, this is the first time I have found the blame in a sexual offence, to be the fault of the girl." The girl was ordered to leave the community while the "punishment" for Sam Barlow's son was an advancement in the Priesthood. About one month later he was ordained an Elder in the Melchizedek Priesthood.

This account is to show the consistency in the handling of the problems of the Polygamists. The sad part of this situation is that the lives of the people who were "out of harmony" were, in some cases, totally destroyed. One of the young men that Sam sent to prison committed suicide. Fred Jessop would not even allow the boy's mother to bring his body home, but rather had the State cremate his remains, disposing of them in any way they chose. Other men lost their wives and families, for no other reason than being "out of harmony."

There was never any effort made by the community leaders to "rehabilitate" any of these offenders, but rather their attitude can be pretty well summed up in this statement of Sam Barlow: "These men are Non-Persons, they never existed."

The Priesthood Split

The men invited to Alma Timpson's home for Priesthood Meeting on the night of May 13, 1984, did not know that Nephi Barlow and Joseph Timpson (Joseph Timpson was a son of Alma Timpson and Ada Barlow) were outside taking down the license plate numbers of their cars. This Gestapo tactic was meant to intimidate any who were bold enough to stand against the Barlows and openly support Hammon and Timpson. It had little effect on those who were attending the meeting. The men inside the house still held allegiance toward "Uncle Roy," but they believed he had been swayed by those aspiring men who surrounded him, and because of his old age and incapacitated condition, they felt he was not responsible for the action he had taken against Hammon and Timpson. They believed that things would eventually be straightened out and if they would stand by the principles that had been taught by the Priesthood Council, they would be blessed for it.

In the weeks and months to come, bitter feelings were generated between the two groups. Leroy wanted to just wash his hands of those who would not place their allegiance with him, letting them go their own way. The Barlows were not so lenient. They wanted the "apostates" to move from the community, leaving everything behind including any interest or control in any businesses, buildings, or property under their jurisdiction. Their one big sore spot was that the "Second Ward" controlled the Colorado City Academy. This must be wrested from them because Marion Hammon had decided to hold the meetings of the Second Ward in the Academy building. This really annoyed Leroy and his "advisors." Any property that belonged to the United Effort Plan should not be used by any Apostate Group to hold meetings. Leroy supposed that if he withdrew from the Board of Trustees of the Academy, it would somehow cripple the institution and it would have to close up.

On May 30, 1984, Marion Hammon called a meeting of the Board of Directors of the Colorado City Academy to plan what to do about carrying on with the school. The meeting was held in Salt Lake City with the four remaining board members of the Academy, namely: Leroy Johnson, J. Marion Hammon, Rulon T. Jeffs, and A.A. Timpson. Also attending was Cyril Bradshaw, Principal of the Academy (The original Board of Directors were the seven members of the Priesthood Council, of which three had died).

At the beginning of the meeting Hammon asked Leroy what he wanted to do about the school. Leroy hastily said, "I don't want anything more to do with it. I resign from the Board." At this, Jeffs spoke up and said: "I resign also."

Hammon then asked Leroy who he wanted to put on the Board to replace them. Leroy answered by saying, "You only need one man," and pointing to Cyril Bradshaw, continued, "you can put Brother Bradshaw on." With that the meeting was over.

Cyril wrote up the minutes and two amendments to the Articles of Incorporation of the Colorado City Academy. The first amendment changed the life of the corporation from 25 years to perpetuity. The second amendment changed the number of trustees from seven to three. The names of the three trustees were: J. Marion Hammon, President; Alma A. Timpson, Member; and Cyril Bradshaw as Secretary. Before he could file the documents with the Arizona Corporation Commission, however, he received a phone call from Rulon Jeffs telling him that he and Leroy had changed their minds and didn't want their resignations to stand. The evidence is that when the Barlows learned what had happened, they could see the danger in allowing the Second Ward to have complete control of the Academy buildings. It would give them a place to hold their meetings and remain a competitive threat if they were allowed to remain in the community. They immediately began telling people in the community that Cyril had forged Leroy's signature of resignation. This was a complete lie because there was no written resignation ever in existence. There were only the minutes of the meeting where Leroy and Jeffs said they resigned.

When Cyril received this phone call from Jeffs, he called Leroy and asked him what was going on (See Note 1 for a transcript of the telephone conversation). Evidently Leroy had not been informed as to what was going on, because he told Cyril, "I'm out of that and I don't want anything more to do with it." Cyril then concluded that Leroy was not behind the change in the resignations and continued to prepare the documents for filing with the Arizona Corporation Commission.

In order to cover themselves, the Barlows had their attorney Charles Ditsch of Phoenix write a letter to the Corporation Commission, telling them to not accept the documents filed by Cyril Bradshaw (Note 2). In the letter Mr. Ditsch states: "It is our understanding that a purported amendment to the Articles of Incorporation of Colorado City Academy has been submitted to your office...my clients, who constitute two of the four members of the corporation and who were not notified of any meeting to vote on the amendment; therefore, it would appear that said amendment was not properly adopted...."

These statements of Ditsch are false, of course. When Leroy told Cyril that no changes had been made, Cyril, at the advice of Hammon, filed the new Articles of Incorporation. Jeffs called the Arizona Corporation Commission and told them not to accept the filed documents. A person from the Arizona Corporation Commission called Cyril Bradshaw and asked what to do in the matter of Jeffs' instructions. Cyril told the lady to ignore what Jeffs had told her because he was acting without authorization, which she did.

There were a few surprises in store for the Barlows in regards to the Academy. One of these surprises was that they supposed the property on which the Academy buildings were situated had been leased to the Academy from the United Effort Plan. The charter for the Academy was for 25 years and they supposed that the lease would run out at the end of 25 years, which would be on about September 1, 1985. The facts were that the United Effort Plan had given the Academy a Warranty Deed for the 20 acres of land, which were now controlled by the Academy Board of Directors. The Barlows were not too worried about the new Board of Directors, reasoning that the charter would soon run out and the control of the buildings would then revert back to the UEP. They may have just sat and waited for this to happen had it not been for actions of the new Board concerning the deed to the property.

Two of the teachers at the Academy, Jack Knudson and Claude Cawley, had been assigned building lots on the same 20 acres that the Academy was on. Since developments (which will be covered, beginning with the next paragraph) had caused great concern among many of the people living on UEP property and since these two men were no longer teaching at the Academy and since the tax burden of their homes fell on the Academy, the Academy Board decided to give Jack Knudson and Claude Cawley the deeds to their homes. This occurred on January 29, 1985. Well, when Jack Knudson received his deed, he immediately went to Leroy to find out what was going on. It is an understatement to say "that really kicked the lid off." We will come back to what happened in regards to the consequences surrounding the issuing of these deeds later, but some very important developments had taken place in late 1983 and all through 1984 that must be covered here.

With Marion Hammon and Alma Timpson out of the way, Leroy began to do some very strange things in regards to running the Priesthood Work. He would make decisions without counseling with anyone on them. Some of these decisions surprised and even angered many people, whose allegiance was still with Leroy, or the First Ward. One such act of Leroy's occurred on the morning of August 12, 1984.

The First Ward holds a priesthood meeting once a month on the second Sunday, where all male members over 12 years old attend. In the August 1984 meeting Leroy stood up before the congregation of about 400 men and called three men to the stand. The men were: Orval Johnson (Leroy's son), Joe Barlow, and David Zitting. Leroy then said: "We are going to ordain these men Patriarchs. If there are any in the building who do not agree with what we are doing, then you can just leave." He then proceeded to perform the ordinations. None of the candidates had been informed in advance of these intentions of Leroy. They were not given any choice in the matter, just took what was given to them. There were some in the audience who disagreed with Leroy's tactics but did not get up and leave. They did, however, stop going to his Priesthood Meetings. This was because they knew the true character of Orval Johnson and Joe Barlow and they knew they would never be able to place any confidence in men whom they considered both immoral and dishonest.

On the 19th of August, 1984, Leroy made the statement: "In two weeks the slaughter will begin. We are building coffins for the good people but we will just dig a hole with a backhoe to put the wicked ones in." After the meeting a group of men went over to his house and anointed their cars and ATV's (all terrain vehicles) with consecrated olive oil, and then blessed them.

Then on August 31, 1984, Leroy called a Board Meeting of the United Effort Plan Trustees to meet at his home in Salt Lake City. This was the first meeting of this kind ever being called since 1946, because all UEP Business was handled in the Priesthood Council Meetings where all the Council Members were UEP Trustees.

When Hammon and Timpson arrived at Leroy's home at the appointed time, they were surprised when a group of men met them at the door and informed them that Timpson could not attend the meeting because he was not, nor had he ever been, a Trustee of the United Effort Plan. Imagine the surprise to these two men who, after thirty-five years of Timpson acting as a Trustee, all the documents filed in the Court Houses of the respective Counties declaring him a trustee, all the Priesthood Council Meetings where he took part in the decision making processes of the UEP, and all the times it had been declared from the stand in public meetings that "all the Council members" were UEP Trustees, then at this late date the Barlows decided he was *not* a Trustee because his name was not on the original document filed in 1942. Such absurd reasoning was beyond belief. Hammon and Timpson made no effort to contest the issue at this time and Timpson turned and left while Hammon went on in.

There were present at this meeting: Leroy S. Johnson, Rulon T. Jeffs, J. Marion Hammon, and Warren S. Jeffs. Leroy began the meeting by saying: "Brother Hammon, I called this meeting of the trustees of the United Effort Plan. The purpose of this meeting is to remove one of our members from the board of trustees, which is yourself.... We'll give you the opportunity to resign if you'd like. If not, we'll present it on the merits of the case."

Jeffs, speaking to Hammon said: "I have a form here prepared if you wish to resign. Or if you decline that, we will go into the merits of the case.... There's been no meeting of the board to appoint any more (trustees). But through the years, affairs of the United Effort Plan were discussed in Council Meetings." Jeffs went on to say that the only UEP business discussed in the Council Meetings were about property being transferred out of the trust.

Hammon asked: Weren't they involved in receiving property?"

Jeffs: "No. Just transferred out."

Hammon: "What was transferred out?'

Jeffs: "Much was to you."

Hammon: "I don't ever remember any going out."

Leroy: "What about the Hatch property?"

Jeffs: "And the Beryl property."

Hammon: "Well, that wasn't in my possession long."

Jeffs: "It was used to pay your debts."

Jeffs then mentioned the Hirshi Ranch and the particulars of Marion Hammon controlling that property.

Jeffs: "I have all income tax records on which these transactions were reported."

Hammon: "That may be so. I haven't any records."

After some discussion about how their lawyer had counseled them that they could put Hammon in prison if they wanted, because of him losing UEP Property, it came down to Jeffs telling Hammon:

"I have a form of resignation if you want to sign it." Hammon turned to Leroy, whose eyes were on the floor, and said: "And I thought we were brethren (Note 3)."

Turning back to Jeffs he took the form of resignation and with much disgust said:

"I'd like to see it. I don't want to sign with my eyes shut."

After some discussion of being exempt of any liability on Hammon's part, he signed the document. He then said: "Well, it took thirty years to get here and just thirty minutes to leave. That puts an end to that. We had high hopes for this thing. We sat in there with Joseph (Musser) and John (Barlow).... There's been lots of conversation over matters. Some things had foundation in truth, but a lot was falsehood...the Lord must handle all men."

In this meeting Jeffs "blackmailed" Hammon into resigning from the UEP Board of Directors under threat of prosecuting him for "losing" the Ranch at Hatch and the farm at Beryl. This threat was only a bluff, because if there had ever been any court action on the matter it would have been shown that it was Leroy Johnson and Rulon Jeffs who "lost" the property when they signed the deeds over to Marion Hammon, with no specific written instructions as to why they "gave" it to him. There are no minutes of any UEP Board meetings explaining the circumstances surrounding the transaction. Some people have made accusations that it was a payoff to Hammon to help him move to Idaho, where he would have nothing more to do with the United Effort Plan, allowing Leroy and the Barlows free reign to do as they pleased at Colorado City. There is very little question that if Hammon could have made a success of running the farm in Idaho, he would never have moved back, thus accomplishing what was planned by his adversaries.

The meeting ended and Hammon left, a much dejected man. He had never supposed there could be such treachery in the hearts of men he had put so much trust in for so many years. It was enough to take the heart out of him. He would never regain any of the old spirit and fire that he had portrayed for the most part of his life. He would forever be a changed man.

When Hammon returned to Colorado City and related to his family and friends what had taken place in Salt Lake, it caused much apprehension among his followers. In view of the recent evictions, a considerable number of them felt that by losing the "balance of power" in the United Effort Plan, it would give the Barlows the power to indiscriminately force from their homes whomever they might choose. Jerry Williams and Marko Dutson felt that if they could visit Leroy they might be able to convince him that he was making a grave mistake by forcing Hammon out of the UEP. On about September 1, 1984, they drove to Salt Lake City and, after calling Leroy to make an appointment to visit him, drove over to his place, where to their great surprise 40 of the Barlow supporters, along with Fred Jessop, were waiting for them.

The meeting with Leroy was a bitter disappointment. They were not allowed to reason with Leroy in any manner. The spokesmen for him were Fred Jessop, Rulon Jeffs, and Truman Barlow, along with all the other 40 men who would "chirp up" whenever one of the men would attempt to communicate with Leroy. When they asked why he kicked Hammon out of the UEP, he would only answer: "If you don't like what we are doing you can hire a lawyer and contact our lawyer, Mr. Ditsch in Phoenix." When they asked how he could legally do what he had done, Jeffs answered them saying: "There have been some documents filed in the Court House at Kingman that gives us the legal right to do what we have done." With this the visit ended. The two men left, not able to comprehend the attitude, and the change in their beloved "Uncle Roy."

After they returned home a meeting was called among those who felt threatened by what was happening. In this meeting it was concluded that an attorney should be contacted to determine if there was anything that could be done to protect themselves. On October 3, 1984, a delegation met with Clay Huntsman, an attorney in St. George. An agreement was discussed with him about a retainer and how payments were to be made for him to handle negotiations between the UEP trustees and those who were apprehensive about the situation.

After this meeting with Mr. Huntsman, two of the delegation went on to Kingman to search what the recorded documents were that Jeffs had told Jerry and Marko about. What they found were three documents: 1) the amended affidavit of disclosure, where the names of the beneficiaries of the United Effort Plan had been changed on November 12, 1983 (Note 4); and, 2) a second amended affidavit of disclosure dated September 5, 1984; and 3) a third amended affidavit of disclosure dated September 24, 1984 (Note 5). The second affidavit of disclosure stated that the original affidavit of disclosure filed in 1976 was in error wherein it listed Guy Musser, Richard Jessop, and Alma Timpson as trustees of the United Effort Plan. The third amended affidavit of disclosure stated that J. Marion Hammon had resigned as a trustee of the United Effort Plan and Fred Jessop had been appointed to replace him.

With regards to these events, the Barlow Cabal, in anticipation of the Colorado City Academy closing down, began to take steps to obtain a public high school in Colorado City, which they could control. There were, however, some problems that needed to be overcome before they could "get their school."

In order to form a high school district in Arizona, a school has to have 200 students attending and a $2 million assessed valuation. The Colorado City School District met the student count, but not the assessed valuation requirement. A big percentage of the Colorado City high school students were attending the Colorado City Academy and if the Academy was allowed to remain open, it would present the question of whether the District would even met the attendance requirement, thus one of the reasons the Academy must close.

Dan Barlow, a Colorado City School District Board Member, and Alvin Barlow, Colorado City School Superintendent, through the district Representative of the Arizona House of Representatives, sponsored House Bill 2238 into the Arizona legislature, which was passed in January of 1984. This Bill, if passed and signed into law, would allow the Colorado City School District to form a new High School District, exempting them from the $2 million assessed valuation requirement. The House and Senate made this exception and approved the bill. Governor Bruce Babbitt then signed the bill on May 4, 1984.

The House Bill did have some opposition. State Senator Ann Lindeman (R-Phoenix) opposed HB2238 for two reasons. First, she said the Colorado City School District, which was a part of Mohave Union High School District, admitted they had never gone to the latter school district to ask for the district's creation. "Their argument was that they were so isolated that the people of Kingman wouldn't support it. But my argument was they should have asked."

Her other argument was the bill's exempting the new school district from the $2 million assessed value requirement. "They were well under that figure and it would be a bad precedent because it would raise several tax problems elsewhere in the state. There would be pockets of high tax rates and the state Legislature would end up having to bail out those areas," she reasoned. "I didn't feel they did their homework properly." While these issues were being raised, the Barlows were careful to keep these developments from the knowledge of most members of the community.

During this period of unstable events, in light of the evictions that had taken place and because of other power grabs that were being made by these "Big Elders," there were some residents of Colorado City who felt something must be done to protect themselves against such a "takeover." The Barlows were aware of the opposition they faced, and hoped that by moving swiftly and secretly, they could obtain their goals before these "dissidents" could hinder their progress. For this reason, there was no local opposition to the passing of the House Bill in May. Had Senator Lindeman known there were people in the community who opposed the forming of the new high school district, she would have undoubtedly moved to debate the issue stronger than she did. The first thing any of the Dissidents knew about the matter was when it appeared on the local ballot to be voted on by the residents of Mohave County.

After the bill was signed into law, it was necessary for the residents of Mohave Union High School District to vote on the issue of splitting the district. The bill only allowed for the *proposal* of the new district to go before the voters, exempting the $2 million value requirement. The issue of forming a new High School District was scheduled to be voted on in the General Election on November 6, 1984. The Dissidents learned of this fact only one week before the election was to take place. In their frustration to thwart the efforts of the Barlows, they sent one of their number to Kingman to place an ad in the local newspaper opposing the forming of the new district. The ad appeared in the Sunday issue of the paper, leaving only one day before the day of the election. It was a half page ad and simply said (in large print):

VOTE NO!
Special Election Ballot.
The Formation Of A New High School District
KEEP RELIGION OUT OF PUBLIC SCHOOLS
Cheaper, More Effective Alternatives Are Available For
The Residents of Mohave County.
Paid For By Citizens of Colorado City.

Needless to say, when Alvin Barlow read this ad in the paper on Monday afternoon (the paper was received in Colorado City through the mail, making it a day or two late), he hit the ceiling. He could not believe anyone in Colorado City would have the courage to oppose the formation of the new high school. To oppose such, to defy not only the Barlow regime, but also Uncle Roy, was to oppose the Mouth Piece of God on Earth. Such outward opposition to Alvin was a new experience for him. Until now he had full control in the school to do whatever he decided. All he would have to do in the meetings with the School Board to get his way was say:

"This is what Uncle Roy wants," and it always worked because to go against what "Uncle Roy" wanted was to spell the end of your career in Colorado City. The realization that there were people living in the community that were not afraid to go against what "Uncle Roy wanted" put an unexpected fear in his bosom. He found himself at a loss as how to combat the situation.

Opposition in political matters are often clouded by throwing in unrelated questions to confuse the public on the real concerns of the opposing party. The Barlows are skilled politicians and know just about all the tricks it takes to confuse the real issues in any situation. Alvin Barlow's first response to the opposition of the new high school was: "I wonder why there is a group of people in our community who would deprive students of their education?" This statement was meant to bring disrepute on those who had placed the ad in the Kingman paper, hoping to distract any from learning the true reasons for the opposition. Some of the concerns of these citizens were as follows:

The School Board at Colorado City was controlled by the religious hierarchy (Leroy Johnson) of the Polygamist society. There were no objections against a public run high school coming into the community, in fact there were a considerable number of the Polygamists who had pulled their children out of the Academy because of their disagreement of the religious subjects taught there and a public high school was desperately needed. The problem with the Barlows having control of a public high school would only mean that the religious views would be theirs instead of Hammon's. It would still be a parochial school, only funded by the Arizona taxpayers.

One of the Dissidents made this statement: "I know that religious subjects are being taught at the public elementary (school). I would rather see a county-run public high school at Colorado City rather than a community administered high school, because I don't think the education being taught is an objective education. I just hate to see too much power centralized. It is destroying the whole community. I'd hate to see our lives governed to the extent that the freedoms of expression, press, and religion are destroyed."

This about sums it all up as to why there was opposition against the new high school. Those opposing it would ask Jim Vandevier, Mohave County School Superintendent, to keep the high school in the Mohave Union High District so it could be controlled by outside influences. His answer was that the County could not afford to support a high school on the Arizona Strip. The only way that a public high school would ever be established in Colorado City would be with state money rather than with county money. To him, this would be the perfect answer, even at the sacrifice of religious freedom for the children at Colorado City. This caused much discouragement among the Dissidents and they did not make much of an attempt to contact any other state officials. "We are afraid to approach state officials with our concerns because the religious leaders in the town have such a strong influence with all the officials," pretty well sums up the situation.

The election of November 6, 1984, went bad for the Barlows. The measure to form a new High School District at Colorado City was defeated at the polls by a vote of 8,383 against and 6,853 for. Jim Vandevier, superintendent of Mohave County Schools cited the half-page advertisement that was published in Sunday's paper as the reason for the measure's failing. He said: "The ad, which was paid for by 'Citizens of Colorado City,' urged voters to cast a 'no' ballot, and 'keep Religion Out of Public Schools.' It needed more positive support, some people I talked to said they weren't even sure what they were voting on."

Richard Dawson, Mohave Union High School superintendent, was disappointed the ballot issue was defeated. He said: "It would have been in the best interest of the young people in the area for the direction of their education to be with their own people. Religious aspects raised by opponents of the formation of the new district must have influenced the voters."

It is no doubt true that the majority of the county voters did not know what they were voting on. Jim Vandevier himself did not know what he was really voting for. He thought he was helping to establish an institution that would provide a free education for some otherwise deprived students in an isolated area. This was only partly true.

In politics there are always at least two reasons why things are done. There is the reason that sounds good (to obtain public support), and then there is the real reason. In the case of the Barlows wanting a new high school district, it was not nearly so much for the benefit of the students, but rather by expanding the school enterprise, it would bring more money into the community, money that they could control and also control who would be hired to teach, work at the school, etc. This was their greatest loss in not getting the new district.

The next Monday morning, November 12, 1984, Alvin Barlow, told the Hildale Town council: "The defeat of not getting the new district will put an added burden on the Mohave Union High School District and it will be one of the most expensive ways that Mohave County can go, for they will have to build a new building. If we had won, the burden would be on the new district and the money would have come from the state, not the county."

The Colorado City Academy Board of Directors had offered the Mohave Union High School District the use of the Academy buildings to establish a new high school at Colorado City. This offer was rejected, the prime reasons being that the Academy lacked the facilities to provide the students with such classes as physical education. There were some concerns about the buildings meeting fire codes as well. At any rate, the County turned down the offer.

The decision was made by the Colorado City School Board to hold a special election and try again to get their high school. They sent Alvin to Phoenix to inquire as to what the procedure was to implement the decision. It was ascertained that the school board could hold as many special elections as they decided was necessary to get a majority vote in their favor. The only catch was that the Colorado City School District would have to fund the cost of these special elections, which they estimated would be from six to eight thousand dollars. They decided to go ahead and plan for an election in March of 1985.

It was during this time that the Dissidents discovered the "secret" documents filed by the UEP Trustees. Some of these Dissidents began mailing out anonymous letters to selected community residents. The letters were an attempt to reveal to the UEP beneficiaries the actions of the new trustees. The letters were not well received by such men as Sam Barlow. One particular letter put him in a very defensive posture. This letter told of a cache of guns that had been purchased by Louis Barlow and were stored in a manmade cavern in the hill above Fred Jessop's home.

Those putting out the letter had done their homework well. The man who had sold the guns to Louis (in Los Angeles) told them that Louis had bought 100 SAM 180 semi-automatic .22 caliber rifles and hundreds of thousands of rounds of ammunition; the guns were stored in the manmade cavern behind Fred Jessop's house. He even sent them a list of the serial numbers. When the letter hit the streets, Sam hurried to the Washington County Sheriff at St. George and demanded that an investigation be launched to find out who was putting out the letters. He, of course, denied that there were a cache of guns stored in the cavern. When those putting out the letter learned that Sam was "making a federal case" out of the issue, they went to the Sheriff and told him who was responsible for the letter. The Sheriff became very concerned about whether or not there were guns in the cavern. He decided that an investigation was in order. He did not reveal to Sam who put out the letter, but rather began asking Sam about the guns being in the cavern. One day when he was questioning Sam about them, Sam asked: "Do you want to come out and inspect the cavern to see if the guns are there?" The Sheriff just said no, he didn't need to do that.

The next morning he showed up at Sam's office in Colorado City and told him he was there to inspect the cavern. This greatly unnerved Sam. It had thrown him completely off guard. He had supposed that when the Sheriff declined his offer to show him the cavern, he was not going to pursue the matter any farther. He began stammering, saying something about there were only two men who had keys to the cavern and they were both out of town. This did not satisfy the Sheriff. He wanted to go into the cavern and the more excuses Sam made, the more determined he became. Someone in Sam's office spoke up, not realizing that Sam was stalling, and told him that one of the boys who helped Fred in the Store House had a key to the cavern. This destroyed Sam's alibi and there was nothing he could do but take the Sheriff and his Deputy to the cavern. The young man was located and did indeed have a key to the cavern. The group then made their way up to the cavern on the hillside.

The cavern is constructed with a corridor leading about fifty feet back into the mountain. There are rooms leading off from this corridor which are used for storing foodstuff and other necessities that would be needed in case of a survival situation. The first corridor leading to the right after entering the cavern leads into a room about forty feet in diameter. After entering this room one finds that it has been divided by a partition made of one-half inch iron bars. There is a gate in this partition leading into this part of the room. On the far side of this divided side of the room is a metal vault door with a combination lock on it. Behind this vault door is a room of about ten feet in diameter that was intended for storing the records of the polygamists. When the group who were accompanying the Sheriff reached the cavern, the young man with the keys opened the padlock on the gate at the entrance. He then led them to the room with the iron bar partition which also had a chain with a padlock on it.

While he was unlocking the gate, the deputy who was with the sheriff looked through the bars and across the room to the vault on the other side. He observed that the vault door was not locked, but was opened about two feet wide. To his amazement, the young man who unlocked the gate immediately walked across the room and slammed the vault door shut. This action, needless to say, surprised the Sheriff and when he asked to see behind the vault door was told by Sam that Fred and his brother Virgil were the only ones in the community who knew the combination and they were both out of town. This flippancy on Sam's part greatly annoyed him, but he was now convinced that there were guns behind the vault door. He decided to contact the Alcohol, Tobacco and Firearms (ATF) agency, to ask their assistance in the investigation of the situation.

The ATF sent an agent down from Salt Lake City to work with one of the Sheriff's deputies on the case and they spent about six months trying to uncover the facts in the matter. This investigation was somewhat a problem for the officers because they were unable to get Sam to cooperate with them. He would never come clean and tell them the truth or any facts in the matter. This was frustrating because local officers will always cooperate with federal officials unless they themselves have something to hide. It was concluded early on in the case that Sam did indeed have something to hide.

After the six months investigation this is what they found out:

Louis Barlow had purchased the 99 guns that matched the serial numbers supplied to the Dissidents. When the ATF tracked down these guns, it was found that Louis had purchased them to put in survival kits he was promoting to sell to those who believed that "Doomsday" was soon to come. This particular venture was a complete failure and Louis eventually sold most of the guns back to the dealer he bought them from at a one hundred dollar loss on each gun. These 99 guns were never stored in the cavern, but were shipped directly to Salt Lake City to a dealer that Louis was working with on the survival kits. But there were another 50 guns in the same shipment that were never accounted for. These 50 guns were unloaded at Las Vegas from the same shipment of 99 guns that were shipped from Los Angeles to Salt Lake. It was these 50 unaccounted for guns that, in all probability, were the ones that Sam was hiding in the cavern. There are two witnesses (young missionary boys) who unloaded the guns from the vehicle and put them in the cavern, who confirmed that the guns were there.

It seems that after six months of investigation, the ATF just became tired of the whole deal and decided to drop it. After all, the guns were legal guns and owning them was not a crime.

There was one thing accomplished that benefitted the community. The Washington County Sheriff withdrew his authorization from Sam to act in any law enforcement capacity in the County and the State of Utah. He withdrew this authorization because he believed Sam was lying to him and he realized that if Sam ever had to make a choice between the civil law and his religious authorities, his loyalties would be with his ecclesiastical leaders rather than with the Sheriff's department. For this reason, the sheriff felt he could no longer trust him. This was the beginning of Sam losing his credibility as a reliable peace office among the surrounding communities.

During the "Gun Episode," there were other events taking place. Due to the recent actions of the UEP Trustees (the evictions, the forced resignation of Marion Hammon from the UEP Board of Trustees, and the disfranchisement of over 100 of the beneficiaries), there were several members of the United Effort Plan who became concerned about their own standing in the Association. About a half dozen of them met together at the Academy building one night and decided to contact an attorney to determine just what their position was. It was after this meeting that the delegation met with Clay Huntsman, attorney in St. George, on November 30, 1984, to discuss what their options were. He was given a thousand dollar retainer and agreed to write a letter to Rulon Jeffs, Secretary of the UEP, asking that they be "given" the deeds to the homes they had built on property titled to the United Effort Plan. The letter caused more than a "ripple" among the Barlows. It surprised them that anyone had the courage to defy them and ask for their deeds. A hurried trip to Phoenix and a meeting with their attorney Charles Ditsch, was immediately executed.

About 40 of the Barlows and their supporters met with Ditsch on December 4, 1984. Leroy Johnson was in this meeting but sat to one side in his wheelchair dozing most of the time. It was Sam and Dan Barlow who did most of the talking with the attorney. Sam especially was doing most of the dictating to him as to what he should write in the return letter to Mr. Huntsman. When the letter was completed, it was read back to Leroy, who only nodded his head in agreement.

It was decided in this meeting that before they would answer Mr. Huntsman's letter, they must have the names of those involved in the request for their deeds. This request was made and the names were given to Mr. Ditsch. The names were as follows: Andrew Bistline, Ben Bistline, Don Cox, Marko Dutson, David Stubbs, Cora Fischer, Mike Pipkin, and Jerry Williams. As soon as these names were received by the Polygamist Leaders, a hate campaign was started against those named. This hate campaign began with Rulon Jeffs' anouncement in a meeting on January 20, 1985, at Salt Lake City, about who those were asking for their deeds. The next attempt at slandering them was made by Fred Jessop in a short paragraph in *The Twin City Courier*, a little one paged newspaper he printed about twice a month. This paragraph appeared in Volume 23, number 1, on January 24, 1985:

"Blessings lost sight of in these days has caused some to become embittered against the hands through which our community's solidarity has been made; and, like all others who have forsaken faith, they have resorted to the outside enemy help, for hoped for comfort (Note 6)."

Then, on February 10, 1985, Fred Jessop read a letter to the congregation in Sunday Meeting. The letter is from Charles Ditsch, UEP attorney, to Clayton Huntsman, attorney for those asking for their deeds.

Fred gave the following short sermon before reading the letter:

"Just by way of a little reminder, that in this dispensation the Prophet Joseph and his successors have striven in great diligence and effort to establish the principles of the gospel among the people. And as all of you know who are somewhat acquainted with Church History, United Order efforts have been undertaken in various places at various times in the early settlement of the Church in the West and in about every instance the situation failed, mostly because of the non-observance of the law of the gospel laid down by the Prophet Joseph, or the Lord through the Prophet Joseph. But in the latter days, nearing the winding up scene of the great work of the Lord, the Prophet has been inspired to set up a system that would last; that would succeed. Now this system that will succeed eliminates men, but not the system. And as you're all aware, Uncle Roy has asked us, young folks and all, to pray for him that he will be able to hold the United Effort Plan. Now this is a system that will succeed, though men fail. And in as much as he has been challenged and threatened with courts of law, and this is not the first time, we have to use the tools unconverted people can be dealt with. So Uncle Roy has engaged the services and blessed the man, Charles Ditsch, to represent him through the law. And he's asked for this letter to be read:

"Now those opposing and challenging Uncle Roy have engaged the

230

services of one Clayton Huntsman of St. George, through which they allege that they will break the United Effort. So this is the letter that Mr. Ditsch has sent to Mr. Huntsman. It's dated January the 23rd from Phoenix to R. Clayton Huntsman, Esq., Courthouse Office Plaza, 180 North 200 East, Suite B, St. George, Utah 84770, with reference to the United Effort Plan Trust."

Charles A. Ditsch Attorney At Law
250 East Sierra Vista Drive
Phoenix, Arizona 85012
(602)265-7106

January 28, 1985
R. Clayton Huntsman, Esquire
Courthouse Office Plaza 180 North 200 East – Suite B
St. George, Utah 84770 Re: United Effort Plan Trust:

Dear Clay:

Since my conversation with you and David Watson on January 15, I have had an opportunity to consider the matters raised and to discuss the various matters with my clients. Concerning the issues of the "evictions" of Cora Stubbs and Andrew Bistline, I understand the following in fact occurred: Cora Stubbs had vacated the home that she had previously occupied in Colorado City and notified Mr. Johnson that the power had been disconnected, the doors were standing open and there was a strong odor of spoiled meat coming from the Stubbs house. He sent several young men who normally perform maintenance duties concerning the United Effort property to the house and they determined that the house was in a state of disrepair, built-in cabinets had been removed and the state was generally one of neglect and abandonment. At some point, Cora Stubbs arrived from Salt Lake, where, we understand, she had established residence, which may have been for the possibility of obtaining the greater welfare payments available in those environs. Apparently, the persons in the home left and thereafter Cora was served with a notice to vacate which gave her thirty days within which to remove her things from the property. It is our understanding that her possessions were moved to David Stubbs's home with help from members of the community. The notice to vacate was served on her as civil service coming through the office of the sheriff in Kingman.

When Andrew Bistline was served a similar notice to vacate, he had for all intents and purposes completed a new residence in Fredonia, where he now lives. He had stated his intentions to move there and, in fact, needed to move there shortly after the notice was served so that he could enter his children in school. The purpose of that notice was merely to make sure that the home which he intended to vacate would be available for use by another member of the community within a reasonable period of time as housing has always been in short supply in Colorado City.

With regard to the "evictions," I frankly see no civil rights violations. They were not forcible and under the terms of the trust, the parties resided on the premises only so long as such was determined to be proper by the trustees. In the two above cases, the residences had been abandoned or the intention to abandon was expressed and the recipients voluntarily complied with the notice.

With regard to the other matters raised at our meeting, you state that your clients are very fearful and that such fear comes in part from the fact that they were deleted as beneficiaries in the Amended Affidavit of Disclosure and that there have been rumors of guns and prospective violence. As your clients well know, the people of Colorado City are a very peaceful people with primarily agrarian interests. This was discovered by the Arizona Highway Patrol in 1953 when they arrived in town with drawn guns only to find the people waiting in the streets to comply with the lawful orders of the raiders. Then, as now, it was not the intent or purpose of the people to react with violence even though their very life was being attacked.

With regard to the rumors of the guns, representatives of the trustees have requested that state and federal officials investigate this matter as they have no knowledge of any weapons other than a few old hunting rifles.

The original Affidavit of Disclosure was prepared and filed to comply with a statute passed in Arizona in 1976 requiring the disclosure of the name and address of persons having an interest in Arizona land under a trust or an estate.

In reviewing the list of your clients, it appears that Don Cox, Mike Pipkin, Marko Dutson and Jerry Williams should never have been listed as beneficiaries because they don't reside on Arizona land and the statute has no requirement concerning Utah land. There have been no court cases construing the statute and, frankly, it occurs to me that the beneficiaries are not sufficiently fixed so as to be amenable to disclosure. I am certain, however, that being on the list does not make one a beneficiary nor does being removed from the list eliminate a person as a beneficiary if they are in fact a beneficiary. In this trust, as in all trusts, the terms of the trust instrument are controlling. The trust instrument speaks of members rather than beneficiaries and authorized the trustees to render assistance to nonmembers as well as members of the trust. The trust instrument in several places specifically states that membership does not create any interest in or title to the trust property or give a member the right to partition the property.

Over the years many people have consecrated property to the trust either by donating land to the trust or by improving land already owned by the trust. Some of them have voluntarily left Colorado City well knowing that property once consecrated to the trust is not returnable. The whole scenario is legally similar to a lessee improving real estate. Without a provision in the lease, the lessee must leave the improvements that have become affixed to the land when his tenancy terminates.

232

The United Effort Plan had been an umbrella which has protected the people of Colorado City since its inception over forty years ago. During this period of time many people have made consecrations to the trust, many people have been permitted to build homes with the help of their neighbors on trust property and they have lived abundantly in these homes, without payment of any rent for the property.

I understand that there has been no question in any residents' mind that they reside on the trust property at the will of the trustees, who are empowered to terminate the permission to reside on trust property when such residence was not necessary or because the residents were acting prejudicial to the spirit of the trust. It is my understanding that the power of the trustees to revoke the permission to live on trust property was discussed on many occasions in no uncertain terms by Alma Timpson and Marion Hammon at meetings in the community.

My clients are duty bound to administer the assets of the trust in accordance with its intent and purpose. It was never the purpose of the trust to transfer property, be it land or money, to persons claiming some unsubstantiated entitlement; rather, it was the purpose of the trust to use its assets to satisfy the just needs of people residing in Colorado City; to do otherwise would make a mockery of all who have contributed.

My clients have had their way of life, their freedom and their families attacked before. United Effort Plan has helped them survive those attacks. It is not now their purpose or intent to take steps which will lead to the eventual dissolution of the United Effort Plan which is such an integral part of the life and values of a majority of the Colorado City residents.

Other than the two people who abandoned or were soon to abandon the residences they occupied, none of your clients have been asked to leave the homes they live in. This is not to say that they will not be asked to leave if they conduct themselves in a manner which is prejudicial to the spirit of the United Effort Plan, however, the same applies to all other residents of the United Effort Plan land whether or not they are on any list.

If your clients are intent upon causing a legal confrontation which will bring untold misery and suffering to the community because of the close relationship between many of the families living there, my clients will resist such actions for as long as it takes to protect and preserve their way of life. There will be no spoils for the victor in such a battle; however, my clients are convinced that they will prevail however painful the victory. Nonetheless, they are convinced, as are the vast majority of the people in the community, that a painful battle is far less painful than to consent to the destruction of the community and life they have worked for so hard and so long.

Very truly yours,
(Signed) Charles A. Ditsch

After Fred read the letter, Leroy Johnson spoke to the people while sitting in his wheelchair. His speech was very halting, pausing several times to collect his thoughts before going on. It was very hard to understand what he was saying as he stumbled through his sermon which follows:

Sermon by Leroy S. Johnson:

"I feel very humble, my brothers and sisters, in trying to say something to you and I pray that the Lord will put in my mouth the words that He wants me to say.

"This ship (Note 7) that has been portrayed to us today is under fire, but I hope that there's someone here that will carry this message to the opposite people, because they haven't been men enough – haven't manhood enough to come out in the open and let us know who they are. We know who some of them are, but we don't know who they all are. So, I'm talking to you today to let you know that there is not going to be any deeds to any part of the United Effort Plan given to the enemy of the United Effort Plan.

"They can take it or leave it. It was given to us by the Lord for a protection for his people, his saints and I'm not afraid to speak in defense of it, because every man who has taken up his arms against the United Effort Plan and against this work that I profess to be the head of, they're fighting against God, not me and they'd better look out because if they push it any farther God will lay a heavy hand on their shoulder, and I'm not afraid to say it, because I have the Spirit of God upon me and He's dictating my words at the present time. And they better take it. They'd better not push me any farther toward the wall, until I can get on my feet and get my people behind me and get the non-believers out of this place. I want them to get discouraged and leave right away, every one.

"Now I want to say a few words to the faithful. The Lord is pleased with your actions so far, you who have determined in your minds to serve God and keep His commandments at all hazards and pray to the Lord, the Savior Jesus Christ and in the Prophet Joseph Smith and his works, but those who try to change the works of Joseph Smith – the words of Joseph Smith as are contained in the Doctrine and Covenants, had better walk carefully because the judgements of God are terrible when they come upon any disobedient people. Now, I pray that the Lord will bless you all, in the name of Jesus Christ, Amen."

After this meeting there was a general spirit of triumph manifest among the Barlows and their followers. They depicted an attitude of arrogance among the people of the community, establishing an illusion of victory over the Dissidents. It was portrayed that a letter from such authority as an attorney was immediately accepted as unquestioned truth. It is true that the denial of Leroy to consider any kind of relief to those who felt threatened was discouraging, but a letter (comprised of lies) from an attorney was not enough to convince them that they were ready to give up. An interesting thing about Ditsch's letter is that the statements, the terminology and the general tone of it, identifies it as being of Sam Barlow's composition. Witnesses to the compiling of the letter say that all Ditsch did was write down what Sam and his brothers told him to write (this is no discredit to Ditsch, as any attorney only knows what his clients tell him about a case, until he has had the opportunity to become acquainted with it himself).

There are statements in the letter that must be refuted here. Concerning the facts in the issue of Cora, she had not vacated her home, and Sam and his cohorts knew this. The state of the house was not "one of neglect and abandonment." It is true that the power had been turned off; this is one of the reasons she had gone to work, to earn enough money to take care of some of these problems because the "charitable" organization she belonged to was not willing to come to the help and support of a destitute member.

Ditsch writes; (she) "arrived from Salt Lake, where, we understand, she had established residence, which may have been for the possibility of obtaining the greater welfare payments available in those environs." This statement is typical of Sam Barlow's procedure of discrediting those he has chosen to eliminate from the community. He exaggerates any little fact (the only true fact in this statement is that she did return from Salt Lake) by embellishing it with his own suppositions. Then he "adds" some other substance by using the terminology, "possibility" in this case, to add credibility to the accusation. These additions are for the purpose of bringing disrepute to his "victim." In this case, establishing the "fact" that Cora only went to Salt Lake so she could take advantage of the welfare program, somehow suggesting that she is a wicked and vile person.

An interesting note here is that Fred Jessop's philosophy is to take advantage of any and all of the government programs he can. Over fifty percent (this is a conservative estimate) of "his" subjects are on either food stamps or WIC (the women, infants and children program), and Sam Barlow himself, is one of these recipients.

Cora was served with a notice to "vacate (of eviction)" after Sam had taken possession of her house. She was not given 30 days to move as Ditsch's letter states, but rather 10 days, after she was forcibly moved out. Much of her personal property had been removed from the premises before she returned home from Salt Lake and most of it was never recovered.

When Andrew was served a notice to "vacate (of eviction)," he had not "for all intents and purposes completed a new residence in Fredonia." It is true that he had purchased an old run-down house in Fredonia (the only fact Sam has stated in the letter), but by no stretch of the imagination was it "completed." He did not "need to move there shortly after the (eviction) notice was served so that he could enter his children in school." He was planning to move to Fredonia the next year, and his intentions were to have his children attend school at Colorado City for one more year. The purpose of the "notice (eviction)" was not "merely to make sure that the home which he intended to vacate would be available for use by another member of the community within a reasonable period of time, but rather was to "punish" him for his defiance of Sam Barlow's "high calling."

The claim that the evictions "were not forcible" is ridiculous in the extreme. How can Sam (Ditsch) claim that Cora was not forced from her home. Her personal belongings were removed (stolen) and she was expelled from her house several days before the "official eviction notice" arrived from Kingman.

The claim that "the people of Colorado City are a very peaceful people with primarily agrarian interests" is a contradiction to Leroy's statement in the meeting where Fred read the letter: "They're fighting against God, not me and they'd better look out because if they push it any farther God will lay a heavy hand on their shoulder…. They'd better not push me any farther toward the wall, until I can get on my feet and get my people behind me and get the non-believers out of this place. I want them to get discouraged and leave right away, every one." This along with the recent beatings of the young men by the "Jerry, Joe-Harryites" destroys the credence of this statement.

The claim that when "the Arizona Highway Patrol in 1953…arrived in town with drawn guns only to find the people waiting in the streets to comply with the lawful orders of the raiders" is a misnomer indeed. The reason the officers came into town with "drawn guns" was because they had been met with many dynamite blasts, with some of these being in very close proximity to the policeman while waiting on the outskirts of the town. The officers were afraid for their very lives that Cult members were determined to fight it out.

The "Dissidents knew" that the Polygamists had the stash of guns and that the reason the "State and Federal officials (were) investigating this matter" was not at the request of Sam Barlow, but rather because he refused to cooperate with the Washington County Sheriff on the matter. They were very uncomfortable about the "threats" that were being made by Leroy of the slaughter of the wicked, etc.

The claim that persons in the group asking for their deeds who were living in Utah "should never have been listed as beneficiaries because they don't reside on Arizona land" is confusing to say the least. If such persons were listed as beneficiaries on an official document filed in the County Court House, how can the fact that they live in a different state exclude them from being such a beneficiary? It is true that just because their names were filed on the document does not "make" them a beneficiary, but it doesn't mean they are not beneficiaries. What made them beneficiaries was their membership in the United Effort Plan; and the property, time, money and allegiance given to the trust, was what constituted them to be such members. Where Sam (Ditsch) uses the word

236

consecrate, he is alleging that such means "giving" as a gift, from those making the consecration to the trust. The definition of consecrate is:

1. To make or declare sacred.

2. To devote to some purpose.

The consecrations made to the United Effort Plan were for the devoted purpose of the consecrating member's own use, not to be "snatched" from them by unscrupulous manipulators. Keep in mind that the improvements (houses) made to the property "given" to the members by the trust for their use, was paid for by the individual member, not by the trust. Sam (Ditsch) states "...that property once consecrated to the trust is not returnable. The whole scenario is legally similar to a lessee improving real estate. Without a provision in the lease, the lessee must leave the improvements that have become affixed to the land when his tenancy terminates."

This statement is another misnomer. If a lessee makes improvements on leased property with the owner's permission and there is no provision for such in the lease, then the owner will be required to pay for such improvements if he attempts to evict the lessee. If the lessee continues to live up to the conditions of the lease, he cannot be evicted and can remain on the property, enjoying the improvements he has made indefinitely. If he chooses to leave, then, and only then, does he forfeit his improvements (AZ Revised Statutes).

This had always been the policy of the UEP, to wait until those who were dissatisfied with living among the polygamists decided to leave on their own volition. Those thus leaving would then forfeit their improvements and would have no claim on the trust for them. It was only when the "new" trustees decided to begin the evictions that the trust was placed in jeopardy of these members having an equity claim on their homes.

The remainder of the letter is only so much rhetoric of Sam Barlow. The statements are misrepresented truths. The people who were asking for their deeds are accused of "acting prejudicial to the spirit of the trust," while in reality the "new" trustees are the ones who are acting prejudicial to the spirit of the trust. The spirit of the trust was one of being charitable and philanthropic, helping members who were in need, not robbing them of their pittance. He further states that "...the purpose of the trust (is) to use its assets to satisfy the just needs of people residing in Colorado City (the only people residing in Colorado City who are using the assets of the trust to satisfy their just wants and needs are Fred Jessop and his Barlow Nephews); ...(and) my clients will resist such actions (legal confrontation) for as long as it takes to protect and preserve their way of life (living off the poor people)."

If the polygamist leaders had been more realistic about settling with these few people at this time, it would have saved them literally millions of dollars. As it was, they chose to make a big issue of not surrendering "their principles" and the cost to their followers has been horrendous.

Two other events of significance also happened in February of 1985. James Zitting was put in as UEP trustee and Sam Barlow retired as deputy of the Mohave County Sheriff Department.

James Zitting was born about 1953, and was about the youngest of Charles Zitting's children. He married Truman Barlow's oldest daughter, securing for him a position of importance among the Polygamists. He had been "given" a house (taken from Jesse Beagley who had allowed him to temporarily live in the house for a short period, but refused to give it up when Mr. Beagley needed it back) to live in and one of the rare jobs in the community. At this time Truman was managing the UEP Service station (J & B Service) and James went to work there.

Because of his position of working for Truman, James was often called on to run errands and perform other small tasks for Fred Jessop. By 1985 he had become Fred's "Little Errand Boy." He was pretty much constantly with him wherever he went. It was because of this very reason that he was called to be a Trustee of the United Effort Plan. Fred was in Phoenix and had been in consultation with UEP attorney Ditsch. He called Leroy at Colorado City and told him that Ditsch had informed him that the Trust Document required them to appoint another Trustee. Leroy asked Fred who was with him. When Fred told him, "James Zitting," Leroy said, "Make him the new trustee." This bears out the fact that trustees for the United Effort Plan are not chosen because of their experience or intellect. The only qualification necessary to be a UEP trustee is the ability to agree with whatever the "President" tells them and then parroting this wisdom on to the other members of the organization. James Zitting, being strong on brawn and slow of mind, fit the requirement perfectly.

In the fall of 1984, Fred Jessop lost the election for the Mohave County Sheriff (Fred himself was not running for sheriff but rather the man he supported lost). He had told the Arizona residents of the Polygamist Community to vote for the incumbent sheriff. Colorado City residents voted almost unanimously as Fred had instructed, but he lost anyway. Joe Bonzelet, an unknown among the polygamists, won the election by a margin of about 9 votes county wide. At Colorado City there were about 350 who voted for the incumbent and about 12 for Mr. Bonzelet. If only 5 of the 12 voting for Mr. Bonzelet had voted for the incumbent as Fred had decreed, the incumbent would have remained in office. This was a very close race and the incumbent demanded that the votes be recounted, not once, but several times because the margin would always favor Mr. Bonzelet. The issue was finally settled and Mohave County had a new sheriff.

Unsure of his position, Sam Barlow went to Kingman immediately after it was decided that Mr. Bonzelet had won the election. He arrogantly informed the new sheriff that in the past it had been the policy of newly elected County Officials to leave intact any of the appointees on the Arizona Strip in their official positions. This, of course, included him as the Deputy Sheriff up there.

Sheriff Bonzelet was unimpressed. He disliked Sam's arrogance from their very first meeting. He asked Sam what benefit it would be to the Sheriff's Department to keep him on as deputy. Sam's reply, "We can give you 350 votes in any future election."

The Sheriff's reply, "I won without you. I don't need your votes."

Sam's attempt to politically "buy" the Sheriff with the votes of the polygamists only convinced him to no longer keep Sam as a deputy. Sam Barlow had been a full time deputy for about 12 years and for this reason it was not a simple matter to dismiss him. However, Sheriff Bonzelet came up with a plan that he felt would work for him and proceeded to implement it.

The deputies of the Mohave County Sheriff's Department were paid an hourly rate for the time they put in for the department. Any overtime hours (over 40 hours per week) put in were to be paid at the rate of time-and-a-half. The policy of the Sheriff's Department had been to not pay for this overtime, but rather let it accrue over the years, calling it "compensatory" or "comp-time." The idea being to allow the deputies to use this comp-time when they needed occasional time off, thus being able to collect their wages for their off time. This plan did not work for all deputies because some of them would accumulate much more time than they could ever use under this arrangement.

By 1985, the payment of this comp-time to the deputies was a very heated issue. Those with the comp-time were asking for a cash settlement from the county because their retirement time was coming up. Sam was about 8 years short of being eligible for retirement but when other deputies began demanding their comp-time payments, he thought he could collect for his also. His comp-time had built up to about 4,000 hours (Note 8) and amounted to a cash payment of about $70,000.00. The amount of compensatory hours accrued by sheriff's deputies added to about 25,000 hours and would cost the county nearly $400,000.00 to pay off. The county's total comp-time, counting all departments, was about 35,000 hours and would cost the county about $500,000.00, if it was all paid off. Under state mandate, when county employees quit, they are paid for their comp-time at the time-and-a-half rate. If their comp-time is "burned up" while still working, it is reimbursed at straight time. It was therefore much more advantageous to keep the employee on the payroll, giving him time off to use up the comp time.

When Sam Barlow approached Sheriff Bonzelet to ask to be paid for his comp-time, the sheriff told him the only way he could get paid was if he resigned from the department. He told Sam that if he would write up a letter of resignation he would present it to the County Supervisors and ask that they pay him off. Sam proposed the idea that he could resign, collect his payment, and then go back to work for the Sheriff's Department for another 8 years, then he would be eligible for the state's public safety retirement money. The Sheriff agreed that such a plan would be entirely legal and it could work if all parties agreed to it. He was careful to not agree to the plan, but Sam, in his mind, believed that he would be hired back after he collected his comp-time money.

Sam Barlow wrote his letter of resignation and gave it to Sheriff Bonzelet. The Sheriff took the matter before the County Board of Supervisors and, after some heated debates with them, it was agreed to pay Sam off.

On May 15, 1985, Sam Barlow was paid almost $70,000.00 for his 4,000 hours of compensatory time, sick leave, and accrued vacation time. It is interesting to note here that the other deputies who had first asked to be paid for their compensatory time did not collect when Sam Barlow did. This caused some bitter feelings among those involved and there would be some lawsuits filed in an attempt to collect this money, using Sam Barlow's case as a precedent.

Sam was very pleased about his good fortune. After a few months from the time he collected the money, he went back to the sheriff and told him he was ready to go back to work. The sheriff simply told him that he did not have a job for him and was not about to hire him back. This was a big shock to Sam. He thought that a deal had been made for him to come back to work after he had collected the money. He threatened a lawsuit if he was not hired back but the sheriff stood his ground, not being intimidated by such a threat. Sam just went back to Colorado City and no lawsuit was ever filed.

Sam's dismissal from the sheriff's department marked a milestone in the history of the polygamists at Colorado City. The young man who took his place as the deputy for the area was more careful than Sam had been about using civil authority to enforce ecclesiastical rules on the young people of the community. This allowed them more freedom of choice and resulted in some loss of control by the religious leaders.

An interesting matter must be brought out here. There was very little real crime among the young people of the polygamists at Colorado City. Most of Sam's time involving these young citizens and their "offences" were crimes against Church rules rather than civil violations. Most all of his comp-time was accrued in this manner, making the matter of his being paid by the county a very controversial issue. There was really no way to prove that such was fact, so no action was ever taken in the matter. The Sheriff (and the young people of Colorado City) were just happy to be rid of him and the business of changing the political climate of Colorado City had begun.

Other developments occurring through this change of the civil authority at Colorado City included the establishment of the new High School District in the Polygamist community.

On March 5, 1985, a special election was held in Mohave County to vote on the forming of the new district. This election was funded by the Colorado City Elementary School District at a cost of $5,000.00. This cost was two to three thousand dollars less than had been anticipated. This was partly due to the combining of some of the smaller districts, resulting in less voter participation (Some of those who were in these combined districts were forced to drive more than a hundred miles one way to get to their assigned polling places).

The result was a majority vote in favor of forming the new district. Out of 26,000 eligible voters, only 1,787 actually cast ballots. Of these votes, there were 1,152 for and 635 against. When the issue was first voted on in November of 1984, there were 15,236 votes cast. Of these, 8,383 were "no," while 6,853 were in favor for the forming of the new district. Holding the election at an inconvenient time for the voters was the principal reason for the low voter turnout. This was no doubt the reason that the Polygamists won their new High School District.

The new High School District was designated "Colorado City High School District No. 2." The new district would have to remain in existence for one year. After the one year period, it would then be combined with the Elementary District, being called "Colorado City Unified District No. 14."

The forming of the new public high school at Colorado City was a local controversial issue to say the least. This was due to the events that were transpiring in the religious aspects of the community. Feelings of animosity between the two religious factions that had formed because of Hammon and Timpson's dismissal from the Priesthood Council by Leroy Johnson, were becoming very bitter at this time. The Hammon and Timpson group (2nd Ward) were still in control of the Colorado City Academy, the only high school available to students in the area. The public school had been granted permission to hold 9th grade the year before, but due to State Mandates, all students in Arizona would be required to either attend school through the 12th grade, or until age 18, beginning in the fall of 1985. This caused a problem for the Polygamist Leaders of the Barlow/Johnson Group (1st Ward); they must either form their own public school, or allow their children to attend the Academy, an unthinkable alternative. If they were able to get their own public school, they would need all the students in the community to attend it rather than the Academy, in order to bring up their ADA (average daily attendance) to properly fund it, so a renewed effort must be made to close the Academy.

The original charter for the Academy was still good for one year because only 24 of the 25 years had elapsed. The Barlows were misinformed on this fact, supposing that the charter would be up in the fall of 1985. They became very bold in their boasting as to how "the Academy would not open again another year." Leroy even made some "prophecies" along these lines. It came as a shock to them to learn that there was no way they could keep the private school from operating another year.

It was in January of 1985 when Jack Knudson and Claude Cawley were "given" the deeds to their homes on the Academy owned property. Although Jack

Knudson immediately gave his deed to Leroy, it was a few months later before the significance of this action fully settled on the Barlows. It took them a few months to check out that the Academy did indeed own the property. When Leroy learned this, he was furious. He began making threats, promising lawsuits if the property was not turned back over to the UEP. In a Sunday Meeting on June 9, 1985, he said that if Claude Cawley did not have "his deed on my desk by Monday morning, he would be served a summons in a lawsuit on Wednesday." The Barlows left for Phoenix after the meeting to see their lawyer, Distch, to see what could be done about getting the Academy property back (Claude Cawley caved in under Leroy's threat and gave his deed back to the UEP). This did not alleviate the matter of Leroy filing a lawsuit, however. A few other developments should be covered here before going on to the matter of this lawsuit.

On March 4, 1985, a new grocery store was opened in Colorado City. This store was severely needed in the polygamist community and had taken over 15 years for its establishment. To relate the story of this store, we must go back to as early as 1958, when Marion Hammon came back to Short Creek to revitalize the United Effort Plan. This story deserves telling as it portrays the problems and characterization of the United Effort Plan and its management personnel.

When the practice of living United Order was changed from the members receiving their commodities from the storehouse to the issuing of script with which to purchase their necessities, a store was in operation at Short Creek. This store, originally called Short Creek Supply, was being operated by David Broadbent and he had changed the name to Dave's Mercantile. David Broadbent was a good business man and as long as he ran the store it was successful to a modest degree.

The problem was that he lacked capital to expand. When Hammon came back to the community and proceeded to ask other people to move there to help build a city, he correctly concluded that a well provisioned store was a major necessity. One of his first decisions was to remove David Broadbent from the management of the store and replace him with someone who was more of a promoter, someone who could hustle credit to more abundantly stock the store. The man he chose for the position was Merril Jessop, a good choice.

Merril Jessop was a promoter and did a good job of establishing a successful store. The name was again changed, to General Supply. About this same time Truman Barlow took over the management of the service station that was just across the road from the store building. It was called J&B Service (Johnson & Black, after Spencer Johnson and Orson Black who had attempted a mechanic repair business, but due to the difficulty of collecting for their services, was forced to close down), where he sold gasoline and other services related to the automotive business.

Merril and Truman were first cousins, had grown up together and were very close friends. They operated these businesses pretty much as though they were one. Their's was a strong partnership and they remained close friends and confidants throughout their lives. At an early age they had dedicated themselves to the "up-building of the Kingdom of God" and worked themselves into a very close position to Fred and Leroy.

The first mistake these inexperienced men (in 1958, they were only 22 years old) made was allowing credit to the people in the community. In only a few months (due to the people not paying their bills), what limited credit had been established with their suppliers was used up. And since they could not pay these creditors, the store and service station were unable to keep the businesses stocked. Consequently those who were paying their bills were unable to obtain goods and services in the community, and so had to go to the outside towns for their supplies. This only increased the problem, not only because those who paid their bills were taking their money out of the community, but those who owed the large bills, when they were no longer allowed credit there, would also take their money outside to obtain their necessities rather than paying anything on their bills. This only made the problem worse for Merril and Truman. Under these conditions the store and service station were unable to either serve the people or to achieve any progress of growth to match the growth of the community.

By the middle of the 1960s these businesses were so bad off that almost all the money of the polygamists was going outside the community for their needs. Marion Hammon, who was still in charge of running the affairs of the polygamists at Colorado City, could see the necessity of alleviating the situation; a new program must be initiated.

The first problem to overcome in establishing a suitable store was to provide a building, because the old building was too small and unsuitable for the foreseeable growth of the community. The problem of financing such a building was the major hurdle. To raise this money, the burden was again put to the people; however, a different approach was taken this time. The people were not just asked to "donate" money for a Priesthood Project as in times past, but rather it was promoted to them as a "business" proposition.

The General Supply, a proprietorship, was changed to a co-operative, or a community owned business. The people were "invited" to buy $500.00 memberships in the Co-op (Note 9); the benefit to them being not only building a business, but that at the end of the year, they would be "given" a dividend on any profit that the company made. The plan was a good one and succeeded in raising enough money to actually construct an adequate building to meet the aspirations of the organizers. The work on the building went forward and toward the end of the decade the building shell was completed, sparking much optimism among the members of the General Co-op. The momentum on the project stopped at this point, however, and the building stood vacant for the next ten years, a monument of folly to the incompetence of the polygamists leaders.

There is more than one reason why the momentum of the General Co-op stopped in the late 1960s: the first being the problem of the Barlows' attempt to rid the UEP of Marion Hammon. This put the management of all the UEP projects in a stalemate condition because a transition was taking place in the control of these projects going from Hammon to Leroy (the Barlows).

During these years, there was much confusion about just who was managing the affairs at Colorado City. Consequently, many of the projects suffered, the General Co-op building being one of these. There are other reasons (bad management personnel that contributed to the problems), but this is the main reason the building sat empty for over ten years.

In about 1984, after Hammon had virtually lost his influence in the community, Leroy again promoted the selling of more memberships in the Co-op to raise enough money to complete the building and stock it with the necessary commodities to establish a store in the community. This was really a Barlow effort because Leroy was not in much of a condition to promote anything. As an example of their using Leroy for their own promotion, at one of their money raising rallies they put him on a platform in the parking lot of the new building, then raised the platform into the air with a lift-truck while they took turns standing on the platform telling the people in the crowd that Uncle Roy wanted them to buy more memberships in the Co-op. He had become nothing more than an icon for them to help raise the money they needed to open the new store.

They were successful in raising the money they needed and on March 4, 1985, the new store was opened. On this opening day of business they took in about $52,000.00, a very impressive amount of money for the community at the time. The operation of the new store was turned over to Joe Barlow to manage and he was able to run it completely broke in less than one year. Again another plea was put to the people to raise the money to bail him out and restock the store. It only took another year for him to again run it broke. The management was then taken from him and turned over to Art Blackmore who, due to his better management ability, has made it a successful venture. There will be more about the status of the General Supply/Co-op and the transitions it has gone through in a later chapter.

In the first part of 1985, there was evidence that the postmistress, one of Fred Jessop's wives, was holding up some of the first class mail. There was later an affidavit made by a teenage girl who was living in the home of Fred Jessop at the time, wherein she swore that the postmistress would bring several letters home each night and Fred would steam them open, read them, then have her take them back to the post office the next day where they could be delivered to their rightful owners. In a deposition of Fred Jessop in about 1989, he testified that his wife had been dismissed from working for the postal department for opening first class mail.

There is no doubt that the only reason she was opening the mail was because Fred had told her to do so, yet she took the punishment while he got off scot free. (The author drives to another town to deposit his mail.)

In the summer of 1985, a movement was started to incorporate Colorado City. This effort would be successful and the city was indeed incorporated on September 17, 1985.

It was in the fall of 1985 that Leroy Johnson and Rulon Jeffs, in defiance of the covenants they had made with Marion Hammon and Alma Timpson, filed a lawsuit against them in an attempt to regain control of the Colorado City Academy. This control was necessary because the Hammon group was holding their religious meetings in the Academy building and Leroy's group would do whatever was necessary to run any religious opposition out of the community.

They must also regain the deeds of the property that was owned by the Colorado City Academy. In the light of these problems, Leroy and Jeffs justified themselves in violating the sacred covenants that he, Leroy, had imposed upon them in their early Priesthood Council Meetings in the 1950s, wherein they raised their hands to the square and covenanted to each other, before God and Angels as witnesses, that they would never hire any lawyers or go to the civil courts to settle any arguments or disagreements that would come among them. Marion Hammon and Alma Timpson felt obligated to keep these covenants, therefore they would succumb to Leroy and Jeffs' demands, returning the Academy back to them without any struggle.

Note 1: The following is a transcript of the telephone conversation between Cyril Bradshaw in Colorado City and Leroy Johnson in Salt Lake City. This call was made after Ditsch had written the letter to the Corporation Commission, and took place on August 14, 1984: Call was received by Mildred Barlow Johnson (one of Leroy's wives). I (Cyril) asked to speak with President Johnson and he answered. I identified myself. He asked how I was doing. I answered that I was doing fine and asked how he was doing. He said "OK."

I then said, "I'd like to talk to you sometime about the Academy, if that's acceptable to you." He replied, "I've nothing to do with the Academy any more. I'm out of that."

Cyril: "President Jeffs gave me to understand that you wanted back in, so I–"

Leroy: "If you want to – if you run that Academy it will be separate from us – from our people."

Cyril: "All right, sir."

Leroy: "Under the direction – you've been operating under the direction of Brother Hammon and that's where you're going to be. If you want to go – be under my direction you're going to be there, so you can take your choice now."

Cyril: "All right, sir."

Leroy: "OK you can tell that to Brother Hammon if you want."

Cyril: "OK – Brother Johnson, while I have you on the phone, are we going to be able to use Sister Johnson in there this year?"

Leroy: "No sir."

Cyril: "All right, sir. I'll consider then – I'll look somewhere else then."

Leroy: "OK."

Cyril: "Thank you so much."

Leroy: "You bet."

Cyril: "God bless you. I sure pray for you continually."

Leroy: "God bless you."

Cyril: "Thank you."

Leroy: "Good bye."

Cyril: "Good bye."

Note 2: This letter of Charles Ditsch is as follows:

June 5, 1984

Arizona Corporation Commission Incorporation Division P.O. Box 6019 Phoenix, Arizona 85005

Attn: Francis:

Gentlemen: I represent Rulon T. Jeffs and Leroy S. Johnson, who have, since its inception in 1961, been members and trustees of Colorado City Academy, a nonprofit corporation. The only other surviving members and trustees are Alma A. Timpson and J.M. Hammon.

Section 3 of Article VII of the Articles of Incorporation requires that any amendment to the Articles of Incorporation requires the unanimous affirmative vote of the members. It is our understanding that a purported amendment to the Articles of Incorporation of Colorado City Academy has been submitted to your office. You are notified that the said amendment was not voted for by my clients, who constitute two of the four members of the corporation and who were not notified of any meeting to vote on the amendment; therefore, it would appear that said amendment was not properly adopted and based on the notification herein, should be rejected by the Corporation Commission. You are further notified that the only members and trustees of the corporation are Messrs. Johnson, Jeffs, Hammon and Timpson. If you have any questions, please contact me.

Very truly yours,
(signed) Charles A. Ditsch

Note 3: Hammon made this remark: "And I thought we were Brethren," because of the covenants the members of the Priesthood Council had made with one another, that they would never take any of the other members to a civil court, or use lawyers to settle differences they may have between each other. That is why it was such a surprise to him when Leroy and Jeffs threatened to take him to court over the matter. He held firm to his part of the covenant, but the covenant meant nothing to Leroy and Jeffs.

Note 4: The First Amended Affidavit of Disclosure was filed by Charles Ditsch, UEP Attorney, in the Mohave County Court House at Kingman, Arizona, on November 27, 1983, in Book 979, p. 741, and is as follows:

AMENDED AFFIDAVIT OF DISCLOSURE STATE OF ARIZONA ss. County of Mohave

LEROY S. JOHNSON and RULON JEFFS, each being first duly sworn, deposed and states as follows:

1. That pursuant to the provisions of Section 33-401 Arizona Revised Statutes, an Affidavit of Disclosure was executed and recorded in Mohave County, Arizona, in Docket 355, p. 818.

2. That Leroy S. Johnson is President and Rulon Jeffs is Secretary of the United Effort Plan, a common law trust, as amended, which is established by a declaration of trust recorded in Book 31 of Miscellaneous Records, at Pages 597 through 600, records of Mohave County, Arizona.

3. That the Trustees of the aforementioned trust hold title to the real property particularly described on Exhibit A attached hereto and by this reference made a part hereof.

4. That this Amended Affidavit of Disclosure is being recorded to correctly set forth the beneficiaries of the trust and their addresses as of the date this Amended Affidavit of Disclosure is executed. The beneficiaries and their addresses are as set forth on Exhibit B attached hereto and by this reference made a part hereof.

5. This affidavit is made for the purpose of complying with the above-referenced Arizona Revised Statute and for no other purpose.

IN WITNESS WHEREOF, the above officers have executed this affidavit for the purposes hereinabove set forth.

(signed) Leroy S. Johnson

Leroy S. Johnson, President

(signed) Rulon Jeffs

Rulon Jeffs, Secretary

SUBSCRIBED AND SWORN to before me this 12 day of November, 1983.
(signed) William S. Shapley.
Notary Public
My commission expires: July 9, 1984.

It is interesting to note that this Amended Affidavit of Disclosure was of such importance as to delete over a hundred of the beneficiaries, and was executed by Leroy and Jeffs without the knowledge of Marion Hammon, who was one of the trustees at the time. It is also interesting to note that Hammon was one of the beneficiaries that was deleted from the list.

Note 5: The second and third amended affidavits of disclosure are as follows:

Fred Jessop P.O. Box 257 Colo. City, Az. 86021

SECOND AMENDED AFFIDAVIT OF DISCLOSURE STATE OF ARIZONA

ss. County of Mohave

LEROY S. JOHNSON and RULON JEFFS, each being first duly sworn, deposes and states as follows:

1. That pursuant to the provisions of Section 33-401 Arizona Revised Statutes, as amended, an Affidavit of Disclosure was executed and recorded in Mohave County, Arizona, in Book 355, p. 818. Said Affidavit of Disclosure was amended by an Amended Affidavit of Disclosure recorded in said county in Book 979, p. 741.

2. That the original Affidavit of Disclosure recorded in Book 355, p. 818, was incorrect in that it listed as trustees Guy Musser, Richard S. Jessop and Alma Timpson, none of which persons were ever appointed trustees of The United Effort Plan, a common law trust, but were erroneously included as trustees in the original Affidavit of Disclosure.

3. That this Second Amended Affidavit of Disclosure is being recorded to correct the erroneous inclusion of the trustees as of June 22, 1976. That as of said date, the trustees of The United Effort Plan, a common law trust, were Leroy S, Johnson, Rulon Jeffs and J. Marion Hammon and no other person.

4. That this Second Amended Affidavit is made for the purpose of correcting the original affidavit of Disclosure and for the purpose of complying with the above-referenced Arizona Revised Statute and for no other purpose.

IN WITNESS WHEREOF, the above officers have executed this affidavit for the purposes herein above set forth.

(signed) Leroy S. Johnson

LEROY S. JOHNSON, President

(signed) Rulon Jeffs

RULON JEFFS, Secretary

SUBSCRIBED AND SWORN to before me this 4th day of September, 1984.
(Signed) Wm. W. Shapley
Notary Public
(Filed in Book 1052, p. 675)
My commission expires: July 9, 1988

CHARLES A. DITSCH
Attorney At Law
240 East Sierra Vista Drive
Phoenix, Arizona 86012.

THIRD AMENDED AFFIDAVIT OF DISCLOSURE STATE OF ARIZONA

ss. County of Mohave

LEROY S. JOHNSON, RULON JEFFS and FRED M. JESSOP, each being first duly sworn, deposes and states as follows:

1. That pursuant to the provisions of Section 33-401 Arizona Revised Statutes, as amended, an Affidavit of Disclosure was executed and recorded in Mohave County, Arizona, in Book 355, p. 818. Said Affidavit of Disclosure was amended by an Amended Affidavit of Disclosure recorded in said county in Book 979, p. 741. Said Affidavit of Disclosure was amended by a Second Amended Affidavit of Disclosure recorded in said county in Book 1052, p. 675.

2. That J. MARION HAMMON has resigned as a trustee of The United Effort Plan, a common law trust, and FRED M. JESSOP has been appointed as a trustee of said trust.

3. That this Third Amended Affidavit of Disclosure is made for the purpose of setting forth the names of the trustees as of the date hereof, said trustees being LEROY S. JOHNSON, RULON JEFFS and FRED M. JESSOP.

IN WITNESS WHEREOF, the above officers have executed this Affidavit for the purposes herein above set forth.

                    (signed) Leroy S. Johnson
                        LEROY S. JOHNSON, President
                    (signed) Rulon T. Jeffs
                        RULON JEFFS, Secretary
                    (signed) Fred M. Jessop
                        FRED M. JESSOP
SUBSCRIBED AND SWORN to before me this 18th day of September, 1984.
                    (signed) Maryett E. Carling
                    Notary Public
                    My commission expires: 12-28-87
                    (filed in Book 1057, p. 244)

The reader should take special note here as to how the United Effort Plan is designated as a COMMON LAW TRUST. Note that nothing is said in any of these Amended Affidavits of Disclosure about the Trust being anything other than a Common Law

Trust and certainly there is no pretext, or claim, of it ever being religious in nature.

Note 6: One of the anonymous letters being circulated by the Dissidents commented on this high handed opinion of Fred Jessop's. It seems appropriate to insert it here. It is as follows:

"Quoting from the *Twin City Courier*, vol. 23 #1, Jan. 24, 1985: 'Blessings lost sight of in these days has caused some to become embittered against the hands through which our community's solidarity has been made; and, like all others who have forsaken faith, they have resorted to the outside enemy help, for hoped for comfort.'

"There are always two sides to every story. Can the readers of the '*Twin City Courier*' accept this statement at face value? In most cases, yes, they will, without even considering what the other side of the story may be. We in this community have been taught since birth to accept without any mental reservations the words of our religious leaders as the truth, the whole truth, and nothing but the truth. The fallacy in this practice is that we become as robots, never thinking for ourselves, thus stagnating any growth potential. The danger here is that much injustice can be perpetrated on unsuspecting persons.

"Let's analyze the first half of the statement in the *Twin City Courier*. What 'blessings (were) lost sight of' in the case of the eviction of a woman and her 11 children? And is there any justification for her to 'become embittered against the hands through which our community's solidarity has been made?'

"In Far West, Missouri, in 1839, a host of women and small children were 'evicted' from their homes, and many were forced to walk over 200 miles, seeking a haven, and necessarily 'resorted to the (so-called) outside enemy help, for hoped-for comfort.' "Inhumane treatment of defenseless women and children by a mob of vicious men is viewed as a cowardly act by any civilized society, whether done in the name of a governor, a dictator, or a religious leader. When a governor or dictator perpetrates such unlawful and inhumane acts, it is regarded as an act of greed or quest for power. But when such acts are performed in the name of religion, it tends to infuriate the civilized and humane element of any society. And, are such acts motivated also by greed and quest for power?

"Do we expect persons who are victimized by such cowardly acts to accept their lot without any murmuring or complaint? And are we justified in starting a hate campaign against dissidents who, with the responsibility of a large family, feel compelled to secure title to their homes?

"We have learned by sad experience that there is no recourse or justice from those 'hands through which our community's solidarity has been made.' It has become necessary, therefore, to resort to the courts of the land to arbitrate the issues. And those who have taken this course are doing exactly what our venerable leader advised them to do. When he was approached by certain members of this community, and asked to help work out a solution to these issues, his very implicit reply was. 'Take me to court! If you don't like what we're doing, you can contact our attorney in Phoenix.' And that's what has been done, just as they were directed, by the man we all love and honor as our leader. If this constitutes going 'to the outside enemy help, for hoped-for comfort,' then so be it. But remember, it was the only remedy given from the one we call our leader. The responsibility of this course of action then can rest only at his door.

"Only God can settle this issue, and he has given his decision in Section 134 of the Doctrine and Covenants. We have been under the impression through the years, that this book was our rule book. But now, we hear that sec. 134 pertained only to the Church back in Joseph Smith's time. Nevertheless, we're going to try one more time...."

"Doctrine and Covenants, Section 134:

"2. We believe that no government can exist in peace, except such laws are framed and held inviolate as will secure to each individual the free exercise of conscience, the right and control of property, and the protection of life.

"9. We do not believe it just to mingle religious influence with civil government, whereby one religious society is fostered and another proscribed in its spiritual privileges, and the individual rights of its members, as citizens, denied.

"10. We believe that all religious societies have a right to deal with their members for disorderly conduct, according to the rules and regulations of such societies; provided that such dealings be for fellowship and good standing; but we do not believe that any religious society has authority to try men on the right of property or life, to take from them this world's goods, or to put them in jeopardy of either life or limb, or to inflict any physical punishment upon them. They can only excommunicate them from their society, and withdraw from them their fellowship.

"11. We believe that men should appeal to the civil law for redress of all wrongs and grievances, where personal abuse is inflicted or the right of property or character infringed, where such laws exist as will protect the same; but we believe that all men are justified in defending themselves, their friends, and property, and the government, from the unlawful assaults and encroachments of all persons in times of exigency, where immediate appeal cannot be made to the laws, and relief afforded."

Note 7: In this meeting of February 10, 1985, Truman and Sam Barlow both spoke before Fred read the letter from Ditsch and before he and Leroy talked. Truman, in this sermon, talked about the "Good Ship Zion." This is what Leroy is referring to in his sermon. Both Truman's and Sam's sermons are entered here. Truman's will be first, Sam's next, although in the meeting Sam talked first.

Sermon by Truman Barlow, February 10, 1985, at a Sunday meeting in Colorado City, Arizona:

"I ask for an interest in your faith and prayers, while I speak for a few minutes and bare my testimony to the truthfulness of the work of God.

"I'm thankful for the life and labors of our prophet, Leroy S. Johnson. And along with you, I pray that his life can continue and that he will have strength and the wisdom to guide us – guide the old ship Zion, so to speak, through snag harbor and that we will have an opportunity of riding on that ship. You know – if we were invited to ride on the old ship Zion and there were certain problems on the ship, and the captain called for us to bail the water out, so she wouldn't sink, and we neglected to help, There would come a time when he would have to bail us out. And if there were certain individuals on the ship, who felt like their job was to bore holes in the bottom of the ship, it would be a great crisis indeed. We'd have to go to work and get our hearts and our hands in to save this ship. We are not carrying it; but it is carrying us.

"When the Lord spoke to the Prophet Joseph Smith and gave him the Priesthood, he right away, shortly afterwards, required him to organize a church, and that church had to be a legal instrument, a legal document. It went along for many, many years and the Priesthood resided in the church.

"And there came a time, when the Priesthood created another entity; and its called: The United Effort Plan; Trust. And that's the instrument, the vehicle, that the Priesthood is riding in today. And we, have an opportunity of being a part of that. And because we are invited in, to ride, to partake with Uncle Roy, does not mean that when we get disgruntled and decide to get off, that we can take a chunk of the ship with us, or that we can destroy it.

"The United Effort Plan Trust, is the greatest instrument, that has been organized and established, since the days of the Prophet Joseph Smith. And the only reason for it to fail, if it should fail, would be because the people would not do, what they knew they should do, when called upon by their leader. The Priesthood will not fail, but the people might, if they don't do what they know they should do."

"Now brothers and sisters, how can we, support, and sustain the United Effort Plan? Let a young man, an unmarried man, a Deacon, look at himself, and say; how can I support the United Effort Plan?' A young lady. The uniqueness of the people of God, upon the earth, has always been their morals, that's the uniqueness of the people of God.

"If we can practice what Uncle Roy, our Prophet Leader, under the direction of the Prophet Joseph, under the direction of Jesus Christ, has called upon us to do, in relation to being morally clean, we will be the people that the prophet Joseph is looking for. If we do not, we can not. I want you to know this applies to me ten times over. The morals of our young people is the thing that is going to see this thing through, that was the uniqueness of the people in 1953. They couldn't find immorality among the people. What would they find today?

"The uniqueness of Uncle Roy, the greatness of that man, is that he is morally clean. Who's responsibly is it, I ask myself, to raise up some children, that will be morally clean, to see this work established.

"Uncle Roy has asked me to read a few words of Brother Brigham. Says Brother Brigham, in Journal of Discourses (vol. 9, p. 220):

"'Now I come to my own experience and say; there is not an individual here, but what has power, and God has given it to him, to drink whisky, or let it alone. To swear, or not swear. To lie, or not lie. To deceive, or not deceive. To cheat, and take advantage of a neighbor, or not do so. Slander, back bite an neighbor, or a sister, or not. This power is our own individual property, and we shall be brought into judgement for the manner in which we use it, and for all our actions in the flesh. Thirty years experience has taught me that every moment of my life must be holiness to the Lord, resulting from equity, justice, mercy and uprightness in all my actions, which is the only course by which I can preserve the Spirit of the Almighty to myself. What is your experience? Is it the same as my own? You can not consistently be sinning a little and repenting, and retain the Spirit of the Lord as your constant companion. My experience up to this time has been to do as I would have others should do unto me, under like circumstances. And if I understand myself, there is not a man or women on the face of this earth that I have dealt with contrary to this rule and this practice, I have continued each day. When Monday morning breaks upon the eyes of this people, they must be as faithful to God and righteousness as they are when they partake of the sacrament; or lose the Spirit of the Lord. We have no permission to sin, for one moment. You ask me; if I ever do wrong? I answer; yes, like every body else, owing to the weakness of the flesh, but if I do wrong knowingly, then I sin. When this people can live and never do a wrong knowingly, if they should sin in their ignorance, God will freely forgive that sin. If they are ready to repent when it is made known to them and refrain from it in the future. Let us live in this way, and the kingdom is ours. It is the Kingdom of God with us, or nothing.'

"I pray my brothers and sisters, that we will be able to stand up to the call that is being made upon us today, by our beloved Prophet and leader, Uncle Roy. And that we will each one be able to do the job that we are called to do, with the Spirit of God upon us. And I ask it in the name of Jesus Christ, Amen."

Sermon by Sam Barlow, February 10, 1985 at a Sunday meeting in Colorado City, Arizona:

"I'm thankful to be here my brothers and sisters and I pray that the Spirit of the Lord will dictate the remarks that I say. I consider it a great opportunity for us to live in this day and time when – ah – the Prophet Leroy S. Johnson's life has been preserved among the peoples of the earth and in -as- much as our Father in Heaven and His son Jesus Christ made a determination, that a certain time, to open up the communication between the heavens and the earth and they initiated that by visiting the Prophet Joseph Smith and delegating to him the authority to act in their behalf among the peoples of the earth and also communicated to him a plan that had been in effect in the earth although the details of it had been lost and the authority to act in it had been for the most part removed from among the people – and subsequent to that the Prophet's life was taken because he had the courage and the – energy – and the vigor – to initiate and bring to pass this action among the people.

"And that same delegation to act for God and to seek his word and reveal to us his will concerning us as a people and also concerning the peoples of the earth is still on the earth and it is vested in the – in the – ah – delegation that is now held by the Prophet Leroy S. Johnson among the people.

"I am aware because of the exposure I have to the people of our neighboring communities that we are a much watched people. We are the conversation piece of our neighbors both in high standing and low standing, it seems that every segment of society feels at liberty to center their discussions around this people and their way of life. We are a light that cannot be hid under a bushel – and in-as-much as the times of the earth is drawing to a close – and the earth's going to be – ah – ah millennium of peace initiated by these same characters that visited the Prophet Joseph, we find ourselves in a period of time when the Lord is going to show forth his power among the people, and I am grateful to be living in this time.

"I hope and pray that any who find themselves troubled because of the stand they've taken in relation to supporting the Prophet Leroy S. Johnson, or any detrimental thing that they've done in relation to the United Effort Plan, which is our instrument of unity which, we are entitled to. I hope and pray that they will repent and show by Godly walk and conversation that they are willing to change, for I know that that's an answer to their problems and any course of self justification could perpetuate – a – an erroneous position, does not constitute an answer, it only adds to them consternation and brings distress upon those that they love. I pray that we as a people can have it in our hearts to forgive all men and to walk in careful obedience. I do not feel that the spirit of obedience nor the spirit of forgiveness requires us to surrender – the – position of obedience. I think that we must maintain that at all hazards. And in studying and learning of sacred history that we now have an abundance of to read and study, we find that many times there were men who were put on – the – had their – a – loyalties challenged to the point that they – that they had to sacrifice their lives, or apparently sacrifice their mortal life in order to maintain their integrity in obedience to the servants of God. Those men, we understand and believe with great confidence, have secured to themselves salvation in the eternal Kingdoms of our Father in Heaven.

"I hope that no child, or no mother, no widow, no family head, would in any way be afraid of the conquest that is before us because, we are on a sound premise, we do have the power of God delegated to men on earth and many, many men, not only in this congregation, but in some other congregations which Leroy S. Johnson presides over, have the power of God delegated to them, and many women have the-the gift of the Holy Ghost. They have received it in authority – to contin – in conjunction just like the men have, in which, one having authority said, to them; receive ye, the gifts of the Holy Ghost,' which entitles them to the spirit of God to direct them and protect them and lead them, as by – as it does their children and their – their husbands. There is no reason to be afraid. There is only a reason to go forward. And – all the history that I can learn of, points out that this thing is coming to a conclusion and that a new era is soon to dawn upon the peoples of the earth. Before that time there – will be a great turmoil and a great consternation, many people who's lives, social lives and religious lives have been more or less secure in their thinking up till now, will be put in a position where they are insecure. And that consternation will cause great turmoil. And may we as a people, actually live by the spirit of peace. And may we be able to follow the direction of this noble man whom God has placed among us, in his wisdom, to show us how to endure pain and suffering and the forsaking of those that should have supported him and financial stress and all manner of perplexities and not get jittery, for he is a man of great faith. It is our privilege to follow him and I hope and pray that we'll live up to that privilege. And I think that we can do it. "May the Lord bless us to do so is my prayer, in the name of Jesus Christ, Amen."

Note 8: The irony of Sam Barlow's building so much comp-time is ridiculous to say the least. He acquired his overtime hours by "enforcing religious policy" among the young people of the community rather than in legitimate law enforcement duties. A big portion of his enforcement activities were entirely unnecessary and there was certainly no justification in having the taxpayers of the county paying the bill.

Note 9: Part of the promotion of selling this plan to the people had been to issue membership certificates for each of the $500.00 membership purchased. None of these certificates were ever issued to the subscribers. In the late 1980s, the Barlows denied that the money paid by these subscribers was to buy a membership into the Co-op, but rather was a "donation to the Church," thereby robbing them of their equity in the General Co-op. One of the bookkeepers who was working at the General Co-Op at the time brought her records to a deposition which showed not only the names of these members, but also showed the amounts they had paid into the Co-op.

The United Effort Plan Lawsuit

On August 2, 1985, Leroy Johnson and Rulon Jeffs filed a lawsuit in Arizona Superior Court, Maricopa County (Phoenix) against J. M. Hammon, Alma Timpson, and Cyril Bradshaw. The purpose of the lawsuit was to regain control of the Colorado City Academy, the local high school.

When Leroy Johnson and Rulon Jeffs resigned from the board of directors of the Academy on May 30, 1984, they did not realize that the 20 acres where the Academy was situated had been deeded to the institution. It was more than a year later that they decided they must take legal action to try and reclaim the property.

When Leroy had dismissed Hammon and Timpson from the Priesthood Council he supposed that they would just fade away, leaving him in full control of the community and all its functions. When Ward 2 began holding their own religious meetings at the Academy, steps were taken by Leroy and Jeffs to force them to stop. At the urging of the Barlows, a lawsuit was filed against their former brethren, even in defiance of Leroy's actions of requiring that all Priesthood Council Members covenant with each other to never use the civil courts to settle their disputes.

This lawsuit claimed that the actions of the Board of Directors of the Academy taken in May of 1984 had been illegal because Leroy and Jeffs had not received a ten day notice that such action as their resigning was to take place in the meeting. The fact is that the meeting was not called to consider the resignation of these two members. The meeting was called to consider what to do about the coming school year in regards to the Academy operating. In the meeting Leroy spontaneously resigned and Jeffs followed suit. In an affidavit of Cyril Bradshaw, who was present at the meeting, he states:

"The affiant attended a meeting on May 30, 1984 at the residence of Leroy S. Johnson, President, J. Marion Hammon, Administrator/Trustee, and Rulon T. Jeffs, Secretary, officers of the Colorado City Academy, a Corporation existing within the State of Arizona, and Cyril Bradshaw, Principal. Since the period of duration of the Colorado City Academy was due to expire in September 1985, and according to Article II of the Articles of Incorporation, 'may be extended upon motion of the board of trustees,' the proposition to extend the period of duration was introduced. At this point President Leroy S. Johnson resigned from the corporation, stating; 'I want out of it.' J. Marion Hammon and the affiant importuned President Johnson to reconsider, but he was adamant in his proposed resignation, reaffirming his desire several times, stating; 'Brother Bradshaw can take my place.' J. Marion Hammon then gave his approval to the nomination of Cyril Bradshaw to the Board of Trustees and Rulon T. Jeffs also approved the nomination.

"Rulon T. Jeffs suggested that Article X of the Articles of Incorporation be amended to reduce the number of members from seven to three, and obtained a typewriter to compose the amendment he proposed. Since the type did not match the printed matter, he composed a rough draft for us to use later.

"At the conclusion of these activities, Rulon T. Jeffs proffered his resignation, which was accepted by those present. Meeting adjourned."

Marion Hammon, Alma Timpson, and Cyril Bradshaw met the next day, May 31, 1984, and, according to the instructions of Leroy and Jeffs, prepared the amendments discussed, signed the pertinent minutes of the meeting and had them notarized. These documents were then filed in the Mohave County Recorders Office. The amendments, together with the appropriate minutes of the Board Meeting, were sent to the Arizona Corporation Commission in Phoenix to be processed.

On June 4, 1984, Cyril Bradshaw received the phone call from Jeffs wherein he alleged "the meeting of May 30 was not valid, since any amendment must be supplied to the board ten days prior to the meeting wherein the proposed amendment would be considered."

In the same affidavit of Cyril's quoted above, he claims this stipulation does not apply here for the following reasons:

"Article II, which was under discussion, states that the period of duration 'may be extended upon motion of the board of trustees.' Also, since there was no action taken at that time, and since the amendment of Article X was proposed by Rulon T. Jeffs during the meeting, and since the only action taken in that meeting was the resignations of Leroy S. Johnson and Rulon T. Jeffs and the appointment of Cyril Bradshaw (by Leroy) to fill the vacancies left, the meeting was in order."

On August 14th, Cyril called Leroy for instructions in the matter. Leroy told him "I've nothing to do with the Academy any more. I'm out of that." Cyril then told him; "President Jeffs gave me to understand that you wanted back in…." Leroy interrupted saying, "If you want to – if you run that Academy it will be separate from us – from our people (a complete transcript of this telephone conversation is in Note 1 of Chapter Eight)." Having received verification that Leroy had in fact resigned in the May 30 meeting and had specifically told him he did not want back in (refuting the statement of Jeffs on June 4th), Cyril went ahead with the filing of the amendments with the Corporation Commission, conforming to the law in all respects.

Charles Ditsch, attorney for the United Effort Plan, informed his clients that the amendments entered by Colorado City Academy with the Corporation Commission were "forged" by Cyril Bradshaw. In the complaint filed against the new Board of the Colorado City Academy, he states: "…The Articles of Incorporation have never been legally amended…. Plaintiffs (Leroy Johnson and Rulon Jeffs), …they having never resigned nor been replaced, and…. No other members or trustees have ever been elected or appointed by or to the corporation."

The complaint further states: "The Articles of Amendment is incorrect; was not adopted in accordance with the Articles of Incorporation of the defendant Corporation; was executed by Cyril Bradshaw, who was never elected as a trustee or member of the Defendant corporation; was adopted without notice to Plaintiffs; and upon information and belief was not signed or executed by the Defendants Hammon and Timpson…. the individual Defendants having conspired to fraudulently amend the Articles of the Defendant corporation other than through process of law." The complaint then requested an order of the Court to:

"Declare that Cyril Bradshaw is not a trustee or a Member of the Defendant corporation. That the purported Articles of Amendment to the Articles of Incorporation to the Defendant corporation are void and of no force and effect. Ordering the Arizona Corporation Commission to correct the annual report of the Defendant corporation; to reflect that the trustees and members of the Defendant corporation; to reflect that the trustees and members are Plaintiffs and Defendants are Hammon and Timpson. Ordering the Arizona Corporation Commission to expunge the purported Articles of Amendment from its records, the same being void and of no further force and effect. Declaring all of the acts of the board of trustees which were done without notice to, or the consent of, the Plaintiffs to be void and of no force or effect. Awarding to the Defendant corporation damages against the individual Defendants and each of them as may be proved at the trial of this cause resulting from the improper and illegal acts of the individual Defendants purportedly acting as the board of trustees of Defendant corporation. For such other and further relief as the Court deems just and proper."

With the filing of this action, Leroy and Jeffs are denying that they ever resigned or that Cyril was appointed (by Leroy) to be on the board of trustees. The matter never went to trial, because Hammon and Timpson would honor their covenants and never use the civil courts to settle differences among members of the Priesthood Council. If it had gone to trial, there is little doubt but what it could have been proven that the Plaintiffs were not telling the truth.

When Hammon and Timpson received their summons of the complaint, they went to Salt Lake to meet with Leroy and Jeffs to try to work out a settlement on the matter without going to the civil courts. They were pleaded with by associates to not go without an attorney because the Plaintiffs would have their attorney Charles Ditsch present. These pleadings were ignored and as was to be expected, they gave in without a struggle. They agreed to "give" the Academy to Leroy and Jeffs and sign the deed of the property back to the United Effort Plan. The Barlow Cabal was not satisfied with this action on their part and demanded that Hammon, Timpson, and Bradshaw all sign a statement admitting their guilt in the "forging" of the documents filed with the Corporation Commission. They all agreed to sign a statement of waiver. This statement was drawn up by the Plaintiffs and Sam Barlow delivered it to the Defendants for their signatures. When the statement was read by the Defendants, they refused to sign it because the Plaintiffs were asking them to admit they had attempted to defraud the UEP. The statement was rewritten by Cyril Bradshaw and was then signed, allowing the Academy to be dissolved on September 10, 1985, the deed to the property to revert back to the United Effort Plan and for the Defendants to totally vacate the premises. No guilt of any wrongdoing on the part of the Defendants was acknowledged.

This agreement was then signed by the parties involved and the moves were made to carry it out. The premises were vacated as agreed to, with the Defendants taking all the furnishings and furniture, storing it at one of their places of residences outside of the community.

The important thing to note here is that this is the first lawsuit involving the United Effort Plan, where "Brethren" of the Priesthood Council used the civil law to sue others in the Council. Leroy Johnson and Rulon Jeffs filed the complaint against Marion Hammon and Alma Timpson, thus destroying any confidence that may have existed at this time and creating a chasm between them that would never be bridged.

On the night of September 10, the day that the Academy ceased to exist, some distraught students, feeling bitter about losing their school, went up to the premises and in a state of confusion over the situation, broke out all the windows in the buildings. This act of vandalism cannot in any way be condoned, but the statement it made was revealing. Fred Jessop had Sam Barlow sleuth out the culprits and demand that they pay him $2,000 for the cost of the windows. The windows were never replaced, but Fred collected the money, keeping it for himself.

After "losing" the Academy, where they had been holding their meetings, the Second Ward (Hammon and Timpson Group) began meeting in Alma Timpson's home. Some of the Barlows (Nephi Barlow and Joe Timpson) began making threats that they were not going to allow them to hold religious meetings on UEP property. These threats were never taken seriously, but it became apparent that in order to "live their religion" the Second Ward was going to have to build their own building, not only to have a place to worship how they chose, but they were determined to continue on with their school The Colorado City Academy.

They realized they would not be able to have a school for the 1985-86 school year, but their goal was to have it in operation by the next year. This seemed an almost insurmountable task. Property would have to be obtained and a suitable building erected in only one year's time. In order to accomplish this objective no time could be wasted; they must begin working on the project right away.

The first hurdle was to obtain property. Hammon stood up in a Sunday meeting held in the Timpson home, and appointed a committee of four men to look for some property in the area that they could purchase. After explaining to the people that they needed a building for their school, in his instructions to this committee he made this statement, "Go buy some property where we can build a building that NO DAMN MAN CAN TAKE AWAY FROM US."

The committee began looking in the Cane Beds area to the south of Colorado City for property. They began negotiating on one parcel about eight miles to the southeast, but just when they thought they could raise money for a down payment, Jack Knudson went to the owners and bought it out from under them. Jack Knudson did not want the property; the United Effort Plan did not want the property; the only reason he bought it was to keep the Second Ward from getting it (Knudson immediately sold the property to a firm in Idaho).

They then began negotiating with Hilda Perkins, a widow who lived in Cane Beds, who owned about 1,000 acres adjoining the UEP on the south of Colorado City but was in the Cane Beds area proper. While these negotiations where going on, Sam Barlow went to see Mrs. Perkins. Taking her to dinner in St. George and using all his charm, he tried to dissuade her of selling her property to the Hammon and Timpson Group; he even offered her more money if she would sell it to the UEP. His scheme failed and she proceeded with the agreement she had made with the other Group.

The Second Ward Group formed a land holding trust to hold title to the property. This trust was in no way a copy of the United Effort Plan Trust, which had been organized by the Priesthood Council in 1942 to attempt the living of United Order. The new Second Ward land trust was organized only for the purpose of holding the property in trust until it could be deeded to those who would build homes on it.

This trust was named Deseret Land and Trust Company. It was governed by a member board of trustees. Each trustee was to serve a three year term, after which would be subject to an election by the members of the trust. An election was to be every year where three board members would be voted on for the respective three year term. The trust would serve no other purpose than to govern the disposition of the land. No claims or attempt was made to live a United Order. The money to buy the property would be raised by people putting money into the trust for that purpose. For every $1,500.00 paid to the trust, a member would be guaranteed one acre of land, which at some future time he would receive a deed.

The agreement that was reached with Mrs. Perkins was a price of about $330,000.00 for the parcel of property, to be paid for over a three year period. Half of the money was to be paid up front with a clear title for one third of the property to be given to the buyers at that time. The remainder of the property was to be paid for in two more annual installments in equal amounts of half of the remaining balance. Another third of the property would be titled to the trust at the end of the first year, the remaining property would be released at the end of the second year.

The money was raised for the down payment and the one third portion of land chosen for the clear title was on the extreme west portion of the property because this was the most suitable area for agriculture purposes, the intent being to first begin a farming operation. The location chosen for the church/school building, however, was on the extreme eastern end of the property and because the main purpose of obtaining the land was to begin construction of this building, this is where the first activity of any kind was commenced, with ground breaking for the building started right away. This would cause some problems with Mrs. Perkins, but the problems would be overcome.

While these developments were taking place, progress was moving forward in Colorado City. An effort was made by the Barlows to incorporate the city. After the necessary elections and preliminary steps were taken care of, the Mohave County Board of Supervisors granted their petition to incorporate, with the actual incorporation taking place on September 17, 1985.

The incorporation of Colorado City was a major move for the polygamists. It gave them advantages of receiving government money to make improvements in the community. It would also allow them to have their own police force, something that they felt they needed because, since Sam's dismissal as County deputy, they had lost control of the law enforcement in the area.

A Town Council was "appointed" with Dan Barlow as the mayor. Leon Johnson, who had been acting as part-time marshal for Hildale, was hired as Colorado City Marshal, to work for both cities, his salary being split between the two municipalities. Sam Barlow's hiring as Town Marshal was not justified at this time (very little crime in the area), but interesting events would come about that would put him back in the position in less than a year, when the problem of having him removed would begin anew.

Throughout the winter months of 1985-86 work on the Second Ward meeting house moved along with impressing expedition. They were holding their meetings at the Timpson home and though there were some instances of harassment (mostly from Joe Timpson, son of Alma Timpson and Ada Barlow), the winter passed with relative peace.

In the spring, however, this peace was shattered with the receiving of a letter sent to Sam Barlow from a Leo LeBaron, threatening the life of Leroy Johnson if "he did not repent and join forces with Leo LeBaron." The letter was received in about March of 1986, and it set a time limit for sometime in April as the date by which Leroy had to "repent," indicating that on this deadline an effort would be made to assassinate him. The letter read:

"On August 16, 1984, a warning was given the fundamentalist Mormons, that God would destroy you all suddenly if you did not answer to the call of repentance. You have chosen to mock God and his Most Awesome Patriarch, Ervil LeBaron. A new Patriarch, Leo LeBaron, will now carry out the order given by the Most Awesome Patriarch Ervil. There are those living in your community guilty of sins that can only be forgiven through the ordinance of Blood Atonement.

"Do not suppose that God will not carry out his commandments, as given by his legitimate Prophet. His work of retribution will be carried out upon those not willing to repent and follow this true Prophet and Patriarch. This last warning is given to you. It is your duty to spread this warning among your people. Repent, or be destroyed by the sword of the Lord!!!

"If no evidence of sincere repentance is observed by the 1st of April, 1986, this work of redemption will begin, starting at the head, even with your false Prophet, Leroy Johnson.
        "This work will be done by the 'Avengers for The Church of The Lamb'."

Sam Barlow turned the letter over to the Washington County Sheriff at St. George (Leroy Johnson lived in Utah) and asked for his help in the matter. The first conclusion the Sheriff considered was that Leo LeBaron was indeed Leo Evonick, a former disciple of Ervil LeBaron, the man who had had Rulon Allred killed some 15 years earlier. (Ervil had just died a few years earlier in the Utah State Prison and Evonick was claiming to be his predecessor). Sam had some letters that had been written earlier by Evonick where he had signed his name as Leo LeBaron. For these reasons the threat was taken very seriously.

As a result of this letter and its threats, the newly incorporated town of Colorado City hired Sam as a deputy marshal to assist the Sheriff in the protection of Leroy. This was a slap in the face for those who had worked so hard to get Sam out of law enforcement just a few short months before. Another effort would have to be made to again rid the community of his warped tactics of "keeping the peace."

Sam Barlow's first action on the case was to invite television reporters in to cover this alleged threat by Evonick. He claimed it would be harder to carry out an assassination under the scrutiny of the news cameras. He also volunteered to the sheriff that the polygamists did indeed have the guns that he had denied having just a short time before. Sam offered to arm selected members of the community to assist the sheriff in the protection of their leader, but the sheriff wisely declined his offer. This admission of Sam Barlow just about destroyed any remaining credibility that he had with the sheriff.

All but one of the roads into town were barricaded off and sheriff deputies monitored everyone coming and going on this one opened road. For about a week, tension in the community ran high, the situation hitting national news. This caused much publicity for the polygamists, something they had always shunned, but when they felt they were in some kind of danger they were willing to call on "their outside enemies for hoped for comfort."

After about a week of this excitement, Leo Evonick, the person being blamed for it all, contacted the Washington County Sheriff and denied having anything to do with the threat. After some investigation by the authorities, it was concluded that he, Evonick, was indeed innocent of any wrongdoing in the matter. He felt that Washington County had harmed his reputation and filed a libel lawsuit against the County. This lawsuit was never brought to trial.

About six months after the incident, he disappeared without any trace, and nothing has been solved on the case. The authorities investigating his disappearance concluded that one of the other LeBaron rival groups was responsible for his vanishing. This led the sheriff of Washington County to believe that the whole thing had been a hoax, with the finger of blame being pointed toward Sam Barlow himself. Many believed he had created a situation where he would be called back to his position in law enforcement. Whatever the truth was in the matter, Sam Barlow was hired by the newly incorporated town of Colorado City, thus restoring him to his lifelong ambition of being a "cop." The matter quietly faded away, leaving the sheriff highly embarrassed over the whole fiasco.

Once again Sam was the Chief Protector of the community. Immediately he began again his religious campaign of "cleaning up the town" of wayward boys. He was acting in Hildale, Utah, as well as Colorado City. He was not hired back as the Town Marshal, because Leon Johnson was already in that position, but rather was hired as a Colorado City Deputy Marshal. Leon was certified by the Utah Peace Officers Standards Training (P.O.S.T.) Academy, therefore qualified to act in Utah, but Sam was not certified to do so. When he began making arrests in Utah, the people involved went to P.O.S.T., asking them to intervene. Eventually this resulted in Sam being denied Utah certification. More will be told about the matter later.

About this time several Baptist Preachers began talking with some of the UEP dissidents about establishing a Bible study class at Colorado City, and they would need a building to hold these classes. Since the Polygamists were using the school building for their religious meetings and had been for the last twenty years or so, the interested parties went to the local school board and asked for the same privilege, offering to pay what rent was necessary. The school board said "no." This did not seem lawfully right to them, so they filled a complaint with the County School Superintendent at Kingman. When the Superintendent learned that the Polygamists were already using the school buildings for religious purposes and had been for the last twenty years, he gave the local school board an ultimatum: the Polygamists could only use the school buildings for religious purposes for one more year, which would give them time to construct a building of their own.

This came as no little shock to Fred Jessop, the person who, since his "appointment" as UEP trustee, was managing the affairs for the Polygamist Group at Colorado City. He went to Leroy Johnson, the aged and incapacitated Group leader, telling him they would have to build a church building. Leroy thought back to the early 1940s and how John Barlow had stopped Marion Hammon from building a church house He had assumed they would never have to build such a building for Church services because they had been able to use the school building all these years. He was reluctant to give Fred the go-a-head on such a project. However, Fred prevailed on him until he gave permission to build a modest building for the purpose of holding their religious meetings. A modest building indeed!

Fred became carried away with the planning of this building, beginning construction on a monstrosity beyond the wildest imaginations of any dreams ever envisioned by the Polygamists. The dimensions of this building when completed would measure about 200' wide by 270' long. Work on "his masterpiece" began in early 1986. It was called the "Activity Center" at the beginning of construction, with hope of obtaining public money toward its construction. In a few months it was decided that in order to keep it under religious control, it would have to be built with private funds. The public money that had been donated by the Town of Colorado City toward construction of the building was denied by Fred of ever being used.

These events were taking place about the same time as the peace movement in the nation called Hands Across America, where it attempted to form a human chain of people holding hands from coast to coast. Fred Jessop copied this slogan, naming his Hands Across The Creek. He had the people hold hands and form a human chain from Leroy Johnson's house in Hildale to the new church building under construction in Colorado City, a distance of about two miles. This distance was the long way around, more than a quarter of a mile directly south of Leroy's house to the new building. For the privilege of standing in this line each participant had to pay Fred Jessop $2.00. The money was supposed to go toward the construction costs of the new building, but just how much of it actually went for its intended purpose is unknown, because Fred's business practices were to put any money he came by into his "slush fund," using it for whatever reason he so desired.

For the $2.00 these people paid, they were "honored" by seeing their prophet Leroy as he was driven by them, sitting in the rear seat of "his" van, attended by "his" nurse (one of his younger wives), and the ever present oxygen bottle and tubes to his nose. This occasion occurred on June 12, 1986, his 98th birthday. It was a big enough event that TV news people covered the episode. Several people were interviewed by the media and were asked why such loyalty was given to their Prophet. The main answer they received: "Leroy is just like Jesus Christ to us." The one astounding news item that was broadcast: "Leroy was not going to die, he would still be around for his 100th birthday." As it turned out, this was his last birthday before he died.

The work on the new church building progressed enough that part of it could be closed in for meetings to be held, thus meeting the one year deadline set by the Mohave County School Superintendent. By the end of August 1986, they began holding their first meetings there, thus vacating the school building for religious services. Prophet Leroy Johnson, who told his people that he would not die until Christ returned at His Second Coming, did not see the completion of this building. He died on November 25, 1986 (Note 1). His funeral was a very elaborate affair, attended by more than 3,500 people.

The funeral was held in the new unfinished church house. It was attended by TV reporters from both Salt Lake City and Phoenix stations. The Polygamists were worried about the possibility of violence at his funeral, so armed Sheriff Deputies from both Washington and Mohave Counties were in the building, along with the Colorado City Town Marshals. It was interesting to see the armed police officers mingling among the mourners. No violence occurred.

The highlight of the service was when Truman Barlow, in his eulogy of the Prophet, made this statement: "Everyone in this building will have to pass by Uncle Roy, getting his permission and OK before you can get into heaven." This statement was puzzling to some of the reporters, not able to comprehend the arrogance of these cult leaders. They wondered why they, just because they happened to be covering the event, would be under such a restriction.

After the funeral, the casket was carried on a horse drawn wagon, driven by Leroy's oldest son Orval to the cemetery, a distance of about two blocks. After the dedication of the grave, the casket was lowered into the ground and Leroy Johnson was buried. A gravestone was placed at the head of the grave stating: "Prophet, Prince Of Peace."

Leroy's death left Marion Hammon as the senior member of the Priesthood Council, but due to his earlier dismissal from the Council by Leroy, he was not accepted by the Barlow Group as the next Prophet. This honor fell to Rulon Jeffs, who now became their new Prophet. Marion Hammon, however, was honored by the Second Ward as the new leader and he carried on with The Work as best he could, making the split with the Brethren of the Priesthood Council a permanent situation. The work on the Second Ward church house was also progressing admirably.

On September 27, 1986, the first meeting was held in their new building at Centennial Park City. This meeting was more of a program that honored the day when the Prophet Joseph Smith allegedly came to John Taylor in 1886, commanding him to keep plural marriage alive after it would be given up by the LDS Church, and resulting in the setting apart of a group of men to carry on in its perpetuation. It was the centennial of this occasion, September 27, 1886, from which the name for their town was derived: Centennial Park City.

It was about this time that some of the citizens of the community became concerned in regards of Sam Barlow's "playing cop" in Hildale. They went to Hildale Mayor David Zitting and asked for a copy of the minutes where Sam had been hired by the Hildale Town Council to act as a police officer. These requests were ignored, so they sent a letter to the Washington County Attorney to force the issue. They in turn referred it to Barbara Hjille, Hildale City Attorney. She advised the mayor to give a copy of the minutes to those asking.

On September 18, the mayor called one of those asking for the minutes on the phone (Ben Bistline) and tried to explain what had happened in the case of Sam Barlow working for Hildale as a cop. A request to meet him in his office was accepted and two of the citizens went up to the Hildale town hall to meet with David Zitting. This turned out to be an interesting session. The mayor told them that he did not have access to the minutes. It seems that Fred Jessop, who was only the town clerk, keep the minutes at his home and they were not available to anyone without his approval. The mayor said he did not particularly like this arrangement, but there was nothing he could do about it.

One of the visitors (Don Cox) asked him why he couldn't just tell the town clerk to bring the minutes down to the town hall where they belonged. David Zitting looked surprised and said, "You mean tell Uncle Fred what to do?" Don said: "Yes." Zitting said, "He wouldn't do what I told him anyway." Don's response: "Then fire him." David was very animated by this, responding with great shock. He exclaimed: "What! me fire Uncle Fred?" (Note 2)

The minutes from the Hildale town meetings were never given to the local citizens asking for them at this time; however, Lorin Webb, a reporter for the *Daily Spectrum*, a St. George newspaper, asked for the minutes and his request was granted. He had to wait two hours for Fred Jessop to send the requested minutes down to the town hall where Webb was allowed to read them. They did not contain anything in them about Sam Barlow being hired as a policeman by Hildale.

A written request was made to Colorado City for a copy of their minutes regarding Sam Barlow being able to work in Hildale. In about two weeks Ben Bistline (who made this request) received a letter from their attorney in Kingman, asking why he wanted the minutes. This letter was answered, explaining that minutes of town meetings were open to public view and asked what were they trying to hide by not supplying them. A letter of reprimand from their attorney was sent to Colorado City, counseling them to send the minutes to those who were requesting them, which they complied with.

Sam Barlow's working in Hildale was addressed in the minutes of Colorado City. It was agreed that he would be allowed to act in Hildale as part of an interagency agreement between the two towns. There were no particulars about how much, if any, of his salary was to be paid by Hildale, only that he was allowed to "play cop." The issue of Sam being certified in Utah to work as a peace office was then taken to the Utah State Police Academy (P.O.S.T) and it was only a short time until he was denied certification in Utah, due to his being a polygamist. This worked so good for those opposed to him that it was decided to go the same route in Arizona, to try and have him decertified there because he was a polygamist.

A petition was drawn up, with over 300 signatures on it, to have Sam decertified in Arizona. The petition was sent to the Arizona Law Enforcement Officer Advisory Council (ALEOAC) at Tuscon, Arizona. The petition is as follows:

PETITION To Review Samuel S. Barlow's Qualifications To Serve As A Police Officer In Arizona, Mohave County, Or Colorado City. Arizona Enforcement Training Academy 560 West Trail's End Road Tuscon, Az. 85745.

We, the undersigned, hereby petition Arizona Law Enforcement Training Academy to refuse certification to Samuel S. Barlow to act in a police capacity in Arizona, Mohave County, or Colorado City. The reasons for our petition are:

1. It is our understanding that a police officer is a peace officer. Sam Barlow does not act as a peace officer, but a trouble maker, in that he incites the youth to rebel by his actions toward them. He allows the youth no latitude to move about, but keeps them hedged in. If they meet on the street and talk for a short time, he accuses them of wrongdoing. He harasses them in their driving, associations, and all activities of Youth. He is particularly active in investigating any and all meeting of youth of the opposite sexes, suspecting them of plotting sex activities.

2. Sam Barlow has been the enforcement arm of the United Effort Plan Trust and the religious hierarchy that governs it during his entire time as a police

268

officer. In his capacity as enforcer, he has harassed men, entered homes illegally, confiscated private property illegally, taken people out of town illegally, harassed "undesirable" young men until they "got discouraged and left," and has stated that he would support "beating up kids" if Uncle Roy approved.

3. Sam Barlow refuses to act, neglects to act, or "forgets" to act properly, such as "forgetting" read a man his rights if the offender is a relative, a close friend, or he has been instructed to leave the offender alone by the religious hierarchy.

4. Sam Barlow acts in the capacity of a police officer outside of his jurisdiction. He recently harassed a juvenile on the county roads outside of Colorado City. He threatened a resident of Cane Beds, Arizona, with bodily harm for interfering with his aspirations to the position of Mohave County Deputy Sheriff.

5. Sam Barlow is a poor influence on the youth in the community, in that in his interrogations of the youth he always brings the conversation around to "sex," asking the party about his (or her) sex experience. If a young man were to admit to any sex activity, he would promptly be arrested and incarcerated or harassed until he left town. If he had a home, he would be evicted, the eviction being enforced by Sam Barlow.

Please consider our petition to review certification of Samuel S. Barlow, and revoke his certification in Arizona.

Sent with the petition were affidavits by young people who had been treated by Sam as described in the petition. The ALEOAC directors reviewed the petition and after contacting some of the people who had signed it, decided in March of 1987 to decertify Sam Barlow. It did not go as smooth, however, for them in Arizona as it had in Utah and it was the beginning of a long battle between ALEOAC and Sam Barlow. More on this later.

One noteworthy development occurred soon after the death of Leroy Johnson. A board meeting of the United Effort Plan was held wherein new trustees were "appointed" by the surviving board members to fill up the vacancies left after the expulsion of Marion Hammon and the death of Leroy Johnson. The minutes of this meeting were recorded in Mohave County, and are as follows:

FIFTH AMENDED AFFIDAVIT OF DISCLOSURE STATE OF UTAH.

ss. County of Washington

RULON T. JEFFS, FRED M. JESSOP, LEROY S. JEFFS, JAMES K. ZITTING, WINSTON K. BLACKMORE, PARLEY J. HARKER, and TRUMAN I. BARLOW, each being first duly sworn, deposes and states as follows:

1. That pursuant to the provisions of Section 33-401 Arizona Revised Statutes, as amended, an Affidavit of Disclosure was executed and recorded in Mohave County, Arizona, in Book 355, p. 818. Said Affidavit of Disclosure was

amended by an Amended Affidavit of Disclosure recorded in said county in Book 979, p. 741. Said Affidavit of Disclosure was amended by a Second Amended Affidavit of Disclosure recorded in said county in Book 1052, p. 675. Said Affidavit of Disclosure was amended by a Third Amended Affidavit of Disclosure recorded in said County. Said Affidavit of Disclosure was amended by a Fourth Amended Affidavit of Disclosure recorded in said county in Book 1088, p. 859.

2. That on the 25th day of November, 1986, Trustee Leroy S. Johnson became deceased.

3. That on November 30, 1986, Winston K. Blackmore, Parley J. Harker, Truman I. Barlow and LeRoy S. Jeffs were appointed as Trustees of the United Effort Plan, a common law trust.

4. That this Fifth Amended Affidavit of Disclosure is made for the purpose of setting forth the names of the Trustees RULON T. JEFFS, FRED M. JESSOP, LEROY S. JEFFS, JAMES K. ZITTING, WINSTON K. BLACKMORE, PARLEY J. HARKER, AND TRUMAN I. BARLOW.

IN WITNESS WHEREOF, the above officers have executed this Affidavit for the purposed hereinabove set forth. The signatures of these trustees follow, notarized by Arthur Barlow. The document is dated, January 18, 1987.

Soon after the filing of this Fifth Amended Affidavit of Disclosure, in the first of the new year of 1987, the UEP bought a 700 acre farm southwest of Colorado City. This property had been homesteaded by Louis Black, one of the early settlers in the 1930s. He had sold it to a couple of Newel Steed's sons who were promoting and selling circle sprinkler systems. They were in debt to the Farm Home Administration (FHA) for close to two million dollars on the project and were unable to meet the payments. In a couple of years the FHA foreclosed and took possession of the farm, called The Berry Knoll Farms. It was put up for auction, requiring a minimum bid of $1,800,000.00. There were no bidders. In another year or so it was again put up for auction, with a lower minimum. There were still no bids. The FHA, being desperate to dump the farm, asked for any offers it could get to try and negotiate a deal. Fred Jessop and Rulon Jeffs sent Parley Harker to contact the FHA, the purpose being to arrange to purchase the property.

Parley Harker was a successful farmer living in the Beryl, Utah area. He also was a polygamist and a member of the Barlow Group. He had had previous dealings with the FHA and therefore had credibility with their agents. He was able to arrange a deal to purchase the Berry Knoll Farms for a fraction of its worth, agreeing to pay $330,000.00 for the property, which included the sprinkler systems, wells and pumps (Note 3).

The money was raised by asking the people to donate to the United Effort Plan. Rulon Jeffs told the men of his (the Barlow) Group in a Priesthood Meeting at the new church house one Sunday morning, "If you want to be a member of the

United Effort Plan, just donate a thousand dollars toward the purchasing of the Berry Knoll Farms." His plea was honored and over three hundred and thirty thousand dollars was raised. Parley Harker paid the FHA and the farm was soon acquired by the UEP. With the addition of this property, the United Effort Plan holdings at Colorado City was almost doubled in acreage.

With such successes under their belts (the acquiring of the Berry Knoll Farms and Sam Barlow's orchestrated evictions), the new leaders of the UEP became quite arrogant and bold.

Due to the 1985 threat of a lawsuit they decided to try and secure their position by establishing that the member/beneficiaries could hold no equity claims on the homes they had built on UEP property.

In a UEP board meeting held in about April of 1987, a letter was drafted and adopted by the board to be sent "TO ALL OF THE PEOPLE RESIDING UPON UNITED EFFORT PROPERTY." The letter was then signed by Rulon T. Jeffs, President of the United Effort Plan, and sent to all these residents. About 600 of these letters were sent by regular mail while about 65 were sent by certified mail. There was no name on the return address, just "Box 459 (Fred Jessop's box number), Colorado City, AZ. 86021 (Those who received the certified letters were mainly those whose names had been removed as beneficiaries on the 1976 affidavit of disclosure).

TO ALL OF THE PEOPLE RESIDING UPON UNITED EFFORT PROPERTY:

As you know and as was explained to you in great detail when you became residents on the property, you are tenants at will and reside on the property at the pleasure of the trustees.

Some or all of you have made improvements to the property with the consent of the administration of the trust. Any such voluntary improvements become part of the land and are not to be moved, transferred, demolished or assigned to other occupants without the consent of the United Effort Plan.

The above policies have been in effect since the creation of the United Effort Plan and this letter is not intended to represent any change but merely the written clarification of pre-existing policy.

Since the incorporation of both Hildale and Colorado City certain additional formalities are required before any improvements can be constructed on the property located in either of those towns. The United Effort Plan is most supportive of the governments of those towns and desires that all of the ordinances with regard to building permits and inspections be complied with. The United Effort Plan will require that building permits be issued by the proper authority before any improvements are made on the property. As the residents have no authority to improve the land without the consent of the United Effort Plan, the application for each building permit must be approved by one of the agents for the Plan and we are notifying the towns of Hildale and Colorado City of this fact and request that they not grant any building permit unless approved by an agent.

The agents of the trust authorized to approve applications for building permits are the trustees of the Plan: Rulon T. Jeffs, Fred M. Jessop, LeRoy S. Jeffs, Parley J. Harker, Truman I. Barlow, James K. Zitting and Winston K. Blackmore.

The willful violation of any of the policies set forth above shall constitute grounds to terminate the violator's tenancy at will on the property.

Very truly yours,
(signed) Rulon T. Jeffs
Rulon T. Jeffs
President of the United Effort Plan by order of the Board of Trustees

The term Tenant At Will was an unknown phrase to most of the beneficiaries receiving the letter. Mike Pipkin looked it up in *Blacks Law Dictionary* to understand just what it was that had been "explained to you in great detail" before they had built their homes on Trust property. Blacks Law Dictionary explains TENANT AT WILL – One who holds possession of premises by permission of owner or landlord, but without fixed term. Where lands or tenements are let by one man to another; to have and to hold to him at the will of the lessor; by force of which lease the lessee is in possession. In this case the lessee is called "Tenant At Will," because he has no certain nor sure estate, for the lessor may put him out at what time it pleases him.

Needless to say, this letter and the interpretation of what a tenant at will was, sent a chill through the people who had been removed from the beneficiary list. In their consternation a committee was sent to the Washington County Attorney Paul Graf to ask his advice on the matter.

When Mr. Graf read the letter, he told the men that it was very evident what their (the Barlows) intentions were. He also told them that if the letter was not protested (contested in court) that in a very short time the statute of limitations would run out and those living on trust property would in indeed become Tenants At Will. He told them they had two choices, 1) start looking for somewhere else to live, or 2) file a court action against the UEP Trustees contesting their actions in the matter.

Judge Burns of the 5th District Court was also approached for advice on the matter. His answer was about the same as was Paul Graf's. The choices for the disenfranchised beneficiaries looked very bleak. Not knowing what else to do and hoping to buy a little time, they filed a protest with the respective county recorders in St. George and Kingman:

"We the undersigned beneficiaries do hereby register our protest and objection to being summarily disfranchised as Beneficiaries of the United Effort Plan Trust without any official notification. As evidence we submit Exhibit A; Affidavit of Disclosure dated Oct. 16, 1976 listing the undersigned as Beneficiaries, Exhibit B; First Amended Affidavit of Disclosure Dated Nov. 12, 1983, disfranchising undersigned without official written or oral notification, in violation of Arizona Revised Statutes #14-77303."

A year earlier several of them had mailed a copy of the following letter (to which they signed their name) to Rulon Jeffs at Salt Lake City, because there was concern as to just what their status in the trust was.

July 1986
Rulon Jeffs, 2452 So. State Salt Lake City, Utah 84115
Dear Sir:
In perusing records made public in the Recorders Office of Mojave County Arizona (Book 355 p. 818), I find my name listed as a beneficiary of the United Effort Plan Trust.

Accordingly, I would appreciate information relating to the Trust itself, and my relationship to it.
Specifically, I would like to know;
(1) What is the nature of the trust (legal description).
(2) What are the trust's objectives.
(3) What is the financial status of the Trust.
(4) What is my standing as a beneficiary.
(5) What are my liabilities, duties, privileges.
(6) What constitutes my beneficial interest.
(7) What does my interest vest.
(8) Who are the current trustees, and are they bonded.
As you can see from the above, my interest is of a general as well as specific nature. As a beneficiary, I would like to have defined for me my formal standing as quickly as possible for use in my own estate planning.
Please forward the information above requested, and everything else you may feel will be helpful for me.

Respectfully,
(signed)

Rulon Jeffs did not answer any of the letters. If the status of the beneficiaries was so well explained to them as was stated in the Tenant At Will letter, then it would have been a simple matter for Rulon to just write back and say, "You are a tenant at Will." But no, they had to wait six months (and after Leroy had died) to concoct this no-equity status for the United Effort Plan Members.

It looked like the only remedy for any of these beneficiaries, if they wanted to stay in their homes, would be to file a lawsuit. Some of these persons who received the Tenant At Will letter contacted Mr. Ruskjer in Victorville, California, an attorney who professed to have some knowledge concerning Cults and their questionable use of Trusts to defraud innocent and gullible people with the intention of bilking them of their money and/or property. A meeting was set up with Mr. Ruskjer and on July 28, 1987, four men drove to Victorville to confer with him.

He told them that because of a commitment with another group, he would not be able to represent them in any kind of court action. He did offer to call Rulon Jeffs, acting as a mediator, in an attempt to negotiate some kind of settlement for the disenfranchised UEP members.

In this telephone conversation, Jeffs seemed to be willing to work out some kind of resolution in order to avoid going to court. This was good news to those who had driven to California for the meeting; however, the euphoria was short lived. In about 30 minutes time Mr. Ruskjer received two telephone calls. One from Dan Barlow and, soon after, another one from Truman Barlow.

After talking to these two men, two things were clear to him: 1) Rulon Jeffs was not the one making decisions for the United Effort Plan, but rather these decisions were made by the Barlow Cabal, and 2) There would never be any settlement made with the "apostates." With this information he could only advise the four men to get an attorney and take them to court. After receiving this counsel, they returned home, determined to look for an attorney to take the case.

Finding an attorney became a real challenge because several they approached required a $40,000 retainer up front before they would even look at the case, and they would have to have a guarantee of at least $100,000 a year for what could last for as many as eight to ten years. This was very discouraging indeed.

The Barlow Cabal knew what it would cost for anyone to challenge them in court, therefore they felt very secure in their arrogant treatment of these victims. Without any assets (their homes were built on trust property) the Cabal "knew" the people could never raise that kind of money. With arrogance and contempt, they went about making their plans as how to get these "dissidents" evicted from the Priesthood Homes.

As sometimes happens, unexplained events transpire to foil the deeds of evil doers. A son of one of these disenfranchised members was working for a legal firm in Salt Lake City, Woodburys & Associates. They dealt mostly in real estate matters. At this particular time the owners of Woodburys & Associates were considering launching out into a new field, that of ligating real estate disputes.

When the young man from Colorado City told them about the dilemma of his parents and others in the community, the owners of the firm became very interested and asked for information on the matter, so they could consider whether to take the case.

On August 9, 1987, the young man took the information to his employers in Salt Lake City and after going over the information, they seemed confident about taking the case. A meeting was set up to meet with 25 of the disenfranchised members. This meeting was held on August 23, 1987, in a private home at Colorado City.

John Kesler, attorney for Woodburys & Associates, was the representative for the firm. He proposed that it would be easier and cheaper to break the disenfranchised members out of the UEP rather than try to break up the trust. He thought that if they could raise a hundred thousand dollars they would be able to force the UEP Trustees to make an out of court settlement. The proposal he made to the group was for 30 people to raise one thousand dollars up front money and then guarantee a monthly payment of a hundred dollars a month until the case was terminated, which he estimated would take one year. Needless to say, this sounded much better than any other offers, so they voted to allow Woodburys & Associates to go ahead with the case.

Mr. Kesler went back to Salt Lake City and began the work of preparing a questionnaire for each of the would-be plaintiffs to fill out, detailing their individual circumstances.

While these developments were going on, another event of interest was taking place. This was the matter of Sam Barlow's decertification as a peace officer in Arizona.

In March of 1987 the Arizona Police Academy (Arizona Law Enforcement Officer Advisory Council (ALEOAC) decided to withdraw Sam Barlow's peace officer certification. This was due to the petition that had been filed a short time before by some citizens of the community regarding his handling of law enforcement duties in the area. The complaints were mostly because of his harassment of the young people, his habit of taking them into his office and grilling them along sexual lines. This problem became so paramount for some of the citizens that they decided to complain to ALEOAC in an effort to stop his molestation of these juveniles. At great difficulty a few affidavits were obtained from some of these juveniles, telling of his abuses. Their names will not be revealed here to protect them from further harassment. A portion of one affidavit from a 14 year-old girl is detailed next to show how bad the problem was.

"The Affiant says that on_____, 1986, Sam Barlow picked her up as she was walking home at about 11:00 PM. He took her to his office, and after questioning her for over an hour about her sexual habits, asked her if she knew what 'giving head' was? He then asked her if she was guilty of 'giving head' to the boys he had been questioning her about."

This was one example of Sam's law enforcement procedures as alleged by those making the complaint. ALEOAC, after reviewing the evidence and conducting interviews with the complainants, decided to hold an administrative hearing to determine if his certification should be withdrawn. Such a hearing was scheduled to be conducted about the first of July, 1987. Sam Barlow was notified of the hearing and given a grace period to protest it if he so wished. And protest he did.

On May 4, 1987, Bill Jameson from the Arizona Attorney General's office and Hank Shearer from ALEOAC went to Colorado City to meet with the complainants about this hearing and discuss with them circumstances surrounding Sam's protest. Sam had filed affidavits with their offices, from the parents of the juveniles who had made affidavits in the case, denying that what their children had testified was fact. And one of the young men (who was now 18) who had made an affidavit of treatment he had received from Sam while a juvenile, had now made a new affidavit disclaiming his testimony in his previous statement. Also, Sam had made a petition exonerating himself of any unlawful or unethical conduct connected with his duties as a peace officer. He was able to collect over one thousand signatures on his petition. In addition to this petition he wrote up several affidavits for other people to sign, wherein "they" testified of his exemplary character (Note 4).

These developments caused some concern with the officials planning to conduct the administrative hearing.

When the young man that changed his testimony was questioned as to why he had done so, he answered that Fred Jessop and Sam Barlow had told his mother, who was a school teacher in the public school, that if her son did not withdraw his accusations against Sam's conduct, she could lose her job. When she emotionally explained this situation to the boy, he felt he had no choice but to protect his mother. He expressed sorrow about his actions, but felt he must consider his mother's position.

Likewise with the other juveniles who had sworn out affidavits, their parents were told that if the charges were not withdrawn that they, the parents, would be evicted from their homes and have to leave the community.

This greatly surprised the State Officials. In all their experience, never had they come up against such a situation, where an entire community was so much under the control of a religious cult. Being all the more determined to remove Sam from his position of control, they resolved to go forward with the process of having him decertified. They felt their case had been weakened by the juveniles' denouncing of their complaints, but still felt they had an ace in the hole with the fact that Sam Barlow was a polygamist. He had taken an oath to uphold the

Constitution of the State of Arizona when he was granted peace officer certification. Since the Arizona Constitution states that polygamy shall forever be prohibited, he had violated his oath and for this cause only, they felt he should be decertified. It would be similar to a criminal serving "silent time," if they could get him out on the polygamy issue, it would still get him out, even though the real reason to get him out was because of his unethical actions. On this reasoning they went ahead with their decision to act in the matter.

The UEP leaders contacted their Phoenix attorney Charles Ditsch and asked him to represent Sam Barlow against the State. Since Charles Ditsch was not a criminal lawyer, only an attorney dealing in real estate and tax matters, he referred them to Marc Cavness, a lawyer who specialized in litigation in criminal law.

Sam Barlow considered Mr. Cavness a "real big gun" in the legal field, and it caused him to act in a very arrogant manner when dealing with the State Officials. Standing on the premise that he had been called to his position by "one of God servants, Leroy Johnson," he would prevail in his cause and proceeded to go all out to vindicate himself.

A meeting was set up between the complainants and Mr. Cavness, with Bill Jameson (the Attorney General's representative) present. The meeting took place in Colorado City, beginning on October 26, 1987. Mr. Cavness grilled these people unmercifully, with some of the interviews lasting for as long as nine hours. The complainants provided excerpts from their journals, showing incidents for the last several years where Sam Barlow had misused his authority. There were numerous allegations in these accounts, but they were mostly second hand accounts, the incidents being related by juveniles to the complainants, thus establishing them as "hearsay evidence." This greatly deprecated the State's case.

At the end of these interviews, neither the State nor Mr. Cavness felt very secure in their positions. There was just enough evidence against Sam to worry Cavness, and Mr. Jameson could see that it would also be hard to prove the State's case. At this point a compromise was reached. Sam Barlow agreed to admit to being a polygamist if the State would drop all of the other charges against him. The State agreed to this, supposing that since he was in violation of the State Constitution, it would be simple on this basis alone to have him decertified.

With these preliminaries settled, both sides settled down to preparing for the upcoming conflict, which would not reach a conclusion until over five years later.

Meanwhile the work on the new Civic Center, First Ward's Church house, was moving along. There were a few setbacks, one being that a great portion (several cubic yards) of the walls had to be torn down because of inferior concrete (an improper mix). This created an unplanned expense for Fred Jessop. When he asked Rulon Jeffs for money to help pay for the blunder, Jeffs went to the people with the problem.

On October 25, 1987, Rulon Jeffs asked his followers to "give" more money for the construction costs of the new building. He told them that for every $1,000 turned toward the new church house, each contributor would be guaranteed a ticket to Jackson County, Missouri (Where the Second Coming was to occur) and title to one lot there. This promise was believed by many of the Polygamists and they would go to great lengths to raise the money asked for to help pay the construction costs of "their" new building. In order to control who could use the building, it was necessary to raise the money from private sources. When work began on this new building it had been designated the Activity Center. This was done in the hope that it may get them eligibility for public money to help in its construction. It was not long until Fred Jessop was able to see that if it was a public building, he would lose control of it.

While the attention of these connivers were turned towards solving these problems, the circumstances surrounding the filing of a civil lawsuit against them was progressing along.

This civil lawsuit was drawn up by Woodburys & Associates and filed in The Utah District of the Federal Court in Salt Lake City on November 25, 1987, almost a year to the day after Leroy Johnson had died. It is impossible to say whether or not such a lawsuit would ever have been filed if Leroy had lived until the year 2000, as he had claimed he would; but there is no doubt in the mind of the author that no lawsuit would ever have been filed against the United Effort Plan if it had not been for Sam Barlow's actions of "cleaning up the town."

This lawsuit was the answer to Sam's childhood dream, for he had boasted all his growing up life that the day would come when he would have to spend his full time "defending the Priesthood" and the time would come when he would "have to run people out of this town."

The author is one year older than Sam Barlow and grew up with him during the early years. He heard Sam make these boasts all of his younger life. Sam Barlow would now realize the fulfillment of these childhood dreams. His complete time would now be spent "in the service of the Priesthood." He would go to Salt Lake City, taking his newest and youngest wife with him, where he would set up residence, spending his full time working with the attorneys that the UEP would hire to defend them against the "Apostates."

This lawsuit would drag on for eight years. The defendants would have their attorneys use every trick in the book to drag it on for as long as they could, knowing full well that when it went to trial they would surely lose. The particulars of the case will be touched on in the remainder of this history, but most of the stalling tactics used by the defendants will be skipped over.

In a memorandum, filed on August 30, 1989, by the attorneys for the plaintiffs, in support of a motion before the court for partial summary judgment, there is a characterization by one of the attorneys of the situation that exists among the Polygamists at Colorado City. This characterization is compiled from the depositions and interrogatories of the Defendants, and is fairly accurate:

In an effort to save money and the Court's time, Plaintiffs voluntarily elected to withdraw a number of causes of action against the Municipal Defendants when they filed their Proposed Third Amended Complaint. Rather than spend additional time and money briefing causes of action which are no longer part of Plaintiffs Proposed Third Amended Complaint, this Memorandum will merely address those causes of action Plaintiffs consider that remain. Should it become necessary for any reason, to defend their position on the earlier causes of action set forth in prior complaints, Plaintiffs reserve the right to brief those issues in a separate memorandum.

Defendants would have this Court believe that Plaintiffs' causes of action against the Municipal Defendants are mere 'window dressing, meritless, specious and brought in bad faith.' Such statements could not be further from the truth and only tend to show the cavalier attitude of Defendants and reaffirm that the communities of Hildale and Colorado City were established for and are totally controlled by one religion.

Hiding from its own past following the 1953 raid, the community of Short Creek ultimately changed its name to Colorado City. The town of Hildale, Utah, was created in 1962 and the Arizona side of the community continued to be called Colorado City. Finally, in 1985, Colorado City was finally formally organized.

There is little question but that Fred Jessop, with the support of church leaders in the past and sustained by the individual Defendants in the present court action, controls virtually every aspect of the communities of Hildale and Colorado City. Wearing almost every conceivable hat while at the same time professing that all he does is church work, Fred Jessop sits as a chameleon as the Hildale town clerk, and effectively pulls strings to control and manipulate all that goes on in the communities. Although their motives may have been pure in the beginning, those in control have become rapacious as they have sought to protect what has transpired in the past from those who have trusted them and preserve their power base in the future. Those motives have led to involvement in the municipalities through rubber stamp town councils and the law enforcement threat of Sam Barlow who was hand picked by church leaders to carry the fear of color of law in enforcement of all of their actions.

Sam Barlow was hand-picked to be 'the man that the priesthood has set as a police officer in this place' in the very words of the former prophet, Leroy S. Johnson. Sam has fulfilled that role by doing the bidding of both President Johnson and now of President Rulon T. Jeffs. Operating in uniform as an employee of Mohave County working in the Colorado City area prior to its formal incorporation and as a Deputy Marshall within Colorado City; and through cross-deputization, acting as a law enforcement officer in the town of Hildale, Sam has brought law enforcement authority to the whims and dictates of the prophets.

Sam was raised in his formative years from ages 12-19 by Leroy S. Johnson and in the waning months of President Johnson's life, he accompanied Leroy Johnson when he traveled until Leroy Johnson's death.

If righteous conduct needed to be enforced, Sam was there. If 'Uncle Roy' needed to see you about your behavior or the behavior of your children, Sam was there in uniform to deliver the message. If you were being evicted from trust property, Sam was involved in serving Notice upon you. His mere presence created an aura of fear in those who felt they may not be entirely in harmony with the teachings or practices of the dominate religious group.

The actions of Defendants and their subordinates have gone well beyond constitutional limits and have severely impacted the lives of Plaintiffs.

Plaintiffs specifically deny that the evidence available in this case involves either non-specific conclusory allegations or claims against a non-party. Plaintiffs do not deny the facts set forth in the memorandum of Defendants in this action, (they) do however specifically deny that Defendants' list of facts is complete. The municipal Defendants appear to have overlooked the significant additional facts brought forth in the form of testimony over the past four months to which this Memorandum shall draw the Court's attention as follows:

Facts gleaned from the Testimony of Fred M. Jessop, Hildale Town Clerk, etc.:

1. Fred M. Jessop is the Vice President and a Trustee of the United Effort Plan, Bishop and a counselor to Rulon T. Jeffs in the presidency of the Fundamentalist Church of Jesus Christ of Latter Day Saints, the Town Clerk of Hildale, the President of Twin City Waterworks, the editor of the Twin City Courier, the only locally printed newspaper of general circulation in the area, as contemplated trustee of the Majestic Security Trust (Note 5), which was created to hold the businesses of the United Effort Plan at a distance from those who may apostatize from the Work, the President and a member of the board of the Colorado City Improvement Association, the owner of the town's only health center, the owner of Standard Supply, the owner of the only restaurant in town, the Early Bird Cafe, the general election Judge for the Town of Hildale, and the municipal election Judge for off year elections. Further, during the last 50 years, Mr. Jessop testified that he has labored full time in church work.

2. In response to a question as to how he has time to do all the things that he does Fred Jessop said 'My whole interest is to carry out the expectations and

hopes and aspirations of Brother Barlow (John Y.) and Brother (Leroy) Johnson and Brother Jeffs and all Presidents of the Fundamentalist Church of Jesus Christ of Latter Day Saints. And all these other incidental so-called hats are just in a day's work. That's the way I view it.'

3. During all the time that Hildale has been in existence there has never been more than one name listed on the ballot for the election of mayor or the election of each position as a member of the town council.

4. Fred Jessop was recommended to become town clerk in 1962 by Marion Hammon, 'since I (he) had been doing some clerical work for the prophet it was recommended that I continue in that capacity when this was done.'

5. Fred Jessop admitted that he was the principal person involved in preparing the list of beneficiaries to attach to the 1983 Amended Affidavit of Disclosure which list deleted 117 names which appeared in 1976 as beneficiaries, This was done while Fred Jessop was serving as town clerk of Hildale but before he was appointed as a trustee of the United Effort Plan.

6. Fred Jessop admitted that he composed the list of beneficiaries which appeared on the original Affidavit of Disclosure filed in 1976, again, years before he was appointed as a trustee of the United Effort Plan but while he was serving as Hildale Town Clerk.

7. Fred Jessop, in talking about his close relationship with the prophet, Leroy Johnson said, 'I felt like I was his right hand man.'

8. Fred Jessop admitted to having the seal of the United Effort Plan for 'quite a long time;' doesn't recall if he used it, but said it was 'just my nature to take care of things.' That was long before he became a trustee of the United Effort Plan and while he was serving as the clerk of Hildale.

9. Fred Jessop holds a private Sunday School in the Hildale town office building 3 times a month for between 150 and 200 people.

10. Sam Barlow, Deputy Town Marshal of Colorado City, was sent by Fred Jessop as the representative of the Fundamentalist Church of Jesus Christ of Latter Day Saints to negotiate with Mohave County officials for the tax exempt status on the Church's meeting house in February of 1988. His negotiations led ultimately to the recording of Notification of Dedication to Religious Use.

11. Fred Jessop has personally leased a building and land owned by the United Effort Plan to the United States Postal Service for a post office in Colorado City and has personally taken the lease money over the years for his own subsistence in amounts in excess of $5,000.00 per year.

12. In his own personal financial statements filed with 3 different banks in 1983, Fred Jessop claimed (and) showed ownership in his own name of his home located on United Effort Plan property with a value of $185,000.00.

13. Fred Jessop prepared a financial statement for the Stockman's Bank in 1983 identifying as his occupation 'City Manager.'

Facts gleaned from the testimony of Rulon T. Jeffs the President of the United Effort Plan and the President of the Fundamentalist Church of Jesus Christ of Latter Day Saints:

1. Fred Jessop, while serving as town clerk and also as a trustee of the United Effort Plan signed as many as 7 different lease agreements between the United Effort Plan and individuals (Note 6) living in the town of Hildale wherein the United Effort Plan leased property to those individuals for a period of 5 years for the purpose of obtaining funding from the Community Development Division of the Utah Department of Community and Economic Development. Each of the leases was signed by Fred Jessop, the Town Clerk, as 'Authorized Representative' of the United Effort Plan, without the knowledge of its president, Rulon T. Jeffs, and without a resolution of its Board of Directors.

2. Rulon T. Jeffs, when he was secretary of the United Effort Plan, gave the seal of the United Effort Plan to Fred Jessop, at Fred's request long before Fred Jessop became a trustee of the United Effort Plan but while Fred was serving as a clerk of the town of Hildale. The seal was to be used on legal documents signed by the United Effort Plan requiring a seal.

3. The beneficiary list attached to the 1983 Amended Affidavit of Disclosure which list deleted 117 names from the 1976 beneficiary list, was prepared by Fred Jessop while he was serving as town clerk and before he was appointed a trustee of the United Effort Plan.

4. The United Effort Plan leased real property to Hildale for the city offices on the 16th of April, 1979 for a 49 year term at $100.00 total rent. There was no meeting of the trustees or a resolution of the trustees to authorize the lease.

5. The Colorado City town hall sits on United Effort Plan land without a lease agreement and is a 'Tenant at Will' on United Effort Plan property.

6. All those who chose to follow J. Marian Hammon and Alma Timpson into what has now been termed as the 'Second Ward' stand in jeopardy of being asked by Rulon T. Jeffs to leave the homes they now occupy.

7. Sam Barlow, while drawing a salary from Colorado City, has served as an agent for the Fundamentalist Church of Jesus Christ of Latter Day Saints in helping it throughout this lawsuit.

8. Rulon T. Jeffs as president of the Fundamentalist Church of Jesus Christ of Latter Day Saints and the United Effort Plan has relied on Sam Barlow to answer interrogatories and requests for production of documents in his own behalf and on behalf of those entities.

9. Rulon Jeffs turned over all of the original files of the United Effort Plan to Sam Barlow at the beginning of the lawsuit 'because he was actively working with our attorneys in preparing the case.'

Facts gleaned from the testimony of Lynn Cooke, Mayor of the City of Hildale from its inception in 1962 until 1985, a period of 23 years:

1. The appointment of Lynn Cooke as Mayor was initially suggested by a member of the Priesthood Council, J. Marion Hammon.

2. During the 23 years Mr. Cooke was Mayor of the town of Hildale he was never opposed in an election due to influence of the United Effort Plan and the Priesthood Council.

3. 'Marked, stray ballots' already filled out were left 'promiscuously around the polling place' in Hildale elections and if citizens asked to see them that request would be made to the election judge.

4. Fred Jessop 'was in fact the real mayor.'

5. Once 'Uncle Fred' stated his opinion, no one on the town board would vote against him.

6. 'Uncle Fred' would often tell the town council what Leroy Johnson (the then President of the Priesthood Council) wanted them to do.

7. Fred Jessop was a mediator between the Priesthood Council and the town Council.

8. Fred Jessop was the mediator between the President of the United Effort Plan and the town Council.

9. As Mayor, Lynn Cooke was asked to pre-sign checks and give them to Fred Jessop 'in blank' to be used by Fred Jessop to pay town expenses.

10. Lynn Cooke, as Mayor, had agreed with Lorin Webb of the Spectrum (local newspaper), in St. George, to send the Spectrum the agenda of the town meetings and minutes of town meetings. He was overruled by Fred Jessop who said that the Spectrum would 'have to go to Court to get them.'

11. In a meeting Cooke had in the home of Fred Jessop, Fred required that they get Sam Barlow on the telephone to have him participate in their conversation regarding Lynn's discussion with Lorin Webb.

12. Fred Jessop holds his weekly Sunday School meeting for friends and family in the Hildale City offices without payment of rent therefore.

13. J. R. Williams was removed as a Justice of the Peace because he had a difference of opinion with Fred Jessop regarding Priesthood Order.

14. Cooke was recently selected by Hildale as a recipient of the largest single grant in Hildale from the Community Development Division of the Utah Department of Community and Economic Development for work on his home in May of 1989. The amount of the grant was $10,000.00 (Note 7). In order to qualify, Mr. Cooke had to demonstrate to the Department of Community and Economic Development that he had at least a 5 year lease from the United Effort Plan on the property on which his home was located. The lease between Mr. Cooke and the United Effort Plan was delivered to Mr. Cooke by David Zitting, the

Mayor of Hildale, in May of 1989. The lease had been pre-signed by Fred Jessop on behalf of the United Effort Plan. Mr. Cooke refused to signed the lease as it was drafted because in two portions thereof it required him to acknowledge that he occupied his property as a tenant at will. Mr. Zitting, the mayor of Hildale, then offered to strike out those portions of the lease if Mr. Cooke would sign it. Those portions were whited-out by Mr. Zitting. At no time did Mr. Cooke have any negotiations with any of the Trustees of the United Effort Plan regarding the lease but only with the Mayor of Hildale and another member of the town council who were in Mr. Cooke's home acting as agents for the United Effort Plan.

15. Sam Barlow, who was not a citizen of the town of Hildale, would occasionally attend town council meetings and express his views. In at least one instance where a decision had already been made by the council, Fred Jessop responded to a late comment by Sam Barlow and recommended that the matter be opened up for further discussion. The decision of the council was changed.

16. Until last year, the audits of the Town of Hildale were always performed by Rulon T. Jeffs, a trustee of the United Effort Plan, and now its president and president of the Priesthood Council, or in later year, by Mr. Jeffs' son, LeRoy Jeffs, who is now a trustee of the United Effort Plan.

17. Lynn Cooke often cast his vote against his will, 'to make voting on the council unanimous because of the psychology of being united, of being one heart, of one mind…it was ecclesiastical psychology that has come down to us through the years, and now I realize that some of the things I permitted and tolerated and participated in wasn't quite right. When they refused to cooperate with me, according to their promise, and send Lorin Webb a report, why I just backed clear out. I didn't say anything to them. I just never did show again.'

Facts gleaned from the testimony of Samuel S. Barlow, law enforcement officer from 1968 to the present:

1. Sam Barlow lived in the home of Leroy Johnson from the age of 12 until he got married at age 19.

2. Sam Barlow finished only the 8th grade; he was able to be certified as a law enforcement officer in the State of Arizona without ever attending high school only by providing an honorary diploma given him by the Colorado City Academy; he was a range Deputy in the State of Arizona in the Colorado City area from approximately 1968 to 1974 and was cross-deputized in the State of Utah during that same period of time as a Deputy Sheriff serving in the Hildale area; he became a Deputy Sheriff in the State of Arizona in approximately 1974; he traveled with President Leroy S. Johnson in the last months of Leroy S. Johnson's life, however he refused to testify from whom he receive compensation at that time; and began serving as a Deputy Marshall for Colorado City in December of 1986.

284

3. In the summer of 1985 Rulon T. Jeffs set up a meeting with Leroy Johnson, J. Marion Hammon, Alma Timpson, Truman Barlow and Fred Jessop at Rulon's office in Salt Lake City. The meeting was an effort to settle a controversy over the Colorado City Academy and the property on which it was located. Sam Barlow testified that 'I was there at the request of the South Salt Lake police department,' indicating that he had told the police department that, 'there had been some threats – not from the persons involved in this contention – but some threats against Mr. Johnson.' He further said, 'and my communications to the police was that I didn't anticipate any violence but I didn't want to be negligent in my responsibilities. And I was not a rookie.'

4. While traveling with Leroy Johnson, he kept his 'duty revolver' in the car with him and carried a radio.

Some application of facts.

The admissions of Defendants and testimony set forth herein as well as the affidavits demonstrate a simple, yet terrifying, reality. There is one dominant religious group with strict hierarchical lines of authority which completely controls the municipal government authority in both Hildale and Colorado City that, with threat of force and under color of law, systematically deprives Plaintiffs of their constitutional rights.

Plaintiffs, who live in those cities and surrounding areas, exist in fear of speaking or acting freely and have no effective redress for grievances which would challenge the civilly imposed opinions and acts of discrimination on Plaintiffs of the leaders of Defendant Fundamentalist Church of Jesus Christ of Latter Day Saints and Trustees of the Defendant, United Effort Plan who are effectively the same individuals. Plaintiffs, who have different religious and trust beliefs, could solve the problem simply by leaving, as these religious leaders want them to do. Yet (under the protection of law), there should be no place in these United States where an individual or a family cannot live peacefully and enjoy the religious and civil diversity and freedom guaranteed by the Constitution.

As adherents of particular religious beliefs, individual Defendants had the right to isolate themselves in a sparsely populated part of the country to practice their religion as they saw fit, but they now have no right to ostracize, persecute and expel people with different beliefs who arise within their midst, particularly by force or through color of law.

The incredible reality is that particularly Defendants Fred M. Jessop and Samuel S. Barlow do not even try to conceal their scorn for the principals of separation of church and state while being employed by the municipalities. They flaunt the subservence of their public duties to their religious allegiance through their current testimony and actions.

Fred M. Jessop is acknowledged generally as running the affairs and being the power behind the scenes in Hildale. For instance, Lynn Cooke, Mayor of Hildale from its inception in 1962 until 1985 stated in his deposition that Mr. Jessop's power and influence in Hildale were such that during all the years Mr. Cooke was legally the Mayor, Mr. Jessop 'was in fact the real mayor.' In other words, he controlled the policy decisions and affairs of the City.

It is clear that Mr. Jessop plays a major and possibly a dominant role in the temporal affairs of the Trust and Church Defendants and the City of Hildale. Fred M. Jessop is the Vice President and a Trustee of the United Effort Plan, a Bishop and a counselor to Rulon T. Jeffs in the presidency of the Fundamentalist Church of Jesus Christ of Latter Day Saints and the Town Clerk of Hildale. He is the President of Twin City Waterworks, the editor of the Twin City Courier, the only locally printed newspaper of general circulation in the area. He is a contemplated trustee of the Majestic Security Trust, which was created to hold the businesses of the United Effort Plan at a distance from those who may apostatize from the Church. He is the President and a member of the Board of the Colorado City Improvement Association, the owner of the town's only health center, the owner of Standard Supply and the owner of the only restaurant in town, the Early Bird Cafe. Mr. Jessop serves as the general election Judge for the Town of Hildale, and the municipal election Judge for off year elections. It is extremely revealing that Mr. Jessop testified that in spite of these public and business designations, he represents that, in fact, he considers himself to be laboring full time in church work.

Mr. Jessop is frank about his true purposes and intentions as the de facto major of Hildale, 'town clerk, town auditor,' election judge and man in charge of other corporations and enterprises. He testifies without equivocation that his 'whole interest is to carry out the expectations and hopes and aspiration of Brother Barlow and Brother Johnson and Brother Jeffs (all presidents of the Fundamentalist Church of Jesus Christ of Latter day Saints). And all these other incidental so-called hats are just in a days work. That's the way I view it.' In other words, his publicly acknowledged loyalties and priorities at all times are to promote and protect the best interests and the objectives of the church leaders. His duties and responsibilities as a public official of Hildale are at all times sacrificed at the alter of his primary loyalty to these religious leaders and Defendant Church.

This loyalty to his religious leaders creates a constant state of fear among Plaintiffs and a dramatic chilling effect on Plaintiffs and other residents of Hildale and Colorado City, who hesitate, for fear of reprisal, to insist on their constitutional rights that the Defendants regularly trample upon.

One of the most blatant and arrogant shows of inappropriate allegiances to the leaders of the Defendant Fundamentalist Church of Jesus Christ of Latter Day Saints and the Defendant United Effort Plan and against Plaintiffs can be found in Mr. (Sam) Barlow's behavior during this lawsuit. This full time Deputy Town

Marshal of Colorado City, sworn to impartially uphold the law of the land and the rights of citizens, is spending virtually all of his time at the tax payers' expense leading the defense of the lawsuit for all the Defendants and functioning as an agent of the Church and Trust Defendants. Defendant Rulon Jeffs, the president of Defendant Church, admits that Sam Barlow is functioning as an agent of the Church in this lawsuit and that Mr. Jeffs as the current leader of the Church has relied on Sam Barlow to prepare answers to interrogatories and requests for production of documents for the Defendant Church and Trust. Rather than being an even handed enforcer of the law and impartial protector of the rights of the citizens in the municipalities where he is employed, Defendant and Plaintiff taking notes and functioning as a paralegal to attorneys for all Defendants. He is publicly acknowledged by most of the parties to the lawsuit as the wholly committed armed enforcer, defender and lieutenant companion of the Defendant Church and Trust and their leaders.

Just as much as Defendant Barlow is the official enforcer of the dictates of the Defendant Church and Trust leaders under color of law, the Defendant Church insists on strict recognition and sustaining support of Defendant Barlow as the Church's armed enforcer.

Defendants make no attempt to conceal their insidious disregard of the principal of the separation of church and state. The actions of Defendants Jessop and Barlow are merely pertinent examples of how the Defendant municipalities of Hildale and Colorado City are permeated by the influence and control of the Defendant Church and Trust and its Defendant leaders.

The governmental practices of the Defendant municipalities, Hildale and Colorado City, are permeated with a strong underlying endorsement of the majoritarian religion. Dissenters are ostracized, discouraged from political office as well as deprived of material benefits such as continued patronage in their livelihood or the peaceable enjoyment of their homes.

Hildale and Colorado City are small and the customs and practices of these municipalities are manifested by a close group of people related by both blood and position in the hierarchy of the Defendant Church and Trust. The Plaintiffs and even Plaintiffs' legal counsel are taking their lives in their hands to oppose these religious and trust leaders who preach a doctrine of blood revenge against those who oppose them and who have armed lieutenants functioning under the banner of civic authority.

This characterization of the status of the community and the United Effort Plan as arrived at by the attorneys of the Plaintiffs was answered by the attorneys for the Defendants in a lengthy memorandum of nothing more than drawn out rhetoric that ended with the following paragraph, the only intelligent claim made in the whole memorandum:

Plaintiffs' effort to portray the United Effort Plan as some sort of selfish 'CABAL' does a base injustice to the selfless struggle of the Trust Defendants and the majority of the community for more than 50 years to create a just, prosperous, and religious community surrounded by the harsh beauty of the Arizona Strip. Quite simply, Plaintiffs' goal in this action is to destroy the 'community chest' and to distribute the 'loot' among themselves, so as to satisfy (in part) their own greed.

This statement of the Defendants' attorneys shows just how badly their characterization of the lawsuit was. The Plaintiffs were merely asking for protection against the Cabal Leaders, that they would not lose their homes, homes that they, the Plaintiffs, not the Cabal Leaders, had built and paid for with their own time and money. For this meager security they were branded as "selfish, greedy robbers."

The first line of defense for the Defendants was to say that all of the United Effort Plan activities were of a religious nature, that it was an entity that was created by a "Church" for religious purposes and all activities of the United Effort Plan were really activities of this "Church," thereby *claiming they did not have to furnish any of the information the Plaintiffs were asking for in the discovery process.* To substantiate this preposterous claim, they produced the document below that Sam Barlow had filed in the Mohave County Court House, claiming tax free status on the new "Church" Building that was under construction.

NOTIFICATION OF DEDICATION TO RELIGIOUS USE

Notice is hereby given that The United Effort Plan, a common law trust, has and does by the execution of this notice dedicate the West One-Half (W 1/2) of the North One-Half (N 1/2) of the Southeast Quarter (SE 1/4) of the Southwest Quarter (SW 1/4) of Section 32, Township 42 North, Range 6 West, Gila and Salt River Base and Meridian, to the Fundamentalist Church of Jesus Christ of Latter Day Saints as a church building and meeting house to be used under the direction of the Bishop residing in Colorado City, Az.– Hildale, Ut, for so long as said property, as determined by the trustees of The United Effort Plan, shall be used in accordance with the tenets of the Fundamentalist Church of Jesus Christ of Latter Day Saints.

The property described above shall not be sold or any interest therein conveyed by the Fundamentalist Church of Jesus Christ of Latter Day Saints and in the event that it ever ceases to be used exclusively for religious activities by the Fundamentalist Church of Jesus Christ of Latter Day Saints, all rights therein shall automatically revert to The United Effort Plan and evidence thereof may be given by the recordation of a notice of such reversion recorded in the official records of Mohave County, Arizona, by The United Effort Plan, which notice shall cause the reversion of all rights to the property to The United Effort Plan.

No rent or other charge shall ever be levied or collected by The United

Effort Plan for the use of such property by the Fundamentalist Church of Jesus Christ of Latter Day Saints.

IN WITNESS WHEREOF, this instrument is executed this 19th day of February, 1988.

ss Rulon T. Jeffs

Rulon T. Jeffs, President of the

Board of Trustees of

The United Effort Plan,

a common law trust STATE OF UTAH

SS. County of Salt Lake

Before me, the undersigned notary public, personally appeared Rulon T. Jeffs, the President of the Board of Trustees of The United Effort Plan, a common law trust, and acknowledged that, being duly empowered so unto do, he executed the foregoing instrument for the purposed therein contained.IN WITNESS WHEREOF, I have set my hand and official seal this 19th day of February, 1988.

ss Patricia B. Birch

Notary Public My commission expires 7/29/88

(notary seal)

Throughout the history of the Short Creek Polygamists, this is the first time that the "Group" had claimed to be an independent church, separate and distinct from the Main Line Church of Jesus Christ of Latter Day Saints. There are two places in Leroy's sermons where he refers to the "Group" as the "Fundamentalist Branch, or Division of The Church of Jesus Christ of Latter Day Saints," but he never claimed to be a separate church, in fact to the contrary; he, along with the other leaders before him, taught that the Polygamists were not the Church, that the Main Line "Mormon" Church was the true church, it was just out of order and the day would come when it would be set in order, with the "true Priesthood" restored to its correct position at the head of the Church. This characterization of the "Group" as a Church was derived at simply to have a religious entity which the trustees of the United Effort Plan could hide behind in an effort to become immune to, or answerable to the laws that would protect the victims of any unlawful actions on their parts. Their strategy did not work for them however because the Plaintiffs just amended their complaint, making the "New Church" a defendant in the lawsuit. This is a prime example of the scheming on their part to just drag the lawsuit out for as long as they could.

One thing that is interesting about this "Notification of Dedication To Religious Use" is the confusion it sets forth as to which is the governing entity, the FLDS Church, or the UEP. The "Church" can be denied use of the building by the "Trustees Of The United Effort Plan" if (It) doesn't use the building "in accordance with the tenets of the Fundamentalist Church of Jesus Christ of Latter Day Saints." If the building "ever ceases to be used exclusively for religious activities by the Fundamentalist Church of Jesus Christ of Latter Day Saints," it then reverts back to the United Effort Plan. This is a prime example of the "tail wagging the dog," the question being: Which is the tail, and which is the dog?

On May 1st, 1988, Rulon Jeffs told his congregation that "the Colorado City Academy was built by Apostates (referring to Marion Hammon whom he now proclaimed was an apostate) and all evidence of its existence must be destroyed." Fred Jessop then told them that the building must be torn down in order to "obey the Prophet" in his admonition of obliterating the institution. He then announced that the work of tearing down "this monument of rebellion" would begin the next day and everybody was to show up in the morning to help with the task. The next day, Monday morning, Fred Jessop's work of revenge was begun with a vengeance.

When Fred Jessop and the other UEP leaders were served with the court orders on the Lawsuit, he immediately initiated a Monday morning Prayer Meeting, where all "faithful members" were compelled to meet at 6:00 a.m. (this was later changed to 7:00 because it was too hard for him to get the people there by six) every Monday morning in the new church house to hold a "circle prayer," asking the "Lord to protect us against the threat of the lawsuit that the wicked enemy has brought against us." After the Prayer Meeting and circle prayer was over, Fred would then direct those attending to spend a "few hours in helping to build up the Kingdom" by participating in Priesthood work projects in the community which had been designated by him as such.

It was at the Monday Morning Prayer Meeting on May 2, 1988, that he designated the tearing down of the Academy Building as the Priesthood work project to be accomplished that morning. This project would take more than a few hours to complete, however, and since it was such an important project, it was "decreed" that once it was started, it would be completed, no matter how long it took to accomplish.

The teachers and high school students of the public school were told that the high school would be let out for all day Monday so they could participate in the work. This provided a substantial work force for Fred to achieve his objective. It did not go over all that well with these young people who were required to do his dirty work, however, for although they participated in his work of revenge, it was with great sorrow and heavy hearts that many of them did so.

Some of the teachers and many of the students in the public high school had spent much of their young lives attending the Colorado City Academy; many of them went about the task of "destroying it" with tears in their eyes. One of the teachers, who had received his high school education at the Academy, was unable to assist in the work of its destruction and had to leave, going home for the day.

In his justification of destroying the Academy, Fred Jessop used the excuse that the buildings would no longer meet the fire code of the city and must be razed. This was not the truth, because the buildings were made of adobe and were virtually fireproof. All the halls were eight feet wide and the emergency exits were adequate. Even if the buildings were no longer needed for educational purposes, they could have been easily adapted to apartments, to be used for young couples as living quarters, especially since there had always been such a great need for homes in the community.

Fred Jessop's act of vengeance was not justified in any way. It was only a matter of demonstrating to the community that he was now the "Boss," and Marion Hammon was no longer in control of affairs therein. Such unnecessary destruction, of not only tangible property, but also of historical and cultural wealth, is one of the greatest detriments that a cult imposes on its members. There is simply no justification for such destruction to be allowed by the members of such an organization as the Short Creek Polygamists, for they, of all people should know better.

The depositions on the lawsuit began with the lawyers for the defendants taking Marion Hammon's on June 27, 1988. They took Alma Timpson's deposition the next day. It should be remembered here that Hammon was the next "worthy senior" member of the priesthood council and according to the "rules" of the "Group" would at this time be their President. The Barlow Cabal, however, had been successful in having him "ousted" by Leroy Johnson before he died and now their recognized leader was Rulon Jeffs.

Hammon, however, was recognized by the Second Ward as the legitimate Leader, with Timpson still supporting him as such. Neither of these two men were either Plaintiffs or Defendants in the lawsuit, but the Defendants were claiming that the lawsuit was filed by their followers to try and regain control of the United Effort Plan. This claim is a misnomer because these two leaders had simply "given up" on the majority of the people, who were following the Barlow Cabal, and they had pretty well established themselves at Centennial Park. They were going ahead with "building up the kingdom," working with those people who had chosen to support them. Throughout the lawsuit, Scott Berry, attorney for the United Effort Plan, would constantly claim before the court, in briefs and in hearings, that the lawsuit was filed for this reason, accusing the plaintiffs of all belonging to a "religious schism" that had broken away from the "true Church," and were just trying to "steal the UEP assets." This could not have been farther from the truth, as the main contenders (plaintiffs) were not members of the Second Ward and claimed no allegiance to either Hammon or Timpson, but rather were Dissidents to both religious groups.

With the beginning of these depositions, the lawsuit got under way. It would be longer than seven years before it would be resolved, costing both sides an enormous amount of money, totaling over $3,000,000 counting the expense on both sides, with the defendants' portion amounting to about five times what the plaintiffs would pay. Other developments among the Polygamists would take place during this time, almost a decade, but the events of the community would revolve around this lawsuit. These events will be covered in the next two chapters.

Soon after his deposition, on August 28, 1988, Marion Hammon died. He died a broken hearted man. Just prior to his death he conceded that his only Priesthood power and calling was to keep Plural Marriage alive. The control he had imposed on the people had merely been because of his ego, in trying to prepare them for entering the Kingdom of Heaven. He died, feeling that his life had been spent mostly for no avail, accusing the people of not obeying the principals that he had tried to instill into their lives.

His funeral was held the next Sunday at the new chapel in Centennial Park. Prior to the funeral, Fred Jessop told "his" followers that they "could not go onto the Devil's ground," thus denying many of his friends and family members from attending the service. He was laid to rest in a family plot, in the front yard of his home, where several members of his family were buried. It was only a matter of a few months after his burial that Fred Jessop attempted to have him and the other buried members in this plot, dug up and moved "off of the United Effort Plan" property. His scheme was somehow foiled and this attempt of his, to "evict the dead," was not carried out.

The death of Marion Hammon left Alma Timpson as the leader of the Second Ward. He felt very much alone under the weight of this calling, and in the spring of 1989, he "called" Frank Naylor as a High Priest Apostle to assist him in the Priesthood Council.

Frank Naylor had been called as a patriarch by Leroy Johnson a few years before and was readily accepted by the Second Ward into this position of being a member of the Council. Naylor was very conscientious and preformed well in his new calling, too well in fact, for his act of living by his conscience rather than by an edict of "his file leader," would soon cause problems in the course of the "Work" at Centennial Park.

The year of 1989 went by without many noteworthy events other than this in the lives of the polygamists. One happening worth noting occurred in the early part of the year. When the attorneys for the plaintiffs were first presenting their "pitch" to their would-be clients, they speculated that the lawsuit could be over within a year, reasoning that the "defendants" would use reason, coming to the bargaining table to negotiate a settlement. This did not happen and at the end of the year and the end of the $100,000 dollars that the plaintiffs had paid their attorneys, the lawyers wanted to negotiate a new contract with their clients, asking them to commit to paying more money.

By now the Plaintiffs could see the position they were in, that of paying their attorneys much more money than any of them had ever dreamed, or trying to settle with the defendants on their own. A few of them did just that, attempting to make such a settlement without going through their attorneys. The response they received was shattering.

They were told by the Cabal that they would not only be evicted, but a counter suit would be filed against any that would drop out of the lawsuit, taking any and every asset they might have. When they were reminded that none of the plaintiffs had any assets, the response was that a judgement would be levied against them, just for the purpose to embarrass and punish them for "fighting against the Priesthood." These plaintiffs were in a position of riding on a tiger; they could not get off for fear of being destroyed and it was a very unpleasant circumstance to have to stay on the tiger's back for as long as it took to subdue it. The ordeal was just beginning for them and the outcome did not look bright.

Note 1: Leroy Johnson had told several people that he was not going to die, that he was going to live until Christ's return at His Second Coming, that he would be here to turn the "Keys of Priesthood back to Him." He had set the date of this event to be in the year 1998. There is one place where this claim is recorded. It is in the minutes of a UEP Board Meeting held at the home of Rulon Jeffs in Salt Lake City, dated September 1, 1984. In this meeting Leroy was asked by Jeffs about making some amendments to the Trust Document, in regarding to its life limit of 100 years. Quoting from the minutes, Leroy says:

"We won't be under any trust law then. It will come under the jurisdiction of the Prophet Joseph Smith and his kingdom.... It's been tested pretty much in the courts. The lawyers are afraid of it so let's not make any changes. There is only 14 years and that won't be long. We'll be dealing with the Kingdom of God then."

Rulon then said: "It will be a very great pleasure to have you govern us in the millennium under the direction of Jesus Christ and Joseph Smith."

In a deposition on May 22, 1989, Jeffs acknowledges his belief that Leroy will live until 1998. He was asked if he knew what Leroy was referring to when he said: "There is only 14 more years, and that wouldn't be long."

Jeffs' answer: "I don't know what he means by 14 years."

Q. Had there ever been a discussion about something happening near the end of this century?

A. Not unless it was meant to be the millennium commencing.

Q. Following Brother Johnson's remarks, these minutes quote you as saying, "It will be a very great pleasure to have you govern us in the millennium under the direction of Jesus Christ and Joseph Smith." Does that refresh your memory as far as what would happen in 14 years?

A. Well, as mentioned in sermons, he is talking about the condition under which we would be alluding after the judgment and the beginning of the millennium.

Q. And did you anticipate that Leroy Johnson would be governing you at that time?

A. I did.

Q. Did you expect him to still be alive at that time?

A. Yes.

Q. How old was he in September of 1984?

A. 96.

Q. So in 14 years, he would have been 110?

A. Yes.

Q. But you anticipated that he would still be Alive?

A. (Nod.)

Q. Is that a yes?

A. Yes.

The next Sunday, May 28, 1989, Sam Barlow, in speaking to the people in Sunday afternoon meeting at the L.S.J. Meeting House at Colorado City, said that when Jeffs acknowledged that he would be governed by Leroy Johnson in 1998, he was met with "titters and jeers," from the plaintiffs who were present at the deposition. He explained that Jeffs, in his acknowledgment, only meant that Leroy would be there, after being resurrected, to govern the people. This explanation by Sam Barlow is totally a cover up, else why did Jeffs agree to the question of Leroy being 110 years old?

Note 2: Fred Jessop's position in the Hildale Town Government is an interesting one. He was never elected as a member of the town council until some years after this, yet, by having himself appointed as the "Town Clerk," he attended every town meeting. Any decision made by the council "had "to be approved by him. In fact, any proposals regarding the town government were almost always his "suggestion." It is a known fact that none of the council members ever opposed him on anything he decided to do, with the possible exception of one person; and that person was the mayor, Lynn Cooke.

Mayor Cooke never really opposed Fred in his "running" the town, just said on a few occasions that he thought the decisions should be made by the town council members rather than by the town clerk. This was enough to have the other council members treat him with contempt and disrespect. In time he just quit attending the meetings, hoping that by his boycotting them someone would inquire as to what his reasons were, thereby giving him an opportunity to voice his complaint about Fred Jessop's absolute power in making all decisions in regards to the community. In this he was terribly disappointed. Not only did no one ever approach him about the matter, but Fred just "appointed" another one of the council members, Dan Jessop, to take his place as Pro-Tem Mayor.

In the meeting with David Zitting, he was asked about him being "elected" mayor of Hildale. Zitting told Don Cox and Ben Bistline that he had never asked to be put on the ballot, but rather was "chosen" by Leroy Johnson to be the mayor. He explained to them that when Fred decided to have a new mayor "elected," he went to Leroy and asked who he wanted as mayor. Leroy asked Fred for suggestions as to whom he wanted. Zitting was one of the names Fred gave Leroy and he is the one Leroy chose to be placed on the ballot. One interesting point here about these elections. In the history of Hildale, since being incorporated, there has never been more than one candidate for each official position on the ballot to be voted on in any of the elections.

All council members were chosen by Fred, and the people just simply voted for whomever he wanted. The same is true for Colorado City, with the exception that Fred does not attend the meetings there, just simply "appointed" Dan Barlow as mayor and he carries out Fred's bidding, as do all the other council members, knowing that whatever Barlow proposes is what Fred Jessop wants.

Note 3: Ron Bradshaw, the man who had drilled the wells and furnished the pumps, had not been paid for some of them. When he could not collect his money he went to the farm and proceeded to pull some of the pumps to try and recoup part of his losses. Sam Barlow showed up with some of his "Goons" and threatened Mr. Bradshaw with physical force if he did not leave the premises. Mr. Bradshaw then filed a claim in the District Court at St. George to either collect the money owed him or repossession of "his" pumps. The day before the scheduled hearing was to take place, his pickup truck was burglarized while parked on the street in St. George and his briefcase, with all the documents and papers, etc. necessary to prove his case in court, was stolen, thus he was unable to prove his claim.

Note 4: Two affidavits that were made in support of Sam Barlow's integrity are copied here. The first one by Lee Bistline is a sample of the control the Barlow Cabal has over its subjects. The second one is made by Rulon Jeffs and is important because it is the first written evidence put out by the Cabal that changes the Polygamists' history of their claimed line of Priesthood authority.

AFFIDAVIT OF LEE BISTLINE STATE OF ARIZONA
ss. COUNTY OF MOHAVE

F. LEE BISTLINE states under oath:

1. I reside in Colorado City, Arizona and my mailing address is Post Office Box 215, Colorado City, Arizona 86021.

2. I am 57 years of age, and have resided at Colorado City since 1945. I am self-employed in fencing and contracting, and have previously been employed as administrator of a nursing home in Cedar City, Utah.

3. I am President of the school board of the Colorado City Unified School District, and in that capacity I have had occasion to remain informed regarding issues concerning the young people of Colorado City, Arizona and Hildale, Utah, some of whose students attend our high school.

4. I have known Sam Barlow since my arrival in Colorado City in 1945; he was then about 8 or 9 years of age, and I have seen him grow up and observed him throughout his adult career.

5. From my observation Sam Barlow has always conducted himself as a law enforcement official in a professional manner. He has not used his badge to advance his personal interests or the interests of his religious faith, but has served as a law enforcement officer sensitive to the feelings of the community.

6. I have had children who have been involved in juvenile (sic) deli(n)quency problems and for whom Sam was the arresting officer. In all of his dealings with which I was familiar Sam behaved in a responsible manner. He acted for the welfare not only of the community but also for the benefit of the children. He build(s) the self -respect of the children and their self- image as law abiding citizens, and he promoted respect for the law.

7. This affidavit was dictated in my presence between 10:00 and 10:30 a.m. Monday, August 31, 1987 at the Holiday Inn Motel, St. George, Utah, following a conversation during breakfast prior to 10:00 a.m. The affidavit was prepared based upon information which I furnished. During the dictation of the affidavit, I was invited to make changes, corrections and additions, and I have done so. This is my voluntary statement, and I swear it is true in substance and in fact.

(signed) F. Lee Bistline
F. Lee Bistline

SUBSCRIBED AND SWORN to before me September 7, 1987.
William S. Shapley
Notary Public My Commission Expires: July 9, 1988.

This affidavit of Lee Bistline was composed and written by Sam Barlow, then presented to Lee for his signature. It is amusing to notice how he (Sam) has gone to such lengths to extol his "virtues."

AFFIDAVIT OF RULON JEFFS STATE OF UTAH

ss. County of Salt Lake

RULON T. JEFFS states under oath:

1. I reside at 3601 Little Cottonwood Road, Sandy, Utah 84092.

2. I am the spiritual leader of a continuing religious congregation which is known as the Fundamentalist Church of Jesus Christ of Latter Day Saints.

3. As spiritual leader of this religious community I am the immediate successor of the prophet Leroy S. Johnson in the Priesthood established by Joseph Smith through revelation of the Lord. The Priesthood so established has been continued under the leadership of the following successors of Joseph Smith: Brigham Young, John Taylor, John W. Woolley, Lorin C. Woolley, John Y. Barlow, Leroy Johnson, and myself, Rulon T. Jeffs.

4. The Fundamentalist Church of Jesus Christ of Latter Day Saints believes on faith and subscribes to the principles which were revealed by the Lord to Joseph Smith and his successors, including those published in Doctrine and Covenants Section 132, which provides in part, and in substance that:

a. Members of the Priesthood which consists of all of the righteous males who accept our beliefs and who are admitted to membership are commanded for the purpose of procreation and to carry out the will of the Lord to marry and with the consent (of) his wife(s) to take additional wives who are not married to others:

b. That all such marriages entered into as an everlasting covenant sealed by the Holy Spirit and his representative on earth are celestial and eternal, and shall last for eternity beyond the time of this earth; and

c. That the glory of heaven cannot be attained except by observance of this law. All those to whom this law has been revealed must obey it, and those who do not abide by it shall be damned; and no one who rejects this law shall be permitted to enter into the Lord's glory.

5. These principles have been consistently held and adhered to by the religious community of which I am spiritual leader since they were revealed through the prophet Joseph Smith, and through the present time, These truths revealed through Joseph Smith are accepted on faith, and are not debatable.

6. Samuel S. Barlow of Colorado City, Arizona was reared in and is a member of the Fundamentalist Church of Jesus Christ of Latter Day Saints, and as a member if its Priesthood conducts his life in accordance with its beliefs.

(signed) Rulon T. Jeffs

Rulon T. Jeffs

SUBSCRIBED and sworn to before me September 15, 1987.

A. L. Barlow

Notary Public My Commission Expires 1-1-91

Note 5: Just prior to Leroy Johnson's death in 1986, Joe Barlow convinced him that many of the assets of the United Effort Plan should be "hidden" in another trust so as to keep them at "arms length" from the reach of any who might apostatize and attempt to claim any equity they felt they might have in the Trust. With "Uncle Roy's permission," he formed a new trust called The Majestic Security Trust. There were only three people in this trust, namely, Leroy Johnson, Joseph I. Barlow and Fred Jessop.

When Leroy Johnson died, he was replaced by Rulon T. Jeffs on this new trust. When the lawsuit was filed in 1987, Joe Barlow and Fred Jessop were in the process of transferring assets of the United Effort Plan into the Majestic Security Trust. In a deposition of Rulon Jeffs taken on May 4, 1989, he testified that he had known nothing of this new trust until just a few days before this deposition when Jethro Barlow, son of Joe Barlow, had handed him a paper showing the names of several companies that at one time were owned by the United Effort Plan but had been changed over to other ownership. These included, besides the Majestic Security Trust, General Cooperative Association, Twin City Improvement Association, Colorado City Improvement Association, Cooperative Mercantile Corporation, General Rock and Sand, General Concrete Products, Danco Manufacturing Co., Color Country Care Center, J&B Service and Cooperative Financial Service. When the lawsuit was filed, it virtually stopped these transfers, thus thwarting the plans of Joe and Fred from gaining complete control of the United Effort Plan assets.

If this lawsuit had not been brought against the UEP at this crucial time in its history, it would have only been a few short years before Joe Barlow and some of his scheming sons would have completely owned and controlled all the property of the United Effort Plan. This is a little known reality that the followers of the Polygamist leaders do not understand, that had these few "apostates" not filed a lawsuit when they did, these followers would have became "Tenants At Will" to Joe Barlow and his son Jethro.

Note 6: Each year a cash grant was given to Hildale Town by the Community Development Division of the Utah Department of Community And Economic Development, to be distributed by the municipality for improvements to be made on homes in the community owned by poor people. Since the United Effort Plan "owned" all the homes in Hildale, the only way the money could be obtained was for a lease to be granted by the United Effort Plan to those living in the home, thus five year leases were given to those whom Fred Jessop selected and determined were "worthy" to receive this benefit. In this manner the money could be "legally" used.

Note 7: When Fred Jessop learned that Lynn Cooke was going to testify in a deposition regarding his experience as the Mayor of Hildale, he attempted to "buy him off" by "giving" him the grant money from the Utah Community and Economic Development Agency that Hildale was eligible for in 1989. The amount of the grant was $10,000.00, the largest the city had ever received.

The new mayor, David Zitting, presented the lease to Mr. Cooke to sign. Mr. Cooke was not happy with some of the wording in the document and would not sign until a change was made. This change was a clause that designated the signer, Mr. Cooke, a Tenant at Will in his home. This clause was eliminated and the five year lease was signed.

This money was spent on Lynn Cooke's home and the improvements were made. Much to Fred Jessop's disappointment, however, Lynn went ahead and testified unfavorably toward Fred's "running of the town board" in his deposition. Because of this unfavorable testimony, when the five year lease was up in 1994, Fred attempted to have him evicted. He would have succeeded in this endeavor had not Rulon Jeffs interceded in Lynn's behalf, thus denying Fred of his "pound of flesh."

Each Side Speaks Out

The lawsuit against the United Effort Plan brought much discord into the community. People were now forced to take sides, either with the "Priesthood" (meaning the Cabal) or with those who were fighting to keep their homes. This placed a burden on the Cabal leaders to convince their followers to choose their side, "the right side." In almost every one of the Sunday Meetings in their new church house the congregation was bombarded with propaganda, most put out by the Barlow boys.

One prime example is a lengthy treatise claimed to be written by Sam Barlow, but read in the meeting by Alvin Barlow in July of 1989, at Fred Jessop's request. Filled with accusations and false claims as to what the situation was at the time regarding the status of the lawsuit and the "Apostates" who had brought it about, the treatise will be copied here in its entirety. Using words from Thomas Paine's "The American Crisis," Alvin begins speaking:

The UEP Crisis

"These are the times that try men's souls: The summer soldier and the sunshine patriot will, in this crisis, shrink from the service of his country; but he that stands it now, deserves the love and thanks of men and women. Tyranny, like hell, is not easily conquered; yet we have this consolation with us, that the harder the conflict, the more glorious the triumph. What we obtain too cheap, we esteem too lightly; 'Tis dearness only that gives every thing its value. Heaven knows how to set a proper price upon its goods; and it would be strange indeed, if so celestial an article as FREEDOM and unity should not be highly rated.

"Apostates, with an army to enforce their tyranny, have declared, that they have a right (not only to divide but) 'to bind us in all cases whatsoever,' and if being bound in that manner is not slavery, then is there not such a thing as slavery upon earth. Even the expression is impious, for so unlimited a power can belong only to God. Whether the unity of the United Effort Plan was declared too soon, or delayed too long, I will not now enter into an argument; my own simple opinion is that had not J. Marion Hammon and Alma A. Timpson defected away from Leroy S. Johnson and Rulon T. Jeffs, it would have been much better.

"We did not make proper use of the last decade, neither could we, while in a divided state. However the fault, if it were one, was all our own; we have none to

301

blame but ourselves. But no great deal is lost yet; all that Harold Blackmore and his associates in this lawsuit have been doing for these months past is rather a ravage than a conquest, which the spirit of the Priesthood work fifteen years ago would have quickly repulsed, and which time and a little resolution will soon recover. I have as little superstition in me as any man living, but my secret opinion has ever been, and still is, that God Almighty will not give up a pure people to division and destruction, or leave them unsupported to perish, who had so earnestly and so repeatedly sought to avoid the calamities of dissension and division by every decent method which wisdom could invent.

"Neither have I so much of the infidel in me, as to suppose that He relinquished the management of the United Effort Plan and given us up to the care of devils; and as I do not, cannot see on what grounds Dell, George, Cyril, or any of their followers can look up to heaven for help against us: a common thief, highwayman, or a house breaker, has as good a pretense as they have. 'Tis surprising to see how rapidly a panic will sometimes run through a community. All nations and ages have been subject to them. Mormondom in the past has trembled like an ague at the report of Judge Zane and the U.S. Marshals; and in 1953, the whole state of Arizona and the state of Utah, after ravaging the community of Short Creek, were driven back like men petrified with fear; and this brave exploit was performed by a few broken forces collected and headed by a man of God named Leroy S. Johnson. Would that Heaven might inspire some young men and women here to spirit up their countrymen, and save the United Effort Plan and the communities from ravage and ravishment!

"Yet trials, in some cases, have their uses; they produce as much good as hurt. Their duration can be short; the mind soon grows through them, and acquires a firmer habit than before. But their peculiar advantage is that they are the touchstones of sincerity and hypocrisy, and bring things and men to light, which might otherwise have lain forever undiscovered. In fact, they have the same effect on secret traitors, with an imaginary apparition, as they would have upon a private sinner. They sift out the hidden thoughts of man, and hold them up in public to the world. Many a disguised apostate has lately shown his head, and shall penitentially solemnize with curses the day on which a counterfeit trust was established in the southern part of the valley.

"As I was with President Johnson in the Raid of 1953, I am well acquainted with many circumstances, which those who live at a distance know but little or nothing of. Our situation there was exceedingly discomforting, the place being an alluvial fill located in the arid southwest during a pioneering time. Our force was inconsiderable, being not one thousandth part so great as Governor Howard Pyle could bring against us. We had no money at hand to have relieved the need for legal assistance. Our resources and light crops and the best part of our stores and our families had been removed on the apprehension that Utah and Judge David

302

Anderson would endeavor to penetrate the faith of our families through the Vera Black case, in which case the Short Creek Valley could be of no use to us; for it must occur to every thinking man, whether in the forefront of the battle or not, that these kinds of attacks on the family unit are only for temporary purposes, and last in use no longer than the enemy directs his force against that particular family, which represents the Priesthood sealing powers of the President and Key Holder.

"Such was our situation and condition in 1953 on the morning of the 26th of July, when a runner arrived with information that the enemy with two hundred cars had halted south of the Berry Knoll, several miles away. Uncle Roy, who loved the Lord and the community, immediately called the people to unite in prayer to the God of Abraham, and to send a message to the Lord that a chosen people were about to suffer persecution.

"Our first object was to secure the children, and secure their faith in God so the enemy could not take them from us and give them over to the world. Uncle Roy stood at the head of the people and declared, "This sand shall drink our blood before we give up our religion or sacrifice these sacred principles." Grandfather Joseph Smith Jessop at the school house stood among the Saints and faced the raiders, and announced, "If it's blood you want, take mine." At which time I expected we should have a brush with them. However, they did not choose to haul our families away then, and the greatest part of our people went back to their homes for a few days, except for some which passed over into Utah on a small creek, between the bridge and the sump and made their way through some marshy grounds up to the town of Hildale, and brought the people out during a storm. We brought off as much baggage as the women and children could carry, the rest was left. The simple object was to bring the women and children to safety and to march them till they could be strengthened by our friends in Salt Lake City and elsewhere, so as to enable us to make a stand. We stayed all night at the Gap, collected in our outposts with the help of friends from Hurricane and Johns Valley, and marched out to meet the enemy on information of their being aware of our location, though our numbers were greatly inferior to theirs.

"Governor Pyle, in my little opinion, committed a great error in generalship in not sending a helping hand to assist the down-trodden citizens of the north land in Arizona, by which means he might have seized all the gory a politician would want, and been re-elected many times over in Arizona. But if we believe the power of hell to be limited, we must likewise believe that their agents are under some providential control.

"I shall not now attempt to give all the particulars of our captivity in Arizona; suffice it for the present to say, that both fathers and mothers of the Mormon Fundamentalist community though greatly harassed and fatigued, frequently without rest, covering, or provision, the inevitable consequences of a long retreat, bore it with a manly and humble spirit. All their wishes centered in one, which was that the country would turn out and help them to survive the attack on their religion. Some have remarked that Uncle Roy never appeared to call for full faith and works, but in times of difficulties and in action. The same remark may be made of Uncle Rulon, for the character fits him.

There is a natural firmness in some minds which cannot be unlocked by trifles, but which, when unlocked, discovers a cabinet of fortitude; and I reckon it among those kinds of public blessings, which we do not immediately see, that God hath blessed him with uninterrupted health and given him a mind that can receive instructions from heaven.

"I shall conclude this paper with some miscellaneous remarks on the state of the present lawsuit against the Church and United Effort Plan; and shall begin with asking the following question. Why is it that the enemy has left Uncle Roy and Uncle Rulon and United Effort Plan lands, and established Centennial Park, and brought a lawsuit into Federal Court? The answer is easy. Could it be the United Effort Plan land is now infested with dissenters?

"I have been tender in raising the cry against these men, and used numberless arguments to show them their danger, but it will not do to sacrifice a chosen people either to their folly or their baseness. The period is now arrived, in which either they or we must change our sentiments, or one or both must fall. And what is a deserter from the principles represented in the leadership of Uncle Roy? Good God! What is he? I should not be afraid to go with an hundred faithful men against a thousand dissenters and apostates, were they to attempt to get into the Lord's Storehouse. Every dissenter is a coward, for a servile, slavish, self-interested fear is the foundation of those turning their backs on Uncle Roy; and a man under such influence, though he may be cruel, never can be brave.

"But, before the line of irrecoverable separation be drawn between us, let us reason the matter together. Your conduct is an invitation to Harold Blackmore and his kind, yet not one in five hundred of you has heart enough to turn him down. Harold is as much deceived by you as the effort toward United Order is injured by you. He expects you will all take up this lawsuit and flock to his standard, with money in your pockets. Your opinions are of no use to him, unless you support him personally, for 'tis greed, and not Christ, that he wants.

"I once felt all that kind of anger, which a man ought to feel against the mean principles that are held by the apostates; a noted one, who kept a home at Hildale, was standing at his door, with as pretty a child in his hand, about eight or nine years old, as I ever saw, and after speaking his mind as freely as he thought was prudent, finished with this un-fatherly expression, 'Well! give me my lot from the United Effort Plan Trust.' Not a man lives on that sacred ground but fully believes that a separation must some time or other finally take place. An honest parent would have said, 'If there must be trouble, let it be in my day, that my child may have peace.' And this single reflection, well applied, is sufficient to awaken every man to duty. Not a place upon earth might be so happy as a home on United Effort Plan land. There the situation is remote from all the wrangling world, and he has nothing to do but to be pure and truthful. A man may easily distinguish in himself between temper and principle, and I am as confident, as I am God governs the world, that Short Creek Valley will never be happy till she gets clear of division and dissension.

"Lawsuits, without ceasing, will break out till that period arrives, and the greed of men must in the end be conquered; for though the flame of liberty may sometimes cease to shine, the coal can never expire.

"The Trustees of the United Effort Plan did not, nor do not, want force; but they want a proper application of pure faith. Wisdom is not the purchase of a day, and it is no wonder that we should err at the first setting off. From an excess of tenderness, we were willing to raise a helping hand and trusted our cause to the permanent defense of the God of John Y. Barlow, Leroy S. Johnson, and Rulon T. Jeffs. A summer's experience has now taught us we are right. And with attorneys, while they were paid, we were able to set bounds to the progress of the enemy, and thank God! They are again assembling. I always considered righteous and pure men as the best troops in the world for a sudden exertion, and they will always do for a long campaign.

"Harold and his crew of apostates, it is probable, will make an attempt on this church; should he fail on this cause of action, he is ruined. If he succeeds, our cause is not ruined. He takes all on his side against a part on ours; admitting he succeeds, the consequence will be that people from the ends of the state will come to assist their suffering friends in this valley. For he cannot go everywhere, it is impossible. I consider Harold and like-spirited men as the greatest enemy the families of our previous friends have; he is bringing lawsuits on to their water supply, which, had it not been for him and partly for themselves, they could have had an improved system even now. Should he now be put down in court, I wish, with all the devotion of a Christian, that the names of Hammonites and Musserites never be mentioned; but should the followers of Alma A. Timpson give Harold encouragement to come, or assistance if he comes, I as sincerely wish that our next contests before the courts may expel them from the United Effort property, and the Judge appropriate their possessions to the relief of those who have suffered in well doing.

"A single successful battle next year will settle the whole. The United Effort Plan lawsuit could carry on a two years war by the confiscation of the property of disaffected persons, and be made happy by their expulsion.

"Say not that this is revenge, call it rather the soft resentment of a suffering people, who, having no object in view but the good of all, have staked their OWN ALL upon a strong faith in the words of the Prophet Leroy S. Johnson. Yet it is folly to argue against determined hardness; eloquence may strike the ear, and the language of sorrow draw forth the tear of compassion, but nothing can reach the heart that is steeled with prejudice.

"Quitting this class of men, I turn with the warm ardor of a friend to those who have nobly stood, and are yet determined to stand the matter out. I call not upon a few, but upon all; not on THIS faithful man and his family or THAT faithful man and his family, but on EVERY faithful man and his family, up and help us; lay your shoulders to the wheel; better have too much force than too little, when so great an object is at stake.

"Let it be told to the future world, that in the depths of winter, when nothing but hope and virtue could survive, that the city and the country alarmed at one common danger, came forth with clean hands and pure hearts to meet and to repulse the spirit of division and greed. Say not that thousands of dollars are gone, turn out your tens of thousands; throw not the burden of the day on Uncle Rulon, But "show your faith by your works," that God may bless you. It matters not where you live, or what rank of life you hold, the evil or the blessing will reach you all. The far and the near, the southern communities, the Salt Lake saints and the Canadians, the rich and the poor, will suffer or rejoice alike. The heart that feels not now, is dead: The blood of his children shall curse his cowardice, who shrinks back at a time when a little might have saved the whole, and made them happy. I love the man that can smile in trouble, that can gather strength from distress, and grow brave by reflection.

"'Tis the business of little minds to shrink; but he whose heart is firm, and whose conscience approves his conduct, will pursue his principles unto death. My own line of reasoning is to myself as straight and clear as a ray of light.

"Not all the treasures of the world, so far as I believe, could have induced me to support an offensive war against the United Effort Plan, for I think it dishonest; but if a thief break into the faith of my household and distress my family or threaten me, or those that are in it, to 'bind me in all cases whatsoever' to his greed and apostasy, am I to suffer it? What signifies it to me, whether he who does it is a religious leader or a common man; my neighbors or not my neighbors? Whether it be them call me up for blind obedience, and welcome, I feel no concern from it; but I should suffer the misery of devils, were I to make a whore of my soul by swearing allegiance to one whose character is that of a greedy, stupid, stubborn, worthless, apostate man. I conceive likewise a horrid idea in receiving mercy from a being, who at the last day shall be shrieking to the rocks and mountains to cover him, and fleeing with terror from the orphan, the widow, and the pure in heart who love the TRUTH for the TRUTH'S sake.

"There are cases which cannot be overdone by language, and this is one. There are persons too, who see not the full extent of the evil which threatens them; they solace themselves with hopes that the enemy, if they succeed, will be merciful. It is the madness of folly to expect mercy from those who have refused to do justice;

and even mercy, where conquest is the object, is only a trick of war: The cunning of the fox is as murderous as the violence of the wolf; and we ought to guard equally against both. The apostates' first object is, partly by threats and partly by promises, to terrify or seduce the people to deliver up their United Effort Plan, and receive mercy. Howard Pyle recommended the same plan to Uncle Roy, Uncle Rich, and Uncle Carl, when hostilities began in 1953. And this is what the dissenters now call making their peace, 'a peace which passeth all understanding' indeed! a peace which would be the immediate forerunner of a worse ruin than any we have yet thought of.

"Ye men of Uncle Roy's training, do reason upon these things! Were the United Effort Plan to give up their lands, they would fall an easy prey to the enemy of righteousness, who are all around. This perhaps is what some dissenters would not be sorry for. Were the home institutions to deliver up their lands, they would be exposed to the resentment of the angels and brethren on the other side of the veil. Who would then have it in their power to chastise the disobedient and call for lives of purity among our people?

"And were any one man to give up his faith, THAT man and his family must be the friend of Harold Blackmore and Ben Bistline, Don Cox, Mike Pipkin, and Cyril Bradshaw, and should rely on them to preserve them from the anger of an offended God. Fear is a principal link in the chain of doubt and failure, and woe be to that saint that breaks the hearts of his friends and family. The adversary of our souls is inviting you to barbarous destruction, and men must be either rogues or fools that will not see it. I dwell not upon the vapors of imagination; I bring reason to your ears, and in language, as plain as A,B,C, hold up the truth to your eyes.

"I thank God, that I fear not. I see no real cause for fear, I know our situation well, and can see the way out of it. While our faith was collected, the adversary and his helpers dared not risk a battle, and it is no credit to him that he decamped south of Berry Knoll and waited a mean opportunity to attempt to ravage the defenseless United Effort Plan, but it is a great credit to us, that, with a handful of men, we sustained an orderly fight for the past ten years, brought off our families in faith and our farm lands into productivity, our store to function, and our meeting house to assemble in, and school houses to learn in. None can say that our defense was precipitate, for we were near the Lord's chosen servant performing it, that our faith might have time to come in. The sign of fear was not seen in our camp, and had not some of the cowardly and disaffected inhabitants spread false alarms through the community, the whole people had never been ravaged, Once more we are again collected and collecting. Our young and middleaged at both ends of the United Effort Plan are recruiting fast, and we shall be able to open the next round of legal battles, with the wisdom of men well armed and clothed with the Spirit of God.

"This is our situation, and who will, may know it. By perseverance and fortitude we have the prospect of a glorious victory, by cowardice and submission, the sad choice of a variety of evils – a ravaged United Effort Plan – a depopulated valley – habitations without safety, and trickery without hope in our churches, schools, and our homes; and a future generation of Fundamentalist Latter-day Saints children whose fathers we shall not honor. Look on this picture and weep over it! And if there yet remains one thoughtless wretch who believes it not, let him suffer it unlamented.

"COMMON SENSE. "The United Effort Plan Crisis, Berry Knoll, July 26, 1989. "Thirty-six years after the Raid:

'The present lawsuit which (should it last) is worth an age, if rightly defended, but if lost, or neglected, the whole religious community will partake of the misfortune; and there is no punishment which that man doth not deserve, be he who, or what, or where he will, that may be the means of sacrificing a season so precious and useful.' – Common Sense.

"Adapted by a common man who believes the words of Leroy S. Johnson, 'The first great commandment is to love the Lord with all thy heart, might, mind and strength, and the second is like unto it, Love thy neighbor as thyself.' These words are worth acting on, and the results possible, worth a lifetime of endeavor, which can be identified as, 'The Spirit of the United Effort Plan.'"
End of sermon.

Alvin Barlow testified under oath that Fred Jessop handed him a copy of this composition as he entered the large Church Building one Sunday afternoon and asked him to read it in the meeting. He claimed he did not know who wrote it, but only read it at the request of "Uncle Fred." This may or may not be the truth. Sam Barlow accepted responsibility for it, but it is suspected that the only reason he did was because he had just recently been dismissed as a defendant in the lawsuit, thus putting him in a position of immunity.

The treatise does ring with the tone of Sam Barlow's literary work when comparing it with some of the memorandums that he complied and were attached to several of the motions for summary judgment being filed with the court throughout the life of the lawsuit. It is reasonable to assume though, after scrutinizing the piece, that he had help, likely from his brother Alvin.

Ben Bistline's Rebuttal

It was a year later that a rebuttal to Sam's accusations in this diatribe was written and distributed throughout the community. It is interesting to note that it was not the author of the rebuttal who circulated it, but rather some of the Cabal who made many copies of the refutation, thus showing it to their colleagues. In his rebuttal, the author occasionally repeats a statement from the UEP sermon and then responds to it. This rebuttal, written on July 26, 1990, by Ben Bistline, author of this history follows:

"The affront to reasoning men by the dastardly parody of Thomas Paine's 'The American Crisis' entitled The UEP Crisis was in the very least reprehensible and bordered on evoking vomiting. The stomach, being a delicate organ, took this long to settle before commencing the composition of a response to this corruption of Mr. Paine's immortal words and place them in the proper light, since they were so defiled.

"Thomas Paine's shroud must be totally spiraled around him from his turning in his grave over the defiling of his noble work to fit the depredations of the UEP and their intentions as noted in The UEP Crisis. Perhaps he will countenance yet another use of his words to counter the previous debasement of his work; therefore, with his indulgence The Age of Reason is affectionately quoted.

"THE AGE OF REASON"
"The UEP Crisis" Response
by Ben Bistline

"'I put the following work under your protection. It contains my opinion upon religion. You will do me the justice to remember that I have always strenuously supported the right of every man to his own opinion, however different that opinion might be to mine. He who denies to another this right, makes a slave of himself to his present opinion, because he precludes himself the right of changing it.

"The most formidable weapon against errors, of every kind, is reason. I have never used any other, and I trust I never shall (Thomas Paine, The Age of Reason).'"

"The only faculty of humans that places them on a higher plane than the other animals with which we share this sphere, this Creation of Deity that we call earth, is the power given to us to reason. Without this power, the power to reason, we would act only on instinct and reflex. If we refuse to use this God-given power, and deny our mistakes and close our eyes and minds against error, we revert to the animal status and become no better than the He-Goat.

"The UEP is in Crisis. An army of apostates are trying to enforce their tyranny on all UEP members. A small percentage of the members have stood against this army of apostates and have declared: 'We refuse to allow you to bind us in all cases whatsoever.' Even God has not unlimited power to make slaves of us. If so, He would cease to be God!

"The unity of the United Effort Plan was destroyed, not by J. Marion Hammon and Alma A. Timpson defecting from Leroy S. Johnson and Rulon T.

309

Jeffs, for this did not happen. The unity of the United Effort Plan was destroyed by men such as Louis, Joe, Dan, Truman, Sam, Alvin, Nephi and most important, Fred!! For it was men such as these that whispered the falsehoods into the ears of Leroy S. Johnson, causing enmity among Brethren, and caused Leroy S. Johnson to tell J. Marion Hammon and Alma A. Timpson they no longer belonged to the Priesthood Council and could no longer sit on the stand at meetings. And had it not been for the benevolent financial help of Harold Blackmore in contributing by the thousands of dollars to the lawsuit, hundreds of innocent people would have been ravaged beyond belief by this time.

"It is nothing more than superstition to suppose that a just God will not allow such an impure people to be divided. This people can never rise above the incompetence of such infidels that have risen up to claim position of leadership. Were we to allow the management of the United Effort Plan to such infidels as Louis, Joe, Dan, Truman, Sam, Alvin, Nephi and FRED, we would have no claim for heaven's help, for a common thief, highwayman or housebreaker has as good a pretense as they have; we would get more justice from devils.

"In 1953, when the State of Arizona planned a raid on Short Creek, Charles F. Zitting, the President of the Priesthood Council, the Key Man and the Man whom Leroy Johnson honored as his file leader, made a trip from Salt Lake City to Short Creek and told Leroy Johnson to take the people and go into hiding. Leroy Johnson defied this man of God, and refused to do as he was told. The consequence of which was that a whole community of people were put through two years of unnecessary suffering. I was at Short Creek in 1953, I witnessed this fact. Because of this disobedience, secret traitors have been allowed to raise up and call the True Believers 'disguised apostates,' and mold the United Effort Plan into a counterfeit trust, in the center of the Valley.

"There were some fiascoes created by such Big Elders as Sam, Truman, and others at the time of the raid. One of the biggest was where it was decided to have the women and children from Hildale subjected to the hardship of walking six or seven miles through sagebrush, mud and rain, to the road by the Gap west of here, only to be met by the Utah law enforcement people who persuaded them to climb on the truck and ride back to their homes in Hildale at sunup. Such poor planning and lack of help from Deity is representative of the help and claimed revelation with which we are being led today by these same impostors.

"Thomas Paine, 'The Age of Reason,' said: 'Revelation, when applied to religion, means something communicated immediately from God to man, No one will deny or dispute that power of the Almighty to make such a communication, if He pleases. By admitting, for sake of the case, that something has been revealed to a certain person, and not revealed to any other person, it is revelation to that person only. When he tells it to a second person, a second to a third to a fourth, and so on, it ceases to be a revelation to all those persons. It is revelation to the first person only, and hearsay to every other, and consequently they are not obliged to believe it.'"

"When Alvin tells us something that supposedly happened some time in the past with regard to some special call given to Uncle Roy, but cannot support the claim with any written background, it is only hearsay and does not apply to the people in general, who, according to the written word, must rely on the revelations written down by the former prophets (including the 1880 Revelation).

"I shall conclude this paper with some miscellaneous remarks of the present lawsuit between the Priesthood Work and the counterfeit trustees of the United Effort Plan. I shall ask a few questions: why is it that these counterfeit trustees cry treason when a few hard working people establish a city (Centennial Park), and built themselves a new school building where they might train their children in the Truth of the Priesthood Work when in light of the fact that a lawsuit was filed against some of these people to rob from them the land and the buildings of the Colorado City Academy? This lawsuit was not brought against Uncle Roy and Uncle Rulon, but rather was brought against Uncle Marion and Uncle Dell by Uncle Roy and Uncle Rulon. Who then was the aggressor? All members of the Priesthood Council were under covenant to NEVER BRING CIVIL ACTION AGAINST ANY MEMBER OF THE COUNCIL IN A COURT OF LAW!! Who, then, are the covenant breakers? Under the moral obligation of the Covenants they had made, Uncle Marion and Uncle Dell refused to go to court against their Priesthood Brethren. Keeping of these covenants was more important to them than to fight over the property and the Academy buildings. They signed a warranty deed of the Academy property back to the UEP.

"Uncle Marion was threatened with another civil action by Uncle Roy and Uncle Rulon if he would not resign as a trustee of the UEP. Uncle Dell was simply robbed of his trusteeship by Uncle Roy and Uncle Rulon simply saying he was 'never a trustee'. With Uncle Marion and Uncle Dell out of the way, the enemy had no trouble appointing a new set of trustees, which are illegitimate in fact. It did not take long for these counterfeit trustees to destroy the Academy in full, by razing the buildings to the ground. Why then are a few people, who are not willing to sacrifice their consciences, branded dissenters, when all they wanted was to establish a place where they could worship God according to their own consciences?

"The counterfeit trustees were not satisfied with their evil work of destroying the Academy, but in order to pour salt into a wound, they proceeded to rob all UEP members of dignity and status. A letter was sent to all members of the UEP from these counterfeit trustees explaining that they had reduced the status of the members to that of 'tenant at will' in their homes they had built and paid for on UEP land. How could the United Effort Plan sink to such a low point as to become a robber of the poor? Could it be that the United Effort Plan is infested and controlled by impostors?

"I have been tender in raising the cry against these men, and used numberless arguments to show them their danger, but a chosen people will never sacrifice their consciences and principles to the folly and baseness of impostors. The period has now arrived in which either these impostors or we must change our sentiments, or one or both must fall.

"What is a deserter from the principles we have held so high? Good God! What is he? I would not be afraid to stand with ever so small a number, be it only five men, against apostates, be they in the hundreds, who are such cowards as these impostors. For a servile, slavish, self-indulgent fear is all that drives them. Though they may be cruel, they can never be brave.

"But before the line of irrecoverable separation be drawn between us, let us reason the matter together. Tell me something, Sam, who sent me the tenant of will letter? Was it Harold? Harold has never proclaimed me an apostate because I would not accept his views on religion or the United Order. These cruel acts and accusations have come from Fred and Rulon. They expect me to quietly succumb to their demands, pick up and leave a lifetime of investment in a plan we were told and believed would be our temporal salvation. They expect me to flock to their standard, not with money in my pockets, for they will rob me of my money if I will so allow. My opinions are of no use to them unless I support them personally, for 'tis greed, and not Christ that they want.

"We were told, and we believed, that not a place upon Earth might be so happy as a home on United Effort Plan land. I once felt anger, as a man ought to feel against the mean principles that are held by greedy apostates. The time I speak of is when I saw a daughter of Uncle Rich standing on the porch of her house, with tears streaming down her face and a number of frightened children clinging on her skirt. She was holding in her hand a document entitled, Notice To Vacate. It had been served on her by a Mohave County Deputy Sheriff, with uniform and gun. The document was not signed by Harold Blackmore, *the cause of all evil in Short Creek valley*, no – it was signed by Leroy Johnson and Rulon Jeffs. Cowards? Even Sam was too big a coward to notify this innocent daughter of Uncle Rich's that she was to be evicted. He had to send Steve Baily to do the Devil's dirty work. If this is an example of the security we have under the UEP, then God hasten its destruction. I am as confident as I am that God governs the world, that Short Creek Valley will never again see peace until she gets clear of the control of such a monster that the UEP has become. Lawsuits without ceasing will break out till that period arrives. The greed of impostors must in the end be conquered; for though the flame of Liberty may sometimes cease to shine, the coal shall never expire.

"The contests of the court between illegitimate trustees and the beneficiaries will no doubt expel these impostors from our land and justice will return to the plundered people the rightful ownership of their homes; it is all that was asked for. After the United Effort Plan war, it may take two more years to accomplish the confiscation of the property of these counterfeit trustees, and the valley be made happy by their expulsion. Say not that this is revenge, but call it the soft resentment of a betrayed people who believed the words of Leroy Johnson when he promised them security. But it is folly to argue against determined hardness. Justice can never come from the heart that is steeled with prejudice.

"There are persons who see not the full extent of the evil which threatens them. These people suppose that if the impostor trustees succeed in winning the lawsuit, they would be forever safe, living at the mercy of these greedy, stupid, stubborn, worthless, apostate men. Better for them to suffer the misery of devils, than to make a whore of their souls by swearing allegiance to such characters as these. What mercy can you receive from beings who at the last days will be shrieking to the rocks and mountains to cover them, and fleeing with terror from the orphan, the widow and the pure in heart who love the truth for the truth's sake. Not all the treasures of the world could induce me to support such characters in their rape and plunder of the United Effort Plan, hiding behind the name of 'Uncle Roy,' when, with a mob they might evict a widow – mother and her children from a comfortable home, put them on the street to find their way as best they can. What man, who claims to be a man, would not rise up in indignation, when thieves break into the faith of a household and bring distress upon a family. What matters – whether such acts are done in the name of a religious leader, or a common highwayman; whether it be done by an individual villain or a group of them? If we reason to the root of things, we shall find no difference, neither can any just cause be assigned why we should permit it.

"Ye men who claim allegiance to 'Uncle Roy,' reason upon these things. Is it any wonder that a lawsuit was filed in Federal Court to protect the other helpless and innocent members of the United Effort Plan? If more of you had the manhood to join such brave souls as Harold Blackmore, Ben Bistline, Don Cox, Mike Pipkin, Cyril Bradshaw, Connell Bateman, and Claude Cooke, we could quickly put down the evil that has the United Effort Plan in a choke hold. The people who have broken the UEP Trust are the greedy sons of John Y. Barlow, and men must be either rogues or fools that will not see it. I hold up truth to your eyes and bring reason to your ears. Fear may be a link in the chain of doubt and failure, but brave men have no time for fear, therefore we will not fail.

"Even though the adversary has gathered in the Large and Spacious Building, and are counseling deep to ravage the defenseless members of the United Effort Plan, just a handful of men have stood them at bay. The sign of fear is not seen in our camp. Even though the cowardly impostors have spread false alarms through the community, their plan to ravage and plunder has been slowed for a season. By perseverance and fortitude we have the prospect of a glorious victory. But if by cowardice we submit to the sad choice of evil, and will allow impostors to expel us from our homes, from this valley we love, and allow them, through their trickery, to rob a future generation of Latter Day Saint children of their Freedom, their churches, their schools, and enslave them forever after, in lies, debaucheries and sorrow, then the blood of these children will curse his cowardice who shrinks back at a time when a little might have saved the whole and made them happy. Look on this picture and weep over it! And if there yet remains one thoughtless wretch who believes it not, let him suffer it unlamented.

"This is my opinion. Ben Bistline, July 26, 1990."

Some months after the first sermon presented by Alvin, Joe Barlow gave a very stirring talk in a Sunday meeting at the Large Church House in December of 1989. This sermon of Joe's was motivated by events that had transpired in the lawsuit. The Defendants (UEP) had asked the judge to delay the court proceedings to allow the attorneys of both sides to attempt a settlement agreement between the parties. As it turned out, this request was only another attempt to drag the proceedings out a little longer, because the strategy of the Defendants was to delay the outcome of the case for as long as they could, *hoping to run the plaintiffs out of money*, thus winning by default.

During these negotiations the Defendants refused to make any compromise whatsoever, thus refusing to even consider any offers made by the plaintiffs. The only "compromise" they offered was that they would allow the Plaintiffs to move out of their houses in peace, not filing a countersuit, if they would withdraw the present lawsuit and reimburse the United Effort Plan their attorney's fees. It was after these negotiations had broken down that Joe Barlow gave his moving speech. This sermon is a little lengthy, so only excerpts are included, but it shows the unreasonableness of the men who were running the Cabal, and their attempt to use the power of religious control they have over their followers to prejudice them against anyone who has the courage to stand against their unrighteous conduct.

"Sermon of Joe Barlow, December 24, 1989 (excerpts).

"I sincerely pray for an interest in your faith and prayers, for I feel that I don't want to say anything that isn't in accord with the Spirit of God, and what Brother Rulon would want said.

"We have the Leroy Johnsons to look to; we have the Uncle Freds and the Rulon Jeffs' and the Parley Harkers, men who would not compromise on the righteous things.

"We've got a group of men who will not listen to the servant of God, because they've already compromised – they've made that compromise. They've compromised their morals. They've compromised their ingenuity. They've compromised their initiative. Everything they've got that was good, they've compromised on it.

314

"May we stand by those principles and give Uncle Rulon our total support, not just when we're in meeting, not just when we're enthused, but when we're in our moment of temptation. Our golden moment comes to us, may we make that right choice and not compromise."

By this time in the history of the Polygamists, the Barlow faction had made many compromises in what was the original doctrine set down by the fundamentalist organizers in the 1930s, and there would be more of these compromises made by them in the coming years. Such a speech coming from Joe Barlow is nothing more than the utmost hypocrisy. His only object in making these accusations was to bring bitter feelings of hatred against those opposing the Cabal in its scheme of taking control of the United Effort Plan assets that belonged to those they wanted to evict. The accusations he makes against his "wicked enemy" are the very things that he and his cohorts are themselves guilty of.

Another concept of thought is that compromises are necessary in the advancement of any organization. In support of this theory, Eric Hoffer, a noted writer and philosopher states:

> "Free men are aware of the imperfection inherent in human affairs, and they are willing to fight and die for that which is not perfect. They know that basic human problems can have no FINAL SOLUTIONS, that our freedom, justice, equality, etc., are far from absolute, and that the good life is compounded of half measures, COMPROMISES, lesser evils, and gropings toward the perfect. The rejection of approximations and the insistence on absolutes are the manifestation of a nihilism that loathes freedom, tolerance and equity."

The Barlow Cabal certainly loathes freedom, tolerance and equity. Keeping this in mind, it would have been much better, and cheaper also, if the Cabal had conceded just a little. If a settlement with their adversaries could have been made at this time, it would have saved their followers about two million dollars.

One of the policies set forth by the Barlow Cabal regarding those who had "apostatized" was to do everything in their power to convince the wives of such that since their husband had lost the priesthood, they could not take them into the Celestial Kingdom, therefore they should be released from them, and be sealed to a (new) worthy man who could "Save Them." Several wives of these "apostates" were convinced to leave their husbands and were indeed "sealed" to other men of the First Ward. Two of such were "given" to Fred Jessop. As could be expected, when this happened it caused some bitter feelings in the hearts of their husbands toward Fred Jessop. Since these wives were plural wives and not legal wives, it was impossible to bring any civil charges of alienation of affection against Fred Jessop. Under the Utah Statutes, however, Fred Jessop was guilty of bigamy, a third class felony. In Utah, bigamy is defined as: if a person is legally married to one spouse and is cohabiting with another partner, as being in violation of this statute. The husband of one of these estranged wives went to the Washington County Attorney and asked him to file a complaint of bigamy against Fred Jessop for living in adultery with "his" wife.

Much to his dismay, the County Attorney refused to do so, telling him that polygamy was a religious issue and if he was to try and prosecute someone living polygamy in Colorado City, he was afraid he would lose on this basis. He also did not feel comfortable prosecuting one polygamist who had taken a wife from another polygamist, just to please one of them (favoring one polygamist over another). After hearing this, the husband, in dismay, went back home and in a few days remarked to some of his friends that he was glad the County Attorney had refused to prosecute Fred Jessop because he would not have felt too good having such a thing on his conscience.

It is unknown to the author whether or not Fred Jessop ever learned about this attempt to have him prosecuted. If he did, he no doubt would have claimed that the Lord had seen him through the ordeal and he had beaten the Devil once more.

Priesthood Shenanigans

The instructions of Leroy Johnson before he died, of not ordaining any "new" members to the Priesthood Council, placed his successor Rulon Jeffs in an awkward position; he could not call any new apostles. He was "stuck" with having only "Councilors," namely Fred Jessop and Parley Harker.

Alma Timpson, (the leader of Second Ward) was not under such a restriction. He had called Frank Naylor in the spring of 1989 as an apostle, and about a year later (April of 1990) proceeded to "fill up the Council." This he did not do, however, without encountering some problems, problems caused by his calling of Naylor the preceding year. It seems that when he approached Apostle Naylor for his endorsement of calling of two men, John Timpson (his own son), and Claude Cawley (his stepson), the first ones he had chosen to call into the Council, Naylor was vehemently against sanctioning them for such a high and holy calling. He had problems with both the moral character and the honesty of these two candidates. Also, they were sons of Guenevere Timpson, wife of Alma Timpson, causing Naylor to think (and correctly so) that there was some nepotism involved (Note 1).

The following account of Timpson calling his two "Sons" is related in the journal of Ben Bistline. A little progress on the lawsuit is also recorded in this same entry. Under date of April 15, 1990 the following is written:

"April 15, 1990

"On the lawsuit; discovery is supposed to be over today. Pre-trial is set for June 15, 1990. We have withdrawn the suit from Colorado City and Sam Barlow, made a settlement. Agreed to pay our own lawyer fees. Sam Barlow has come back in as representing the F.L.D.S. Church.

"Dell Timpson ordained John Timpson and Claude Cawley apostles.

"On about the 10th of April (1990), I went to see Frank Naylor at his home in Centennial Park. He had been ordained a High Priest Apostle about one year previous to this visit. When I knocked, he opened the door and asked me to come in. We went into his office and sat down. He was very agitated and could not sit still, getting up from time to time, pacing the floor. He first handed me a copy of the instructions that Charles Zitting had written down on the order of how men should be called into the Priesthood Council. They read:

"'Every man must be called of God by revelation given to the senior

Apostle or President of this Priesthood Council. This one man is known as the Senior President or President of Priesthood. When he dies, the next worthy or qualified Apostle in seniority in this council becomes President of Priesthood automatically as they all hold the same keys, power and authority.... He said, he had no right to even suggest a name to heaven for this high position.... A person is first chosen by the Council in heaven and then a messenger comes here to reveal the man chosen to the President of Priesthood. Then the Priesthood Council here votes on him and the results are taken back to the Priesthood Council in heaven, who, calls the man by revelation through the President of Priesthood.'

"He then proceeded to tell me that Alma Timpson had ordained John Timpson and Claude Cawley to his Priesthood Council. He said that Brother Timpson had come to him on three different times and asked him to give his consent to their being called. He told Brother Timpson that he believed that these two men were not honest, and he also questioned their morals. When Brother Timpson came to see him the last time, and Frank Naylor told him he could not sustain the calling of these men, Brother Timpson left in anger.

"He then went ahead and ordained them anyway without Brother Naylor's consent (much the same story as when John Barlow called Leroy Johnson and Marion Hammon back in 1942). He then sent someone down to Frank Naylor and said he wanted a copy of the Temple Endowments, because he thought that Guy Musser had them (when Guy Musser died Frank Naylor married some of his wives, thus he had received most of Guy's papers and records. Alma Timpson supposed that Guy had a copy of the Temple Endowments in his effects). Frank Naylor had searched through Guy's papers but had not found any such copy. He sent word back to Timpson that he did not have such a copy. Timpson was very wroth and sent word back down to Naylor that he knew he had such a copy, and he was demanding that Naylor send it to him.

"At this point in my visit with Frank, he began to chuckle, and pulling a few sheets of paper from his desk, he handed them to me and said: 'This is what I gave them to take back to Brother Timpson as it is all I have regarding those ordinances.'

"What he handed me to read was a copy of an article that The Tanners (Mormon apostates who had been publishing anti-Mormon literature) had put out. It was supposed to be a copy of the Temple Ordinances that they had compiled from memory after going through the Temple themselves. He then told me that Brother Timpson had used these 'Apostate' ordinances and had 'given' the Temple Endowments to John Timpson and Claude Cawley in the living room of his home. He thought this to be quite humorous that they would think they had a proper endowment when all they had was a mockery before God."

When Guenivere Timpson (the mother of these two men and who also assisted

318

Alma Timpson in administering these ordinances to them) was confronted with these facts, she became very defensive, not accepting that such was the truth; in fact she went to great lengths to discredit the veracity of Naylor's account of the incident. She vehemently claims that the ordinances they used were a true and correct copy obtained from the papers of Guy Musser. This places those receiving these ordinances in a very precarious position, not only as to the question of being administrated by correct authority, but also as to the validity of the ordinances themselves; the seriousness of which should be considered as no small matter to anyone looking to them for ecclesiastical leadership.

In the next year Alma Timpson called four more men into his Council: Clayne Wayman, Jed Hammon, Joe Knudson, and Lorin Zitting, thus filling it up to the required number of seven.

This action on Timpson's part caused another split in the Priesthood Work. When Frank Naylor learned what he had done, he was very disturbed about the matter. His conscience would not allow him to support Timpson's actions, for according to what he had been taught, Timpson had violated the most important rule that governed the calling of new members being called into the "Priesthood Council." In his frustration, he withdrew himself from the people and went into the hills to pray and ponder just what he should do about the matter.

One of his sons owned a mountain cabin near Duchesne, Utah. He took part of his family, some goats, and moved up to live in this cabin. He did not want to be bothered. He just wanted to hide out and be left alone, not knowing what he was supposed to do. There were others who also did not agree with the actions of Timpson and sought Naylor out, attempting to convince him that because of what Timpson had done, acting contrary to "Priesthood Doctrine," that he, Naylor was duty bound to step up and lead those who were willing to follow him. Naylor, very reluctant to do so, told these people that he had received no revelation to lead anyone, that he just wanted to be left alone and let the Lord work things out. These people would not be satisfied with this decision and persisted in trying to convince him that it was his duty to come home and lead the people.

He was finally convinced and after a few months he came back to Centennial Park to take up the duties of presiding over the flock. By the fall of 1990, he began holding regular meetings, alternating between Centennial Park and Salt Lake City, meeting every other Sunday respectively. About one half of the Second Ward members in Salt Lake City chose to follow him while only about ten per cent of those in the Colorado City/Hildale/Centennial Park area gave him their allegiance.

Frank Naylor is an honest man. He has tried to lead his followers in a righteous manner and has enjoyed some success among his group, but things have not gone all that well for them. There has been dissension among his followers and a number of them have "fallen away," not knowing just what they should do. He eventually moved to Missouri, pretty much abandoning the Colorado City area, and taking some of his followers with him.

In November of 1990, Judge Jenkins of the Federal Court in Salt Lake City ordered the Defendants (UEP) to turn over their bank accounts and all United Effort Plan records to the Plaintiffs. This was very upsetting to them and they again made another effort to try an out of court settlement. Rulon Jeffs decided that the lawsuit was too costly and told Fred Jessop to "give them their deeds," to which Fred remarked, "over my dead body." This, of course, broke down any chance of settlement at this time, but it did gain the Defendants a few more months of dragging out the lawsuit; it was now February of 1991, more than three years after it was filed in November of 1987.

A major change in the doctrine of the Polygamists was made by the Colorado City First Ward in the year of 1991. This change was a complete turn around on one of the Fundamental stands taken by them since the 1930s; that stand being the "Adam God Doctrine," wherein it was taught that Adam is the creator of the earth and is our God. On June 2, 1991, Rulon Jeffs gave a discourse on "The Godhead" at Colorado City, explaining a new and foreign doctrine to the Polygamists, that Adam was not the creator. This change in doctrine is so dramatic for the polygamists that it seems fitting to present the following excerpts:

Rulon's Godhead Sermon

June 2, 1991 (Rulon T. Jeffs is RTF) (Larry S. Johnson is LSJ) (Joseph Smith is JS)

"A good many questions have been raised from a reading of a sermon of the Prophet Leroy Johnson, July 25, 1976, in which the matter of the Godhead is treated. It is a very good introduction to the subject that we have at hand. The following are the quotations to be considered:

(LSJ) . We have been taught that there are three personages in the Godhead – God the Father, God the Son and God the Testator or the Holy Ghost. Now, these three governing powers were called and set apart to come forth in their day and time to govern the destiny of the peopling of this earth.

(LSJ) One reason I speak upon this subject, the question was asked me this morning: When Adam met with His posterity at the close of His time upon this earth, He called His posterity together and blessed them and He said that He had been instructed by His Father to do this work. Who was the man that He had reference to in the Garden of Eden when He was asked by Lucifer; 'Why do you offer sacrifice?' He said; 'I know not, except I have been commanded by my Father.' do you think it was some foreign spirit other than the ones that had been

the Fundamental religionist court case, which you now preside over. We desire this note to offer some outsider views. During our current visit to Utah, we have again looked for answers. How incredible that the dissident side has yet to come up with sufficient viable cause. That at this late date – discovery for the dissidents is still being allowed? That motions for the defense are thrust off to pre-trial or quashed?

Also very strange, is this return to anonymous poison letters that the dissidents are circulating. These writings are worse than the articles we find in the NAC papers from time to time. "Those that are high on disinformation and long on propaganda." It is disgusting at best to see efforts made to sway opinions by such "immoral methods."

An article in the *Spotlight* Newspaper, for August 19, 1991, becomes the impetus for this writing. This article – "Judicial Ethics Questions. An interesting premise here!" That the Bar Association defines the action of a judge to "recuse" himself. "If there is an appearance of impropriety?" Not necessarily real – just an appearance!

To quote from an article by Dawn House of *The Salt Lake Tribune*, on June 28, 1991:

"In a status conference on Thursday, Judge Jenkins assured attorneys for the church leaders he has no conflict of interest stemming from his employment with the Utah Attorney General's Office more than 30 years ago." ...."Judge Jenkins said in open court that he reviews all cases assigned to him for any connection to prior cases. He said he would consider a motion on the matter. But as far as he can recall, he knows none of the parties named in the 1987 lawsuit."

We must apologize to your honor; but a few of us old gray heads, who are yet around – have a recollection of your personal involvements many years ago. Records and personal experiences if you please, with those who were then being persecuted and who were up for prosecution; and from there, to some of the connecting relationships of today. As we can visualize this present case being: "A potential extension of those events of years gone by;" this then – can really make our old heads wag and reel!

We have long ago come to consider: That the matters here are those of: – "internal religious struggle – not a bona fide judicial issue!" To our minds and feelings, there is very strong "appearance" still existing; and we understand it shows dramatically within this current case!

Judge Jenkins – To the honor of the U.S. District Court, and especially for consideration to your own personal status; there are those of us who would still, occasionally, like to realize justice happens!

As we prepare to depart from Utah, we have very mixed feelings about the outcome; about the "quality of justice" dealt to this subject case. Isn't it justice –

that all levels of American jurisprudence "claims" to champion? Thank you very much for your indulgence.

Yours truly,
(signed) Alfred – Gust Benson
Alfred & Gust Benson
6949 Burnham St.
Citrus Heights, CA. 95621
cc: Mr. Jeffery C. Swinton

If Sam Barlow had signed his name to this letter, it could not have proven any more that he had written it. The letter itself provides the proof that he was its author. There is no "outsider" who would have been interested enough to criticize and condemn the "dissidents" as Sam did in the letter. For these reasons, the plaintiffs made an effort to locate the alleged authors, Alfred & Gust Benson. An investigation was made as to who actually occupied the premises at "6949 Burnham St. Citrus Heights, California 95621." Interesting enough, it was a man named Blair Rountree. A letter was sent to him, asking if he knew the Bensons. This letter in part asked Mr. Rountree: "whether you are renting to a Alfred and Gust Benson and if not, where can I reach those people for communication?"

Mr. Rountree wrote in long hand on the bottom of the letter: "I don't know that person, B. Rountree" and returned the letter.

In a memorandum sent from Cyril Bradshaw to Nick Hales, attorney for the plaintiffs, he reported that: "Mike Pipkin followed through on the Alfred/Gust Benson letter.

"He tried to find a phone number for Alfred or Gust Benson at the address given, without success. Next he called the County offices in Sacramento and found that Mr. Blair Rountree owned the property at that address.

"Mike also asked if they had any record of an Alfred or Gust Benson and was told that no record of either could be found in that county. He then wrote a letter to Mr. Rountree at the Burnham St. address, together with a copy of the envelope addressed to Jeff Swinton with that return address on it, and received an answer stating 'I don't know that person.'

"In another call, he determined that the tax notice for that property was sent to Blair Rountree at that address.

"The letter is filled with intimate details of the lawsuit that could only have been known by a defendant or Sam Barlow.

The Judge was astute enough to realize the charade connected with these letters he received at this time and simply ignored them.

The motion of the Defendants to have Judge Jenkins recuse himself was denied, but it did bring about another stall on their part to keep the case from coming to trial.

Another stalling tactic they used was successful in keeping it from coming to trial for over a year: Their appeal to the 10th Circuit Federal Court in Denver. This was an appeal on the decision of Judge Jenkins to have them make an accounting and of turning over their bank account records to the plaintiffs. The appeal was based on their claim that this information was of a religious nature and therefore the courts had no jurisdiction under the freedom of religion clause in the Constitution; that the plaintiffs were apostates and were not entitled to what they claimed "were sacred records." It would be like "casting pearls before swine," if such was allowed to happen.

This appeal did accomplish what the UEP Defendants had hoped for: Stalling Time. The lawsuit was virtually put on hold and for more than a year there was very little action on the main case. There were several sparring efforts made by the Defendants to "harass" the plaintiffs in such things as encroaching on their premises; moving fences to "cut down" their lots; attempts to take possession of buildings they claimed were not being used "properly" by the plaintiffs; and any other thing that could cause hardship for them. These efforts were mostly repulsed by the plaintiffs, either through court action (in most of the cases the local courts ruled that no decision could be made until after the Federal Case was settled) or by the plaintiffs just bodily standing up to the "trespassers" and "moving" the fences back to the proper location, sometimes, just a half dozen or so, while 50 or more hoodlums were standing by heckling them.

Some of these episodes would become quite tense, with the local police force (First Ward Colorado City Marshals) standing by but never moving to protect the property and rights of the victims, but rather doing everything possible to assist the intruders, threatening those who were trying to protect their property with arrest if any violence were to erupt. Only those who supported the First Ward religious leaders were ever hired by the city, giving the advantage in any conflict to the UEP, thus depriving any semblance of justice to the real victims in the issue. This, of course, was all part of the plan, to "harass the dissidents" until they would get discouraged and leave.

We will come back to the lawsuit a little later, but another important development was taking place among the Polygamists that would bring an unexpected change into the community.

On June 21, 1992, the President of the Kanab, Utah, Kaibab Stake of The Church of Jesus Christ of Latter-Day Saints held a missionary meeting in the Second Ward Chapel at Centennial Park. There were about 50 people (Stake Leaders) who came with him. Only about that many (50) local people attended the meeting, but even so, it was a significant event.

This was the first time in over 50 years that a meeting was held by the "LDS Church" among the Colorado City Polygamists. It was surprising that the Second Ward Leaders allowed them the use of the building, but it does show their open-mindedness in comparison with the First Ward. The message that was given in this meeting was basically the Articles of Faith (Statement of beliefs) and an invitation to any who desired to hear more about the LDS Church to participate in future missionary meetings that were to be held in the area.

The LDS Stake Officials, however, were unable to obtain a building where these meetings could be held on a regular basis. Their only option was to hold them out-of-doors in one of the parks until the weather turned too cold in late November. They were then invited into a home of a non-member who, although she did not intend to join the Church, still had enough Christian compassion to offer her home. The LDS Stake Mission President went to the local school board and requested permission to use the County school house for these meetings, but after giving him the run-around for several weeks, he was told that the LDS Church could not use the public school house, this in light of all the years that the Polygamists had been allowed to use it for these same purposes.

The president of the Colorado City School Board, Lee Bistline, called Rulon Jeffs in Salt Lake City and asked whether or not he should allow the LDS Church the use of the building. Jeffs told him that he was not going to make that decision, that the school board would have to do so. Lee then asked Fred Jessop and Fred made no hesitation, "Don't give it to them." Fred then announced in "his" church house that the people should not allow their children to attend any of the LDS Meetings or any of their activities (The LDS Church was also sponsoring weekly activities for the young people of the community where the attendance sometimes would reach up to a hundred people).

This un-Christian behavior of Fred Jessop is in marked contrast to the attitude of the Second Ward Leaders, for although they did not offer their building to be used for these regular meetings (they were never asked), they did allow the first meeting to be held there, displaying charity that is lacking among their First Ward counterparts.

Sad to say, these "missionary" meetings were stopped in January of 1993, not because of the opposition of the First Ward, but because of the LDS Church Leaders themselves. The General Authorities of the LDS Church were suspicious that people living in Colorado City would only join the Church to gain access to the Temples and after getting their endowments return to the Fundamentalist Cult where they could continue living polygamy. They where somewhat justified in this concern because some members of other Polygamist Groups in the Salt Lake City area were guilty of this charade, but none of the Colorado City Polygamists had ever attempted it. The teachings and beliefs of these polygamists are that the Temples are *out of order*, that the LDS Church does not have the Keys to

326

Priesthood, so all temple work being done at the present time is not efficacious and will all have to be redone when they, the Polygamists, are established as the true Priesthood Leaders.

This action of the General Authorities was a disappointing blow to the local LDS Church leaders, but recognizing them as having the authority to set Church policy, they complied with the instruction given, thus suspending all missionary activities in the Colorado City area on the Stake level. This placed any LDS Church activities in the Colorado City area at the Ward level (local congregation) because there were a number of active members now living there. By the end of 1993 there were over 20 active members living in Colorado City and Hildale, who were members of the Kaibab/Moccasin Ward. Although the missionary work was stopped, a spark was lit and that spark has the potential to grow into a blossoming flame. There are active members living among the Polygamists and the influence of The Church of Jesus Christ of Latter-day Saints is being felt in the community, thus opening the way for a great number of people to some day find the truth of their religious history.

On June 16, 1993, Judge Bruce Jenkins dismissed the UEP lawsuit in the Federal Court, ruling that the disputes were equity issues and did not come under the jurisdiction of the Federal Court and must be adjudicated in a state court. This was quite a shock to the plaintiffs (dissidents) because the case had been in the Federal Court for *almost six years* and they felt that the securities violations of the new UEP trustees would be cause enough to keep the case there. The Defendants, on the other hand, were ecstatic. They claimed this ruling as a great victory and told their people that the lawsuit was over and they had won.

The biggest question about this action of the judge: why did he wait for six years before making this ruling, causing such a long delay and untold thousands of dollars for both parties involved? Before handing down his ruling, however, he made an observation in the courtroom. He stated his opinion that the issues were bona fide and that the plaintiffs may receive a favorable ruling in a state District Court. He further stated that it seemed ironical how the once persecuted Polygamists had now become the persecutors.

The plaintiffs (dissidents) were not so easily whipped as their persecutors had supposed. They were expected to just lie down and give up in the face of this ruling of Judge Jenkins, but this did not happen. Their attorneys began drawing up a new complaint to be filed in the District Court at St. George in Washington County, narrowing the issues down to equity claims rather than claims of fraud. This complaint was filed in the Washington County, Fifth District Court on July 26, 1993.

The Defendants (UEP) were not served until a couple of months later, thus causing them to believe that no action would be taken against them. This caused them *to become bold in their actions* against those whom they considered to be "apostates" and take the following action.

On August 15, 1993, Sam Barlow announced in a meeting of the first ward group that the *apostates must be removed from the homes* belonging to the Priesthood. He read off a list of 45 names, people to whom *letters were being sent*, people who were considered unworthy to stay in the community. These letters were sent by certified mail and the recipients began receiving them the next week.

FUNDAMENTALIST CHURCH OF JESUS CHRIST OF LATTER DAY SAINTS

Rulon T. Jeffs, President, 3611 Little Cottonwood Road, Sandy, Utah 84092
87 East Utah Avenue P.O. Box 39, Hildale, Utah 84784 U.S.A.
August 13, 1993
(Name of recipient)

The United Effort Plan, created in 1942 by the church now organized as the Fundamentalist Church of Jesus Christ of Latter Day Saints, is a religious and charitable institution operated through a board of trustees on behalf of the Presidency of the Church. The United Effort Plan was established to advance the principles and purposes of the United Order. These principles are described in many places in the scriptures, including Doctrine and Covenants, Section 42:33-37; Section 82:14-24; Section 104:55-56, 70-80; Section 119; Section 120; Section 85:1-5.

All contributions, in any form whatever, including those used by the Fundamentalist Church to meet the needs of the United Effort Plan, are deemed to be religious consecrations, freely donated to support the work of the Church.

The Fundamentalist Church recognizes a solemn obligation to preserve and advance the religious purposes of the United Effort Plan. To meet that obligation, those individuals who voluntarily and publicly reject the Priesthood must be disassociated from the United Effort Plan, and from its parent, the Fundamentalist Church (see Section 84, verses 35 through 44; Also see the *Teachings of the Prophet Joseph Smith*, pages 155 and 156). To allow otherwise would result in compromise of the effort to implement the eternal principles of the United Order, as restored by revelation through the Prophet Joseph Smith.

The United Order effort, to be acceptable to God, must be directed by the President of the Church and the holder of the keys of the Holy Priesthood. President Rulon T. Jeffs holds those keys and that responsibility at the present time. Those who have altogether turned away from the President and his teachings are apostates, and must be excluded from the congregation of saints whose labor and devotion give visible expression and vitality to the principles of the United Order.

Your words and actions over a period of many years show that you have forsaken the Fundamentalist Church and the teachings of President Johnson and President Jeffs. The Fundamentalist Church hereby recognizes your withdrawal from the congregation of saints, and declares you disassociated from the Fundamentalist Church, including the United Effort Plan.

For this reason, the Fundamentalist Church declines to accept any further donations or offerings from you.

For the Fundamentalist Church of Jesus Christ of Latter Day Saints, and the United Effort Plan Trust:
(signed) R.T. Jeffs

Rulon T. Jeffs, President of the Fundamentalist Church of Jesus Christ of Latter Day Saints, and President of the Board of Trustees of the United Effort Plan Trust.

An interesting fact concerning these letters is that they were all copies made on a copy machine, including Rulin Jeffs' signature. Sam Barlow made as many copies as he saw fit to make, then at his discretion, typed on the name and address of whomever he pleased, then he mailed them. It was not Jeffs who was sending out the letters, but rather Sam Barlow.

One of the recipients of "Sam's" letter (an aged widow) became very distraught over thinking she was going to be removed from her home. She called Jeffs on the phone and asked him why she had been singled out to be "excommunicated" from the Church. Jeffs told her that he did not know who Sam had sent the letters to and that she had no need to fear, that he would see to it that she would not be asked to leave her home.

These letters were indeed viewed by Sam as "letters of excommunication" and he supposed that those receiving them would accept them in that light. In contradiction to Sam's claim that he could excommunicate these United Effort Plan beneficiaries, lies the fact that none of them were ever members of The Fundamentalist Church of Jesus Christ of Latter Day Saints. The F.L.D.S. Church did not even come into existence until February 6, 1991, almost four years after the "apostates" had filed the lawsuit. It was only "organized" then so the Defendants could have a religious entity to hide behind, claiming that the courts had no jurisdiction in religious matters (Note 2).

On September 3, 1993, these same persons who had received the first letters from Sam Barlow (with Rulon Jeffs' signature on them) were sent another letter under the same pretext. The letterhead was the: Fundamentalist Church of Jesus Christ of Latter Day Saints; Rulon T. Jeffs President:

(Dated) September 3, 1993
(Name of Recipient)

The Fundamentalist Church of Jesus Christ of Latter Day Saints, including the United Effort Plan, has always deemed all improvements to land owned by the United Effort Plan to be religious consecrations to the Fundamentalist Church, freely donated to support the work of the Church. All persons who actively participated in Church services during the last half century are aware that President Johnson and other Church leaders always included this principle in their religious teachings, based on holy scripture.

As I stated in my letter to you dated August 13, 1993, the Church has recognized your withdrawal from the congregation of the saints, and declared you disassociated from the Fundamentalist Church, including the United Effort Plan. The Fundamentalist Church declines to accept offerings or contributions from you, or any improvements which you may desire to make to United Effort Plan property.

Because donations or offerings from you are not acceptable, you are hereby directed to not make any substantial improvement to the property at the above mentioned address. A substantial improvement is any improvement in which the cost of materials and/or labor exceeds five hundred dollars. Until arrangements are made for your relocation, you are directed to maintain the property in its present condition, and to take reasonable care to protect the safety of the persons residing on or using the property.

This decision is based upon scriptural references included in my letter to you of August 13, 1993, and in the teachings of President Johnson, delivered in his sermon of February 10, 1985, a copy of which is included for your review.

For the Fundamentalist Church of Jesus Christ of Latter Day Saints, and the United Effort Plan Trust:

s.s. Rulon T. Jeffs
Rulon T. Jeffs, President

The following excerpts from a sermon given by Leroy Johnson some years earlier on February 10, 1985, were included with this letter:

"I feel very humble, my brothers and sisters, in trying to say something to you, and I pray that the Lord will put in my mouth the words He wants me to say.

"This ship that has been portrayed to us today is under fire – the United Effort Plan. I can't see who is in the room, but I hope that there is someone there who will carry this message to the opposite people, because they haven't had manhood enough to come out in the open and let us know who they are. We know who some of them are, but we don't know who they all are. So, I am talking to you today to let you know that there is not going to be any deeds to any part of the

330

United Effort Plan given to the enemy of the United Effort Plan. You can take it or leave it.

"The United Effort Plan was given to us by the Lord for a protection to His people – His saints – and I am not afraid to speak in defense of it. Because every man who has lifted his hand against the United Effort Plan and against this work that I profess to be the head of, is fighting against God and not against me. They had better look out because if they push it any further, God will lay a heavy hand on their shoulder, and I am not afraid to say it because I have the Spirit of God upon me, and He is dictating my words at the present time, and they had better take it. They had better not push me any further towards the wall until I can get on my feet and get my people behind me and get the non-believers out of this place. I want every one of them to get discouraged and leave right away.

"Now, I want to say a few words to the faithful. The Lord is pleased with your actions so far – you who have determined in your minds to serve God and keep His commandments at all hazards and believe in the Lord our Savior, Jesus Christ, and in the Prophet Joseph Smith and his works.

"But those who try to change the words of Joseph Smith as they are contained in the Doctrine & Covenants had better walk carefully, because the judgments of God are terrible when they come upon a disobedient people. Now, I pray that the Lord will bless you all, in the name of Jesus Christ. Amen."

The threats made in this 1985 sermon of Leroy Johnson were included in this "eviction notice" by Sam Barlow in hopes that it might intimidate his victims. It had little or no effect on them, however, because by this time the lawsuit had been filed in the State Court at St. George. The Barlow Cabal likely supposed they had been blessed from above and that by having the case thrown out of the Federal Court in Salt Lake City, they had won the lawsuit. In fact, this is what they told the people of the Barlow/Jeffs Group in their Sunday meetings. They were wasting no time in getting the message to all "apostates" that they were going to be evicted.

When the complaint was served on the Defendants (UEP) it shocked them. They had supposed that the plaintiffs (dissidents) would be unable to raise enough money to entice the law firm of Woodburys and Associates to continue the case any further. One thing that caused the UEP concern was that the state statutes would not allow them to drag the case out with ridiculous motions. These Statutes allowed only about one year for such cases to be resolved. This meant that the issue would soon appear in a court of law and they had very little confidence that the UEP could win against the plaintiffs in such a forum; however, they determined to move ahead, using all their former stall tactics. They had very little success, however, because Judge J. Philip Eves divided the issues of the lawsuit into two different phases, seeking to determine two facts:

1) whether the plaintiffs had any equity in the homes they had built and,

2) whether or not they were beneficiaries of the United Effort Plan Trust. This decision was not formally rendered by the Court until June 24th, 1994, with other interesting developments transpiring in the meantime.

Depositions began on December 6, 1993, at St. George, Utah. These depositions began with the lawyers for the defendants taking plaintiffs' (dissidents) testimony first, which took about two weeks. The plaintiffs' attorneys then took testimony from the defendants. The most significant factor surrounding these depositions is the involvement of Sam Barlow and his role in the case.

Sam Barlow was not a defendant, but he was appointed by Rulon Jeffs to be the official representative for the United Effort Plan. A person who was a non-party to the lawsuit read his deposition and commented: "The only truthful statement Sam made in the whole deposition was at the first part where he stated his name."

A few of these inconsistencies will be entered here.

One of the first questions asked of Sam: "Do you receive any income from the Trust (UEP)?"

Sam: "I don't receive any income from the Trust. The Trust has no income. I don't receive any income from the church either, but the church does allow me to continue on my mission that sustains me on my mission."

The next set of questions were whether or not the "Church" claimed the language in the trust document as being ambiguous. Sam's answers were of such that Scott Berry, attorney for the defendants jumped in and answered for him.

Mr. Berry: "Obviously Sam, you haven't gone to the Trust or the president of the Trust or the president of the church and asked him to give you guidance on the questions that Reed is asking you. So, the fair answer in the case would be that you don't know what the Trust claims."

This statement by Scott Berry is so inconsistent that it causes one to ask why Mr. Lambert, attorney for the Plaintiffs, would not stop the depositions and insist that if Sam Barlow was going to answer questions for the trust that he indeed go to the president of the trust and the "church" and learn what "his guidance on the questions" were. This little stalling act on the part of Sam and Scott is a prime example of how the deposition of Sam Barlow went.

A few more examples:

Question: "My question is, does the Trust agree that the trustees are liable to the members for acts that they might commit in bad faith?"

Answer: "They (fundamentalists) do not believe the priesthood leadership over them are accountable to the members of the church."

Question: "Okay. If a trustee were to do something in bad faith...would the Trust agree that they could be subject to the civil laws?"

Answer: "Absolutely."

Going to the trust document, Mr Lambert then asked:

Question: "Let's look on page 6…Short sentence. 'Evidence of membership shall be shown in the books of the association.' Have such books been maintained by the Trust?"

Answer: "Maintained by the church."

Question: "And there is a book that records membership?"

Answer: "No, records of baptisms into the church."

Question: "Does the Trust admit that at some point the plaintiffs were members of the Trust?"

Answer: "They were at one time regarded as members of the church."

Question: "Were their names ever noted in the book of the Trust or shown in the books of the association?"

Answer: "I think you'll find that they were baptized and recorded as being members of the church, designated the Fundamentalist Church."

The reader is reminded here that there was no Fundamentalist Church organized until the late 1980s, several years after the Plaintiffs had initiated the lawsuit, so Sam's answer is a falsehood. None of the Plaintiffs ever belonged to any so-called "Fundamentalist Church."

Question: "Are you aware of anything that you have seen that is a separate record, not a baptism record, but a separate trust record of membership in the Trust?"

Answer: "No."

Question: "(From the trust document) A membership certificate may, in the discretion of the trustees, be issued to each member. My question is, were such certificates ever issued?

Answer: "I don't think they were, I have never seen them."

Question: "Rulon Jeffs testified in deposition that there were some – there was some kind of agreement and he testified that it was possibly a dozen pages long."

Answer: "I've never seen that."

Then Sam was asked why Leroy Johnson and Rulon Jeffs gave Marion Hammon the deeds to certain large parcels of land.

Question: "The Trust at one time conveyed real property to Marion Hammon and I realize Marion Hammon lost that property."

Answer: "I don't know entirely what arrangements was made, but I know quite a degree what arrangements were made. And it was not giving the property, it was allowing him to use it to establish a contingent in Idaho which he wanted to do…when it didn't work out, they called him into an accounting for that and asked him to step down as a trustee."

This answer only leaves more questions that should be answered.

First question: Wasn't the property (the ranch at Hatch and the farm at Beryl) "given" to Marion as a pay-off that he would move to Idaho and allow the Cabal to "have Short Creek?" Second question: How was "'giving" the deeds of these properties to Marion "allowing him to use it to establish a contingent in Idaho," if Leroy and Rulon didn't expect him to either sell it or at least mortgage it? Either way would have been in violation of what Sam claims is the policy of the Trust.

And if this whole scenario of Sam's had been the truth, then why did Leroy refuse to help Marion when he got into trouble with the farm in Idaho and try to save UEP assets? The real question here is, who were the true violators of trust policy: Marion Hammon for losing the property after it was "given" to him, or Leroy Johnson and Rulon Jeffs for "giving" the property to Marion in the first place. Sam Barlow's logic has no consistency.

A major falsehood told by Sam Barlow in this deposition was that when asked if those members who turn property into the trust were told at the time where they could read a copy of the trust document and he said that they were told that the document was filed in the courthouses of two counties and they could find it there if they wanted to read it.

When he was asked: "How would the trust define support of the priesthood?" This question came about because Sam said that this was the way a person became and remained a member of the trust, supporting the Priesthood. His answer, "Speak well of the leading brethren and to not do things that damage the faith of others and cause dissension or division (the very thing that he and his brothers had done to get Marion Hammon and Alma Timpson removed as trustees of the trust)." Another prerequisite was that you give generously of "your treasure."

He was asked about the accusation of the defendants that the plaintiffs had violated the standards of moral conduct of the trust.

Question: "Does the Trust contend that any plaintiff has violated one of the standards of moral conduct that it referred to in the excerpt we have read?"

Answer: "That's set forth for the reason that moral standards are important and not for the reason we want to go and ferret out somebody's misbehavior, but certainly gambling and lying and misrepresenting and filing non meritorious, fictitious lawsuits is outside of the purview of the gospel plan."

Besides these misdemeanors, Sam included the act of apostasy and adultery as being paramount sins, giving the trust cause to disassociate members.

He was asked to be specific as to which individual plaintiffs were guilty of these moral faults.

Answer: " I don't wish to accuse these folks. I wish to defend the church and the United Effort Plan and in the process of that defense, it's really gauged on how you make your attack on the church. I can't answer that question you just asked about without some time to work on it."

Question: "So at this point, you haven't – you don't know of any specific instance of the type I'm talking about that the Trust would contend is, other than what you've told me about, the lying and apostasy, being disassociated with the church, other than those things, you can't point to any specific instance of conduct by any plaintiff that you would say is conduct inconsistent with these moral standards we're talking about?"

Answer: "I think bringing publicity upon our people, that is designed to create a collision between this small religious community and the world in general, is a breach of moral conduct."

Question: "That's a good example. Can you tell me which plaintiffs you believe have done that?"

Answer: "Yes. Some of them have said it in deposition that they had participated in alleging that we were a gun-toten people, that we're using the Bishop's store house to store firearms. And some of them worried in front of the television about bloodshed and that sort of thing, which has never ever been proved at all."

Question: "Do you know who those individuals were?"

Answer: "Yes, Ben Bistline, Harold Blackmore, Cyril Bradshaw, Don Cox, and some of them."

Question: "Is there any other conduct, the type we're discussing, that you can identify at this time?"

Answer: "Claiming a women is your wife while she's married to someone else."

Question: "Tell me who's engaged in that kind of conduct?"

Answer: "David Stubbs was reportedly engaged in that."

Question: "At the present time?"

Answer: "I don't know about the present time."

Question: "And the position of the Trust is that at that (same) time she was someone else's wife, not his?"

Answer: "Someone else claims she was."

It is interesting to note here that this was the only evidence that Sam could come up with to support his accusation of any of the plaintiffs living with the wife of someone else. It must be pointed out that at this very time, his Uncle Fred Jessop, one of the leaders that the plaintiffs had been so badly ridiculed for because of their disrespect of him, was living in adultery with wives of two of the plaintiffs whom he had convinced should be "married" to him instead of the men to whom they had been "sealed to by the Priesthood."

When Sam was asked about businesses once owned by the UEP his answer: "United Effort Plan only holds property. It's a receptacle for real property."

Question: "When property is sold, the United Effort Plan maintains no records of the sale, or doesn't have any books that it keeps track of it?"

Answer: "United Effort Plan is a child of the church and the church designated what happens."

He was denying that the UEP ever handles any money, it's all church money. When he was asked about the tax assessments made on the members by Truman Barlow, he said that the members had been told it was a donation to the church and not to pay taxes for UEP property.

He was then asked: "Can you tell me the first time the Trust expressly told the members that they, when they paid their taxes, they were really paying a church contribution and not paying – and paying something other than taxes, that they were paying a church contribution?"

Answer: "I don't know if this trust expressly told them, but the priesthood leaders told them."

Question: "Can you tell me when they told them that for the first time?"

Answer: "I don't know about the first time, but many times in over a long period of years, in the general meetings particularly."

Question: "Is it true people were assessed separately for taxes by being given a notice?"

Answer: "No, that's not true. They weren't assessed for taxes at all."

Question: "Did they receive separate notices for taxes?"

Answer: "They received requests for contributions."

Question: "Did the request for contribution have the name of the Church on it?"

Answer: "The faithful members receive a reminder that contributions are in order (never answering the question)."

The tax notices had the name of the United Effort Plan on them up until the late 1980s.

When Sam was asked if people could be evicted for no reason at all, he said they would only be asked to leave if they had done something prejudicial to the trust. This then makes them not a tenant at will.

Question: "Okay. Is it inconsistent with the way the Trust operates today that the general manager was under the direction of a Board of Directors?"

Answer: "It's inconsistent with how it was managed at any time. It may have been what Brother Musser had hoped would happen, but it never was a practical way that it operated."

Sam stated that no leases are given. This is untrue because Fred Jessop had been given many leases on which he has built income-producing businesses, making sure that any income produced on the property would not be income him, not to the trust.

Guy Musser, one of John Barlow's Priesthood Council members, made this statement shortly before he died:

"The Barlow boys have wrested the keys from the Priesthood." This deposition of Sam Barlow confirms the truth of Guy Musser's statement. Although the Barlow Cabal has been able to gain control of the "Priesthood" assets, they cannot change historical facts. They may attempt to do so, and teach the followers of the Barlow/Jeffs schism that policies of the United Effort Plan set up in the 1940s *were only the ideas of Joseph Musser*, making it appear that John Barlow was in total control and was establishing his "One Man Doctrine" and that such was accepted by most of the members of the Priesthood Work at the time; but the facts are entirely different. The facts are that the "Group" was operating just exactly as Joseph Musser said it was when he recorded it, both in the letters that exists and in his journal. More explanation concerning this controversy will be covered later.

In the spring of 1994 the Barlow Cabal decided to make "One Last Amended Affidavit of Disclosure" to try and set the record straight as to just what they claimed the policy of the United Effort Plan was in regard to Beneficiaries.

In this sixth amended affidavit of disclosure they now claim that "the only beneficiary of the United Effort Plan is the 'Fundamentalist Church of Jesus Christ of Latter Day Saints' and has always been so. All other affidavits of disclosures filed, under oath, prior to this time were made in error." Because of the ridicules nature of these claims, it seems necessary to submit the complete document here; This new affidavit of disclosure is as follows:

AFFIDAVIT OF DISCLOSURE
NOTICE OF CORRECTION OF BENEFICIARY
Filed in Mohave County Court House; April 21, 1994, 8:30 AM.
Book 2391; Pages 735...748.
STATE OF UTAH   )
) SS.
County of Washington   )
    RULON T. JEFFS, FRED M. JESSOP, LEROY S. JEFFS, JAMES K. ZITTING, WINSTON K. BLACKMORE, PARLEY J. HARKER AND TRUMAN I. BARLOW. Trustees of the United Effort Plan Trust, a religious and charitable trust, operated on behalf of the Presidency of The Fundamentalist Church of Jesus Christ of Latter-Day Saints, each being first duly sworn, deposes and says as follows:
    Pursuant to the provisions of former Section 33-401 Arizona Revised Statutes, as amended prior to 1987, an Affidavit of Disclosure was executed and recorded in Mohave County in Book 335, page 818. Said Affidavit of Disclosure was amended by Amended Affidavits of Disclosure recorded in said County as follows:
    1. in Book 979, Page 741;

2. in Book 1052, Page 675;

3. in Book 1057, Page 244;

4. in Book 1088, Page 859;

5. in Book 1285, Page 986.

The original Affidavit of Disclosure was recorded under the requirements of A.S.S. 33-401, which became effective on June 22, 1976. Although the statute did not specifically address the disclosure requirements of charitable trusts, it made the failure to disclose the names of beneficiaries of land held in trust a crime in Arizona.

The Trustees at the time and others who were then leaders of the Church which established the United Effort Plan Trust, although unsure of the application of A.R.S. 33-401 to religious and charitable trusts, attempted to comply with the spirit of the statute by recording an Affidavit of Disclosure erroneously listing as beneficiaries the head of each family permitted to occupy trust land because the households were receiving charitable benefits. The Trust document refers not to beneficiaries but to "members," and while under the broadest definition anyone receiving any benefit from the Trust could be construed as a beneficiary, under Utah law (this being a Utah Trust), as explained hereinafter, the only true beneficiary of the Trust is the Church.

The amended Affidavits of Disclosure referred to above were recorded as a continuing effort to comply with the spirit of the statute and to give notice of the actions described therein.

On February 6, 1991, the Corporation of the President of the Fundamentalist Church of Jesus Christ of Latter-Day Saints, Inc. was incorporated in Utah by Rulon T. Jeffs, the current President of the Church. The religious association which was legally organized by the incorporation is also known as the Priesthood Work. The corporation sole was incorporated to give legal recognition to the Church which has existed for more than 100 years.

The United Effort Plan Trust was created as a charitable and religious trust in 1942 by the Church, now legally organized as The Fundamentalist Church of Jesus Christ of Latter-Day Saints. The specific purpose of the Trust was to foster and support the living of the religious principle of the United Order by the members of the Church in accordance with the teachings of the Prophets Joseph Smith, Brigham Young, John Taylor, John Y. Barlow, Leroy S. Johnson, Rulon T. Jeffs and other Presidents of the Church. The Church has always used the Trust to hold property consecrated to God by the members of the Church.

The charitable benefits available from the United Effort Plan Trust are administered by the Board of Trustees, at the direction of the President of the Church. They are available to members of the Church who are faithful to the tenets of the Church and who support Church leadership.

In view of the foregoing, the undersigned Trustees therefore declare that the true and sole beneficiary of the United Effort Plan Trust, which is the owner of the property, which is particularly described on Exhibit "A" attached hereto and by this reference made a part hereof, is and always has been The Fundamentalist Church of Jesus Christ of Latter-Day Saints. Any recordation to the contrary has been determined to be incorrect and is now corrected by this instrument.

IN WITNESS WHEREOF, the undersigned Trustees have set their hands this 4th day April, 1994

Rulon T. Jeffs, President (S.S.)   Fred M. Jessop (S.S.)
Leroy S. Jeffs (S.S.)   James K. Zitting (S.S.)
Winston K. Blackmore (S.S.)   Parley J. Harker (S.S.)
Truman I. Barlow (S.S.)

SUBSCRIBED AND SWORN to before me this 9th day of April, 1994 by Rulon T. Jeffs, Fred M. Jessop, Leroy S. Jeffs, James K. Zitting, Winston K. Blackmore, Parley J. Harker and Truman I. Barlow.

Ron Steed

Notary Public
My Commission expires:
8/8/94

In the spring of 1994 the Cabal began requiring those who were "given" a lot to put up a sign before they began any improvements, stating that the lot belonged to the UEP and acknowledgment that they would be a Tenant at Will on the property. This was done at the suggestion of their lawyers, contemplating it would alleviate any future disputes concerning equity claims if the occupant would become discouraged and decide to "apostatize." Strange as it seems, these recipients of a lot were all eager to comply with this rule, thinking no doubt that the rules of the cult would not change and they would be secure in "their" homes forever. Reality is much harsher.

At the end of May 1994, there was a hearing in St. George before Judge Eves on the lawsuit. Both sides had filed motions for him to consider. The Defendants were asking that the lawsuit be dismissed on the basis of religion. The plaintiffs asked the judge to compel the Defendants to turn over their bank records and give an accounting to the plaintiffs. The results of this hearing are best explained in a letter that was sent to the plaintiffs from their attorneys. The first part of this letter is as follows:

June 30, 1994
Dear (Plaintiff),

This letter, is to bring you up to date regarding the State Law Suit, since

Judge Eves has handed down his ruling on the motions brought before him.

A hearing was held on May 20, 1994, before Judge Eves to consider the Defendants' motion for summary judgement to dismiss our law suit against the UEP. We had three motions before him, (1) to let us amend our complaint, (2) to force the trust to give us an accounting and (3) to let us look at their bank records.

The Judge granted our motion to amend our complaint immediately.

Scott Berry argued that the UEP was a religious and charitable trust because it had such words and phrases included in the Declaration of Trust as "just wants and needs" and "consecration", etc. Reid showed that the term "consecration" as used in the Declaration of Trust defined a transaction. The argument on our motions to compel were very emotional – the Defendants' attorneys stating that they didn't want the "apostates" to see those records.

The Judge denied the Defendants' motion for summary judgement, stating that the nature of the trust was not defined in the Declaration of Trust, but that there were ambiguous references in that document that needed to be considered. He also denied our motions to compel, stating that he would like to determine if we are indeed beneficiaries, as we claim, and he left all of the motions open to be reconsidered at a later date, if needed.

The Judge determined to split the Plaintiffs' claims into two groups; to bring the first six claims to trial immediately and if the last three claims then need consideration, to have another trial to hear them. The first six claims contain the core issues in our case:

1. Breach of Contract
2. Implied Contract
3. Negligent Misrepresentation
4. Constructive Fraud
5. Estoppel
6. Unjust Enrichment/Occupying Claimants

We have all the discovery we need on these six claims to go to trial immediately. The additional three:

7. Breach of Fiduciary Duty
8. Accounting
9. Distribution of the Trust

To do all would require further very expensive discovery involving time, appeals and further expenses before coming to trial.

The Judge has placed before us the opportunity to get to trial speedily, without opportunity of the Defendants to stall proceedings through appeals and other tactics. This will be far less costly than other possible strategies.

The long awaited trail on the UEP lawsuit finally got under way in St. George on November 30, 1994. It took three weeks for the plaintiffs to present their case at the end of which the judge asked the attorneys of both sides to have their clients consider an out-of-court settlement. His suggestion was that the defendants allow the plaintiffs ten years to live unmolested on the property, at the end of which they would willingly move, forfeiting all claims of ownership. He asked that they meet with their clients and report back to him the next day, hoping to stall off any further trial. The next morning the attorneys reported back to the judge the desires of their clients in the matter.

The defendants' offer for settlement was to allow the plaintiffs two years to move, after which forfeiting all claims of ownership, assuring them that they would not file any counter-suit in the matter. The defendants felt they were being very generous in their offer of not "punishing" the apostates for bringing such a hardship upon the "Lord's anointed."

The plaintiffs on the other hand felt that they should be compensated in some way for their equity. Most of them did not even want to move but were willing to do so, if they could receive enough money to at least buy the material to construct themselves another home to live in. Their offer of settlement was to be allowed to live in their homes for so long as they desired. If the defendants wanted them to move, they would "sell" their equity for 75 percent of the assessed valuation.

Needless to say neither side would accept either of their opponent's offer. The trial resumed its course with defendants putting their witnesses on the stand.

On the weekend before these developments Warren Jeffs, son of Rulon Jeffs conducted a Priesthood Meeting class in Salt Lake City, wherein he proclaimed the "One Man Doctrine" of the Barlow Cabal. This meeting was held on December 17, 1994.

"President Jeffs would like me (Warren Jeffs) to read tonight the story of what took place in President Barlow's day. This is from the journal of Joseph Musser, his own words. You will see the opposition that President Barlow experienced by men who should have been perfectly obedient, one hundred percent with him. President Jeffs has explained that those who were ordained by Lorin Woolley to the apostleship, the other five, in one way or another, turned against President Barlow. That is why President Johnson became the keyholder after President Barlow was taken. This is the Private Journal of Joseph W. Musser, November 1936.

Warren Jeffs quoting from Joseph Musser's Journal (November 8, 1939).

(J.W. Musser) That when the Lord wanted any man to know who holds the keys of Priesthood, and that man was prepared to receive the fact, He would reveal in a clear way. He expressed his unshaken faith in the fertility of the soil and that the section involved would yet become a very choice spot, yielding in abundance, and would be a place where protection would be assured the Saints against their evil enemies; but that this condition would be brought about through the faithfulness of the Saints and not otherwise. There must be no autocratic rule.

(Author note: It is interesting that Joseph Musser, in his journal, often has written "keys *of* Priesthood" then crossed out the word *of* and replaced it with keys *to* Priesthood. Whether this has any significance or not is hard to say.)

(Warren Jeffs) "Or no one man rule, in his view."

(J.W. Musser) The agency of every individual must be respected. That no man should refuse his neighbor help when it was needed, even though the neighbor may not be a member of a TRUST GROUP.

(Warren Jeffs) "Uncle Sam (Barlow) handed me this to read from John Y. Barlow on June 27, 1943:"

(J.Y. Barlow, 1943) Bro. Lorin came and took me to the Priesthood on the other side. I heard things discussed there. I know those things. This work has started – not only the work of celestial marriage, the work of united order. We may not accomplish it, but if we don't our sons will (this was in a dream John Barlow claimed to have had, not an actual event [added by Ben Bistline]).

(Samuel S. Barlow said the following) "A couple of weeks ago, I pointed out this reference to the folks down south, and another reference where Dad said that he had been visited by the Prophet Joseph Smith, and that the call was made for a man to come and witness in regards to the dissension that occurred, as has been recorded here in the journal of Joseph Musser. The man that was called was Isaac Carling.

"Uncle Roy had told us the story of being at Big Bend when President Barlow was there, and he said: 'I have got to go home. The Lord needs a man, and it has got to be either you or Isaac Carling.' Then they learned that Isaac Carling had picked up a log, and had developed a hernia, the hernia strangulated, and he died within a few days (this account of Sam's does not correspond with Leroy's account he gives of the event in his journals [added by Ben Bistline]).

"We also learned that Uncle Isaac Carling had attended the meeting (with Joseph Musser in 1936) at which this dissension developed, and was amplified and explained. Uncle Roy had not been to that meeting. He was in Hurricane with this hurt hand. His testimony was that a man came to him the next day, and said to him: 'Roy, you should have been there. Joseph Musser sure put John in his place.' Uncle Roy said: 'I am glad that I wasn't there.' Nevertheless, when the Lord called a witness, He called for a witness a man that had been there and saw those things.

"But brethren, an important thing happened down south after we talked about this. I am not sure that everyone caught it, but it certainly went through me like it was important. The Prophet Rulon Jeffs spoke at the end of the meeting, and he said: 'I have had Uncle John and Uncle Roy right at my elbow helping me to get the things done that I have to get done.' This explained to us that this pattern is continuing, just like John Y. Barlow was saying that the Prophet Lorin Woolley took him and directed him on what to do. This same thing is occurring in our day, brethren, and the Prophet bore that testimony to us. I trust that we will remember it and believe it."

(Warren Jeffs) "All this training is to prepare us for the tests ahead. For these many years now since Uncle Roy passed away, there has only been one man holding the Apostleship alive in mortality. By now, we should have permanently sealed in our minds that there is only one man who holds the keys of Priesthood, and all others work by a delegated authority. All of us are here today only through our connection with him.

"There are tests ahead of us to prove if we are truly with him. Please know that anything opposite to what he wants us to do is wrong. 'Right,' to know what is right is to do the will of this man who has the right to rule over us. What is going to come, we don't know exactly. When the court case is through, there will be greater tests come. So we need to tie ourselves to President Jeffs, read his words, and through our agency go and do it. If we are having to be dragged, the tie is being broken. The sweet Spirit is not staying with us. We have to move with the same Spirit. That is how exacting, and challenging, and terrible the times will be. We have to move with the same Spirit in a perfect oneness with him.

"I rejoice in what he is calling on us to do in our efforts to unite. It is only blessing. It is a preparation for greater events. He has had these things revealed to us now, the challenges of the Prophets before. May we be part of that five hundred who will move as one man, truly understanding Priesthood, that this man is god over us, and through him comes all things of any value in our lives, I pray in the name of Jesus Christ. Amen."

Rulon Jeffs said, "I feel impressed that we should have a day of fasting and prayer on Monday. The Judge will be making a decision, or he may postpone it sometime. Let us pray that God will overrule, and answer the prayers of His servant."

Warren S. Jeffs concluding the session by stating: "I am very impressed with the lessons we have had tonight, and ask that Heavenly Father's Spirit will be with me as I try to fulfill President Jeffs' purposes here. I know that he is god over me, which means, I owe him my all. I belong to him, for he is God with us, he being the key holder and God's representative to us. You will only see the face of your Heavenly Father through coming to a perfect obedience to this man, President Jeffs."

The class was "taught" that only one man on the earth held the keys to priesthood and all must honor him as "God over us."

The decision the judge made was to continue the trial. This he did after his attempt to get the litigates to come to an out of court settlement.

On December 19, 1994, the Plaintiffs finished their presentation to the court in St. George. Afterwards the Judge called the attorneys into his chambers. He told them to try and come to a settlement, suggesting that they give the Plaintiffs a ten year time period to move off the property. They met in court again the next day and the Defendants "offered" to allow the Plaintiffs two years to move off the property, leaving without any equity. The Plaintiffs "offered" that they would settle out of court if the UEP would allow them to live on the property, unmolested, for the rest of their lives. If any of the Plaintiffs decided to leave, they would forfeit any claims on the property. If the UEP decided they wanted them to leave, they would pay for their homes at 75 percent of the assessed valuation. Needless to say, there was no out of court settlement.

The trial resumed with Scott Berry, attorney for the defendants (UEP), attempting to put into evidence a packet of information that Sam Barlow had compiled, taking excerpts from sermons etc. The Judge would not allow that it be evidence, upsetting Scott Berry very much. He spent 30 minutes arguing with the Judge, but to no avail, the Judge still would not allow it.

The trial only lasted for a few more days with only a few of the witnesses for the defense testifying, before the time allotted by the Judge ran out. The hearings were then postponed until some future date, with Scott Berry telling the Judge that he was prepared to put 125 witnesses on the stand when the trial resumes. The Judge asked him to proffer what they would say but Scott Berry refused to do so. The trial was scheduled to continue in May and to take place in Parowan at the Iron County Court House.

The next Sunday after these court events, Sam Barlow announced in church to the followers of the UEP, that neither side would win the lawsuit and it would have to go to settlement. This seemed a little strange because they refused to settle just two weeks before his announcement.

The hearings resumed on May 17, 1996, in Parowan, Utah. The defendants began putting their 125 witnesses on the stand. The testimonies of those put on were all pretty much identical, just what Sam Barlow had instructed them to say. After the first half dozen or so witnesses, the Judge proposed to the attorneys for the defense that they began proffering the testimony of the remaining witnesses because the testimony of all witnesses seemed to be just about the same. After considerable bickering on their part, Scott Berry somewhat agreed to the Judge's proposal. There were a couple of witnesses whose testimony was different than "Sam's party line." This was of Fred Jessop and Ken Driggs.

Ken Driggs had made considerable effort to study the history of the Polygamists. He had spent several hours in the LDS Church archives, studying the journal of Joseph Musser. He was not allowed to make a xerox copy of any of the journal but was allowed to type much of it. He had put together a brief history of the Polygamists and had relied very much on Musser's journal in this account. There was nothing in his quotes of Musser's journal that contradicted any of the claims of the Plaintiffs. Many of the claims of the defendants, however, were not substantiated in this journal; in fact their claims of the "One Man Doctrine" was strongly disputed by Musser in his journal. Ken Driggs' testimony really did nothing for either side in a legal sense, but it certainly disputed the claims of the "Cabal" in the religious issues.

Fred Jessop's testimony did much more to favor the Plaintiffs' claims than it did to help the UEP defendants'. He said: "There has never been anyone forced to move from their homes if they were asked by the 'Priesthood' to move and they refused to do so." The Judge questioned him on this statement and he assured him that such was the truth.

While one of the witnesses for the defendants was on the stand, Scott Berry told the Judge that if the plaintiffs (dissidents) were allowed to remain in the community, it would be an infringement on the religious freedom of the UEP supporters. The Judge asked the lady testifying if it would infringe on her religious rights if the Plaintiffs were allowed to remain in the community. She answered: "Yes, it would." When the Judge asked her how it would be so, she could only stammer and finally said: "Well, if the children of the apostates are allowed to live in the community they would set a bad example, their form of dress etc., for our children." The Judge questioned her as to how this could be so, but she could not give him any further explanation.

The trial was postponed on this note with the Judge saying he would set a date later on which it would resume (The UEP lawsuit supposedly ended on November 13, 1995. The lawyers gave their closing statements with the Judge saying he would rule on it later).

On July 2, 1995, Truman Barlow's house (a virtual mansion, built and paid for by the UEP) caught fire and was a complete loss. This seemed a big hardship on him because he had to move into Uncle Roy's house while the UEP rebuilt his house for him. It took several months before his new house was rebuilt, but when finished, it was by far more imposing and grand than had been the old one. And this all done and paid for by the Priesthood, or the UEP, at no cost to Truman. The Priesthood takes care of its own.

In October of 1995, Fred Jessop "sent down a decree" that no one in the community could any longer own guns. All guns were to be disposed of. Only those who had been commissioned by proper authority could any longer have guns in their possession. This edict was followed almost implicitly by the First Ward followers. This was the third time in the Colorado City Polygamists' history that the people have had their guns taken away. The first time was in the early 1960s and was ordered by Marion Hammon. The second time was in the late 1970s. The order was handed down by Leroy Johnson, but was orchestrated by Fred Jessop and his Barlow nephews.

The Attorneys for both sides in the UEP lawsuit gave their closing statements on November 14, 1995. This pretty much marked the end of an era. It was near the end of the year (1995) and seemingly the end of an eight year legal conflict that had literally torn the community and families apart, spawning the most bitter feelings of hatred that the community had experienced in its history. With anxiety running high in the hearts of the people, the community moved into the new year, nervously awaiting how the Judge's decision would affect the lives and the future of everyone living there.

Note 1: There is a parallel with this "calling of the "Prophet's son(s)" in Joseph Musser's journal. He claims that Joseph Fielding Smith was "called by his mother." The following is taken from his journal, dated December 21, 1936:

"Been in Salt Lake since above entry. Prepared copy for *Truth* (magazine). One Article, 'Slander Refuted,' I prepared correcting Joseph Fielding Smith. He is young and inexperienced; has never had to work or get along in the world without either his father's help or his salary from the Church. He was, as I am reliably informed, chosen as an Apostle not by the Lord, but by his mother. He lacks lots in knowledge and in 'human touch.'"

Note 2: Because of the Lawsuit, the Polygamists began claiming that not only were they "A Church," but that they were the "True Church as set up by Joseph Smith in 1830." They claimed that all their actions, evicting people from their homes etc. were of a religious nature, therefore the courts had no jurisdiction over their conduct. By 1991 they were advised by their attorneys that if they were going to claim such immunity they should organize some kind of a legal church. On February 6, 1991, they filed the following articles of incorporation for the corporation of the president of "their" church. The interesting thing about this document is that the Fundamentalist Church of Jesus Christ of Latter Day Saints, the name they gave to "their" church, has only three members, Rulon Jeffs, Parley Harker and Fred Jessop.

Articles of incorporation for the corporation of the President, of the President of The Fundamentalist Church of Jesus Christ of Latter Day Saints Inc.

I, Rulon T. Jeffs, having been duly chosen and appointed President of The Fundamentalist Church of Jesus Christ of Latter Day Saints, in conformity with the rites, regulations and discipline of said Church, being desirous of forming a corporation for the purpose of acquiring, holding and disposing of Church or religious society property, for the benefit of religion, for works of charity and for public worship, hereby make and subscribe these Articles of Incorporation for a corporation sole pursuant to the provisions of Sections 16-7-1 et seq. of the Utah Code Annotated (1953, as amended).

ARTICLE I

The name of the corporation shall be THE CORPORATION OF THE PRESIDENT OF THE FUNDAMENTALIST CHURCH OF JESUS CHRIST OF LATTER DAY SAINTS INC.

ARTICLE II

The object of the corporation shall be to acquire, hold, or dispose of such real and personal property as may be conveyed to or acquired by said corporation for the benefit of the members of The Fundamentalist Church of Jesus Christ of Latter Day Saints, a religious society, for the benefit of religion, for works of charity, for public worship, for the establishment of schools and for the advancement of both religious and secular education, and for all other lawful purposes necessary or incident thereto. Such real and personal property may be situated, either within the State of Utah, or elsewhere ((including foreign countries), and this corporation shall have power, without any authority or authorization from the members of said Church or religious souiety, to grant, sell, convey, rent, mortgage, exchange, or otherwise deal with or dispose of any part or all of such property.

ARTICLE III

The estimated value of property to which I hold the legal title and which I desire to place in this corporation for the purpose aforesaid, at the time of making these Articles, is the sum of $568,000.

ARTICLE IV

The title of the person making these Articles of Incorporation is "President of The Fundamentalist Church of Jesus Christ of Latter Day Saints Inc."

ARTICLE V

In the event of the death or resignation from office of the President of The Fundamentalist Church of Jesus Christ of Latter Day Saints, or in the event of a vacancy in that office for any cause, the First Counselor of the First Presidency of said Church (or in the event such First Counselor shall not then be living or shall be disabled, the Second or nest subsequent Counselor in the First Presidency as the President shall have designated prior to his death or disability) shall, pending installation of a successor President of The Fundamentalist Church of Jesus Christ of Latter Day Saints, be the corporation sole under these articles, and the laws pursuant to which they are made, and shall be and is authorized in his official capacity to execute in the name of the corporation all documents or other writings necessary to the carrying on of its purposes, business and objects, and to do all things in the name of the corporation which the original signer of the articles of incorporation might do; it being the purpose of these articles that there shall be no failure in succession in the office of such corporation sole. At the time of signing of these Articles, the First Counselor in the First Presidency of said Church is Parley J. Harker, and the Second Counselor is Fred M. Jessop. The President shall have authority to designate new counselors in the First Presidency of said Church, or to change the office of existing counselors, as he shall see fit.

ARTICLE VI

In the event of the ending or dissolution of this corporation, after paying or adequately providing for the debts and obligations of the corporation, the remaining assets shall be distributed to a nonprofit fund, foundation or corporation, which is organized and operated exclusively for charitable, educational, or religious and/or scientific purposes.

ARTICLE VII

This corporation shall exist perpetually unless sooner dissolved by law.

DATED this 6th day of February, 1991.

s.s. Rulon T. Jeffs

Rulon T. Jeffs, President

The Fundamentalist Church of Jesus Christ of Latter Day Saints, 3611 East 9400 South Sandy, Utah 84092

Notarized by Patricia B. Buirch, Notary Public residing in Salt Lake City, Utah. Commission Expires on 7/10/92.

Final Judgment In The UEP Lawsuit

Judge Eves handed down his ruling in January of 1996. The important issues that most affected the litigates were the questions of Plaintiffs' (dissidents) equity and the status of the trust, whether it was religious or business in nature. The Judge ruled that the UEP was a religious trust, charitable in nature. Also, according to his interpretation of the trust document, the Plaintiffs were not members of the United Effort Plan, but if the trust were to evict them from the homes they had built, it would be unjust enrichment. Therefore he ruled that the Plaintiffs would have equity interest in the property on which their homes were situated and could remain in them for the remainder of their lives. If the UEP desired to evict them, they would be required to pay the current assessed valuation of the homes to the occupants. If any Plaintiffs chose to leave their homes on their own volition, they would forfeit any equity claims.

In light of this explanation, a portion of the Judge's decision will be entered here.

IN THE DISTRICT COURT OF THE FIFTH JUDICIAL DISTRICT IN AND FOR WASHINGTON COUNTY, STATE OF UTAH MEMORANDUM DECISION RULON T. JEFFS, trustee for the United Effort Plan, a Utah trust, and KENNETH STEED, Plaintiffs, VS. CASE NOS. 89-2850 930500305 QT CORA FISCHER STUBBS and 930501020 CV DAVID L. STUBBS, Defendants.

These consolidated cases came before the Court for trial on the following dates: November 30, 1994; December 1, 2, 5, 6, 8, 12, 13, 14, 19, 20, 21, 22, 23, 1994; May 17, 18, 19, 24, 25, and 26, 1995. The parties were represented by their respective counsel of record, Reid W. Lambert representing the 21 plaintiffs in the Amended Complaint filed February 16, 1994, (Plaintiff Boyd Dockstader having been dismissed by stipulation and with prejudice prior to the commencement of the trial) and the defendants in the two consolidated cases (hereinafter referred to collectively as the claimants); Raymond Scott Berry representing the United Effort Plan Trust; and Reed L. Martineau and Rodney R. Parker representing Rulon T. Jeffs, Fred M. Jessop, Leroy S. Jeffs, Parley J. Harker, James K. Zitting, Winston K. Blackmore, and Truman I. Barlow, Trustees of the UEP Trust. The presentation of evidence was concluded on May 26, 1995, and the parties sought, and were given, time to submit memoranda prior to closing argument. The parties submitted their memoranda and the matter came before the Court on November 13, 1995, for closing argument. The Court took the matter under submission and now enters the following memorandum decision and order.

GENERAL FINDINGS OF FACT

This case presents complex issues of fact and law. The Court has heard dozens of witnesses and has received over 100 exhibits. After a thorough review of the evidence the Court finds the following facts have been established.

Plaintiffs and defendants herein generally all contend that in approximately 1886, John Taylor, then President of The Church of Jesus Christ of Latter-day Saints, directed several of his followers to continue the practice of polygamy outside that Church. The movement that resulted has been called The Priesthood Work (hereinafter The Work), and the adherents to that movement have continued the practice of plural marriage within their own religious organization to the present day.

As may be expected, the adherents to The Work claim to have suffered legal prosecution and illegal persecution because of their beliefs over many years. Sometime in the early part of this century the leadership of The Work determined to locate its membership in an isolated area where they could practice their religion without interference from those outside their faith. The Work's leaders taught, and the adherents believed, that the chosen area would become holy ground intended for the use and protection of the faithful. There was even a widely publicized report of a vision received by Joseph Musser in which he was told by God that the unfaithful residents would become discouraged and leave, implying that only the faithful would reside in the community.

At some point, probably in the 1930s, the area now known as Short Creek, composed of Hildale, Utah, and Colorado City, Arizona, was selected for that purpose. Those in charge of The Work set out to obtain land for the development of a city for the adherents to their faith to occupy.

The Work was directed by a group of religious leaders called the Priesthood Council during most of the history relevant to this case. The number of members of that Council varied from time to time. Under the direction of the Council a large tract of land was secured and those faithful to The Work began to migrate to the area to settle.

A common way for The Work to obtain land to occupy was to have its followers and sympathizers buy land and then deed it to The Work. To hold title to the land as it began to accumulate, the leadership of The Work formed a trust which was the predecessor to the current United Effort Plan Trust. The predecessor trust eventually failed and the land was deeded back to those who had contributed it, for the most part. Finally, in 1942, the 5 members of the then existing Priesthood Council signed, and later caused to be recorded in Mohave

County, Arizona, a Declaration of Trust of the United Effort Plan, the trust in question in this law suit (hereinafter UEP).

After the UEP was formed, most of the land held by the predecessor trust was deeded to the UEP. As other land was made available by the adherents to The Work, it was also deeded to the UEP. The UEP currently holds legal title to much of the land around the Short Creek area, including the lands occupied by the claimants in these cases. Taxes on the UEP held land are paid by assessment of the persons occupying the land and other faithful members of The Work, if necessary. Tax money would be solicited as a donation and collected by religious leaders. No penalty was imposed on the land users who could not pay the taxes assessed to them. The shortfall would be made up by The Work, even using other donation money if necessary. The plaintiffs herein participated in this tax arrangement to one degree or another.

In the early days of the UEP, it also owned various cooperative enterprises in the community and engaged in business activities which were formed to serve the adherents of The Work living in the remote area, such as stores, a gas station, dairy, and other operations. In the 1940s many of these enterprises failed and the trust closed its accounts and determined that it would limit its functions to holding title to the land in the area. Such has been the case since the 1940s.

Also in the early days of the UEP there was an effort by the religious leaders to provide food and other necessities to the faithful. In 1953 The Work's policy in that area changed and the adherents were encouraged to be independent and to "begin paddling their own canoes" to quote Fred Jessop. From the beginning of the operation of the UEP, it was apparently the practice of the trustees, who were also the religious leaders of The Work, to invite certain of the adherents to build their homes on the land owned by the UEP. The adherents were aware that they were building on land to which they did not hold title. No deeds were issued and no written agreements were formalized spelling out the terms for the use of the land. The use of the land was conditioned upon religious teachings and beliefs commonly held and widely known in the community.

The Work's leaders often preached that the purpose of the UEP was to advance the group toward the United Order, which was an economic concept taught in the scriptures held sacred by The Work. To accomplish this goal, the UEP was intended to provide a means for all real property of the religious group to be held in common and for its use to be managed by a benevolent and inspired group of God fearing leaders. Accordingly, it was not unusual for those occupying UEP lands or houses to be asked to move so those more needy or more deserving in the eyes of the trustees, or their agents, could take over the premises. Generally such requests were complied with willingly by the adherents to The Work. Some adherents of The Work built homes only to see the UEP move another family into the partially or fully completed structure. These occurrences were common knowledge in the community.

Another purpose of the UEP, as taught by leaders of The Work, was to protect the adherents from legal suits by enemies of The Work. The adherents were told that having a home on UEP land was better than having a deed because it couldn't be foreclosed for the adherent's debt. For the same reason, the adherents were frequently told that they were not free to mortgage or sell the land they occupied and that if they ever determined to leave the land, for any reason, the land and all improvements would belong to the UEP.

The leadership of the Work also taught that the UEP constituted a communal effort to build up the Kingdom of God on Earth by developing a community for the adherents to occupy. As a result, many of the adherents, as part of their religious practice, spent countless hours on volunteer projects for the community, such as setting up water and sewer systems. They often went on work missions in which they would work without compensation for the community, or they would take jobs outside the community and contribute their pay to their religious leaders. It was also common among the adherents of The Work to serve as volunteers doing construction work on the homes of the other adherents. Some were compensated for those efforts, either with money or by trade, but many were not compensated.

Some residents did become discouraged and leave the community, as life there could be hard and lonely, and their improvements became the property of the UEP. Some were invited to leave by the leaders and some of these left voluntarily while others were bought out, "prayed out" or allowed to remain. Until recent times, the trust had not resorted to legal action or force to require occupants of the land to vacate.

Most of the communications to the residents from the UEP, or the Priesthood Council about the UEP, came from the pulpit during the frequent religious services that the adherents attended. In addition, some of the claimants in this suit claim that they had private conversations with representatives of the UEP in which they received additional representations about their right to use the UEP land. These communications will be discussed later in this opinion. All of the claimants have built improvements upon land to which title is held by the UEP.

Although the verbal arrangements for the use of UEP land were usually made with members of the religious leadership, who were also UEP trustees, or their agents such as J. Marion Hammon or Edson Jessop, the evidence clearly indicates that the provisions of the UEP Declaration and the amendments thereto were roundly ignored by everyone in the process.

A copy of the Declaration and amendments is appended hereto and incorporated by this reference as Exhibit A. The Declaration is clear in some particulars and ambiguous in others. Having heard the evidence presented by the parties as to the intention of the subscribers or settlers, the Court is now prepared to assign meaning to the Declaration provisions. (See 76 Am. Jur. 2d, Trusts, Sect 35, p. 62)

The structure of the UEP is somewhat unusual. It has subscribers who created the trust who are also the initial members and the trustees of the trust and some of its potential beneficiaries. In addition there is provision for others to become "members" of the trust (See Article XII) and also for others to become potential beneficiaries (See 1946 Amendment and Article XII, paragraph 3). Under the terms of the declaration the distribution of benefits from the trust is entirely discretionary with the Board of Trustees who are to administer equitable and beneficial interests from the trust according to the "just wants and needs" of the members and beneficiaries and in accord with the trust's ability to respond to those wants and needs. (See Declaration, page 1, 2nd paragraph.)

The Declaration clearly provides that the trust is to take action only through the trustees *acting together* (See Articles II and III) except for the specific duties delegated to the President (See 1946 Amendment). The trustees and their successors were to hold title to all property in the trust estate and to exercise exclusive management over it under the terms of the trust. (See Article V.) The Board of Trustees was to select additional trustees and could increase or diminish the number of trustees. (See Article VII)

In the declaration the trust is specifically designated as a charitable and philanthropic trust to be operated in the spirit of brotherhood, and is empowered to engage in legitimate business enterprises to further its objectives. (See Article VIII.) The declaration designates no specific beneficiaries, but only shifting, potential beneficiaries, whose identity is to be determined in the future, depending upon the discretionary decisions of the trustees. The members of the trust have no entitlement to benefits since the trustees have discretion to distribute benefits to members or non-members alike as the trustees see fit.

The Court finds that the trust is a classic charitable trust established with the intention to serve those in need of help through charitable and philanthropic activities, regardless of whether they are members of the trust or not. Additional members may be added to the UEP by "consecration of such property, real, personal or mixed, to the trust in such amounts as shall be deemed sufficient by the Board of Trustees..." *and members can be expelled* by vote of the Trustees. (See Article XII, last paragraph). The members buy nothing by their contributions to the corpus of the trust, as the members and other potential beneficiaries have no right to claim any benefit unless the trustees declare it (See Articles XIV and XV). Those seeking benefits from the trust do so as suppliants, not as a matter of right. The Trust is to terminate no later than 100 years from 1946 and the corpus, if any, distributed to the then current membership. The UEP was declared a non-profit organization in the 1946 Amendment to the declaration.

The plaintiffs in this case have argued that the trust was actually a common law business trust or a Massachusetts business trust. The Court is persuaded that the trust was intended as a charitable trust, even though there is evidence to the contrary, and even though the trust itself has demonstrated confusion on this point by variously referring to itself as a common law trust and a charitable trust over its history.

Plaintiffs make the following points in support of their view:

1. The Declaration authorizes the trust to engage in business; 2. the members are entitled to equitable and beneficial interests in the profits and property of the trust; 3. the ability of the members is limited, implying some entitlement; 4. there is reference to membership certificates; 5. the trust is to endure "for such time as the business proves to be advantageous"; and 6. the trust states that its creators meant to create a trust, not a partnership.

The Court finds as follows regarding the factual assertions contained in those points:

1. This statement is true. 2. This statement is incorrect. The members' interests in the trust are subject to the discretion of the trustees who are to distribute benefits based on the just wants and needs of the beneficiaries and members (See 2nd paragraph of the first page of the Declaration, Article XIV, and the 1946 Amendment). 3. The first part of the statement is true, the implication stated is not. 4. This is true. 5. The original declaration contains that language but it was amended out in 1946. 6. This statement is true.

The mere mention of matters normally related to a business enterprise is not the determining factor in deciding the nature of the trust. The Court is aware of no legal authority prohibiting a charitable trust from engaging in the activities set out above. The primary focus of the inquiry must be to ascertain the intent of the settlers and to give full effect to that intent, so long as it is not contrary to law or public policy. (See 76 Am. Jur. 2d, Section 35, p. 62)

The Court has found, based on the evidence presented at trial and the clear language of the unambiguous portions of the declaration, that the creators of the trust were motivated by their religious beliefs to create a trust to hold title to the property donated by adherents to their religious faith, including themselves, and to engage in business enterprises for the benefit of the followers of The Work. The property was intended to be used to benefit those that the trustees chose as beneficiaries in the future according to the "just wants and needs" of the beneficiaries at the time benefits were being considered. At the time the trust was created, and at all times thereafter, the identity of the beneficiaries was unknown until the trustees designated beneficiaries. The trustees were free to confer benefits upon trust members and non-members alike and to do so only restricted by consideration of whether the wants and needs of the beneficiary were just in the view of the trustees. In the process the trustees were free to distribute all the holdings of the trust. In the event that they chose to do so, there would be nothing to be divided among the trust members at the time the trust terminated.

Although the declaration provides for the business of the trust to be conducted by the trustees as a group, the evidence shows that the presiding religious officer of The Work was allowed to make the decisions for the trust, often without consulting with the other trustees.

The trust kept few records. Membership lists were not maintained. Certificates of membership where issued rarely and sporadically. The trustees did not meet to create new members or to determine who should become beneficiaries of the trust. The UEP was often referred to in religious discussion but the formalities of the administration of the trust were ignored, as was the actual language of the trust. In fact many within The Work felt it would be an indication of a lack of faith if the declaration of trust were to be obtained and examined.

The claimants all claim to be members of the UEP. The Court finds that the evidence does not support that position. No evidence was introduced by any claimant to show that he was made a member of the UEP by vote of the Board of Trustees after they had determined that a sufficient consecration had been made. The parties generally assumed that they were members of the UEP *automatically* because they were adherents to The Work, or because they were allowed to live on UEP land, or because someone told them they were a member, or for some other reason. No action by the Board of Trustees was demonstrated granting membership to any of the claimants in this case. The Court finds that none of the claimants are members of the UEP. However, that does not mean that they are not beneficiaries of the UEP since all are receiving the benefit of being allowed to use and occupy UEP land. The terms "member" and "beneficiary" are not interchangeable in the UEP Declaration. Each claimant has constructed substantial improvements on UEP land since being allowed to enter into possession and use of the property.

In approximately the late 1960s or early 1970s there arose some dissention among the adherents to The Work. The priesthood council then in place was apparently split by a doctrinal question. The situation festered until the death of President Leroy S. Johnson. At that time the dispute surfaced and in approximately 1984 the adherents to The Work split into two camps. One, under the direction of President Rulon T. Jeffs, holds control of the UEP and has since formalized and organized the Fundamentalist Church of Jesus Christ of Latter-Day Saints (hereinafter referred to as the First Ward). The other, initially under the direction of J. Marion Hammon and Alma Timpson, is the camp to which the claimants belong, for the most part, although some claimants now assert no affiliation with either group. (Hereinafter referred to as the Second Ward.)

Pres. Jeffs has appointed trustees for the UEP who are not members of the Priesthood Council. He has declared all those occupying UEP lands to be tenants at will. He has declared the claimants herein are apostates and has disassociated them from the religious organization which he heads. The Second Ward claims they are the true adherents to The Work. The Court has repeatedly held that it has no jurisdiction to resolve such a dispute.

In 1987 the claimants herein brought suit in the Federal Court to determine the rights, if any, that they may have in the UEP land which they have occupied. This action was commenced after the claimants received notification that they were considered to be tenants at will by the UEP. In 1989 suit was also filed in Washington County, Utah raising many of the same issues. The State case was stayed pending the resolution of the Federal case. Eventually the Federal case was dismissed for lack of subject matter jurisdiction. The stay on the State action was then lifted and this matter has proceeded in this forum. During the pendency of this original case, the UEP brought suits against the defendants Stubbs and Harker seeking relief under the unlawful detainer statutes of the State.

Legal Analysis

For trial, the Court ordered bifurcation of the issues in the consolidated cases. The issues tried to date are those raised in the first six claims for relief in the Amended Complaint filed February 16, 1994, by 22 plaintiffs. By the time of trial Boyd Dockstader had been dismissed with prejudice as a plaintiff, leaving 21 with claims pending.

The six causes of action tried are 1. Breach of Contract; 2. Implied Contract; 3. Negligent Misrepresentation; 4. Constructive Fraud; 5. Estoppel; and 6. Unjust Enrichment/Occupying Claimants.

The elements of these claims are as follows:

Express Contract

To establish the existence of an enforceable express contract, there must be proven, by a preponderance of the evidence, an offer with present contractual intent or mutual assent, and acceptance of that offer by the other party, supported by consideration. In this case the claimants assert, among other things, that they were promised an interest in real property belonging to the UEP, which raises issues of the Statute of Frauds. The law is clear in Utah that part performance of an oral agreement will satisfy the Statute of Frauds, but only if the existence of an oral contract and its terms are clear and definite, the acts done in performance are clear and definite and those acts are in reliance upon and strictly referable to the contract and not readily explainable on any other ground. [See Martin v. Scholl, 678 P.2d 274 (1983)]

358

Implied Contract

An implied contract is based upon the same elements as an express oral contract, except that the contract and its terms are inferred from conduct, rather that expressed in words. The burden of proof is the same.

Negligent Misrepresentation

The elements of this cause of action have varying formulations which seem to contain the same legal principles. One such is, a "party injured by reasonable reliance upon a second party's careless or negligent misrepresentation of a material fact may recover damages resulting from that injury when the second party had a pecuniary interest in the transaction, was in a superior position to know the material facts, and should have reasonably foreseen that the injured party was likely to rely upon the fact". [See Price-Orem Investment Company v. Rollins, et. al., 713 P.2d 55 (1986) and Maack v. Resource Design & Const-Inc., 875 P.2d 570 (1994).]

Another definition, cited by the plaintiffs herein, is, "one who, in the course of his business, profession or employment, or in any other transaction in which he has a pecuniary interest, supplies false information for the guidance of others in their business transactions, is subject to liability for pecuniary loss caused to them by the justifiable reliance upon the information, if he fails to exercise reasonable care or competence in obtaining or communicating the information". [See Atkinson v. IHC Hospitals, Inc..798 P.2d 733 (1990)]

The elements of this claim must be proven by clear and convincing evidence. [See Pace v. Parrish, 247 P.2d 273 (1952); and Jardine v. Brunswick Corp., 423 P.2d 659 (1967)].

Constructive Fraud

A claim for constructive fraud arises out of a confidential relationship between the parties such that one party, having gained the trust and confidence of the other, exercises extraordinary influence over the other and in so doing fails to make full and truthful disclosure of all material facts in connection with any transaction in which the other party could be expected to rely upon the information provided with resulting injury to the other party from the transaction.

The existence of a confidential relationship must be proven by clear and convincing evidence. [See Bradbury v. Rasmussen,. 401 P.2d 710, 715 (1965)]

Estoppel

"Elements essential to invoke the doctrine of equitable estoppel are: (1) an admission, statement, or act inconsistent with the claim afterwards asserted, (2) action by the other party on the faith of such admission, statement, or act, and, (3) injury to such other party resulting from allowing the first party to contradict or repudiate such admission, statement, or act." [See Celebrity Club, Inc. v. Utah Liquor Control, 602 P.2d 689 (1979)] Estoppel can also arise from silence when one ought to speak and in failing to do so induces another to believe certain facts exist. [See Leaver v. Grose, 610 P.2d 1262 (1980).] The burden of proof is preponderance of the evidence.

Unjust Enrichment/Occupying Claimant

Unjust enrichment has the following elements: (1) enrichment of one party; (2) an appreciation or knowledge of the benefit by the enriched party and (3) the acceptance or retention by the enriched party of the benefit under such circumstances as to make it inequitable for the enriched party to retain the benefit without payment of its value. [See Berrett v. Stevens, 690 P.2d 553 (1984)] The burden of proof is preponderance of the evidence.

The parties apparently agree that the law in the State of Arizona is in agreement with that in the State of Utah as to those claims discussed above. They likewise agree that Arizona has no counterpart for the Utah Statute on occupying claimants, 57-6-1 et. seq., UCA. Therefore the claims under the occupying claimant statute would apply only to those claimants occupying land in the State of Utah.

APPLICATION OF LAW TO VARIOUS PLAINTIFFS

The Court will decide the issues presented as to each plaintiff in the order in which the plaintiffs appear in the Amended Complaint.

Since the Judge's ruling on the other Plaintiffs' claims were almost the same as the rulings on Mr. Bradshaw, the remainder of his original ruling will not be included here.

Cyril Bradshaw

Mr. Bradshaw became associated with The Work in 1953. He was highly educated, holding a Ph.D, and had experience in real estate matters. At time of trial he testified that he is also a master electrician. Bradshaw moved to Short Creek in 1960. He was invited to move to the area from Northern Utah after becoming affiliated with The Work. He agreed to do so. He had a home in Northern Utah which he donated to The Work prior to moving to Short Creek. He was to be the teacher at the Colorado City Academy, a high school level institution which operated in Colorado City for 20 plus years under his direction.

Bradshaw had seen the Declaration for the UEP in the 1950s but claims he did not actually read it until about 1984. He knew it was recorded and could be obtained but he did not take action to read the Declaration because it just didn't seem important. He claims that he was told by J. Marion Hammon when he moved to the area that he was a member of the UEP. He presented no evidence that the trustees had taken the action required under the provisions of the Declaration to make him a member.

Bradshaw was assigned the use of a small house while he taught school at extremely low wages for about the first 8 years. Finally J. Marion Hammon assigned him a UEP lot upon which to build a home. Bradshaw could not remember the exact words used in the conversation but did recall the use of the word "forever."

He knew that he could not mortgage, sell or leave the lot. He knew he had no ownership of the lot. He had been told from the beginning that the UEP was to be operated for charitable and benevolent purposes. He assumed that his use of the lot was secure because of his membership in the UEP. He freely admitted that he moved to Short Creek out of religious motivation.

After he was assigned a lot to use, Bradshaw spent money and labor constructing a large home where he raised his family. He was assisted in constructing the home by others in the community who worked on his home and contributed materials. Many of these helpers were uncompensated volunteers associated with The Work and the UEP. He was never told that his right to use the UEP lot could be terminated by the trustees and he never asked about his status. He did pay tax assessments made by Truman Barlow to help pay for the property taxes levied against UEP lands by the counties.

On cross examination Bradshaw testified that he has a selective memory that allows him to remember facts without remembering where he learned them. He has difficulty remembering dates and some details. He admitted that he joined with The Work after undergoing a "personal conversion." He began attending religious meetings in Salt Lake where he heard requests for help in Colorado City. Even before he moved to Short Creek he often came down on weekends to help build up the community and donated money for the projects underway there.

Bradshaw admitted that he often heard J. Marion Hammon speak in religious meetings about the UEP but he ignored the speeches because he "already had that tapestry woven."

Breach of Contract Claims

Bradshaw is one of the ten plaintiffs who have asserted contract claims. He alleges that conversations between him and J. Marion Hammon in 1960, when he moved to Colorado City, and again in 1969, when he was assigned the use of a lot to build on, constituted an offer that he could build on a lot owned by the UEP and use it "forever." He claims that he accepted that offer and that his construction of a home on that lot constitutes part performance sufficient to remove the oral agreement from the operation of the Statute of Frauds. The burden of evidence is, of course, upon the claimant to establish his claims by the applicable evidentiary standard.

The Court finds that Bradshaw has failed to demonstrate the existence of an express oral contract, even taking his testimony at face value. The Court is concerned about the deficiencies in Mr. Bradshaw's memory and cannot accord his unsupported assertions full credibility. Setting aside those concerns, however, the Court finds that the alleged conversations with the now deceased J. Marion Hammon fail to prove that the UEP was offering Bradshaw perpetual and everlasting use of the lot upon which he was allowed to build his house. In fact Bradshaw remembers very little of the conversation. To establish an oral contract, one must present definite evidence of its terms and existence. No such evidence was contained in the testimony of Bradshaw. In fact, his testimony establishes, beyond question, that he went to Short Creek, taught school, engaged in various commendable religious works and activities, taught school for a very low wage and built a house on a UEP lot because of the depth of his religious convictions, not because he had been promised life long, or perpetual, use of the property.

In addition, the construction of the home on UEP land does not avoid the application of the Statute of Frauds, as the alleged part performance is not exclusively attributable and referable to the oral contract, even if one had been established. An equally plausible reason for the construction of the house was Mr. Bradshaw's admitted motivation to build up the Kingdom of God in Short Creek, as everyone else in the area was doing.

Likewise, and for the same reasons, the Court finds that the implied contract claim of Mr. Bradshaw has not been proven. Nothing in the actions of the parties demonstrates a tacit agreement that the plaintiff would have anything other than the temporary use of the UEP lot until the Trustees determined that the benefit would be withdrawn. A contract does not arise from the unsubstantiated assumptions of one of the parties.

In the Amended Complaint, under the First Claim for Relief, the ten listed plaintiffs allege other contract claims. They first assert that they became members or beneficiaries of the UEP by contributing valuable property to the UEP as required by the Board of Trustees. As stated above under the General Finding of Fact, the evidence does not support that assertion. There was no proof that any of the plaintiffs was ever approved as a member of the trust by action of the Board of Trustees or that the trustees ever determined that any contributions made by the plaintiffs were sufficient for membership. None of the plaintiffs can claim a contract based on membership in the trust. Since plaintiffs were never members of the UEP they cannot claim that they entered into the agreements listed in paragraph 16 (a), (b), and (c) of the Amended Complaint.

The plaintiffs also claim that they were beneficiaries of the UEP and they entered into contracts with the trust based on that status. The Court finds that the evidence does not support that claim as to any of the plaintiffs, as will be discussed hereafter.

The Court finds that the contract claims of Plaintiff Cyril Bradshaw have not been proven by a preponderance of the evidence.

Negligent Misrepresentation

Mr. Bradshaw is also one of the plaintiffs named in the Third Claim For Relief of the Amended Complaint. In that claim it is asserted that in connection with contributions made by the plaintiffs to the UEP, agents of the UEP made certain oral representations of material fact, specifically:

1. that the principal purpose of the UEP was to provide security for its beneficiaries by protecting their property and enterprises from loss for any reason, including bankruptcy, foreclosure or legal actions by enemies from without the movement,

2. that each plaintiff would be a co-owner of the enterprises of the community and would thus share in the prosperity of those enterprises,

3. that each plaintiff would be secure in his home on his assigned building lot and could only lose that home if he chose to abandon it,

4. that the UEP would provide long-term security to the beneficiaries and would provide for them according to their needs.

None of the plaintiffs has presented evidence sufficient to prove this claim. The Court has found that one of the purposes of the UEP, as taught by the trustees in their religious gatherings, was to protect those on UEP land from losing the land to enemies of The Work. No such loss has been proven by any plaintiff.

On the other hand, the evidence does not support the allegation that anyone promised any one of the plaintiffs that he would be a part owner of any enterprise or share in any profits from the trust. No plaintiff claimed that and the vast weight of the evidence is contrary to that assertion.

In fact Mr. Bradshaw did not even think the UEP important until some 24 years after he moved to Short Creek and until the religious dispute had arisen and he realized he was among those no longer in control of the UEP. He never read the Declaration of the UEP, even though he knew it existed. He ignored speeches about it. He assumed that the UEP owned certain business enterprises in the community, but had no authoritative evidence of that. He never made any contributions to the UEP but did to his religion and its leaders. His testimony simply does not support this claim.

The evidence does not support the claim that the plaintiffs were told that they would be secure in their homes and could only lose them by abandoning them. No such representation was made to any plaintiff. Mr. Bradshaw recalled no such representation as his only recollection was that J. Marion Hammon used the word "forever" when he assigned the use of the UEP lot, but Bradshaw could not remember what else was said. The Utah Supreme Court has not included due diligence as an element of this cause of action but has required the analogous element of reasonable reliance. [See Maack v. Resource Design & Construction, Inc., 875 P.2d 239 (1994).] The plaintiffs herein, including Mr. Bradshaw, could not have reasonably relied on the off hand, and abbreviated comments to which they point to create a right of ownership or perpetual use in view of all they knew about the operations of the UEP. The evidence does not support this claim.

Likewise the evidence presented does not support the claim that any plaintiff was told that he would be provided long-term security by the UEP according to his needs. Mr. Bradshaw testified that he was promised, as part of his employment as a school teacher, a place to live, a low wage, and medical care, all of which he received. There was no persuasive evidence of any representation that his long-term security would be met by the UEP.

In paragraph 31 of the Amended Complaint, Bradshaw claims that the UEP omitted to disclose material facts to avoid misleading him.

(a) Mr. Bradshaw was well aware that the UEP was governed by a Declaration recorded on the public records and had been prior to his association with The Work. He chose not to read it, even knowing that it might relate to his right, or privilege, of occupying a UEP lot. If he was mislead by lack of the information in the Declaration, he was as much at fault as the UEP.

(b) Mr. Bradshaw was not specifically told that he would be a tenant at will on the UEP lot until he had already constructed improvements on the lot, nor did he ask. He was apparently satisfied that his "just wants and needs" would be met by his religious leaders and chose not to ask about the terms of his use of the land provided by the UEP. One who seeks relief because of injury from misrepresentations of another cannot simply believe whatever is said. Such a person has a duty to exercise the degree of care to protect his own interests as would be exercised by any reasonable and prudent person under like circumstances. [See Jardine v. Brunswick, 423 P.2d 659, 662 (Utah1967)]. To rely on one word in a conversation in a matter of this import is not reasonable.

(c) The Court is persuaded that Mr. Bradshaw and the other plaintiffs herein were aware, because of the purpose and nature of the movement they were with, that the Short Creek area was being developed as a refuge for the faithful adherents to The Work. Each plaintiff was invited to help build up the community and to practice his own religious beliefs there because he was in harmony with others living there.

If Mr. Bradshaw had read the Declaration which he knew was recorded in Mojave County, he would have learned that even if he was a member of the UEP, he could be expelled and lose all claim on the trust by a majority vote of the trustees for actions prejudicial to the trust, and that as a non-member beneficiary, he could be deprived of benefits conferred by the Trust in the event that the Trustees deemed it unwise to confer the benefit. Mr. Bradshaw cannot now claim misrepresentation because he didn't understand that if he fell out of

364

harmony with the trustees of the trust his right to use trust land could be terminated. Such knowledge was widely available in the community to anyone who inquired.

(d) Mr. Bradshaw never testified that he made contributions to the UEP or its enterprises to gain an interest therein, nor did the other plaintiffs. The inference from their statements was that they considered their contributions to be religious donations to The Work, although the UEP may have benefitted.

Mr. Bradshaw's motivation for his labor and money was to comply with the requests of his religious leaders, regardless of the ownership of the project. He never claimed in his testimony that he was mislead by the failure of the UEP to tell him that the trust did not own the projects he worked on. It simply was not a matter of concern to him when the contributions were made as they were religious contributions.

(e) The accountability of the trustees to the beneficiaries is spelled out in the Declaration of which Bradshaw was aware. In addition, no evidence at all was presented on this point during the trial by any plaintiff. No one testified that he or she was mislead by the lack of this information.

The Amended Complaint seems to state that the plaintiffs are seeking reimbursement for all the contributions ever made to the UEP. If so, the evidence is completely lacking in this particular. The evidence presented on contributions was not sufficient to allow the court to determine the contributions made to the UEP, as opposed to The Work. No accounting was presented by any plaintiff. There was no persuasive evidence of any amount of damage claimed.

Nothing in the evidence presented demonstrated that Bradshaw made contributions to the UEP, with the possible exception of the house he built. He stated no claim for damages other than for the house. The Court finds that he has failed to prove his claim for reimbursement for other contributions to the UEP. Likewise, the Court finds that Mr. Bradshaw was not mislead by the representations made, or the omissions claimed. He knew that he could obtain all the information available to J. Marion Hammon by asking, or by reading the UEP Declaration. He was not in an inferior position to the trust in regard to the extent of his right to use UEP land. In addition, it was not reasonable for an educated man, experienced in real estate transactions, to assume, without investigation or inquiry, that he could build a home on the land of a trust and expect to keep the land "forever" without specific agreement as to that term.

For the reasons stated, Mr. Bradshaw's claim for negligent misrepresentation fails.

Constructive Fraud

Each plaintiff alleges that he was in a confidential and fiduciary relationship with the trustees of UEP because they were the trustees of the trust and also his religious leaders. He then alleges that the trustees had a duty to make full and truthful disclosure of all material facts and to act in his interest. He claims the trustees or the trust breached the duty by failing to disclose the following material facts.

1. That the trust was governed by a recorded Declaration limiting the plaintiffs' right of use of UEP land. Mr. Bradshaw's testimony, and the other evidence in the case, does not support this claim. He testified that he knew of the existence of the Declaration and that it was recorded long before he began constructing improvements on UEP land.

2. That Mr. Bradshaw would be a tenant at will on UEP land and could be removed at the will and pleasure of the trustees. It is true that Mr. Bradshaw testified that no direct communication of this fact was made to him before the tenant at will letter in 1984. However, Mr. Bradshaw was an educated man with prior experience in real estate matters, which should have made him curious about the rights of one who builds on another's property without an agreement as to the term of the tenancy. Mr. Bradshaw did not even inquire as to the terms when he was assigned a lot nor did he seek out the Declaration to clarify the situation before beginning construction. The evidence does not demonstrate that Mr. Bradshaw's will and intelligence were overcome because of his relationship with the trustees. In fact Mr. Bradshaw testified that he turned down lots which J. Marion Hammon offered him and held out until he got one.

The Amended Complaint is not clear as to who breached the duty to make full disclosure as it actually alleges that it was the plaintiffs who breached the duty of full disclosure. (See paragraph 41 of the Amended Complaint.) The Court is convinced that the reason Mr. Bradshaw built his home on UEP land was because he wanted to continue in his association with The Work. He understood fully the operations of the UEP, having discussed it with one of the subscribers to the trust before ever associating himself with The Work. He never conceived that he might find himself at odds with the UEP or some of his religious leaders and he now seeks to blame them for his own lack of foresight and judgment.

A confidential relationship is the basic prerequisite for a claim of constructive fraud. The mere fact that the trustees of the trust and the plaintiffs were members of the same religious organization does not automatically create such a relationship. [See Thatcher v. Peterson, 437 P.2d 213, 214 (1968)]. Mr. Bradshaw made his own choices based on his own desire to be a fully participating member of The Work. He cannot now blame the trust or its trustees for allowing him the privilege it offered to many of its adherents, the use of UEP land for whatever term the trustees felt wise. Equitable Estoppel

Mr. Bradshaw alleges that UEP should be estopped from removing him from UEP land because the UEP had taken the position that he had an interest in the corpus of the trust. The Court has already found that the evidence does not support either the claim that the plaintiffs were members of the UEP or the claim that membership created any right to the corpus of the trust.

He also claims that the UEP had taken the position that those occupying UEP land had the right to do so in perpetuity. The Court finds that the weight of the evidence is to the contrary. Mr. Bradshaw may have taken the position that he ascribes to the trust but no evidence was presented that the trust ever agreed to allow anyone to occupy property held by the UEP in perpetuity. The best Mr. Bradshaw could come up with was the word "forever" and he could not even place that word in context. To the contrary was the vast body of evidence presented by others who live in the Short Creek community and who knew the leaders and practices of the UEP well, as well as evidence from those leaders. That evidence clearly showed that the UEP often moved people around on UEP property, asking some to move in favor of others. Some were even asked to leave the community. Some built houses, only to see others move into them. Many testified that it would have been contrary to the very purpose of the UEP to allow permanent use of a lot. J. Marion Hammon himself, by deposition testimony, denied that he ever told anyone they could use a UEP lot forever. The evidence preponderates in favor of a finding that the UEP did not promise permanent use of lands it controlled to individuals using the land. The Declaration of Trust provided that the UEP could extend benefits, or not, as its trustees thought wise. The weight of the evidence was inconsistent with the claims of plaintiffs.

Mr. Bradshaw never testified that the UEP made representations to him about long-term security, funeral insurance, retirement, and so forth. The evidence does not support that claim as to this plaintiff or any other.

For the reason that the plaintiff has failed to prove that the UEP made statements, or took actions, or did acts inconsistent with statements, actions, or acts later taken, the estoppel claim fails as to Mr. Bradshaw.

Unjust Enrichment/Occupying Claimants
Mr. Bradshaw testified that he resides in Arizona and thus would have no protection under Utah's Occupying Claimant Statute. He does assert a claim under the theory of unjust enrichment, however. There can be no doubt from the evidence presented that Mr. Bradshaw has conferred a benefit on the UEP by improving the lot he was allowed to use by the installation of a home worth far more than the land. There can also be no doubt that the trust was aware of the benefit as its representatives encouraged the construction and the improvement of the lot by the occupant and watched the building going in. The issue is whether, given the facts in this case, it would be inequitable to allow the UEP to retain the benefit without compensation to Mr. Bradshaw. The Court is of the opinion that such a result would be inequitable.

At the time Mr. Bradshaw was assigned a lot, he was encouraged, as were many other plaintiffs, to improve the lot and to build on it. The Court is convinced that neither the trust and its representatives nor Mr. Bradshaw ever thought about what would happen to the improvements if Mr. Bradshaw became estranged from the UEP, or The Work, but wanted to remain on the property. The prevailing thought within the community at that time was that God would take care of the disaffected by causing them to become discouraged and to leave. Mr. Bradshaw claims he built his home with the intention that he would occupy it "forever," even though the Court has found that he has failed to prove that the UEP agreed to that term. As a practical matter "forever" would necessarily be limited to his lifetime, as there was no indication, even in his version of the facts, that the use of the lot would pass to his heirs upon his death. Nonetheless, he expected to use the property into his foreseeable future. As a result he has invested lots of money and time in the improvement of the property and now, because of a religious disagreement, he faces the possibility of losing the occupancy of the home he has built. Should the UEP chose to remove him from the property he now occupies, the UEP would acquire a large home suitable for housing another of its adherents at little or no cost. The UEP must bear a large share of the blame for the confusion as to the terms of occupancy since it did not communicate to Mr. Bradshaw directly the conditions of his occupancy of the lot, even though the trust was engaged in a long term and wide spread program of settling its people on UEP lands. It would have been easy to prepare a list of the conditions of occupancy and to distribute the list to those preparing to invest heavily in improvements with the encouragement and agreement of the trust.

The Court finds that the circumstances here present would make it inequitable for Mr. Bradshaw to be forced from the home he occupies, during his lifetime, without any compensation from the UEP for the improvement of the lot he is using. The Court finds that the UEP owns the land and the improvements thereon but imposes a constructive trust thereon in favor of Mr. Bradshaw during his lifetime. In the event that the UEP discontinues benefits to Mr. Bradshaw and discontinues his use of the property prior to his demise, he is entitled to compensation for the then current value of the improvements conferred upon the UEP, minus any contribution to the value of the improvements made by the UEP in the first place, including, but not limited to, aid in the construction or contribution of materials, if any. If Mr. Bradshaw is allowed the use of the home he constructed until his death, the improvements will then belong to the UEP without the necessity of payment therefore. Mr. Bradshaw's right of occupancy is also subject to loss without reimbursement for improvements if he tries to sell or mortgage the property or the improvements, or if he abandons the use of the lot, as those limitations were known to Mr. Bradshaw at the time he built the improvements. Mr. Bradshaw and his co-occupants, if any, shall be liable to the UEP for waste committed upon the property, beyond normal wear and tear, during this occupancy.

Declaratory judgment will be entered to that effect.

The Judge told the attorneys for the Plaintiffs to write the Order and he and the attorneys for the Defendants (the UEP) would sign it. After the Order was written, however, the attorneys for the Defendants refused to sign. There would be two more hearings to clear up the questions of the attorneys, held on June 10, 1996, and on August 13, 1996. The results of these hearings will be written later. Some events of the community and the society will be entered first.

One development that had taken place in the first part of 1994 was that the Town of Colorado City bought out Garkane Power Company's power system within the community and began operating the system as a municipal utility. This resulted in the power rates going from about 5.5 cents a kilowatt hour to over 9 cents per kilowatt hour and the service was poor. The majority of the people in the community voted for this changeover, with very few objecting. It was impossible to get an intelligent message to them because Erwin Fischer went around to the homes and told them that before Uncle Roy had died, he told Erwin to change the power company over to a municipal system if he could because it would make the community more self sufficient. Erwin's plan was to pipe natural gas into the community to run a power plant, selling the surplus power to the outside communities, thus being able to sell power to the "saints" at a cheaper rate than what Garkane was now selling it for. The glitches that have accompanied this plan are now legend and the people are the real losers, paying much higher rates for their power, while Erwin (in 1994) was running a diesel generator, selling electricity to the city power company.

In January of 1996 the town of Colorado City began construction of a natural gas pipe line from Hurricane, about 20 miles away. They also began construction of a power line back to Hurricane about the same time. The plan was to install an electrical power generating plant fueled by natural gas. They would then transport power they did not use back to St. George where they offered to sell for less than Utah Power and Light was selling to St. George City. Mountain Fuel, the utility company from which the gas was to be purchased, offered to construct the gas line to the power plant and also service the community with natural gas.

This would have been very advantageous for the citizens of the community because their energy costs would have been reduced considerably. Colorado City Town refused their offer. Since Mountain Fuel has the franchise in the area, Colorado City cannot service the homes in the community for about a three year time period. Since they are a municipality they can set power rate prices, both electrical and gas, at whatever price they choose. Mountain Fuel on the other hand is subject to the Public Utilities Commission for the setting of their rates. There is no question that when the gas is piped to the homes the price to the consumer will be much greater than had Mountain Fuel been allowed to service the community. Since Colorado City bought the power lines from Garkane Power, the electrical rates in the community have raised about 80 percent. The only explanation from city officials as to why they choose to take over the power companies is that "it will supply some members of the community with employment."

On May 20, 1996, "Aunt" Lydia Jessop, wife of Fred Jessop, died after a short battle with cancer. While Fred Jessop, in the opinion of the author, symbolizes all that is bad in the community, his wife Lydia can be said to have symbolized all that was good. She was the epitome of courage and never will she receive the praise that is her due.

Lydia Jessop was born in Fredonia, Arizona, on February 29 (leap year), 1920, to Warren Elmer and Viola Spencer Johnson. She came to Short Creek in 1931 at the age of 11 years. She married Fred Jessop in about 1935, his first wife. Due to a childhood disease, Fred Jessop was sterile and "Aunt" Lydia never had any children of her own but she made up for this misfortune by becoming a midwife at a very early age and delivered literally thousands of babies for other mothers. Her children were everyone else's children and she was much loved by them all. She was also the "doctor" of the community for many years, setting broken bones, sewing up cuts and nursing the sick through fever and other sicknesses. Her heart was free from the enmity and bitterness that has been displayed by her husband and his Barlow nephews. If any person in the polygamist society deserves sainthood, it is surely "Aunt Lydia."

One of the events of the summer of 1996 was that Rulon Jeffs publicly announced in church that he had made a mistake when he gave his "Godhead Sermon" in the late eighties, wherein he had denounced the "Adam God Theory" and he was recanting it, now being in support of that doctrine. About the same time Truman Barlow made a public apology to the people because he had gone to Rulon Jeffs and asked to be given the apostleship. Rulon had refused to give him such and only scolded him for asking, telling him that no man ever asks for such a calling.

The June 10th hearing before Judge Eves was brought about because Claude Cooke had moved to a new house he had built outside of the community and was allowing his daughter, along with some other people, to live in his house on UEP property. Sam Barlow set up a "spy ring" to keep a 24 hour watch on the house, taking pictures and monitoring, with binoculars, every move of those living there. An account of the happenings at Claude's house was filed with the court. This account was greatly exaggerated, making claims that Claude was allowing people to desecrate the UEP property by their immoral conduct in the house. The

Defendants at this time asked the Judge to declare that Claude had abandoned the home and the UEP could take possession of the premises.

They also filed two other motions; a Motion to Dismiss the 6th Claim for Relief (hereinafter referred to as the Motion to Dismiss) and a Motion to Alter or Amend Memorandum Decision and Final Judgment to Address Omitted Issues Pursuant to Rule 60 U.R.C.P. (hereinafter referred to as the Motion to Alter). The Motion to Dismiss was asking the Judge to change his decision on the unjust enrichment claim, wherein the Plaintiffs could remain in their homes, claiming that this was an infringement on their rights of religious freedom. The Motion to Alter was asking the Judge to set some rules in regards to the paying of taxes.

After this hearing and the hearing of August 1996, the judge offered his Memorandum Opinion on September 5, 1996. This Memorandum will not be quoted fully because the Order following this Memorandum will be copied and most of the ground will be covered in that document. There are some interesting "facts" brought out in the Memorandum however and some of these will be entered here.

The following is Judge Eves' Writing:
During the trial and in related pleadings and motions in this matter, the Defendants raised and argued issues as to the applicability to this case of the Religious Freedom Restoration Act of 1993. The court held in its Memorandum Opinion that the act was not applicable to the issues in this case, but probably did not accord to the issue as full a discussion as the Defendants wished. By this Motion the Defendants apparently seek clarification and amplification of the court's views on the applicability of this provision of Federal law. They argue again that the court should dismiss the unjust enrichment claims of the plaintiffs and allege that the relief sought, and now the relief awarded by the court, constitutes an impermissible "substantial burden" on the Defendants' free exercise of their religion and is without a compelling state interest and is not the least restrictive means available for furthering any existing governmental interest. The Defendants' Motion is, of course, opposed by the plaintiffs.

The court is of the view that its decision in this case does not substantially burden any person's free exercise of religion, that even if there is some burden it is incidental and is justified by a compelling state interest and that the approach taken by the court is the least restrictive means available to further that interest.

Both parties cite the same case for the definition of what constitutes a "substantial burden" within the meaning of the Act. In Sasnett v. Sullivan, it was determined that to be a substantial burden, the government action must: significantly inhibit or constrain conduct or expression that manifests some central tenet of a (person's) individual (religious) beliefs; must meaningfully curtail a (person's) ability to express adherence to his or her faith; or must deny a (person) reasonable opportunities to engage in those activities that are fundamental to a (person's) religion.

Defendants take the position that the court's decision granting equitable relief on the grounds of a claim of Unjust enrichment is violative of this definition. The Defendants struggle in specifying, however, and the court fails to see, just how the court has burdened the free exercise of religion within the above stated definition of those terms. Nothing that the court has done in fashioning an equitable remedy to resolve the dispute between the United Effort Plan Trust and those who occupy its lands infringes in any way upon the religious practices, beliefs, activities or expressions of adherence of members of any religious group.

The Defendants seem to argue that their right to practice a religious principle called the United Order is impaired by the fact that those who are not members of their faith are occupying land which belongs to a trust administered by leaders of their church. The Defendants have presented no evidence in these proceedings to demonstrate that assertion. The evidence does indicate that the United Order is a goal of the Defendants' church but that it is not being lived presently nor was it being lived when the plaintiffs were allowed by the trust to occupy UEP land and build improvements thereon. The evidence also was that the trustees have and do allow non members to continue to reside on UEP land independent of the court's decision. No evidence was presented as to what constitutes the United Order and how the practice of that principle would be impacted adversely by the presence of non-believers in the community. The fact that the adherents of a religion may wish to live among others who believe similarly does not mean that they have the right to remove non-believers from their midst nor does the evidence in this case indicate that the Defendants' church so teaches. In fact, the evidence is that the Defendants' church has taught that those who move onto UEP land and then become estranged to The Work will become discouraged and leave by themselves, without the need of removal by the faithful. Therefore the court fails to see that a part of the United Order principle had been burdened by the remedy fashioned by the court.

The Defendants also assert that their religious practice is somehow infringed by the fact that non-members of the Fundamentalist Church of Jesus Christ of Latter Day Saints are living on UEP land by order of the court rather than under the direction of the trust. It is important to note that the court did not place the non-believers in possession of the United Effort Plan's land. The trust, or its representatives, decided who could live on the land and under what circumstances. Unfortunately, the trust did not make clear to the occupants of the property that their right to stay on the property was limited by various factors, including faithfulness to the same religious beliefs as the UEP's trustees espouse. The occupants have now constructed improvements on the property at considerable expense which would be forfeit if the occupants were required to simply vacate the UEP's land.

The issues presented to the court, and which both sides asked the court to decide, raised questions as to the relative rights of the UEP and those occupying UEP property in view of the situation they had jointly created. The court sought in its decision to define and clarify the rights of all parties under concepts of equity and to allow the UEP and the occupants of its land to continue to co-exit without further contention or hostility. In doing so the court sought to apply non-religious, neutral principles of law. The court specifically avoided making decisions about the religious practices of the parties or their religious differences.

This court fails to see how the application of neutral legal and equitable principles to resolve an important civil dispute involving significant property rights and issues has created any burden, let alone a substantial burden, on any person's free exercise of religion. The adherents to the UEP's views are still free to practice their religion in full. The court's decision simply means that if the trustees of the UEP wish to remove those living on UEP land, for what ever reason, they will have to compensate them for the value of the improvements acquired by the UEP in the process. That may mean that the UEP will incur additional expense to remove these occupants but that does not create a substantial burden on anyone's free exercise of religion. Of course, if the UEP does not desire to pay for the improvements installed on its land by those the UEP allowed to occupy UEP land, they, the UEP, need only wait until the occupant abandons the improvements or dies and the land and the improvements revert to the UEP without compensation to the occupant or the estate or the survivors of the occupant.

It appears that the UEP is really arguing that anything the court does that interferes with its desire to conduct its affairs as it sees fit is a violation of the Act. The court sees the purpose of the act differently. The act does not prohibit government regulation of religious organizations. In fact, it contemplates that there will be general laws which apply to the activities of such organizations. The act simply prohibits regulation that interferes in a substantial way with the ability of a person to practice his or her religious beliefs, unless a compelling interest of the state is demonstrated and the state is properly restricted in the application of its laws to that person.

The court has held herein that there is no burden on free exercise of religion in this case but assuming for argument's sake that there is a substantial burden, the court is also of the opinion that any such burden is clearly justified by a compelling state interest in resolving issues relation to real property rights. Our constitutions, state and federal, secure to all citizens certain rights which are considered basic. Among those are the right to due process of law before being deprived of property and equal protection of the law. The plaintiffs in this case are entitled to those protections in this case where the opposing party is a legal entity set up to further religious goals just as they would be if the opposing party were any non-religious entity. The issues decided here involve basic property rights and are typical of disputes routinely heard and decided by courts across the country. The state has the obvious and compelling interest of providing a forum and a mechanism for the resolution of disputes about such matters, regardless of the involvement of a religious organization. The property laws of the state must apply to religious organizations as well as to non-religious litigants. If the laws were to be applied otherwise churches could not acquire title to property, or convey title to others, or protect their lands and rights. Clearly the state has an interest in assuring that all of its citizens, religious and otherwise, enjoy protection for the basic rights afforded by citizenship in this country and any of the states.

Although Mr. Berry has decried the use of examples to clarify this argument, the court finds them instructive on occasion. For example, suppose the religious organization in question believed in the practice of ritualistic human sacrifice and sought to subject members or non members to murder during such worship services. There can be little doubt that the state would be able to interfere with such practices and declare them illegal and to punish those participating in such activities. The right to life, established in our Constitutions as a paramount of citizenship must take priority over the right to practice religion.

Likewise the rights afforded in a society of law, such as due process, equal protection of the law, the right to own property and the ability to access a forum to resolve property disputes under universally applicable and neutral law must be recognized as having priority over an individual's right to free exercise of his of her religion. The state has a compelling interest in enforcing the rule of law in our society.

In deciding this matter the court has adopted the very least restrictive approach in developing an equitable remedy. The decision recognizes the rights of the occupants in the permanent improvements which they have installed on UEP land but gives the UEP ownership and ultimate control over the use of the land it owns. If the UEP wants to divest an occupant of the possession given by the UEP, it can be done but the UEP is required to pay for the benefit it receives in the process. No one has been able to suggest a less restrictive approach to the problem. The only approach less restrictive would be for the court to simply turn its back on the situation, refuse to determine the rights of the parties and let the parties battle it out among themselves. Ultimately, for one side or the other, and maybe for both, that approach would ultimately prove more costly than the one adopted by the court.

For the reasons stated here, the court denies the Motion to Dismiss brought by the Defendants (UEP). Mr. Lambert is to prepare the appropriate order.

The question of Claude Cooke allowing other people to live in his house was answered by the judge verbally in open court. He told them (UEP) that so long as Claude had personal property stored on the lot, either in the house or the shop behind the house, it was evidence that he had not abandoned his lot. As long as such was the case he could allow anyone he wished to live in the house. The issue of those living in the house being judged immoral by Sam Barlow and his snitches was outside the jurisdiction of the Court. That if there were any laws being broken then the matter should be referred to proper police authority but the Court was not in the position to Judge the moral conduct of persons according to the religious judgement of their neighbors. Even if there was a violation of civil law it would not warrant them being denied the right to live in the house so long as Claude allowed them to do so.

The Motion To Alter; concerned the paying of property taxes by the occupants and is covered in the Order which will be copied in its entirety here. The Order is as follows and is THE FINAL JUDGEMENT:

Nicholas E. Hales – #4054
Reid W. Lampert – #5744

WOODBURY & KESLER, P.C.
265 East 100 South, Suite 300
P.O. Box 3358
Salt Lake City, UT. 84110-3358
Telephone: (801) 364-1100
Attorneys for Plaintiffs
IN THE FIFTH JUDICIAL DISTRICT COURT
FOR WASHINGTON COUNTY, STATE OF UTAH
FINAL JUDGEMENT
UNITED EFFORT PLAN, et al.
Plaintiffs,

	Case Nos.	89050250CV
		930501020QT
vs.		930500301QT
		930500303QT
STUBBS, et al.,		930500305QT

Defendants
Judge J. Philip Eves

On November 24, 1994, the Court bifurcated the above consolidated cases for trial. With the exception of the Seventh, Eight and Ninth claims for relief set forth in the Amended Complaint in Case No. 930501020 CV, all matters and issues raised in the consolidated cases came before the Court for trial on November 30, 1994; December 1, 2, 5, 6, 8, 12-14, 19-23, 1994; and May 17-19, 24-26,

1995. Reid W. Lambert appeared representing all Plaintiffs in Case No. 930501020 CV except Boyd Dockstader (referred to herein as "plaintiffs"); R. Scott Berry appeared representing the United Effort Plan Trust ("UEP"); and Reed L. Martineau and Rodney R. Parker appeared on behalf of Rulon T. Jeffs, Fred M. Jessop, Leroy S. Jeffs, Parley J. Harker, James K. Zitting, Winston K. Blackmore, and Truman I. Barlow, Trustees of the UEP Trust ("Trustees").

Following trial, the parties submitted written Memoranda, and closing arguments of all parties were heard on November 13, 1995. Following closing arguments, Plaintiffs prepared a proposed Declaratory Judgment, and Defendants filed an Objection to Proposed Declaratory Judgement and a Motion to Alter or Amend Memorandum Decision and Final Judgment to Address Omitted Issues Pursuant to U.R.C.P. 60. Defendants also filed a Motion to Terminate Plaintiff Claude Cooke's Permission to Occupy UEP Property. After a hearing on June 10, 1996, at the Court's request the parties submitted further briefing on the issues of Plaintiffs tax liability and future improvements to U.E.P. property. Defendants also filed a Motion to Dismiss Sixth Claim for Relief (Post Trial), based on application of the Religious Freedom Restoration Act ("RFRA"), 42 U.S.C. 2000bb et seq., and a Motion for Summary Judgment on the Seventh Claim for Relief; Breach of Fiduciary Duty. Having heard testimony and examined the evidence presented at trial, having heard the closing arguments of counsel, having reviewed the Post Trial briefs of the parties, having been fully briefed and having heard the arguments of counsel regarding all of the above Motions, and now being fully advised herein, the Court now adopts its Memorandum Decision dated January 11, 1996, and its Memorandum Opinion dated September 5, 1996, as its findings of fact and conclusions of law and enters the following Final Judgment:

1. Declaratory Judgment is hereby rendered in favor of the following identified Plaintiffs and against the United Effort Plan Trust and its Trustees, both current and prospective, in their representative capacity only, on the Sixth Claim for Relief in the Complaint in case no. 930501020 CV, unjust enrichment. Specifically, the Court hereby orders that each property commonly described by the address below, including the improvements thereon, is owned by the UEP, but orders that the UEP owns such property in a constructive trust in favor of the identified plaintiff during his lifetime:

Plaintiff   Property (addresses deleted for this book)

Cyril Bradshaw
Connell Bateman
Benjamin Bistline
Alma J. Burnham
Claude S. Cooke

376

Donald B. Cox
Harvey J. Dockstader
T. David Dockstader
Marko J. Dutson
George R. Hammon
 J. LeGrand Hammon
Merrill Harker
J. Michael Pipkin
David L. Stubbs
Ray D. Timpson
John M. Williams
Rodger E. Williams
Thomas J. Williams
Don D. Timpson
John W. Timpson

2. In the event that the UEP discontinues benefits provided by the UEP, such as utility easements over UEP property, to any Plaintiff or discontinues any Plaintiff's use of the property prior to his demise, such Plaintiff shall be entitled to compensation for the then current value of the improvements conferred upon the UEP, minus any contribution to the value of the improvements made by the UEP in the first place, including but not limited to aid in the construction or contribution of materials, if any. In such calculation, the UEP shall not be responsible for the value of any improvement installed on UEP land after the earlier of the filing date of this lawsuit or the date when it can be shown that such Plaintiff first received actual notice that no further improvements should be constructed on UEP land.

3. The Court further orders that upon each Plaintiff's death, the land and improvements shall then belong to the UEP without the necessity of payment therefore.

4. Each Plaintiff's right of occupancy shall terminate without reimbursement for improvements if he tries to sell or mortgage the property or the improvements, or if he abandons the use of the lot. Each Plaintiff shall be liable to the UEP for waste committed on the property by him or his co-occupants, beyond normal wear and tear, during his occupancy.

5. Plaintiffs shall not construct any further improvements on UEP land if under applicable law the project requires a building permit, without the express written permission of the UEP, and any such project shall be submitted to the UEP for approval before it is submitted to any governmental authority or agency. Each Plaintiff may perform maintenance and construct improvements not requiring a building permit under applicable law, but must notify the UEP of the intent to do

so at least 7 days before any work on the project occurs so that the UEP can inspect and catalogue the existing improvements and the new improvement or maintenance project if it desires. In the event that any Plaintiff constructs unapproved improvements on UEP land without complying with the procedures set out herein, the UEP is hereby authorized to seek to evict that Plaintiff by judicial proceedings and, if successful, can be awarded costs and attorneys fees as consequential damages for the failure to comply with this court's order.

6. Each Plaintiff is hereby ordered to pay all real property taxes accruing on the property he occupies from the date of this Judgment forward. The procedure for such payments shall be as follows:

(a) For each tax year the UEP will make arrangements to obtain from the county governments assessing taxes against UEP land, as soon as possible after the final assessment notices are issued, an individual listing of the taxes assessed to each Plaintiff's holdings. Within 10 days after those individual listings are available, the UEP will notify each Plaintiff of the amount of taxes assessed against the UEP for which the occupant is responsible and the due date for payment. The date for payment shall be the same date for payment imposed upon the UEP by the taxing authority.

(b) The Plaintiffs shall pay to the UEP, in lawful currency of the USA, their proportionate share of the UEP tax assessments on of before the date the taxes are due from the UEP to the taxing entity. Any taxes not paid by the due date will be delinquent and will be subject to interest at the highest rate allowed by law from the due date forward. The UEP shall maintain records of payments received and issue receipts for payment. The UEP will also issue notice to the occupants annually, within 30 days after the tax due date, of those taxes not paid and delinquent.

(c) In the event that any Plaintiff fails to pay the proportionate share of taxes assessed to his holdings, then the UEP may pay those taxes to the taxing entity to preserve its interest in the land. The UEP will allow a grace period of 3 months after the taxes become delinquent before ommencing collection efforts, except that interest shall be added to the amount due during that 3 month period. If the taxes have not been paid current during the 3 month grace period, the UEP may then file suit against the occupant in any court of competent jurisdiction and obtain a judgment against the occupant for the delinquent taxes plus interest at the highest rate allowable by law and costs of court. The judgment may be collected in the same way as any judgment under the law, excluding foreclosing the occupant's interest in UEP land by paying the delinquent taxes, plus accumulated interest, at any time prior to the filing of a suit to remove the occupant from UEP land, as set out hereafter.

(d) In the event that the occupant fails to satisfy any judgment obtained under these provisions for 3 years after its entry, or fails to pay delinquent taxes for

4 years after the initial due date, which ever comes first, the UEP may seek through the courts to remove the non-paying occupant from UEP land based on the delinquent taxes. The failure to pay taxes within the time frames provided herein shall constitute an adequate basis in equity to allow the UEP to remove an occupant and to require the occupant so removed to forfeit any interest in the UEP land or the improvements thereon.

7. For the reasons set forth in Memorandum Decision dated January 11, 1996, all other claims of the Plaintiffs set forth in the first through sixth claims for relief of the Amended Complaint in Case No. 930501020 CV are hereby dismissed with prejudice.

8. The Defendants' post trail motions to dismiss the Plaintiffs' Seventh (breach of fiduciary duty), Eighth (accounting), and Ninth (distribution of trust) claims for relief are hereby granted based on the findings of the Court set forth in the Memorandum Decision of January 11, 1996, and each such claim is hereby dismissed with prejudice.

9. All claims of David L. Stubbs relative to the real property located at 415 Jessop Avenue, Hildale, Utah set forth in the first through sixth claims for relief of the Amended Complaint in Case No. 930501020 CV are hereby dismissed with prejudice, and the UEP is hereby entitled to possession of that property.

10. David L. Stubbs was also a party to Case No. 890502850, an unlawful detainer action brought by the UEP against him relative to the property located at 415 Jessop Avenue, Hildale, Utah. Based on the Court's finding that David L. Stubbs has abandoned the property, the unlawful detainer action is hereby dismissed with prejudice.

11. All claims of Fayila M. Williams set forth in the first through sixth claims for relief of the Amended Complaint in Case No. 930501020 CV are hereby dismissed with prejudice.

12. At a hearing held on August 12, 1996, Defendants' moved in open court to dismiss their claims against Merrill Harker for unlawful detainer contained in Case No. 930500305 QT. Based on the stipulation of counsel for Merrill Harker, the motion to dismiss is hereby granted and the unlawful detainer claim is hereby dismissed without prejuduice.

13. In Case No. 930500305 QT, the UEP also asserted a quiet title claim against Merrill Harker relative to the property located at 350 West Uzona Avenue, Hildale, Utah. The Declaratory Judgment set forth herein conclusively resolves the respective rights, title, and interests in the property of the UEP and Merrill Harker, and title is hereby quieted in the UEP subject to the constructive trust described herein.

14. The Case No. 930500301 QT, the UEP asserted a quiet title claim against J. Michael Pipkin relative to the property located at 375 North Lauritzen Street, Hildale, Utah. The Declaratory Judgment set forth herein conclusively

resolves the respective rights, title, and interests in the property of the UEP and James M. Pipkin, and title is hereby quieted in the UEP subjected to the constructive trust described herein.

15. In Case No. 930500303 QT, the UEP asserted a quiet title claim against Donald B. Cox relative to the property located at 725 North Lauritzen Street, Hildale, Utah. The Declaratory Judgment set forth herein conclusively resolves the respective rights, title, and interests in the property of the UEP and Donald B. Cox, and title is hereby quieted in the UEP subject to the constructive trust described herein.

16. For the reasons set forth in the Memorandum Decision, the Court makes the following findings regarding the nature of the United Effort Plan Trust:

(a) The UEP is a charitable trust and not a private trust. The creation of the UEP was motivated by religious beliefs. Those seeking or obtaining benefits from the UEP do so as supplicants and not as a matter of right.

(b) The Plaintiffs have not proven that they are "members" of the trust as that term is used in the Declaration of Trust.

(c) The trust is intended to serve those in need of help through charitable and philanthropic activities, regardless of whether such persons are members of the trust or not.

17. For the reasons set forth in the Court's ruling in open court at the hearing dated June 10, 1996, the Motion to Terminate Plaintiff Claude Cooke's Permission to Occupy UEP Property is hereby denied.

18. For the reasons set forth in Memorandum Opinion dated September 5, 1996, the Motion to Dismiss Sixth Claim for Relief (Post Trial), based on the Religious Freedom Restoration Act ("RFRA"), 42 U.S.C. 20000bb et seq. is hereby denied.

DATED this 15th day of October, 1996.
BY THE COURT
ss. Judge J. Philip Eves
Fifth District Court

Approved as to form:
GREEN & BERRY
ss. R. Scott Berry
Attorney for the United Effort Plan
SNOW, CHRISTENSEN & MARTINEAU
ss. Reed Martineau
Attorney for the individual Trustees

Needless to say, the Trustees of the UEP decided to appeal this Final Judgement of Judge Eves. The Notice of Appeal follows here:

PLEASE TAKE NOTICE that the United Effort Plan, Rulon T. Jeffs, Fred M. Jessop, Leroy S. Jeffs, Parley J. Harker, James K. Zitting, Winston K. Blackmore, and Truman I. Barlow appeal to the Utah Supreme Court from the final Judgment of the Fifth Judicial District Court of Washington County, State of Utah, entered by the Honorable J. Philip Eves in consolidate cases Nos. 930501020, 8905502850, 930500301, 930500303 and 930500305, on October 15, 1996. This appeal is taken from the entire judgment.
Dated this 15th day of October, 1996.
(ss. by attorneys for the Defendants).

It is unknown how long the appeals will go on in this case. One of the important points of the Defendants' appeal has been rendered void by the U.S. Supreme Court. That court nullified the "Religious Freedom Restoration Act," which was the basis for much of their appeal. It is very doubtful in the mind of the author that the UEP will win a favorable decision from the Appellate Court. The likelihood of the outcome is that they will lose a big part of their victory and the Appellate Court will overturn Judge Eves' decision regarding the nature of the trust. If it is found that the United Effort Plan is a business trust and not a religious trust then the Plaintiffs will stand to gain much more than the Defendants will from the appeal. The outcome of the appeal will have to be told sometime in the future.

There was one encouraging note. The General Authorities of The Church of Jesus Christ of Latter-day Saints gave their approval for the establishment of a Branch of the Church to be organized in Colorado City. A building was appropriated and would be moved into the community, probably in the spring of 1997. The plan was to establish a Church Institute in connection with the Mohave County Community College, using the building not only for a chapel and activities building, but for the Institute classes as well. This would have been a big milestone in the history of the community, it being over 60 years since there was a Branch in the community.

But in January of 1999, representatives of the General Authorities of the LDS Church met with Dan Barlow, mayor of Colorado City and David Zitting, Mayor of Hildale, to discuss the legal aspects of building permits etc., to begin construction of a building for the establishment of a Colorado City Branch of The Church of Jesus Christ of Latter-day Saints. Dan Barlow's answer: "We want you to build your church house in Cane Beds; we don't want it here. If you attempt to build here, we will condemn the property and build a road through it." Needless to say, this put an indefinite hold on any "Church" activity in Colorado City.

It had been my hope that it would have made the biggest impact on the community in bringing about the changes necessary for its growth in a *normal environment* of today's standards. These developments would have allowed a choice for the young people growing up who have never seen nor heard anything other than the teachings of an "apostate Priesthood." I wanted the opportunity for these young people to be led from their state of bondage into an era of freedom and choice, where they can find a far greater degree of happiness, a greater happiness than is ever possible in their present condition. But it was not to be so.

Dramatic Changes

In October of 1997 The Utah Supreme Court heard the appeal on the UEP Lawsuit. The Defendants' appeal was on the judgment of the lower court wherein it ruled that The Plaintiffs could live in their homes until they died.

All other causes of action were denied the Plaintiffs (dissidents) and the court ruled in favor of the Defendants (UEP) in the matter. The Defendants appealed on the basis of religion, claiming that the courts had no right to rule in religious issues. The Plaintiffs counter appealed, claiming that the lower court erred in its judgment. The attorneys for the Defendants told them not to appeal, telling them they could end up worse than they were. The Defendants were very arrogant, claiming that God would win it for them.

Before the Utah Supreme Court handed down their decision in the matter (which was in September of 1998) Sam Barlow, under the urgings of Fred Jessop, once again began evicting people from their houses. He started by picking on widows, whom he supposed would not have the courage nor the will to oppose him. He was successful in running out a couple of old defenseless widows and was going through court proceedings to evict a couple more. This was entirely illegal because some of these people had been plaintiffs in the lawsuit and no action in these matters should have been taken until the appeal had been ruled on by the Utah Supreme Court. This action of these two zealots was totally out of propriety and caused them trouble before it was over.

Also, in January of 1998, Parley Harker, First Councilor to Rulon Jeffs, died. Rulon then appointed his son Warren Jeffs as first councilor to fill Parley's place. He left Fred Jessop as the second councilor. A few weeks later, there was a notice filed in the Salt Lake County Recorder's office declaring that a document had been filed in the same office declaring that Warren and LeRoy Jeffs had been appointed UEP agents. But there is no document on file. The clerk, when asked why there was no such document on file, explained that those filing the declaration would have had to have taken the document with them when they left, assuring that the document would not be available for anyone to read. It is unclear as to what information is in this document, or what power these two sons of Rulon Jeffs might have in the control of the UEP.

A few months later in 1998, another notice was filed in the same County Recorder's Office stating that a document had been filed, titled: "Corporation of

The Presiding Bishopric of the Fundamentalist Church of Jesus Christ of Latter-Day Saints." The same situation exists with this document as with the one mentioned above; it is not on file. For some reason, Rulon Jeffs and his sons do want anyone reading these documents.

In September, 1998, The Utah Supreme Court handed down its ruling on the appeal that was heard in October of 1997. The Judges ruled against the Defendants and ruled for the Plaintiffs in the case, thus overturning the ruling of Judge Eves at St. George. This puts the Plaintiffs as the winners in the Lawsuit. At this time, November, 1998, Judge Eves has not yet rewritten his Order. When he does so, it will then be up to the Plaintiffs to decide what action they will want to take to extract justice from the dishonest trustees of the UEP. This decision of the Court also stopped the evictions by Sam Barlow and Fred Jessop.

Soon after these developments, Warren Jeffs, acting in the name of his father, who had just had a mild stroke, got up in Church and told all the Barlows they could no longer sit on the stand, doing in effect what Leroy Johnson had done to Marion Hammon and Dell Timpson a few years before. Dell Timpson died in 1998, thus leaving his son, John Timpson as the leader of the Second Ward.

On December 8, 1998, Warren Jeffs, under the pretense of acting on his father's direction, sent a letter and a copy of a new United Effort Trust Document to most of the members living on UEP property. Interesting enough, he did not send this information to any of the plaintiffs in the lawsuit, leaving a lot of questions. First one is: does he plan a settlement offer to the Plaintiffs? And the next big question is: How can any such changes be made regarding the UEP while in litigation?

This letter and the new document:
UNITED EFFORT PLAN TRUST
985 West Utah Avenue
Hildale, Utah 84784
December 8, 1998
(Name and address of the recipient).

Dear Resident:

On November 3,1998, President Jeffs and the Board of Trustees approved and adopted an Amended and Restated Declaration of Trust of the United Effort Plan. The trustees were sustained in this action by members of the Priesthood assembled during the month of November, 1998.

The Amended and Restated Declaration of Trust sets forth the terms of use of United Effort Plan Trust property. It is therefore an important document.

A copy of the amended and Restated Declaration of Trust is enclosed for your review and study. Please retain this document in your permanent records.

> The Kingdom of God or Nothing
> Yours in the Faith,
> (Signed by) President Rulon T. Jeffs
> Leroy S. Jeffs, Secretary.

The new trust document then is as follows.

AMENDED AND RESTATED
DECLARATION OF TRUST
OF THE
UNITED EFFORT PLAN TRUST

The United Effort Plan Trust is a religious and charitable trust. It is the legal entity of the United Effort Plan. The Trust was created by Declaration of Trust dated November 9, 1942, and was amended April 10, 1946.

The United Effort Plan Trust is a spiritual (Doctrine & Covenants, 29:34) step toward living the Holy United Order. It exists to preserve and advance the religious doctrines and goals of the Fundamentalist Church of Jesus Christ of Latter Day Saints, previously known as "The Priesthood Work," or "The Work" (The church). The United Effort Plan is under the direction of the President of the Church, who holds the keys of Priesthood authority (which keys have continued from Joseph Smith, Jr. to Brigham Young, John Taylor, John W. Woolley, Lorin C. Woolley, John Y. Barlow, Leroy S. Johnson, and Rulon T. Jeffs). The doctrines and laws of the Priesthood and the Church or bound in the Book of Mormon, the Doctrine and Covenants, Pearl of Great Price, The Holy Bible, the sermons of the holders of the keys of Priesthood authority, and present and future revelations received through holder of those keys; and are the guiding tenets by which the Trustees of the United Effort Plan Trust shall act.

The United Effort Plan Trust was created under the direction of John Y. Barlow. The original subscribers and Trustees of the United Effort Plan Trust were John Y. Barlow who died December 29, 1949; Leroy S. Johnson who died November 25, 1986; Joseph W. Musser who died March 29, 1954; J. Marion Hammon (now deceased) who resigned August 1, 1984; and Rulon T. Jeffs.

Fred M. Jessop became a Trustee September 1, 1984; James K. Zitting became a Trustee January 18, 1985; Winston K Blackmore became a Trustee February 25, 1986: Parley J. Harker, Truman I. Barlow and Leroy S. Jeffs became Trustees November 30, 1986; Parley J. Harker died January 29, 1998; and Warren S. Jeffs became a Trustee April 11, 1998.

Rulon T. Jeffs holds the keys of Priesthood authority and so serves as the

President of the Church. President Jeffs is also the sole remaining original Trustee and subscriber of the United Effort Plan Trust, and President of the Board of Trustee of the United Effort Plan Trust. In those capacities he, and Fred M. Jessop, Leroy S. Jeffs, Warren S. Jeffs, Truman I. Barlow, Winston K. Blackmore and Jame K. Zitting, as Trustees, hereby amend and restate the Declaration of Trust to more clearly set out its purposes and manner of operation. This document is a total restatement and amendment of the Declaration of Trust. It supersedes all previous documents, including all documents filed of public record in Utah and Arizona and with various courts. The President of the Fundamentalist Church of Jesus Christ of Latter Day Saints, a corporation sole, hereby ratifies this amendment. This Amended and Restated Declaration of Trust has also been approved by the Priesthood and sustained by the Church membership. Because the Trust is a charitable trust, this Amended and Restated Declaration of Trust will be recorded in the public record but no future affidavits of disclosure will be recorded.

The original real estate constituting the Trust Estate of the United Effort Plan Trust was consecrated to the Trust, and consisted of property located in Mohave County, State of Arizona, described as follows.

(Legal description of this property is then described in the document. It does not seem necessary to copy the description here. It will be passed over).

Since the original conveyance substantial additional real estate has been added as consecration to the Trust Estate, and parcels have been purchased, traded, subjected to rights=of=way, and dedicated as roads and streets. It is anticipated that property will continue to be added as consecrations to the Trust Estate. Property has been conveyed as consecrations to the United Effort Plan Trust in the name of the United Effort Plan, as well as in the name of Fred M. Jessop, as trustee. All properties now included or hereafter added to the Trust Estate are consecrated and sacred lands, dedicated to the United Effort Plan's religious purpose.

The United Effort Plan is the effort amd striving on the part of Church members toward the Holy United Order. This central principle of the Church requires the gathering together of faithful Church members on consecrated and sacred lands to establish as one pure people the Kingdom of God on Earth under the guidance of Priesthood leadership. The Board of Trustees, in their sole discretion, shall administer the Trust consistent with its religious purpose to provide for Church members according to their wants and their needs, insofar as their wants are just (Doctrine and Covenants, Section 82:17-21).

A consecration is an unconditional dedication to a sacred purpose. Consecration of real estate to the United Effort Plan Trust is accomplished by a deed of conveyance. Church members also consecrate their time, talents, money, and materials to the Lord's storehouse, to become the property of the Church and, where appropriate, the United Effort Plan Trust. All consecrations made to or for the benefit of the United Effort Plan Trust are dedicated to the sacred purpose of the United Effort Plan and without any reservation and or claim of right and/or ownership. Improvements made by persons living on United Effort Plan Trust property become the property of the Trust and are consecrations to the Trust.

The privilege to participate in the United Effort Plan and live upon the lands and in the buildings of the United Effort Plan Trust is granted, and may be revoked, by the Board of Trustees. Those who seek that privilege commit themselves and their families to live their lives according to the principles of the United Effort Plan and the Church, and they and their families consent to be governed by the Priesthood leadership and the Board of Trustees. They must consecrate their lives, times, talents and resources to the building and establishment of the Kingdom of God on Earth under the direction of the President of the Church and his appointed officers. All participants living on United Effort Plan Trust property must act in the spirit of charity (Moroni 7:6-10, 45-48). They must live in the true spirit of brotherhood (Matthew 22:36-40) and there shall be no disputations among them (3 Nephi 18:34). The Trust is most firmly committed to these goals. People who are granted the privilege to live on United Effort Plan Trust property acknowledge by their presence upon the land their acceptance of the terms of this trust.

Participation in the United Effort Plan and use of property owned by the United Effort Plan Trust is not and does not become a right or claim of anyone who may benefit in any way from the Trust. Use of Trust property must be within rules and standards set by the Board of Trustees. The Board of Trustees may require individuals and their families to relocate to different locations on United Effort Plan Trust property or to share a location with others. Participants who, in the opinion of the Presidency of the Church, do not honor their commitments to live their lives according to the principles of the United Effort Plan and the Church shall remove themselves from the Trust property and, if they do not, the Board of Trustees may, in its discretion cause their removal. At such time as they reform their lives and the lives of their family members and are again approved by the Priesthood and the Board of Trustees they may again be permitted to participate in the United Effort Plan. The Board of Trustees shall have no obligation whatsoever to return all or any part of consecrated property to a consecrator or to his or her descendants.

To carry out its religious mission and charitable purpose, the Trust shall be administered by a Board of Trustees consisting of not less than three nor not more than nine Trustees appointed in writing by the President of the Church. Trustees shall serve at the pleasure of the President of the Church and may be removed or replace at any time by the President. Dismissal of a Trustee shall be by a written notice, effective on the date the notice is exceuted. A Trustee may resign by written notice to the President of the Church. Each successor Trustee shall have the same powers and authority, and shall be subjected to the same duties and restrictions, as predecessor Trustees.

The President of the Church shall serve as a Trustee and President of the Board of Trustees. The President shall execute any necessary documents on behalf of the Trust, including contracts, deeds, transfers, assignments and other documents to carry out the purposes of the Trust, unless the Board of Trustees designates one or more Trustees to execute such documents.

The Board of Trustees shall act by majority vote of the number of Trustees in office and shall have all rights, powers, and privileges of an absolute owner in carrying out the purposes of the Trust, including without limitation all powers of trustees under Utah law. The Board of Trustees, subject to the approval of the President, may designate representatives to perform one or more of these functions on its behalf.

This Declaration of Trust may be amended at any time and from time to time by the President of the Church and a majority of the Trustees. The Trust is intended to be a charitable trust of perpetual duration; however, in the event of termination of this Trust, whether by the Board of Trustees or by reason of law, the assets of the Trust Estate at that time shall become the property of the Corporation of the President of the Fundamentalist Church of Jesus Christ of Latter Day Saints, corporation sole.

This Decaration of Trust shall be construed, administered and governed by the laws of the State of Utah in effect from time to time.

IN WITNESS WHEREOF. Rulon T. Jeffs, Fred M. Jessop, Leroy S. Jeffs, Warren S. Jeffs, Truman I. Barlow, Winston K. Blackmore, James K. Zitting, constituting all of the Trustees, and Rulon T. Jeffs, President and Corporation Sole, for the Corporation of the President of the Fundamentalist Church of Jesus Christ of Latter Day Saints, a corporation sole, have executed this Amended and Restated Declaration of Trust on the 3rd day of November, 1998.

(Signed by) Rulon T. Jeffs.

Notarized by: Boyd Knudsen of Hildale, Utah.
The following signatures are also notarized by Boyd Knudsen:
Fred M. Jessop
Leroy S. Jeffs
Warren S. Jeffs
Truman I. Barlow
Winston K. Blackmore
James K. Zitting

THE CORPORATION OF THE PRESIDENT OF THE FUNDAMENTAL-
IST CHURCH OF JESUS CHRIST OF LATTER DAY SAINTS.
(signed) Rulon T. Jeffs, President and Corporation Sole.

This document does not affect the Plaintiffs in the lawsuit because the court will
decide their standing and equity in the Trust. It will, however, affect all other
members living on Trust property if none of them contest it in court before the
legal statutes of limitations runs out. If no one contests this illegal actions of the
impostor trustees before the statutes of limitations run out, it will then become
binding. The opinion of the author is that there will be no one who will contest it,
thus allowing the perpetrators of the crime to get away with their vile deed.

May God have mercy on their poor souls.

The "Certificate of Authority" that was filed with the Corporation Commission
establishing Warren and LeRoy Jeffs as agents for Rulon Jeffs, was found in the
county recorders. It is copied here.

CERTIFICATE OF AUTHORITY
KNOW ALL MEN BY THESE PRESENTS:
That I, Rulon T. Jeffs, do hereby certify that I am the Presiding Bishop of
The Fundamentalist Church of Jesus Christ of Latter Day Saints, a religious
association, and by virture of such office I am the Corporation Sole of THE
CORPORATION OF THE PRESIDING BISHOP OF THE FUNDAMEN-
TALIST CHURCH OF JESUS CHRIST OF LATTER DAY SAINTS, a
Corporation Sole, organized under the laws of the State of Utah; that I am the
person designated in the Articles of Incorporation of said Corporation Sole to sign
and execute deeds and other instruments of writing and to transact all of the
business of said Corporation Sole pursuant to the provision of Title 16, Chapter 7,
Section 8, Utah Code Annotated, 1953, as amended and that pursuant to said
Section 16-7-8, thereof, I hereby designate and appoint WARREN S. JEFFS and
LEROY JEFFS, each individually, as an agent authorized and empowered to act
and execute documents on behalf of the Corporation of the Presiding Bishop of
The Fundamentalist Church of Jesus Christ of Latter Day Saints for the following
purposes:
1) To assign and endorse for transfer, certificates representing stocks,
bonds, or securities now registered or hereafter registered in the name of the
Corporation.
2) Execute deeds and other instruments of writing and to transact all
business of the Corporation.
3) To establish bank accounts to be operated by and in behalf of this
Corporation, as well as for schools, welfare units, United Effort Plan, and other

field offices of The Fundamentalist Church of Jesus Christ of Latter Day Saints, and to certify to the appropriate banks the names of those individuals authorized to sign checks on or deposit funds in said bank accounts, and to attest to signatures of the authorized signers.

DATED this 7th day of April, 1998.
THE CORPORATION OF THE PRESIDING
BISHOP OF THE FUNDAMENTALIST
CHURCH OF JESUS CHRIST OF LATTER DAY
SAINTS, a Utah Corporation Sole
Signed by: Rulon T. Jeffs, Corporation Sole
Notarized by Ron Steed,

Early in 1999, the lawyers for the UEP, filed an appeal to the U.S. Supreme Court regarding the decision of the Utah Supreme Court, wherein the decision of the State District Court had been reversed. In June of 1999, the U.S. Supreme Court turned down this appeal, thus putting the burden on the lower court to rewrite its earlier decision. These events will now result in further court action on the lawsuit.

Blood Atonement

During the 1990s Rulon Jeffs published several volumes of his sermons and doctrine. In 1997 one of these volumes contains a talk about the doctrine of blood atonement. The following is taken from these teachings.

"I could refer you to plenty of instances where men have been righteously slain, in order to atone for their sins. I have seen scores and hundreds of people for whom there would have been a chance (in the last resurrection there will be) if their lives had been taken and their blood spilled on the ground as a smoking incense to the Almighty, but who are now angels to the devil, until our elder brother Jesus Christ raises them up – conquers death, hell, and the grave. I have known a great many men who have left this Church for whom there is no chance whatever for exaltation, but if their blood had been spilled, it would have been better for them. The wickedness and ignorance of the nations forbid this principle being in full force, but the time will come when the law of God will be in full force.

"This is loving our neighbor as ourselves; if he needs help, help him; and if he wants salvation and it is necessary to spill his blood on the earth in order that he may be saved, spill it."

Soon after issuing these teachings he told the people in a public meeting that they should come forth and confess their sins to him that he may let them be rebaptised and their sins forgiven. A number of people did go to him and confess to sins of immorality. He did not forgive their sins and have them rebaptised but

390

instead he excommunicated them and in the case of men, he took the wife or wives from the them and gave them to someone else. These unfortunates were then expelled from the society and forced to leave the community.

It was reported by John Dougherty in the *Phoenix New Times* on January 29, 2004, that "Warren Jeffs…may have been secretly making audio and video recordings of confessions by church members…in the decade before assuming control of the church…according to allegations made by a longtime member of the church who was recently excommunicated. Reportedly he has accumulated thousands of audio and video tapes that detail church members'…confessions…."

End of World Warnings & Preparations

In the fall of 1998 and in the early part of 1999, there was a lot of hype and rumor among the polygamists of the First Ward, that the righteous people among them were going to be lifted up into the heavens while the wicked people would be destroyed. The righteous people would then return to the earth and continue to live their religion in peace. There were dates set, when these events were supposed to take place; the first dates being September of 1989. When it did not happen there were later dates set; first in October, then in December. When those dates came and went, the date was then set for it to happen on June 12, 1999, the 111th anniversary of Leroy Johnson's birthday.

The people gathered in the parking lot of the LSJ Meeting house at 6:00 a.m. on that morning. Fred Jessop welcomed every one there on "this beautiful morning," after which they sang "We Thank Thee O God For A Prophet." After the opening prayer and another song, the people were addressed by Louis Barlow. Then "Uncle Rulon's Sons of Heleman," were marched past the Brethren, presenting an honor guard before them. A circle prayer was then performed, where the people stood in a circle holding hands. A procession of the people then made their way to the Cottonwood Park, a distance of about two blocks away and there engaged in a day long celebration. During the day, people went to the store to buy a supply of groceries to take with them to Heaven. The Lift up event was supposed to take place at midnight. Needless to say, it did not happen, when at that time the people were told that the Lord had given them a six-month extension.

The following is the basis for the above actions of the Polygamists.

Statement of Rulon Jeffs: "WE MUST BE LIFTED UP TO BE PROTECTED. KEEP SWEET IS OUR ONLY PROTECTION." He then quotes from Leroy Johnson's sermon given in 1984.

"We will have to have the spirit of God upon us enough to be caught up when the judgments of God go over the earth, then we will be let down again. That

391

is the only way the Lord will protect his people. He says he will protect his Saints if He has to send fire from Heaven to do so; and this he will do."

In 1992 Rulon Jeffs said: Keep sweet, Keep the Holy Spirit of God, it is the only way we are going to get through the narrows and overcome this complacency, lack of faith. Keep sweet means keep the Holy Spirit of the Lord, until you are full of it. Only those who have it will survive the judgments of God, which are about to be poured out without let or hindrance upon the earth, beginning at the house of God, where the Mormons are. I mean the Mormon Church which is now apostate, completely, and will never be set in order. We have the true and living Church of Jesus Christ of Latter Day Saints, under our administration. We add the word "Fundamentalist" in order to distinguish the true Church of Jesus Christ of Latter Day Saints from the name of the one that now is a complete Gentile sectarian church, The Lord has rejected it."

Before the Winter Olympics came to Salt Lake City in 2002, Rulon began telling the polygamists living in Salt Lake that terrorists would strike at that time and there would be great destruction and devastation in Salt Lake Valley, therefore he told them to begin to move to Colorado City. All of his followers in Salt Lake City did move to Colorado City. Many of them abandoned the homes they were buying and allowed them to be foreclosed on therefore losing any equity that they may have had in the property. At the time of the Olympics there were no terrorist strikes, only great hardship on the people who abandoned their property at a loss and moved to Colorado City.

Warren Jeffs Takes Over

Soon after the year 2000 Rulon began experiencing confrontation from some of the Barlow boys who were pressing him to ordain one of them to the High Priesthood because he was getting old and was not expected to live much longer. He rejected their efforts toward this end telling them that he was not going to die, that he would live long enough to witness the the second coming of Jesus Christ and return the keys of the priesthood back to him. Continuing with this reasoning, he could see no reason why he should ordain anyone else to the higher order of priesthood. What he did do, however, was begin to turn operations of the cult over to his son Warren Jeffs. Warren Jeffs became a real tyrant when he began experiencing opposition from the Barlow boys toward his position as leader of the cult. He began making unreasonable demands on the people of the community. He forced them to acknowledge his position as leader and told anyone who would not accept and believe everything he said that they would be excommunicated and forced to leave the community. He organized a group of young men 13, 14, and 15 years old whom he designated "Uncle Warren's Sons of Helaman," and he would send these young boys into the homes of the people in the community, forcing them to make a statement that they would acknowledge him as their leader and would accept whatever doctrine he preached to them.

In September of 2002 Rulon Jeffs died, contrary to his prediction. At the time of his death Fred Jessop and Warren Jeffs were standing at his bedside. Warren turned to Fred Jessop and said, "I guess you're the one who takes over now." Fred responded, "No, you're the one to be the leader." This exchange between these two men was the only ceremony that took place allowing Warren Jeffs to become the cult leader. Warren's father, Rulon, had never ordained Warren to a position of leadership such as apostle or prophet, thus effectively ending the line of special priesthood authority that had been passed on from Lorin Woolley. This is the authority to perform plural marriages outside of the church after the Manifesto had been issued by Wilford Woodruff in 1890. Since there is no longer a priesthood Council among the polygamist group at Colorado City, Warren Jeffs has no priesthood authority and can only be classified as an impostor.

Prior to all this, a dispute had arisen between Winston Blackmore and Warren Jeffs over a girl that rebelled against Warren Jeffs dictates. It is rumored that he asked her to marry one of his brothers when she was 16. It is further rumored that after about three weeks she left the community with another brother. The two began living together but after a short time their consciences began to bother them and they decided to seek forgiveness.

Rulon Jeffs had commissioned Winston Blackmore to be the leader of a branch of the polygamists at Bountiful, British Columbia. This commission entitled him to forgive sins and to perform ordinances such as marriages. The young couple that had fled Colorado City decided to go to Canada to seek forgiveness of their sins from Winston Blackmore. Blackmore contacted Rulon Jeffs by telephone, seeking his permission to perform the forgiveness. Rulon gave his permission and this infuriated Warren, feeling that Blackmore had bypassed his position in the priesthood line of authority. He immediately chastised Winston and excommunicated him. He then ordered him off the United Effort Plan property at Bountiful to which he supposed he held title, only to find that Winston had placed much of the property in his own name. Winston claimed that the commission given him by Rulon entitled him to authority equal to Warren.

This only added fuel to Warren's indignation and he severed all ties with Winston at this time. When Warren discovered that the property was in Winston's name rather than the United Effort Plan, he filed a lawsuit attempting to reclaim the property. Before this lawsuit went to court Winston offered to make a concession to Warren. He offered to split the assets and the debts with Warren, each taking half. Warren, with indignation, refused this offer, telling Winston he must take all the debts and Warren would take all the assets and the property. This lawsuit has yet to be resolved. However, Winston had purchased other property in his own name without any United Effort Plan strings attached to it, both in Canada and also in northern Idaho.

Back in Colorado City Warren had ordered all business owners within the community to turn ownership of their businesses over to him. He also demanded that they draw out all their money held in 401(k) programs and give it to him. A number of the people rebelled against this demand and several families began leaving Colorado City, moving to northern Idaho settling on property that belonged to Winston Blackmore. Winston therefore acquired a following and is now a rival group to Warren Jeffs and his group at Colorado City.

Eviction Lost

A sixteen year-old daughter of Lenore Holm was told to marry a man 23 years older than her, as a second wife. The girl's mother did not object to her daughter's marriage, only stating she did not want her to marry the man until she was 18 years old. Warren Jeffs agreed to this request but wanted the girl to live in his home until she became 18 so as to receive proper training. Lenore objected to this arrangement, demanding that her daughter remain in her own home until she became of age. The girl however, was not in agreement, she wanted to leave her mother's home and so did so, running away. Her mother went to the Colorado City police department seeking help to locate her daughter. Although the police knew where her daughter was (either in Warren Jeffs' home or in the home of the man she was to marry), they wouldn't assist Lenore in returning her daughter.

Because of Lenore's rebellious attitude, her husband was told to divorce her and expel her from his home and the community. This he refused to do, and was served an eviction notice from the United Effort Plan. He and Lenore refused to move and the case was taken to trial at Kingman, Arizona. The judge in the case ruled in favor of Lenore and her husband and ordered that the United Effort Plan would have to pay for the equity in their home if they wanted them to move. This was a big loss for the UEP because it set a precedent that people could not be evicted from their homes in Colorado City unless they are paid for their equity.

Rodney Holm

Rodney Holm, a Colorado City police officer, had married Ruth Stubbs when she was 16 and he was 30, as a third wife. After having two children and pregnant with a third, Ruth became disaffected in her marriage to Rodney and decided to leave the community. She was unable to take her children with her, because she had to sneak out in the night and flee the area. After making her escape she sought help from the local law enforcement people of Washington County at St. George, Utah, to try and retrieve custody of her children. She was granted custody of her children and agreed to press charges against Rodney for his illegal sexual conduct with her. Rodney was arrested and charged with one count of unlawful sex with a 16-year-old girl and one count of unlawful sex with a 17-year-old girl and also one count of bigamy. At his trial in August of 2003, he was convicted of all three counts. He was sentenced in October of 2003 by Judge Beacham, Fifth District Court of Utah at St. George.

Rodney was sentenced to three years probation and one year in prison on work release for each offense, all three sentences to run concurrently. This was merely a slap on the wrist and caused much complaint among the citizens of Southern Utah. However, it is a well-established fact that a policeman cannot be sent to general population in any prison. Prior to the trial of Rodney Holm, the Utah State Attorney General's office solicited the help of the Colorado City police department in serving a subpoena on Warren Jeffs to be called as a witness in the trial. Sam Roundy, Colorado City police chief, not only refused the help asked for, but actually dispatched a policeman to barricade the way to Warren Jeffs home when investigators attempted to serve the subpoenaed. This was very discouraging to the Utah State Attorney General. He has since taken steps to decertify all Colorado City policeman of their Utah peace officer status.

First Ward Split Begins

Since the death of Rulon Jeffs, a split began developing between the Barlow boys and Warren Jeffs. In an effort to force their allegiance Warren began to restrict privileges that the Barlows had formerly been granted. The community had always celebrated the birthday of the former prophet Leroy Johnson. On June 12, 2003, Warren would not allow this annual celebration to take place. Also on the 24th of July (Pioneer Day), the community had always sponsored a large parade down the main street of Colorado City. Warren also did not allow this parade to take place. Also, Fred Jessop has sponsored a Fall Festival Fair in October of every year. Warren would not allow this event to take place.

The controversy between the Barlow's and Warren came to a head when on the 26th of July 2003, the 50th anniversary of the Short Creek Raid, a dedication ceremony was held for the unveiling of a monument on the grounds of the old schoolhouse sponsored by the Mayor of Colorado City Dan Barlow. Inscription on this monument read: Early Morning July 26, 1953 The Prophet Leroy Johnson stood on this site with the people and met the raiding police officers. He later declared that the deliverance of the people in 1953 was the greatest miracle of all time.

On August 5, 2003, LeRoy Jeffs ordained Warren Jeffs to be the President of the FLDS Church. Prior to this time, Warren had ordained LeRoy Jeffs to be the Patriarch of the church.

In a general meeting on August 10, 2003, Warren Jeffs delivered a sermon that lasted more than an hour and a half. In this sermon he severely chastised the people, speaking to the Barlow's but not mentioning any of their names, he told them that they are going to be chastised by the Lord. Near the end of this sermon he read a revelation which follows, wherein he orders the destruction of the monument that was unveiled two weeks earlier.

False Gods

Revelation given to Warren S. Jeffs at his home in Hildale, Utah, Sunday, July 27, 2003. Verily I say unto you, my servant Warren, my people have sinned a very grievous sin before me in that they have raised up monuments to man and have not glorified it to me. For it is by my almighty arm that my people have been preserved if they are worthy. I use men as instruments to perform my work.

And my prophets of all ages who have endured faithful to the end have acknowledged me, as their lawgiver, their protector, and their God, and have taught and instructed my people the same. Those are some outward evidences.

Reparations have to be made. What else is upon us? My people, let thee repent of their idolatry, which is covetousness loving anything more than God and His will; partaking of the world and its sins and all their wicked doings. For there are many elders who continue partaking of the spirit of the world and its wickedness.

And behold I say unto you, my elders, beware, for what you do in secret I shall reward you openly. And you must seek my protection through the repentance of your sins, and the building up of my kingdom, my storehouse, my priesthood on the earth. And if you do not, I shall bring a scourge upon my people to purge the ungodly from among you. And those righteous will suffer with the wicked if I will preserve the pure in heart who are repentant. I the Lord have spoken it and my word shall be obeyed if you would receive my blessings. Honor me, through obedience to my celestial laws, and set your family in order, to abide the spirit of oneness, which is the spirit of the celestial kingdom.

My holy love burning in your minds and hearts, bonding it together as one in a new and everlasting covenant, the laws of my holy priesthood. Hear the warning voice, oh ye my people, and repent and make restitution unto me that I may own and bless you in the day of trouble and also in Zion, if you will, for my arm of mercy is stretched out still unto those who will repent and come unto me with full purpose of heart, and I will preserve my servants among you to lead and guide you through my revelations and my power, otherwise you will remain unto those who will receive. Abide in my word. Let my people make restitution unto me, through the repentance of their sins and building up my storehouse and all other things, as I shall direct through my servants even so. Amen.

After reading this revelation, Warren then proceeded to chastise the people, accusing them of being unworthy of any future blessings. He said there would be no more meetings held, priesthood meetings or general meetings, he said there would be no more marriages performed, there would be no more baptisms, no more confirmations, only allowing the people the blessing of paying their tithing to him and supporting his storehouse, meaning that all men of the community would be forced to pay tribute to him of $500 per month. He then told them that the monument at the old schoolhouse must be destroyed. It must be broken into many pieces and scattered among the hills where no one could find it and restore it. This was because of the wickedness of those who had sponsored the monument. It is wicked to build monuments unto man and to do things in secret as the City Council had done this without his permission. In Canada, Winston Blackmore did not conform to these commandments. He is still performing marriages and holding meetings.

Of particular interest is how Jeffs declared himself the FLDS's new leader and how he has organized the new power structure. First he ordained LeRoy Jeffs a Patriarch, then LeRoy Jeffs ordained him President of the Church.

On August 15, 2003, Warren had a revelation calling other men to positions in the church. He called these men ordaining them High Priests and setting them apart: James Allred, Fredrick Merrill Jessop, Edson Jessop, LaMar Johnson, Edmund Barlow, Steve Harker, Joseph Steed, Rulon Jessop, Gerald Williams, Boyd Roundy, Leroy Steed, and Paul Stanley Jessop, Sr. Jeffs then said that Kevin Barlow was to be the superintendent of all priesthood schools and that LeRoy Jeffs and Richard Allred would act as councilors. Wendell Nielsen would be the first councilor, Fredrick M. Jessop remains as the second councilor to Warren Jeffs.

In 2002 an organization of interested people in St. George, Utah, began bringing awareness to people outside the community of Colorado City of the child abuse that was going on among the polygamists, namely that of marrying underage girls to much older men. As a result, state authorities have been taking interest in the situation in Colorado City and changes are beginning to take place among the polygamists.

Disappearances & Wives Reassigned

On January 3, 2004, Warren Jeffs announced that he had released Fred M. Jessop as bishop and that Fred Jessop was in full agreement with these matters. No one has seen or heard from Fred Jessop since this incident. Many people from within the

FLDS Church are concerned in regard to Uncle Fred's whereabouts. It is reported that Fred Jessop, with five of his wives, was sent to a compound in Mexico, by Warren Jeffs, where he is being held against his will. Soon after Fred's disappearance Warren Jeffs appointed William Timpson, age 32, to fill Fred's vacancy as bishop. He has moved into Fred Jessop's home, taken over his family, and is teaching and directing them in doctrine different from what Fred Jessop was teaching them.

It is evident that Warren Jeffs supposed he must remove Fred from the vicinity of the community in order to accomplish his next vengeful move. Fred Jessop, has been a leading father figure in the community for 65 years. He is much honored and respected and in any disagreement between himself and Warren, the majority of the people would support Fred Jessop. In order to avoid this confrontation Warren had him moved from the area.

On January 10, 2004, in a Saturday morning prayer meeting at the LSJ meetinghouse, Warren Jeffs stood before a group of about 1500 people (men and women). He berated them for their many sins and the lack of respect they rendered to the priesthood (himself). After about 30 minutes he read off a list the names of about 20 people, asking them to stand up, telling those who were standing that he had excommunicated them from the church. They must immediately remove themselves from UEP property and leave the community.

They must leave their wives and children for him to reassign to other men. Most noteworthy of this list were: Louis, Joe, Dan and Nephi Barlow. Also Louis's son, Tom and Dan's son, Roland. Among the select group were also four of Warren's brothers: David, Hyrum, Blaine, and Brian Jeffs. He then asked those standing to show by uplifted hand that they accepted his action as the word of the Lord. All of the group raised their right hands. He then asked the audience if they accepted it as the word of the Lord. They all raised their right hands. He then asked the audience to all kneel while he led them in prayer. In the prayer he instructed those who had been excommunicated to repent, keep their nose to the grindstone, and continue giving him their money. If they were to faithfully do so, they may have a chance to someday return to the fold.

The Barlow's Fight Back

On Tuesday, January 12, 2004, copies of the following letter were mailed to 453 random post office box numbers in Colorado City and Hildale. It is reproduced here as it was written.

January 11, 2004

I am a young man. I am simple and do not know the proper way to address you. But I have been commanded of God to stand upon the wall as Samuel and to tell you of a dream I had. For this reason I have chosen to send you letters describing this dream. I do this with humility and with trust in God.

I beheld this valley before it became Short Creek – before it became Colorado City. I saw a stream that had cut its way into this sandy valley and I saw children playing on the banks of this sandy creek. And while they were children, I recognized them as the town fathers I have come to trust and love. I beheld the children of John Y. Barlow. And a voice that filled my soul and my heart spoke to me in this dream and it said, "Behold, these children are pure in blood and hold the birthright to this sacred valley. They were chosen by god to carve out of the very wilderness you see a community where the people can raise themselves up unto God's glorious work."

And, I beheld this happen. I watched as our beloved prophet, Leroy S. Johnson, clung to John Y. Barlow's words. I watched as Leroy S. Johnson became the steward of these lands administering the just laws of God to this people. I watched him govern over the children of John Y. Barlow in a just and fair manner. And I saw how this place we live in was carved out of the wilderness by the will of God through these men. And I beheld that within their hearts they knew of their birthright and their duty to act as protectorates of this sacred place. And I saw that in all things they acted to this end, that by their sweat, their tears, and their very blood they stood true to their birthright.

I witnessed the Fifty-three Raid. I watched in tearful reverence as Dan Barlow ran himself near to death to warn of the police cars he saw coming. I saw the tears upon the cheeks of the mother's of this community who lamented for their husbands and feared for their children. I saw the life blood of this place in secret and strange places praying, pleading, and begging unto God that he might restore them to there sacred homes, to their sacred priesthood husbands. I beheld the sons of John Y. Barlow through these difficult times become true priesthood men, true defenders of god's work. I beheld, in particular, Dan Barlow apply himself to the building up of this kingdom unto God. And I saw that he was given great wisdom to understand the workings of government and man and that he did use his understanding to bring peace to this community, that he cultivated many important relationships of respect with the world.

I witnessed a great speaker raised up under Leroy S. Johnson and I witnessed this speaker fill the hearts of his children and this people with unbridled love and devotion to God. I stood in awe ready to stand the tide forever having been so moved by his words for he stood as Aaron stood to Moses. And I beheld that this man knew the prophet better than any man of his time. I beheld that he received special knowledge through the mouth of God and that many things he was told he held near and dear to his heart and that he has yet to reveal some of these things. And I beheld that this man carried the true birthright of John Y. Barlow; I beheld that it was Truman Barlow and that he was a just and true man worthy of his calling.

I watched as many men with their wives and children became disillusioned and left the care of our beloved prophet Leroy S. Johnson. And I saw that in this time of sorrow the sons of John Y. Barlow did hedge up the rift that formed in our prophet's heart having lost so many dear friends and that through the strength and love of the sons of John Y. Barlow he was able to continue on down the road together with the faithful, the pure, the meek and the mild.

I witnessed a great patriarch, Joseph I. Barlow, raised up unto God's work under the direction of Leroy S. Johnson. And I did witness this patriarch apply himself with a fervor to the defense of God's work and God's sacred land and to the institution of the UEP. And I saw that some were fearful and did resent him.

I watched as the sons of John Y. Barlow placed the mortal frame of their prophet into the ground and unto God. And I beheld that in this time the sons of John Y. Barlow did receive a new steward, Rulon Jeffs, to administer the laws of God unto them. And I saw that he was a just and fair prophet and administrator. And I beheld the mortal frame of this prophet also placed onto the sacred earth.

And darkness crept into my dream and a great fog did form. I witnessed as many of the labors of our forefathers went unrecognized and unappreciated. And I did see the world's respect begin to whither for the people's work. I beheld a harsh time in which forgiveness was abandoned. And I beheld too many families destroyed for petty reasons. I beheld children torn from their fathers and mothers torn from their husbands. I beheld the people of God crying in the darkness for God to deliver them. Fear filled my heart and I too prayed for deliverance.

And in the darkness a light began to form and rays of light penetrated everywhere and bathed my heart in joy. I beheld the prophet John Y. Barlow before me and he did speak unto me and told me many things that did fill my heart with cheer, things that I cannot share. For this reason I shall not reveal my identity. The prophet then instructed me to look and I beheld a great meeting of men and I beheld the prophet Rulon Jeffs in glowing glory before me and I beheld the mantle of the prophet pass onto the pure blood of John Y. Barlow. And I beheld the eldest of the sons of John Y. Barlow, Louis Barlow, did receive the mantle and that his being was filled with wisdom and words of God. I beheld John Y. Barlow command unto his son to step up to his calling and to forsake his birthright no more, that his time remaining quiet has passed, that he was chosen before the world was created to do an important work and that the time for his calling has come. I then watched as he addressed each of his sons telling them in turn to defend their birthright and that God had marvelous plans for his people should they stay true, should they stay pure in heart, meek, and mild.

I beheld John Y. Barlow address our beloved bishop, Fred M Jessop who had been put away from the view of his people. And I saw that our bishop had become weak and feeble and that age had crept upon him. And I saw that through vices of man he was stripped of the right to share the love of God with his people and I beheld he wept. And my heart ached and I wept not alone for I saw the pure and the meek and the mild weeping with me. I witnessed the great prophet, John Y. Barlow, thank him for the lifetime of love's labor that he put into building this community. And I saw the bishop true and honorable in his methods, give this compliment to God. And I wept for I felt in my heart that he might pass from us too soon.

I woke and marveled at this dream and the sprit of God did burn in my bosom and I resolved to do as I had been instructed. I wish also to express my love and devotion to the prophet as shown to me by God and to commit myself to God through his wisdom. (End of letter)

A few days later another letter was mailed to several people of the community. It is reproduced here as it was written.

1-15-2004

A simple word to those in Colorado City/Hildale who are currently following Warren Jeffs. Never and nowhere, in the known history of God's work upon this earth, has He condoned the marriage of a mother to her son. It is an abomination in the eyes of God and should be shouted from the roof tops. In spite of Uncle Roy's teachings to all parties, the fact that Warren Jeffs, convincing his own mothers to wed and bed him, does not make a prophet of him. A true prophet of God has a testimony of Jesus Christ and <u>correctly</u> foretells the future. One of the many examples of Warren Jeffs (as proclaimed prophet at the death of his father) giving an incorrect prophecy quite some time ago was when he told us to flee California and come back to Colorado City/Hildale because California was to be immediately destroyed. We were so obedient that when the urgent call came, we rushed back home "to be spared of the destruction", dropping everything, jobs, contracts, obligations, materials, equipment, etc. By the end of that day not one of us was in the state of California and we still haven't returned to work in that state. Warren, in making a prophecy about Satan gathering his forces to come against us, then publicly thumbing his nose at the united states government, along with the continuing use of severe dictatorship-like powers as well as still giving and taking underage girls to wife after severe warnings, is a no-brainer. Of course "Satan will rage." Duh!!!

Uncle Roy felt concern for our future and so should we. He taught us something publicly in one of his last sermons, after returning from Salt Lake City, Utah, that he had never mentioned before. He said that he had run in to, or was almost overwhelmed by, a power in Salt Lake City that was almost stronger then he was. He told us that he would never go to Salt Lake again and he never did. While acknowledging how sinister this sounded, most of us didn't understand what he was talking about and just shelved this statement. Others, on our own, or perhaps at the subtle suggestions of others, bent Uncle Roy's words around until we thought the Mormon Church, who seemed to us to be leaving more and more of their original tenets and doctrines behind, was what he had been referring to. Had Uncle Roy been awakened to something subtle and insidious that we were not yet aware of?

Seeing things from hindsight is not so difficult. What is difficult is honestly admitting to seeing things as they are, not as what we are told they are, or as we wish them to be. One or two weeks after Uncle Roy made the statement, Uncle Rulon, the only other ordained apostle as well as the Salt Lake community bishop who we understood was to be the next in line if Uncle Roy died, in public sermon Stated, " I hope and pray that I was not the cause of that statement by our prophet." We hoped so too. But did Uncle Rulon suspect that he, or something connect to him, was the cause of that statement?

Thru hindsight, we can recognize that there was indeed, an insidious new power gaining a foothold, that was slowly creeping into the fold. This wasn't an old established power that was easily recognized. This statement of Uncle Roy's occurred at the time in our history when Warren Jeffs had been given control of the Salt Lake City Alta Academy by his father, Uncle Rulon. This new school administrator began a somewhat foreign era of physically and mentally forcing young children to be righteous through fear. Fear of being physically whipped so bad by the principal of the academy that you could hardly walk and couldn't sit down comfortably for days. Fear of being publicly expelled from school and ostracized from your friends for small infractions of rules. This being done to scare the remaining children into being totally submissive and obedient. And, because of something you had said or done, (or not said or done) the fear of having our parents brought in and questioned by Warren about intimate things in their personal lives and beliefs they may have that may have conflicted with "correct teachings." The repercussions from this sort of treatment are traumatic and disastrous to a young person's mind.

As Warren's strength among the children grew, he fostered the need in these children to seek out what they were taught by him was evil and "humbly reporting" it in anticipation of a perceived position of superiority. This included, "humbly" informing Warren about any doctrinal or differences of opinion their own parents or family members might have had with those in authority. Warren planted small seeds in the minds of those young people that after "humbly and sweetly" informing on someone, they felt more elevated than those around them and "more worthy of building up the kingdom of God." These kinds of seeds grew and created a yearning for perceived power, position or authority, even at the expense of friends, neighbors, relatives, and even parents. Informants were everywhere. Children against parents, wives against husbands, and brethren against brethren. You didn't know who you could trust. Independent thinking, of any kind, was driven further underground. This force disguised as "love", began to slowly spread beyond the confines of the school and into our Salt Lake City community. During the administration of Uncle Rulon, it slowly, but surely, began to make its was into the Colorado City/Hildale community. This could go on and on, history repeating itself. The clues to our future are hidden in Warren's past, even preceding Alta Academy. Seek it and you will find it if you earnest and are willing to put forth the mental and physical effort, in addition prayer, that will be required.

Friends, this insidious wickedness has covertly crept among us, almost unawares, except for the many small hints that we were taught and trained to "just put on the shelf of belief" with the accompanying statement that "understanding would come later if we would just be obedient and go forward in faith, nothing wavering." This evil force, now among us, is a child no longer and needs to be exposed, Uncle Roy only warned us about this. He then withdrew from the saints on the Salt Lake community and permanently resided "down south." What knowledge did he suddenly acquire when he exclaimed, "oh, my God?!"

Uncle Fred, removed from power last month, and who has our bishop been for more years than most of us can remember, publicly said, "In case you elders haven't noticed, this work has done 180 degrees turn." Elementary students know that a complete circle is 360 degrees. If we do a one half turn 180 degrees, it is exactly the opposite of the way we were headed. Were we going to Hell under Uncle Roy's administration and to Heaven now? Were we going to Heaven under Uncle Roy's administration and to Hell now? You do the math. You can't have it both ways. Divide and conquer seems to be the motto of the day.

When Uncle Rulon was <u>still alive and sitting on the stand,</u> his son, Warren Jeffs, publicly speaking about John Woolley, (the father) and Lorin Woolley, (the son) both being prophets one after the other. Warren then made a revealing statement when he said, "then was the time for the reign of the Woolleys. Now is the time for the reign of the Jeffs." What exactly did Warren mean by the plurality of the statement? Slip of the tongue, perhaps?

Uncle Rulon had told us God revealed to him that his body would be renewed. His 67 mostly young wives, yearning for motherhood, would have children, and that he would live an additional 350 years into the millennium. He said he would be our last and only living prophet. That is why he didn't ordain any more apostles. With that kind of a life span there was no need to set up any chain of command. It simply wasn't needed. What was needed for the next 350 years was the trusted bishop and counselor Uncle Roy and Uncle Rulon had counted on for year to be with them. Before his stroke, Uncle Rulon said many times, "Uncle Fred and I are one." Uncle Rulon, at Priesthood meeting, in front of all the men, told Uncle Fred that God had also revealed to him, (Uncle Rulon) that Uncle Fred would also live to be an additional 350 years old and that his body would be renewed as well. He then asked Uncle Fred to move to the front of the stand and sit on a chair. He then requested that his new first councilor, Warren Jeffs, seal upon Uncle Fred, the same blessing of a renewal of his body and long life into the millennium that had been given to him.

From that time on, until the death of Uncle Rulon, believing in the actual bodily renewal of Uncle Rulon and Uncle Fred was an absolute requirement to staying in this religion. To even wonder if our beloved Uncle Rulon was getting old and feeble minded, after his terrible stroke, or that he may one day die, was cause to be turned into church authorities by those "humbly seeking out sin from among the people". If caught, the "heretic" would be called in and questioned by Warren and if found guilty of lacking faith that Uncle Rulon and Uncle Fred would be renewed, the offender would be cut off from the church and expelled from the community.

Warren constantly preached renewal of Uncle Rulon and kept it foremost in our minds. With the people truly believing that Uncle Rulon would be "our last prophet", as he said, and that he and Uncle Fred would lead us for the next 350 years, what was the need for the rule of the father and son Jeffs? Unless of course, one of Rulon's sons, beneath his "humble" pretense, was an aspiring man. Remember Uncle Rulon died on Sunday, dissolving the First Presidency. Warren was still only an elder. The following day, at Monday morning meeting, Uncle Warren, besides giving us details on the passing of Uncle Rulon, made this statement. "I won't say much, but I will say this, "Hands off my father's wives." Speaking to the newly bereaved widows, he said, "You women will live as if father is still alive and in the next room." I remember thinking to myself, "Who in the world, at a time like this, would be lusting after Uncle Rulon's wives?" The thought sickened me.

This was said on Monday. By that Friday, Warren moved in on those women so fast, and with such finesse, that only two of his "mothers" had enough fortitude to stand up against him. Those stunned women, who had sincerely believed that their husband and prophet would live 350 years and give them children, went through the shock of losing their husband to death, seeing him buried, Warren proclaiming himself prophet quickly thereafter and then immediately receiving revelation to marry those women "those found worthy of him" in secret ceremonies. Before committing that kind of sin before the eyes of God, one of his mothers, seeing the futility of fighting him off, bravely fled the compound and left the community at a run. Another of Warren's young "mothers" flatly refused to go along with the marriage. She was sent back to live with her father and told him she would live the rest of her life out without ever being married.

As Jesus said, " Those who have ears to hear, let them hear. Those who have eyes to see let them see." This undercurrent of fear that we now have, but won't admit to having for fear that it proves us "wicked", has already been fully experienced by the first test cases at Alta Academy and is now being felt in full force by us as people.

Friends, there is only one power that governs or rules with the use of fear. The danger is no longer at the gate. The wolf is in the fold and the shepherds are down.

A Concerned Friend.

Anonymous Letter of Warning to Ben Bistline:

On the 22nd I received the preceding "Concerned Friend" letter addressed to Ben Bistline. On the same day I received the following letter addressed to Benny Bistline. The following letter was one of a kind, sent to me only. It was not a Xerox copy but rather was typed on lined looseleaf paper with holes on the edge. This letter does not seem as much of a threat to me but rather the scary part is the mentality expressed by the writer, which is revealing as to the danger of potential violence that lies among the followers of Warren Jeffs.

The personal letter is now in the hands of the FBI. The letter is reproduced here exactly as it was written.

Cover Page to Letter
Benny Bistline
I know that you're an evil man and that you're not a friend to the righteous in Colorado City or to the UEP but sometimes God uses the evil to do a righteous purpose. You stand for apostates and gentiles and you as well as your kind should take this letter as a warning. Hopefully after reading this the gentiles will understand our point of view and have a little more respect for us. When you take on God's chosen people you are playing with his fire.

The Letter:

I'm from Colorado City and that means that you view me as a polygamist. We don't believe in polygamy. We believe in plural marriage which is the new and everlasting covenant of marriage as laid down by the prophet Joseph Smith. The difference is one is commanded of God and the other is not. I have a job to do. My job is to protect the prophet Warren Jeffs and the Lords chosen people from you cockroaches and scum. I'm sick and tired of the harassment we get here. It seems like every day you gentiles and apostates are looking down our throats trying to make trouble. Why don't you just leave us alone! The truth is, you're jealous because you can't have what we got. We got the priesthood and that makes our women and children obedient to us. We live a different more religious way of life and you shouldn't hate us because of it. You're green with envy because your wifes argue and will leave you if you don't bow and scrape to their needs. Your children don't obey you. All they want to do is watch TV and play computer games. You gentiles don't know how to direct women and children because you don't know about priesthood. You don't understand what it takes to be the priesthood leader of a family. We have to raise our children like calves in a stall. Why do you think we don't allow gentile women as wifes or allow gentile people to move into our town. We work with our children everyday to make sure they don't know too much about you. You'd just destroy them in a matter of minutes. That's why were glad our prophet commanded us not to go to public school. We don't want our children being asked stupid questions that'll just destroy their lives. To much worldly influence destroys children. That's why we make our children dress with long dresses with jeans underneath them. The long clothes and all make them stand out so that you gentiles will leave them alone. Besides they'd never talk to you because they know that all you people are servants of Lucifer and that given half a chance you'd put your foot in the door and pry them wide open to sinning. That's another reason why you'd better leave us alone. You can't have these girls. They know better than to be associating with you all. You gentiles and apostates have no business here at all. Under the constitution we're guaranteed our religious freedom. We can do what we want here and you people should have nothing to do about it. We should be allowed to set up our own government and laws. The courts did not follow the headings of God and let us use our own laws. The courts accused us of trying to make a lawless society. The prophecies will come true to fix it. There won't be a yellow dog here to greet us or stand in our way when it comes time for the prophet to rule this world. Besides we already control everything here in the town anyways. You accuse us of marrying our cousins and relates. The Lord tells us who to marry not you. Rodney did the right thing. When it comes to choices you have to choose to do what the prophet wants even if you are sent to prison. The thing here is obedience. We're obedient to our prophet and in turn our wives and children are obedient to us. But that's none of your business because it's our religion!!! The world frowns on us for living our religion. But were not worried because God will protect us. We believe in following God's laws. Our prophet tells us that God's laws are more important than the laws of the land and so we choose to not follow the laws of the land. It doesn't matter what the people are doing here. It's a matter of principle. God brought these children into the world and he'll do with them what he wants. God raised these people up for this purpose. That's what the whole plan of Colorado City and the UEP is about. The UEP makes it so that if somebody disobeys the prophet then he can make them leave so they don't destroy the lives of our children. These things are to keep our children protected. Our children must be protected from the evil ways of gentiles. We can't have people hanging around giving our children stupid ideas. Our children are scared of the world. They don't want to leave this town because they can see the ruined mess their lives would be if they do leave. God will curse them and destroy them. We've seen it time and time again that when people leave this town, satin possesses them and they go crazy. You gentiles don't have a right to get in the way with the way we raise our children or our women. The way we do things here is part of our religion and the constitution guaranteed freedom of our religion. You should know we don't force our children to do things like getting married anyway. Uncle Sam says in our priesthood meeting that we tell the world we don't force marriages. Is what we do is invite people to obey. The prophet then tells them which guy to marry. There's no force involved. People can choose to disobey. They have that right. Without perfect obedience we do not have priesthood. Obedience is the first law of heaven and when you disobey you break the first law of heaven. When they disobey they make a choice and the Lord tells the prophet to tell them to leave town. He has the right to forbid them to ever speak to even their families again. If a family chooses to disobey the prophet then they choose to disobey. If they choose to disobey then they make a choice to leave. They weren't forced because they made that choice. And their house wasn't theirs anyway it was the Lords. You see if they choose to disobey they turn themselves over to Lucifer who will destroy them. The prophet says the only hope for a person who disobeys is blood atonement. He hasn't told anybody to kill anybody else. He's working very hard to get us to a point where God will clean up the world.

That's why you see all the stuff happening here in our town. He's destroying the seeds of contention. If we're good enough then we'll get to help the prophet do his work. Then God will be able to order the destroying angels to go forth and they will kill off all the wicked. The only way you'll be saved is if you're wearing the priesthood garments and if you don't have the markings of the beast on you. We are ready to answer the call when our prophet asks it. He said it will be the young that will do this. We young priesthood boys have the most special privilege of getting to serve our prophet in the last days that are upon us. We meet in special priesthood meetings to learn special things that are special. This is the greatest time for a priesthood man to be alive. The prophet has promised us that the destructions are here and we will get to witness them.

I have a message for the person who wrote the letter in the newspaper. Uncle Louis supports our prophet with all his heart. You did a most evil thing in trying to stir up trouble with us. I hope you know the penalty for making false prophecies. If you really did have a dream then you are the most inspired man of satin I've ever known. God will reveal to the prophet who you are. I shudder to think what will happen to you. If I were you I would be shaking in my shoes with fear for your life because the Lords going to take your life. You have brought down a scourge and condemnation upon yourself. At this point there's no place you can hide that the prophet can't find.

The best plan for you gentiles and apostates is to leave us alone. It doesn't matter what you do cause the Lord will deal with you shortly. The more you gentiles bother us the harder you are going to get judged and the more terrible will be your destruction. We down to every single last man in Colorado City will gladly die to protect our prophet. As the mouthpiece of God on this earth we will do whatever the prophet commands us to do to protect the work of God. The best advice I can give you is to stay away from us and let us do God's will as revealed to us by the prophet Warren Jeffs. (End of Letter)

In his new book *Polygamy Under Attack: From Tom Green to Brian David Mitchell*, author and retired Sheriff's Lieutenant John Llewellyn devotes a chapter to the potential for violence that can and has occurred in some cults. And he made a similar presentation to a law enforcement conference in St. George in January 2004, at the request of the Utah Attorney General.

He states: "The likelihood of aggressive violence initiated by 'leaders' of the prevailing organized groups is remote unless they are backed into a corner. Violence is more apt to come from deluded people like the Laffertys, who without warning suddenly take it upon themselves to avenge the prophet or the principle of plural marriage.

"However, there is always the possibility of armed resistance on a grand scale much like occurred at Waco, Texas. The organized fundamentalists sects still believe in the doctrine of Blood Atonement that was preached by early leaders of the LDS Church." He then discusses other cult tragedies that have occurred in the past.

As they should, the FBI and law enforcement are taking seriously the possibility that someone, believing they act in the name of God or their prophet, will begin to avenge what they believe has been an assault on their leader. I called Ross Chatwin the day I received the threatening letter and cautioned him. And during his press conference, law enforcement was everywhere present.

Ross Chatwin

The next day, January 23, 2004, Ross Chatwin held a press conference at his home in Colorado City. Ross Chatwin is a young man in his early thirties who was recently told to leave his home and his wife and family, and leave the community. This message was sent to him from Warren Jeffs by James Zitting. The following is taken from a prepared speech that he read to about 50 reporters from all over the country who attended his press conference. It reads as follows:

Recently, I joined a growing list of men who have been told to leave their homes. I can't be sure as to why I've been told to leave behind everything that I've worked for.

I do know, however, that the owner of the UEP land trust, Warren Jeffs, has claimed to be receiving revelations of whom to evict. Typically he requires that the person in question quietly vacate their home and leave their family under the auspices that if they show complete humility he may restore to them what was lost. As part of the process, he requires the evictee to write a letter listing all of their sins. He says that if the list of sins does not match the list of sins that God gave him through revelation then their eviction becomes permanent. This is essentially the ultimatum that was given to me and it is the same ultimatum that was given former Mayor Dan Barlow and his brothers along with approximately 20 other men. My list of sins obviously did not match up with the list of sins Jeffs put together. I want James Zitting to know that what I have to do is stand up to Warren Jeffs and to the UEP. My family and I do not plan on leaving our home anytime soon. I am pleased to report that my wife has submitted to stay by my side regardless of Jeffs commandment to leave me. It was ultimately her choice to preserve our family. It is difficult for me to find the words that can express to her how much I appreciate her.

One of the messages I want to leave people of Colorado City is that they don't have to leave if they don't want to. I've come to realize that a few men stood up to the UEP, and paved the way for a better life for us all.

The young men of the FLDS church are taught that if they want advancement in the organization they must build a home upon UEP land. It's quite an exciting time for a young man. He knuckles down and puts everything he has into building his home all the while anticipating the possibility of marriage and of getting to start a family.

When I was a young, impressionable, a little ignorant, and maybe even a little over zealous, I wanted more than anything to build a home. As all marriages within the FLDS organization are assigned, I felt that as a 17 year-old boy at receiving a building lot from the UEP, it can only be matched by the dread of finally realizing the UEP might be used as an instrument to forcibly take my home from me.

If the UEP should try to evict you I would recommend that you resist leaving your home. The UEP has been known to send out notices asking that people move. I suggest that you ignore these notices. If you leave your home for more than 30 days, your home reverts back to the UEP.

When the possibility of losing your home is frustrating, the real travesty in Colorado City is the possibility of losing your family. The second message I would like to leave with the people of Colorado City is to not let some whimsical notion be the reason you break up your family. It's not fair to you and its especially not fair to your children. I've talked with individuals who, being stunned by the magnitude of the situation, allowed Jeffs to remove their families from them. They now deeply regret having allowed this to happen. Houses can ultimately be rebuilt. Once a family is destroyed, it leaves broken hearts that can never be healed. Please, give it some thought before you throw it all away. There are few systems of checks and balances to govern how Jeffs operates. One of the only ways we can affect what he is doing is by letting the world know about the things that go on inside this town. In this way, pressure from the outside world restricts to a degree what he can do. The Barlows have preached a concept of one man leadership that has come full round to ultimately remove them from the power. Jeffs has refined this doctrine even further. He claims to govern the FLDS church by way of a "benevolent dictatorship." Now Jeffs has been initially accepted a renegade from Salt Lake City to come into the position of the "one man" and have absolute power.

However, it is possible that Jeffs will abandon many of the members of the FLDS church. This does not mean that he plans on giving up the UEP anytime soon as it is his only source of income. My sources tell me that Jeffs is in the process of building a new community in a secret location and that he plans on taking a few of the elite to live there. Some evidence points to this compound being in Mexico. One of my resources tells me that the compound is being called Zion. In the last year, Jeffs has become extremely paranoid and is essentially gone into hiding. This is probably the actual reason as to why he's building a secret compound. Lately an entourage of bodyguards and wives attend him wherever he goes.

The compound as well as other responsibilities has obviously cost a great deal. The members of the FLDS church are being required to provide huge amounts of money to Jeffs. Last week on January 17 in the Saturday work meeting directed by the new bishop, the elders were instructed to come up with another thousand dollars each to give to Jeffs. Jeffs has obviously become increasingly frustrated with people being unable to pay. This latest demand also carries with it *a threat of being left behind* if you fail to come up with the money. And, this is just one of many required thousand dollar donations in the past little while. His need for cash has severely taxed the people of the FLDS church.

Overall, Jeffs' leadership has been reckless at best. It's shocking to realize that the owner of a 100 million dollar asset could act so carelessly. I am sickened by the number of families Jeffs has been instrumental in destroying. It's baffling to see the men who choose to stay around after they've had everything taken from them. At least 50 men have been essentially turned into eunuchs. They continue to consider themselves members of the FLDS church. They watch while other men take their children and wives. It is their lot in life to put their noses to the grindstone and hope that in the next life they may be given families again.

Jeffs' methods are cruel and final. He operates his benevolent dictatorship with a cold indifference. Most of the people he ostracizes are humiliated in public meetings before thousands of people. In my case, he told the congregation that I was a master deceiver. He said that he planned on publishing a list of names and that my name as well as two others would be listed in that publication. Jeffs defined what this meant by saying that "anybody who thinks they have priesthood when they don't are master deceivers." In the case of 20 men who were recently ostracized he told them to stand up in the audience of more than 1500 so that everyone could see who they were. He then publicly rebuked them. At the end of this meeting he required that the congregation get on their knees while he stood and prayed.

Some people are concerned that I might be endangering my life for sticking up for my rights. I do fear that some overly zealous person from within the FLDS Church might take it upon themselves to do something rash. But more than that, I fear what would happen if Jeffs was allowed to act unchecked. I feel it's my responsibility to let the world know about the situation here in Colorado City and that in doing so, I ultimately make things safer and better for everyone by limiting what Jeffs can do. Jeffs claims that "he fears no man or set of men." And yet he has walled his compound in Hildale with an 8 foot fence and has surrounded himself with bodyguards. I believe that Jeffs actions show that in fact he is afraid to face the troubles he has created. I believe that what I am doing here today does impact Jeffs in ways that are helpful to the people of the FLDS organization.

Some of the zealous young people within the FLDS organization need to be made aware of the implications of acting in a rash manner. Anything you do that might harm another individual will bring down a thorough investigation of this people. The very religion you are trying to protect will be exposed beyond your wildest imagination.

I know that most people within the FLDS Church will reject the advice I'm offering them. But at least the information will be out there. There may come a time they'll be able to use this information in order to react in an appropriate way. It is my hope that more people will stand up to Jeffs. If you are scared, just stand up and you will find that you have lots of support; just make sure that your family is standing with you. I'm your friend and will gladly help in any way that I can.

I am deeply concerned for the young people who are choosing to run away. I feel that these people need a tremendous amount of support. I am concerned that the world may not be aware of how sheltered these young people have been. They were raised in a culture that is quite different from what they are moving into and I fear that they are extremely vulnerable to some of the pitfalls of being a teenager. I would like to extend an offer of friendship to anyone who needs help. Please contact me and I will be happy to stand with you.

I want to say, "Lets stand up for what's right and help stop this evil dictator from destroying more families." Almost all the people here really are good people and I love them all. They just follow blindly and they are taught to not ask questions.

I just want to get the ball rolling and to help pave the road for others to add to. Almost all the families in this society are really good and hard working people. They are just taught (brainwashed) from infancy to just trust, believe, and follow like sheep and not to ask questions. If we don't understand something then we were told, "just put it on the shelf of belief."

When I'm tired of being kept ignorant, my shelf was so stacked up it broke.

We need your help to stop Warren S. Jeffs from destroying families, kicking us out of our homes, and marrying our children into some kind of political dollar browney point system.

This Hitler-like dictator has got to be stopped before he ruins us all and this beautiful town."

Ross then held up a book saying, "Warren has studied this book for many years. It is what he uses as a guideline to govern this community and control the people."

Someone then asked: "What is the book?"

Ross replied, "THE RISE AND FALL OF THE THIRD REICH."

Conclusion

It is February of 2004 and I'm often asked the question, "What will happen next at Colorado City?" I offer two scenarios.

First: Warren Jeffs will take a select group with him and escape to Mexico. He has borrowed millions of dollars on the property and homes that the people have built and paid for with their own money. He will abandon Colorado City, leaving those who stay to try and pick up the pieces from the destruction he has created.

Second: The civil authorities will indict him for his crimes. These include extortion, exploiting and destroying the lives of teenage girls, income tax violations, money laundering, and overall fraudulent activities.

If either of these happen, the way will be clear for the Barlows to take over. The community was promised to them by their father John Yates Barlow as their heritage in the Barlow dynasty. Perhaps the Barlows truly believe the Keys of Priesthood remain in their family. I strongly suspect the Barlows have long waited for an opportunity to assume full leadership of the Group. I believe Rulon Jeffs and Warren Jeffs both knew this and it would account for why Warren has acted swiftly in excommunicating so many Barlows. An underlying power struggle has gone on for years. Given all that has occurred, I suspect the Barlows will create a somewhat more open atmosphere within First Ward. Because of all the public and government scrutiny, it would be politically smart to do so, and the Barlows are very articulate and very politically astute.

There is still the problem of what to do to protect the young people of the society and to free the people from bondage. In the case of the young people, the state authorities must take some action to protect them from further exploitations. There are very few polygamist wives who will leave the community to seek a better life. We can only hope to make changes that will affect the next generation. State authorities must have facilities in place (local sheriff's sub-station, for example, staffed by law enforcement from outside Colorado City) to accommodate any young people who wish to flee the society. There will be more boys wanting to leave than girls. This, however, is only a short term solution.

Much has been done to help victims of domestic violence leave their abusers and restart in society. Similar action is needed for our people. Safe houses, education, child care, learning a skill or trade – all are needed to help these polygamist girls and women (and boys), some of whom have lived in a third-world environment and will feel frightened about entering mainstream society. Those helping them must remember that the people leaving have never been taught to think for themselves. Many are easily misled, easily manipulated. Therapy is needed. Patience and kindness are needed. Creating a new life structure in which they can live day to day is essential.

The bottom line solution that may produce the greatest gain to free the people is to decriminalize polygamy. We can see what making polygamy illegal has done, not unlike prohibition in the last century. Let these people come out into the world. And as they do so, they will see clearly that they have choices. Stay in polygamy. Or leave. But the choice is theirs. And I suspect fewer people will enter plural marriage.

If it is decriminalized, over zealous leaders will have less control. It would remove the power of self-proclaimed religious leaders in controlling its people and their marriages, particularly of young girls. The child rape trial of Tom Green and the new book by John Llewellyn teach the world a great deal about why Tom wanted his wives "young," so he could "train" them. A girl must be allowed to mature so she can make a legitimate decision about her future. And it would be good if First Ward children returned to public school.

The next step would be to dissolve the United Effort Plan Trust, placing ownership of the homes and property in the hands of those who paid for and built the houses, so that the threat of being evicted for perceived infractions to their leaders is removed.

A comparison between First Ward at Colorado City and Second Ward at Centennial Park shows a significant difference. The people living in Centennial Park are much freer and live a more normal lifestyle. Their dress is more modern and less conspicuous than their First Ward neighbors. Two reasons for their freedom and open-mindedness: Young girls are not forced to marry older men, and the people own the property on which their houses are built. Thus they can't be threatened with losing their homes for disagreeing with or for perceived lack of devotion to their leaders.

In associating with the people in both communities (my wife and I are related to 90 percent of them), the attitude and feelings we encounter are many times more friendly and truly warmer among those of Centennial Park Second Ward than those of Colorado City First Ward.

We have a daughter living in a polygamist relationship in First Ward and another living in a polygamist relationship in Second Ward. We have a good relationship with both. They each chose their lifestyle and are happy and satisfied with their choice. They feel they have the right to make this choice and desire to be left to pursue their own mode of happiness. This is not the case with all polygamist wives living in the society, however.

There are many human rights abuses of men, women, and children, and these abuses must be addressed. Evicting people from their homes must stop. It is my hope in writing this history that those of my many relatives, friends, and others in the community who are living in unhappy circumstances might read it, and that it might have some influence in giving them the courage to take the necessary steps to change their lives for the better.

Opportunities are available for young people who desire to leave and there are facilities and helping agencies to assist those desiring to make their way in the world.

We face a monstrous problem that must be overcome, but I do believe that all things are possible.

Benjamin G. Bistline was born in Logan, Utah, on April 21, 1935, the son of John Anthony Bistline and Jennie Johnson Bistline. He was the sixth of ten children. His parents were active members of the Mormon Church but became involved with a few polygamist families in Millville, Utah, and were excommunicated by LDS Church authorities in 1937.

The family moved to Short Creek, Arizona, in 1945 to join a united order movement, also known as The United Effort Plan. His father soon became discouraged by Barlow's ineptness in governing his Order, and by 1948 he had repented of his decision to join with Barlows' group at Short Creek. He then decided to rejoin the Mormon Church, but his wife refused to leave, taking a firm stand. Ben's father died in April of 1949, before rejoining the LDS Church because of their policy of a one year repentance probation period after being excommunicated.

Ben's mother had always wanted to live polygamy and this gave her the opportunity to do so. She married Richard Jessop as his fifth wife and they moved into his large household of four wives and about thirty children.

Ben lived in this polygamous household for the next three years until the raid on Short Creek in 1953. While living with his stepfather, he became romantically involved with one of the daughters, but the Raid interrupted the courtship. Ben was eighteen and Annie was fifteen. All minor children in the community were declared wards of the state of Arizona, and were transported with their mothers to Phoenix, Arizona, in 1953. They were released and allowed to return to Short Creek in 1955

Annie and Ben were married June 24, 1955, and remained in the society where they parented and raised sixteen children. He was never allowed to marry any other wives, after being deemed unworthy of the privilege by polygamist leaders because of his "rebelliousness." He refused to take what he was told at face value, he refused to join one of the cliques, and he refused to live in blind obedience. Thus he was never a polygamist. He and his wife would have accepted plural marriage.

In the early 1980s Ben became discouraged with the polygamists due to their changes in religious doctrine. He was a plaintiff in a lawsuit filed in 1987 in an attempt to win title to the property on which he had built his home. The court granted him equity ownership in his home but not ownership of the property (land). In March of 2003, Fred Jessop, bishop for the polygamists, negotiated an equity agreement with Ben whereby he was able to move away from the community. He now lives on his own property in an area called Cane Beds, about two miles south of Colorado City. He and his wife are still very much involved with the polygamists due to extended family relationships.

Ben and his wife Annie joined the LDS Church in 1992. They believe the same doctrine as the LDS Church in regards to polygamy. They are members of the Kaibab Moccasin Ward where they have served in several church callings. Ben presently serves on the high council of the Kanab, Utah Kaibab stake.

Bibliography

The references given here are among the main ones utilized in the preparation of this book. However, they are by no means a complete list of all the works and sources consulted; rather, the list merely indicates the substance and scope of reading upon which some of the material is based. The bibliography is intended to serve as a convenience for those who wish to pursue further the study of fundamentalist polygamist history, and related issues.

Allred, Byron Harvey. *A Leaf in Review*. Salt Lake City: Caxton Publishers, 1933.

Anderson, Max. *The Polygamy Story: Fiction or Fact*. Salt Lake City: Publishers Press, 1979.

Baird, Mark J. and Rhea A. Kunz. *Reminiscences of John W. Woolley and Loren C. Woolley*. 4 vols. Draper, Utah: N.p,n.d.

Bradlee, Ben, Jr. and Dale Van Atta. *Prophet of Blood—The Untold Story of Ervil LeBaron and the Lambs of God*. New York: G.P. Putnam's Sons, 1981.

B. H. Roberts. *Comprehensive History of the Church of Jesus Christ of the Latter Day Saints*. Provo: Brigham Young University Press, 1965.

Jessop, Edson, with Maurine Whipple. "Why I Have Five Wives: A Mormon Fundamentalist Tells His Story." Colliers, 13 November 1953, 27-30.

Johnson, Leroy S. *Sermons*. 6 vols. Hildale, Utah: Twin City Courier Press, 1984.

Journal of Discourses. 26 vols. Liverpool and London: Latter-day Saint Book Depot, 1854-86.

Musser, Joseph W. *Celestial or Plural Marriage*. Salt Lake City: Truth Publishing Co., 1944.

____, Joseph W. Musser Journal. N.p., n.d. These published excerpts are available from Pioneer Press, Salt Lake City.

_____, *The New and Everlasting Covenant of Marriage an Interpretation of Celestial Marriage, Plural Marriage.* Salt Lake City: Truth Publishing Co., 1934.

Musser, Joseph W. and J. Leslie Broadbent. *Supplement to the New and Everlasting Covenant of Marriage.* Salt Lake City: Truth Publishing Co., 1934.

Newell, Linda King and Valeen Tippetts Avery. *Mormon Enigma: Emma Hale Smith.* New York: Doubleday and Co., 1984.

Short Creek Historical Calendar. Hildale, Utah: Twin City Courier Inc., 1992.

Smith, Joseph. *Teachings of the Prophet Joseph Smith.* Salt Lake City: Deseret Book, 1976.
Joseph Smith

Solomon, Dorothy Allred. *In My Father's House.* New York: Franklin Watts, 1984.

Van Wagoner, Richard S. *Mormon Polygamy: A History.* Salt Lake City: Signature Books, 1986.

Index

Y

Z

Polygamy Under Attack: From Tom Green to Brian David Mitchell
by John R. Llewellyn

Polygamy expert, former polygamist, and retired Salt Lake County Sheriff's Lieutentant John Llewellyn provides a dramatic inside look at each of the polygamist groups, how they began, how they rule their people, and their beliefs. He explores serious human rights abuses that occur such as forcing young girls to marry men old enough to be their father. A former friend of Tom Green, the author provides deep background on Tom's life and polygamist activities. John explores the fascinating underground fraud by the various groups, and evaluates Brian David Mitchell's efforts to turn Elizabeth Smart into a compliant plural wife.

And finally, he takes a hard look at the possible value of decriminalizing polygamy so that the many hidden abuses, including tens of millions of dollars of welfare fraud when polygamist wives pose as single mothers with children, can be brought out into the open and finally be dealt with realistically.

Table of Contents: Brief History of the Mormon Fundamentalist World, A Profile of Each Group and the Independents, Anti-Polygamy & Pro-Polygamy Movements, An Inside Look at AUB Fraud, An Inside Look at TLC Fraud, Tom Green and His Wives, Bleeding the Beast for Your Tax Dollars, Authority versus Love in Mormon Fundamentalism, Legal Issues and Four Attitudes Towards Polygamy, Are There Realistic Solutions for Polygamy Abuses, Rights of Children vs. Rights of Parents, Decriminalizing Plural Marriage, From Tom Green to Brian David Mitchell, The Potential for Violence

John R. Llewellyn appeared on *The Today Show with Matt Lauer & Katie Couric, NBC Nightly News with Tom Brokaw,* Fox News Channel's *The Edge* with Paula Zahn, MSNBC, *Inside Edition,* and *Good Morning America.*

Murder of a Prophet: Dark Side of Utah Polygamy
by John R. Llewellyn

A riveting story of intrigue, murder, and sex. Lusting for worldwide power, the fanatical leader of a Utah polygamist group launches a plan to become the "prophet" over the entire Mormon Church. Detectives fear a doomsday Waco-type standoff with women and children. Investigator John Llewellyn, polygamy expert, creates a fascinating tale of fiction taken from real-life events, based on the Rulon Allred murder by Ervil LeBaron.

A Teenager's Tears: When Parents Convert to Polygamy
by John R. Llewellyn

The author wanted people to be able to walk in their shoes and feel what they feel, to be on the inside looking out. An emotionally charged and tender fact-based fiction.

Review by Laura Chapman. "Llewellyn accomplishes the incredible task of exposing the many diverse dynamics of Utah polygamist groups and their members in *A Teenager's Tears*. The characters of the women, children, men and self-proclaimed apostles are both astounding and precise. The display of male privilege, abuse of power in leadership, and struggles within families is triumphantly accurate. The feminists within the groups are still captured in a basic belief that without a man there is no heavenly glory in the hereafter."